SAVAGE FORTUNE

AN ARISTOCRATIC FAMILY IN THE EARLY SEVENTEENTH CENTURY

SUFFOLK RECORDS SOCIETY

Elizabeth Savage, later Countess Rivers, date and artist unknown, possibly Sir Peter Lely. One version of this painting is known to have been at Hengrave. This version hangs in Melford Hall. *(Reproduced by courtesy of the National Trust)*

SAVAGE FORTUNE

AN ARISTOCRATIC FAMILY IN THE EARLY SEVENTEENTH CENTURY

Edited by

LYN BOOTHMAN and
SIR RICHARD HYDE PARKER

General Editor

DAVID DYMOND

The Boydell Press

Suffolk Records Society
VOLUME XLIX

A Suffolk Records Society publication
First published 2006
The Boydell Press, Woodbridge

ISBN 1 84383 199 6

Issued to subscribing members for the year 2005–2006

The Boydell Press is an imprint of Boydell & Brewer Ltd
PO Box 9, Woodbridge, Suffolk IP12 3DF, UK
and of Boydell & Brewer Inc.
668 Mt Hope Avenue, Rochester, NY 14620, USA
website: www.boydellandbrewer.com

A CIP catalogue record for this book is available
from the British Library

This publication is printed on acid-free paper

Printed in Great Britain by
MPG Books Ltd, Bodmin, Cornwall

CONTENTS

ILLUSTRATIONS

Colour plates

Black and white plates

ACKNOWLEDGEMENTS

We would like to express our thanks to the many individuals and organisations who have helped us with this work. First, we would like to thank the Suffolk Records Society, and in particular its general editor David Dymond, for assistance at all stages. David helped in many ways with his valuable advice, and also contributed to the volume with his translation of Document 13 and part of Document 62. The volume would not have been conceived in its present form, nor completed, without his help. The volume includes documents from many repositories and institutions, and we wish to thank staff at all of them who have helped us with our identification of records, and given their permission for the transcripts to be included in this volume. However most of the records used are held by the Cheshire and Chester Archives and Local Studies Service or by The National Archives (formerly the Public Record Office), and we are particularly grateful to their staff for their aid and support. Lancashire and Cheshire Record Society kindly allowed us to use their edition of the Inquisition Post Mortem for Thomas Viscount Savage.

Before beginning this project the authors of this volume were not particularly conversant with national politics in the early seventeenth century nor with the workings of the royal court. We have learnt an enormous amount from scholars in these areas who have been very generous with their support and expertise. In particular we would like to thank Caroline Hibbard who over several years has contributed references relating to Henrietta Maria, the royal court and related matters. Richard Cust has also been particularly generous in his advice and supply of references and copies of documents, and Santina Levey offered much needed advice and references in relation to the inventory. We would also like to thank Edward Chaney, Noel Cox, N.R.R. Fisher, John Guy, John Heward, J.A. Hilton, Ralph Houlbrooke, John Lawler, Father Albert Loomie SJ, Roger Lockyer, John Morrill, Fiona Podgson, Michael Questier, Glyn Redworth, the Earl of Scarborough, John Schofield, David Smith, Simon Thurley and Andrew Thrush. In addition we would like to thank Tony Bland, Gill Clegg, Alex Cowan, John Herod, Elizabeth Lawrence, Christopher O'Riorden, Bill Robinson and H.R. Starkey for references we would have been very unlikely to find without their assistance or searches.

Melford Hall is a National Trust property, and we are grateful to the Trust for their co-operation with and encouragement of this work.

Lyn Boothman
Richard Hyde Parker

ABBREVIATIONS

Repositories

AGS	Archivo General de Simancas
BCA	Birmingham City Archives
BL	British Library
Bodl.	Bodleian Library
BRO	Berkshire Record Office
CCALS	Cheshire and Chester Archives and Local Studies
CLRO	Corporation of London Records Office
CUL	Cambridge University Library
DRO	Devon Record Office
ERO	Essex Record Office
ESRO	East Sussex Record Office
HLRO	House of Lords Record Office
LMA	London Metropolitan Archives
MAE	Ministerio de Asuntos Exteriores, Madrid
HPP	Hyde Parker Papers, Melford Hall
RBM	Biblioteca Nacional, Madrid
SJSM	Sir John Soane's Museum, London
SRO	Staffordshire and Stoke-on-Trent Archive Service: Staffordshire Record Office
SROB	Suffolk Record Office, Bury St Edmunds branch
TNA	The National Archives (formerly the Public Record Office)
UH	University of Hull, Brynmor Jones Library
UWB	University of Wales, Bangor
WCRO	Warwickshire County Record Office

Other

BA	Bachelor of Arts
c.	circa
CP	*Complete Peerage*
d.	died
DNB	*Dictionary of National Biography*
doc./s	document/documents
ed./eds	editor/editors
edn	edition
f./ff.	folio/folios
HMC	Historical Manuscripts Commission (now The National Archives)
ibid.	*ibidem* (Latin), 'in the same place'
IPM	Inquisition Post Mortem
KB	Knight of the Bath
KG	Knight of the Garter
MA	Master of Arts

MS/MSS	manuscript/manuscripts
ODNB	*Oxford Dictionary of National Biography, 2004*
OED	*Oxford English Dictionary*
PSIA	*Proceedings of the Suffolk Institute of Archaeology*
q.v.	*quod vide* (Latin), 'which see'
Trans	*Transactions*
VCH	*Victoria County History*

ANCESTORS OF THOMAS SAVAGE

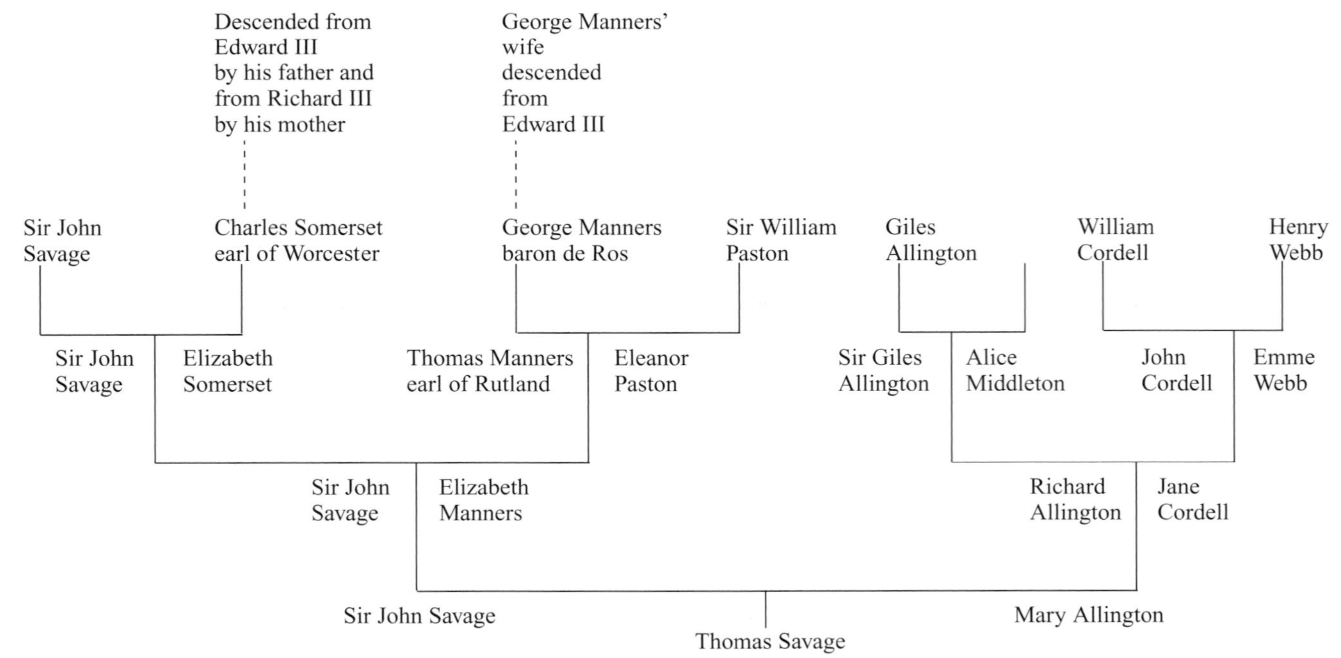

ANCESTORS OF ELIZABETH DARCY

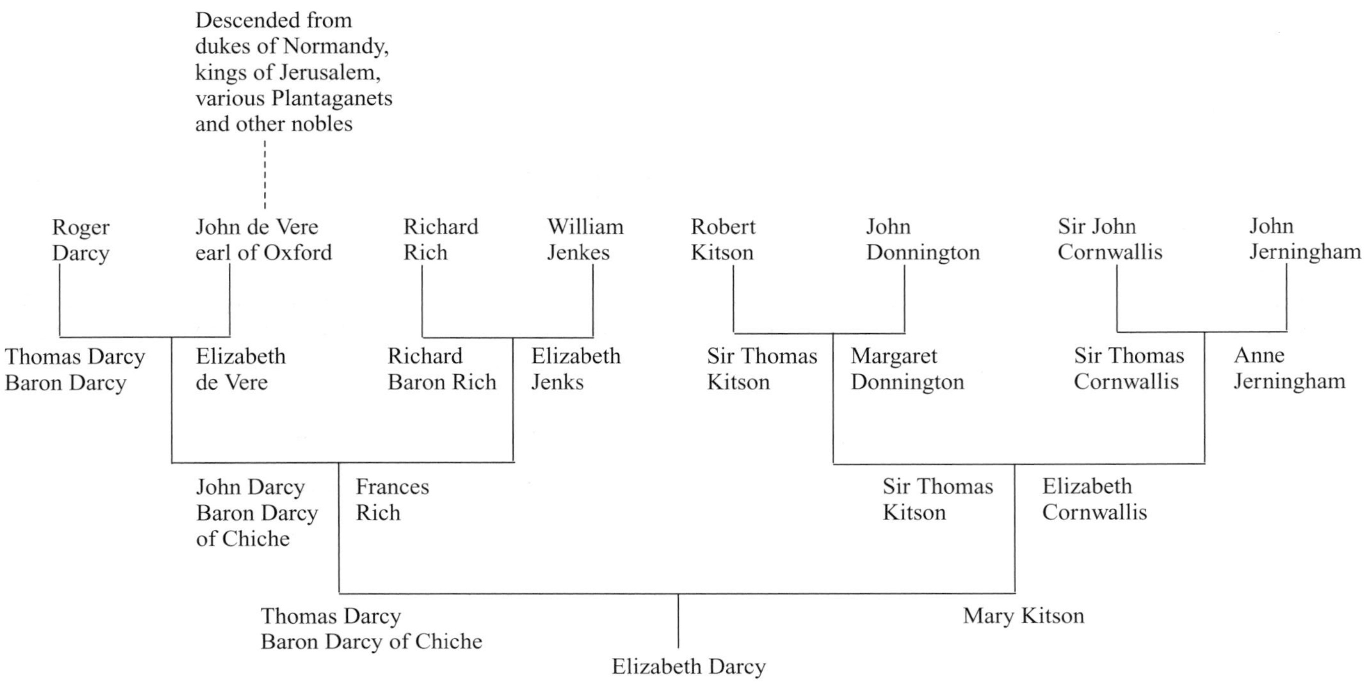

INTRODUCTION

This volume is an unusual publication for a county record society. It concerns people from Suffolk, Essex, Cheshire, London and elsewhere, and properties in Suffolk, Cheshire, Isleworth and central London. The constituent records are not from one collection, but have been gathered from a wide variety of archives and repositories. Some, such as the inventory and wills, are of types well known to local and family historians; others, such as those from the royal court, will undoubtedly be less familiar. The thread holding the collection together is the multi-faceted and eventful life of one wealthy aristocratic family which had influence at various levels – local, regional and national.

The centrepiece of this collection is an inventory of the movable goods of Thomas Viscount Savage, who died in 1635. The inventory lists the contents of Melford Hall at Long Melford in Suffolk, Rocksavage at Clifton in Cheshire[1] and Lumley House on Tower Hill in London. Melford Hall is the only one of the three to survive. The inventory is part of the Cholmondeley-Savage archive held at the Cheshire and Chester Record Office. Although well catalogued there, it was unknown in Suffolk until 'discovered' in 1999 by one of the authors, who has long worked on the history of Long Melford.[2] Once the inventory had been transcribed, the authors began work to put it in context, to find out more about the man and family whose belongings were described, and to use the inventory to reconstruct the layout of Melford Hall in the early seventeenth century.

It became clear that although Melford Hall is the only one of Savage's houses to survive, the inventory of goods there has to be seen alongside those of the other two houses; it would have been foolish to separate the Suffolk material from the remaining evidence of Rocksavage and Tower Hill. It also became evident that although the Savage family is well known in Cheshire history, little existed in print about Thomas Viscount Savage, and indeed in Suffolk his wife Elizabeth is rather better known under her later title of Countess Rivers.

The records in this volume are documents and letters written to, by or about Thomas or Elizabeth Savage, their properties or their children. They cover the years of their marriage and Elizabeth's widowhood, essentially the first half of the seventeenth century. This fairly lengthy introduction summarises their lives so far as we can discover them from the surviving records, and describes the three houses included in the inventory. In an appendix, the inventory is interpreted against the surviving structure and other evidence to suggest the layout of Melford Hall in the

1 In present-day Runcorn, Cheshire.

2 L. Boothman, 'Mobility and Stability in Long Melford, Suffolk in the Late Seventeenth Century', *Local Population Studies*, 62, Spring 1999, pp. 31–51; 'The plague of 1604 in Long Melford', E. Wigmore (ed.), *Long Melford, The Last 2000 Years* (Long Melford, 2000), 36–40 and 'Sitting in Church 1774', *ibid.*, 56–62. She has also written a research paper on the 1604 plague and her Cambridge M.St dissertation (unpublished) is entitled 'Mobility, Stability and Kinship – the Population of Long Melford in the Late Seventeenth Century.'

1630s. The volume also includes biographical notes on many of the individuals mentioned in the various documents.[3]

In its nineteenth-century form local history concentrated on the aristocracy, gentry and clergy, the descents of manors, heraldry and the patronage of churches, but in the twentieth century it developed into a much wider study of whole communities. As a result, record societies have often concentrated, rightly, on records relating to that wider approach. This particular study is a reminder, however, that many communities were directly or indirectly affected by the activities of their social élites, whether resident or non-resident, and that local historians should never forget the importance of aristocrats and gentry operating at various levels from the strictly local to the national.

The records in this volume may serve as a reminder of the range of information that can be found for aristocratic families, for those involved at court or in government and others whose lives went 'beyond the local'. As local historians used to having few documents relating to each individual, the range of material surviving for this relatively unknown aristocratic couple and their children has fascinated us. Documents have been chosen for this volume either because they illustrate major points about the lives of the family, give particular insights about the individuals involved or are illustrative of certain classes of evidence. The first few documents, which are mainly long and legal, relate to Thomas's inheritance of his lands, particularly (but not exclusively) those at Melford. They are balanced to an extent by other long legal documents towards the end of the collection that outline the process by which the Melford lands left the Savage family. All these legal documents provide a framework within which the family lived; although dense and wordy they are given in their entirety as examples of their type, which are rarely printed in full. We hope that publishing a few examples may help other historians faced with this type of material when investigating the lives of gentry or aristocratic families. The remainder, and majority, of the documents relate to Thomas's and Elizabeth's family and working lives, and are predominantly shorter and less dense.

Thomas died in November 1635 at his house on Tower Hill in London.[4] His entrails were interred under the chancel of St Olave's Hart Street, just a few yards from his home, and his body was taken to Macclesfield in Cheshire, where he was buried in the Savage family chapel on 16 December. To appreciate the sources of wealth that enabled Thomas and his family to live in the relative splendour suggested by his inventory (Doc. 60), we have to look first at the families to which he and his wife belonged, and through which they inherited their wealth.

The Cordell family

The Cordell family, from whom Thomas inherited Melford Hall, came from the most modest background amongst these families. John Cordell, yeoman, said to be son of a London merchant, appears in Melford in the 1520s as a servant, possibly

3 Throughout this introduction, Thomas and Elizabeth Savage are referred to as Thomas and Elizabeth, unless it is essential to add 'Savage' to ensure clarity. Their official titles changed over time: 1601–26 Sir Thomas Savage and Lady Savage; 1626–35 Thomas Viscount Savage and Elizabeth Viscountess Savage; 1635–41 Elizabeth is the Dowager Viscountess Savage; 1641–51 Elizabeth is Countess Rivers.

4 *Complete Peerage* (*CP*) gives his date of death as 20 November 1635. This is the date on which his entrails were buried, so it is likely that he died slightly earlier. The inventory of the Tower Hill house, where he was living when he died, states that it was taken on 14 November 1635; see Doc. 60 and its introductory note. V. Gibbs, H.A. Doubleday, G. White and others (eds), *Complete Peerage of England, Scotland, Ireland, Great Britain & the United Kingdom* (2nd edn, London, 1910–59), XI, 458.

steward, of the Clopton family at Kentwell Hall.[5] There is a suggestion that he may have been legally trained.[6] John's son William was called to the bar and became one of the most successful lawyers of his period, very much a 'new come up' man, whose property speculations brought him lands in Yorkshire and elsewhere, as well as in Suffolk. In the late 1540s William Cordell leased Melford Hall and its associated lands, and was finally granted them in 1554. A year earlier he had become solicitor general and one of Queen Mary's privy council. In 1557 he was knighted and made master of the rolls. He retained this latter post when Elizabeth I came to the throne, and held it until his death in 1581. A few years earlier, in 1578, his importance had been underlined when Elizabeth I spent some days at Melford Hall as part of her progress through East Anglia.[7]

Sir William had married Mary Clopton, cousin to the Cloptons of Kentwell. None of their children survived, so he turned to his brothers and one of his sisters to find his successors at Melford Hall. He left the manor and the hall to his wife for her life, then to his sister Jane Allington for her life. After her death the property was to go to their brother Francis and his male heirs; if there were none, to the next brother Edward and his male heirs. If neither had male heirs, it was to go to their female heirs. If neither brother left heirs, the Melford properties were to go to Jane Allington's heirs. William Cordell's other sister Thomasine Gager, who had married a local man, and whose family seems to have caused Cordell various problems, was not mentioned in relation to the inheritance of the house and land.[8] Cordell's will gave his house in High Holborn directly to Jane Allington; this became known as Allington house.[9] Both Francis and Edward Cordell died before their sister Jane, and neither had any direct heirs, so Melford Hall, its manor and lands were fully inherited by Jane Allington in 1590.

The Allington family

The Allingtons were a gentry family from Horseheath in eastern Cambridgeshire, where they had lived since at least the early fifteenth century; they had been at Bottisham in the same area from the thirteenth century. Horseheath church has surviving monuments to various members of the family, and did have one to a William Allington who served as speaker of the House of Commons and died in 1446, and another to a William who died on Bosworth field.[10] Many leading members of the family had been knighted.

---

5 The Cordell family are said to have come from Enfield (although other sources say Edmonton) and Cordells appear in Enfield records from at least 1411. Most appear to have been tilemakers or maltmen: Enfield Parochial Charities, LMA, Acc. 903. However the genealogy of Thomas and Elizabeth gives John Cordell's parents as William Cordell of Long Melford and his wife Thomasine née Smith. It is possible that the Enfield connection is through Sir William Cordell's grandfather rather than his father: Genealogy: CCALS, D5913.

6 The lay subsidy of 1525 includes the first known mention of John Cordell in any government records: TNA, E/179/180/152. However he first appears as a witness to the will of Simon Hall, husbandman in 1520: SROB, J 545/6/138.

7 Sir W. Parker, *The History of Long Melford* (London, 1873), pp. 235–6; Z. Dovey, *An Elizabethan Progress* (London, 1996), pp. 39–47.

8 Will of Sir William Cordell: TNA, PROB 11/63/42.

9 'Unto my loving sister Jane Allington, and to her heirs forever, all that my messuage, with the appurtenances, set, lying and being in Holborn, in the county of Middlesex, within the parish of St. Andrew': *ibid.*

10 The name is given as either Allington or Alington: C.R. Elrington (ed.), *VCH Cambs* (Oxford, 1978), VI, 71.

Jane Cordell had married Richard Allington, son of a Sir Giles Allington. Richard had died in 1561, leaving his wife with four young daughters. After 1581, and possibly earlier, Jane lived for much of the time at Allington House in High Holborn, London, the property left to her in her brother's will. In Thomas's lifetime the head of the Allington family was another Sir Giles Allington, whose mother Mary was a Spencer of Althorpe, and cousin to Elizabeth Savage.[11]

Two of Jane Allington's daughters married: Mary, the eldest, to Sir John Savage of Rocksavage in Cheshire and her sister Cordell to Sir John Stanhope of Shelford in Nottinghamshire. When she made her will Jane left Melford Hall and its lands to Thomas, eldest surviving son of Mary and Sir John Savage. He also inherited Jane's house at Brentford and (after his mother's death) half of Allington House in High Holborn. The other half of Allington House went to his cousin, Sir Philip Stanhope, who later became 1st earl of Chesterfield.[12] Thomas was one of the executors of Jane Allington's will.

The Savage family[13]

The Savages were one of the long established élite families of Cheshire. The family could trace their lineage to Thomas le Savage who came to England with the Norman army in 1066, and since the late fourteenth century a succession of nine John Savages had owned lands at Clifton, on the Weaver near Halton, and elsewhere in Cheshire. The Cheshire branch of the family had been founded when a John Savage of Derbyshire married the Danyer heiress to Clifton in 1375, and lands in Derbyshire were amongst Thomas's inheritance after his father's death in 1615.[14]

Thomas must have been proud of his family's long history for in 1631 he paid a herald of the College of Arms to produce a long family tree which shows his ancestors along with those of his wife.[15]Amongst Thomas's ancestors were a Sir John Savage probably knighted at Agincourt; a Sir John Savage who, with his father-in-law Lord Stanley, helped Henry VII to his crown on Bosworth field, and that John's brother Thomas Savage, archbishop of York.[16] Where land and money were concerned, marriages were vitally important. Thomas's great grandmother Savage was daughter of an earl of Worcester and, more importantly, his grandmother Savage was Elizabeth Manners, daughter of Thomas, 1st earl of Rutland. Her husband Sir John Savage had built a grand new house at Rocksavage (just yards away from their existing home at Clifton) in 1565.[17] This eighth Sir John was the holder of high office in Chester and Cheshire and several times an MP; later his

---

11 Giles Allington d. 1573, cousin to Thomas Savage's mother Mary, married Mary Spencer (sometimes given as Margaret); Mary Spencer's mother was Catherine née Kitson, aunt to Elizabeth Savage's mother.

12 Notes on People (pp. 159–95 below) includes information on many of the individuals mentioned in this Introduction.

13 The name is variously given as Savage, Savadge, Savedge, Savege; in this volume all have been given as Savage.

14 For the Savage family pedigree and a summary of family history: G.R Armstrong, *The Ancient and Noble Family of the Savages of the Ards* (London, 1888); IPM of Sir John Savage, 1615: TNA, CHES 3/91/7.

15 Savage genealogy: CCALS, D 5913. The roll is around 12 feet long.

16 The Sir John Savage who led the left at Bosworth had an illegitimate son who was grandfather of Bishop Bonner, notorious for his activities in Queen Mary's reign.

17 Elizabeth Manners' sister Gertrude married George Talbot, 6th earl of Shrewsbury. Two generations later Thomas was to be closely linked with his Manners relatives through much of his career, and the 7th earl of Shrewsbury acted on his behalf and called him cousin.

second marriage brought him lands at Beaurepaire in Hampshire where he lived for the latter part of his life.[18] These southern lands he left to his second son, Edward, who entertained Queen Elizabeth at Beaurepaire in 1601.

The next John Savage was born in 1554 and spent time at Lincoln's Inn before he married Mary Allington, probably in 1576; he spent a short time in London and then went to Ireland with Sir William Norreys in 1579. He had returned by 1585, so his eldest children were possibly baptised in London or Ireland. This John was not knighted until 1599, two years after he inherited the Savage lands from his father. He appears to have played his major role in Cheshire and Chester, rather than being closely involved with the royal court in London.[19] He was mayor of Chester and high sheriff of Cheshire. He may have served as a MP again in 1606, but appears not to have sought such office for many years; in a letter to the earl of Salisbury (Robert Cecil) in 1605 he said that he would now be prepared to take office in Cheshire, where formerly he had avoided it.[20] The inventories made in 1616 after his death suggest that a considerable amount of his movable property was not at Rocksavage but in Chester where he lived for at least some of each year. Sir John's belongings in the city were in other people's houses rather than in one he owned himself.[21] He also had goods at Allington House in London. Like his father before him, this Sir John Savage held his public positions despite being from a known catholic family.[22] Unlike his father and his son he had a quiet funeral, held in the evening.

John and Mary Savage had not intended to end the unbroken line of John Savages; they named their eldest son John, but he died very young and the succession settled on Thomas, their second son.[23] When Sir John Savage died in 1615 Thomas inherited substantial lands in north-east and north-west Cheshire. Many other family holdings in Cheshire and Derbyshire went to his mother as her jointure; those lands were due to revert to Thomas after his mother's death. However the dowager Lady Savage lived to a great old age, well into her eighties, and was buried on the same day as Thomas in 1635, so he presumably never received any income from that part of his inheritance.

The Darcy family

On Thursday, 13 May 1602, Thomas Savage married Elizabeth Darcy. 'On ascension day young Sir Thomas Savage was exalted and married to his fair mistress Darcy' wrote John Chamberlain in a letter to Dudley Carleton on the

---

18 He had been sheriff of Cheshire seven times, and three times mayor of Chester. Details of his very grand funeral survive: BL, Harleian MSS 2129. Some sources suggest that the John Savage who was MP for Cheshire in the 1580s was his son John, Thomas's father.

19 *The History of Parliament* records that John Savage was in trouble in London in 1576, before his marriage, for not taking sufficient care of his mistress. Sir William Norreys/Norris died later in 1579, so John may have returned considerably earlier than 1585.

20 The HMC calendar gives this as, 'whereas he has formerly endeavoured to be dispensed from the bill of sheriffs for Cheshire for divers reasons much importing his poor estate', he was now ready to take such a post 'if it shall seem good to the state': *HMC Salisbury (Cecil) MSS*, XVII (London, 1938), 483. Although his name does not appear on any of the lists of people selected as MP in the 1604–10 parliament, a Sir John Savage is mentioned as MP by the *Journal of the House of Commons* in 1606.

21 Inventory of Sir John Savage: CCALS, Savage WS1616–18.

22 The records do not survive to let us know whether he paid fines as a recusant, or was a 'church papist', attending just enough to avoid the fines and exile from public office.

23 John Savage died in 1580 aged three. It is probable that Thomas, the second son, had been born and baptised before this; if he had been born after the death of his brother he would surely have borne the usual name of the Savage heir; instead John and Mary named their third son John. Thus the most likely estimate for Thomas's birth is sometime in 1578–9.

17 May.[24] Her father was Thomas, third Baron Darcy of Chiche and her mother Mary was heiress of the Kitson family of Hengrave Hall in Suffolk.[25] Thus Thomas, soon to inherit a large Suffolk estate, married into two of the more important catholic land-owning families of the eastern counties. Whether Jane Allington's decision to leave Melford directly to Thomas followed or preceded the idea of an East Anglian marriage is impossible to know, but Chamberlain's letter suggests a match based on mutual attraction. Thomas's and Elizabeth's life and their careers at the royal court were to be intimately bound up with her Darcy family's fortunes.

The Savage family was long established by the time the sixth Sir John Savage led the left at Bosworth field, but it seems to have been Henry VII's favour that led the Essex branch of the Darcy family to national notice.[26] Thomas Darcy's great grandfather (Roger) was esquire of the body to Henry VII; his grandfather, the first baron (Thomas) rose through a variety of royal appointments under Henry VIII to be lord chamberlain to Edward VI in 1551–3. His marriage to Elizabeth de Vere daughter of the earl of Oxford was another alliance of powerful families in the eastern counties. This first baron Darcy signed the letters patent in 1553 settling the crown on Lady Jane Grey, so the family was out of favour in Queen Mary's reign. But the second baron (John) was knighted in 1559 at Elizabeth I's coronation and married the daughter of Baron Rich, another lord chamberlain. By this marriage John Darcy later became uncle of the earl of Warwick.[27] John Baron Darcy twice entertained the Queen at the family home at St Osyth, but died while still relatively young; his son Thomas, the third baron, inherited while in his mid teens.

Elizabeth came from a broken family. In 1583 Thomas Darcy had married Mary Kitson, daughter and co-heiress of Sir Thomas Kitson of Hengrave Hall in Suffolk, and his wife Elizabeth.[28] James Watney tells us that Darcy competed with Lord Percy for Mary Kitson, that she was thought to prefer Lord Percy, and that it might have been better if she had followed her inclinations. The Darcys had four children but 'groundless suspicions', or to use the words of Sir Harbottle Grimston, 'peevish jealousies', in her husband led to differences, which no interference of friends could reconcile. It appears that in 1594 the couple separated by mutual consent and never came together again, although both lived until the 1640s.[29] Lord Darcy lived at St Osyth and in London, while Lady Mary lived with various relations, before finally moving to Colchester. To quote from John Gage, 'The earl seems to have been a weak, perverse man careless of the affections of his consort, while the countess, with a proud heart and a masculine understanding, despised her husband.' Shortly

---

24 N. McClure, *Letters of John Chamberlain* (Philadelphia, 1939), I, 47. For John Chamberlain and Dudley Carleton, see Notes on People, below. For the family background of Darcy of Chiche, see *CP*, XI, 25–30 and J. Watney, *A Sole Account of St Osyths Priory* (London, 1871). There is another Baron Darcy involved in public affairs at this period, from Aston in Yorkshire.

25 Chiche (Essex) was the original name of the place later known as St Osyth, after the priory built there.

26 Thomas's great grandfather was Roger Darcy of Chiche; his ancestry can be traced back another three generations to a Sir Robert Darcy of Maldon who died in 1449.

27 John Lord Darcy's wife Frances Rich was aunt to Robert Rich, 1st earl of Warwick, so their son Thomas Darcy was his cousin. The earl of Warwick's wife was sister to the earl of Essex. When Thomas Lord Darcy was summoned to serve as a member of the jury at Essex's trial in 1601, he was called to condemn someone he probably regarded as a close relation.

28 Elizabeth Kitson was daughter of Sir Thomas Cornwallis of Brome Hall; see Notes on People, below. Both families were catholic. Elizabeth Cornwallis brought to Hengrave John Wilby, madrigalist, who remained at Hengrave until her death. Wilby has been called the 'most polished' of English madrigalists.

29 Watney, *St Osyths Priory*, p. 221. For Harbottle Grimston, see Notes on People, below.

after the separation her parents had wanted Mary to move back to Hengrave but she refused. Mary's maternal grandfather, Sir Thomas Cornwallis, wrote to her mother and called Mary 'your stubborn and ungreeting daughter'.[30]

The Darcy children were three daughters (Elizabeth was the eldest) and a son, another Thomas Darcy. Even more than usual was invested in this son because many of the Darcy lands would revert to the crown if there were no direct male succession.[31] We have no way of knowing where Elizabeth and her siblings spent their remaining childhood after the separation, although Elizabeth appears to have been on good terms with both her parents. A letter from the Hengrave collection suggests that Lady Kitson, his grandmother, was responsible for engaging a tutor for young Thomas, who made a promising start in court life in 1610, being appointed page to Prince Henry, prince of Wales.[32] But the prince of Wales died the next year and his page Thomas Darcy shortly after; although the latter had married, he had no children. Lord Darcy's brother had also died without heirs, so Darcy was now without a male heir. He and his son-in-law Thomas Savage were able to persuade James I to recognise Thomas as his successor.[33]

Thomas and Elizabeth and their children were to inherit not only from Elizabeth's father but also from her aunt Elizabeth, Thomas Darcy's sister. This older Elizabeth Darcy had married John Lord Lumley, a major figure in Elizabethan England, and another highly placed catholic.[34] Lumley's first wife, Jane, had been daughter to Henry Fitzalan, 12th earl of Arundel. Jane and John Lumley's children all died young, and Jane died in 1577.[35] While she was still alive the earl of Arundel had given the couple his house on Tower Hill, but they spent much of their time at his country home, Nonsuch Palace, near Cheam. Although Lumley was widowed by the time his father-in-law died, he still inherited much of the earl's goods and property, including Nonsuch.[36]

Lumley was living at Nonsuch when he married Elizabeth Darcy in 1582, and the couple continued using the palace as their principal home even after Lumley arranged, in 1592, to give it to Queen Elizabeth to release him from debts inherited from the earl of Arundel.[37] Edith Milner quotes a description of Elizabeth Lumley as 'a woman not only of an ancient pedigree and race, but, which is greatly to be praised, with the virtues of modesty, truth and conjugal love'. It seems highly likely that Elizabeth Darcy, as a favoured niece, spent some of her childhood at Nonsuch, and it is possible that her new husband Thomas made some of his early contacts with Prince Charles there, for King James and his two sons spent a considerable time at Nonsuch in the early years of his reign.[38] In 1604 when the earl of

30 J. Gage, *The History and Antiquities of Hengrave in Suffolk* (London, 1822), p. 216.

31 McClure, *Letters*, I, 489.

32 Gage, *Hengrave*, p. 216. Thomas Darcy is not listed in Prince Henry's household printed in T. Birch, *The Life of Henry Prince of Wales* (London, 1760), pp. 449–52.

33 Gage, *Hengrave*, p. 216; grant to Thomas Savage (in reversion from his father-in-law) of the dignity of Baron Darcy of Chiche: TNA, SP 14/141.

34 John Lord Lumley's life is summarised in *DNB*, xxxiv, 272–4, but see also Notes on People, below.

35 Called Joan in some records.

36 Grant of the house on Tower Hill to Jane and John Lumley: CCALS, DCH/O/75. For the earl of Arundel and Jane Lumley his daughter, see Notes on People, below.

37 Elizabeth Lumley originally received Nonsuch for her jointure; this was replaced by the manor of Stansted in Sussex after Nonsuch was given to Queen Elizabeth.

38 The *DNB* describes the earl of Arundel as the 'leader of the old nobility and the catholic party'. See also E. Milner (ed.), *Records of the Lumleys of Lumley Castle* (London, 1904), p. 90. The Lumley connection with the palace is described in J. Dent, *The Quest for Nonsuch* (London, 1970), chs 8 and 9.

Shrewsbury wrote to Lord Cecil on Thomas's behalf, he had obviously recently come from a visit to the Lumleys at Nonsuch (Doc. 6).

When Lumley died in 1609 his family lands, Lumley Castle near Chester le Street, County Durham and lands in Yorkshire and Sussex, went to his widow Elizabeth and to Richard Lumley his cousin. His famous library was divided up between James I, the Bodleian Library, Cambridge University Library and the Harsnett Library at Colchester. Those left to the king are now of the Royal Library, in the British Library. His Surrey lands, including his property near Nonsuch, went to his sister's children; most of his other possessions went to his widow.[39] When Elizabeth Lady Lumley died in 1617, George Lord Carew wrote that she had bestowed most of her estate and movables upon her niece, lord Darcy's daughter and wife to Sir Thomas Savage. In fact in her will she left the house on Tower Hill to her brother Thomas Darcy, to Elizabeth Savage after his death, and then to her grandson John Savage.[40]

The Kitson family[41]

The Kitsons were another family whose fortune had been made early in the sixteenth century. Thomas Kitson, who bought Hengrave Hall in 1520, was a merchant and one-time sheriff of London; he was knighted in 1533. One of his daughters married Sir William Spring, heir to a fortune made in the cloth industry in Suffolk. Sir Thomas Kitson died in 1540; his only son, another Thomas, was born posthumously. Margaret Kitson, his widow, married John Bouchier, earl of Bath, who was a catholic and a supporter of Queen Mary. The marriage settlement stipulated that the couple should live at Hengrave.[42]

Thus the second Thomas Kitson of Hengrave had grown up in a catholic household and he married Elizabeth Cornwallis, daughter of another major East Anglian catholic family.[43] In the early years of Elizabeth I's reign, Kitson and Sir Thomas Cornwallis, his father-in-law, were both clients of the duke of Norfolk. They suffered after his downfall, with Thomas Kitson being imprisoned for some time; however he wrote to the queen declaring his intention of adhering to the Protestant faith, and was released. Although he continued a traditionalist, and was consistently suspected of recusancy, he must have convinced the queen. She knighted him in 1578 on her way north through Suffolk on the same East Anglian progress that had taken her to Melford Hall, and she visited Hengrave on her way back to London.

Thomas and Elizabeth Kitson had only daughters (one son had died in infancy). Mary married Thomas Lord Darcy and her sister and co-heir, Margaret, married Sir Charles Cavendish. Margaret died soon after her marriage, leaving Mary as sole Kitson heiress; however she had to wait some time for her inheritance, for her mother lived on at Hengrave until a great age.[44] The family had lands in Devon as well as Suffolk.

---

39 Will of John Lumley: TNA, PROB 11/114/72.

40 IPM of Elizabeth Lumley: TNA, C142/377/50. Letter of George Lord Carew to Sir Thomas Roe: TNA, SP 15/95/165. Will of Elizabeth Lumley: TNA, PROB 11/129/13.

41 Often given as Kytson.

42 Dovey, *Progress*, pp. 104–6.

43 Elizabeth's father Sir Thomas Cornwallis had been in the service of the duke of Norfolk and had served Queen Mary. When she died he retired to his home at Brome, Suffolk.

44 For Sir Charles Cavendish, see Notes on People, below. It is possibly through this link that Thomas Darcy became closely involved with Gilbert Talbot, 7th earl of Shrewsbury, who had family links to Sir Charles. However Darcy's brother-in-law Lord Lumley was a close friend of the earl and this is perhaps a more likely link.

Thomas and Elizabeth Savage – their family and careers

There are just a couple of glimpses of Thomas before his marriage, and none of Elizabeth. Thomas had spent his childhood as the 'son of the heir' to the Savage inheritance as his grandfather, the eighth Sir John Savage, was still alive. When Thomas was admitted to Lincolns Inn on 28 October 1596 he was described as 'of Cheshire, gentleman'; his sponsors were a John Goodman and Ranulph Crewe.[45] Just over a year later his grandfather died and a splendid funeral took place at Macclesfield; this appears to have been when the world first took notice of Thomas as heir to the Savage lands, and the promise he showed. William Webb, who was present at the funeral, wrote of the greatness of old Sir John Savage and then of the new heir apparent:

> And why should not I add also that which even then the writer's muse was prophetically inspired with, concerning the great hope and worth of his issue, in the person of his grandchild, then a young plant and newly set to the Inns of Court to be trained up answerably to his birth and dignity, which she sang thus:
>
> That hopeful plant, that is the apparent heir
> Of all his glory, and this great descent:
> Oh! be the rest as his beginnings are
> That Savages may still be excellent.
> Sweet youth! who now, within these sacred bowers
> Where England's purest bloods do make abode
> In fruitful study, spends his happy hours,
> While nature him with blessings rare doth load.
> There he a mirror shines amongst his peers
> In all his carriage right heroical
> Pleasant in show, discreet beyond his years
> Well spoken, courteous and judicial.[46]

Thomas was probably still at Lincolns Inn in 1601, but the turn of the century had seen him recognised as an adult.[47] In 1598 he became joint steward of the lordship of Halton and keeper of Halton Park with his father, and a land settlement was made in 1600 which rehearsed much of the information given in the settlement made at his marriage, where his father identified the lands which would come to him (Doc. 1).[48] But Thomas possibly had military experience as well as legal training. When he was knighted on 31 October 1601, it was by Charles Lord Mountjoy, lord deputy of Ireland.[49] The place is not given, but must have been in or near Kinsale in Munster, where Mountjoy had been besieging Spanish troops since the start of October. It is doubtful that Mountjoy left the area until after the decisive battle of Kinsale on Christmas Eve 1601, where the Spaniards and the Irish leader

45 For Randolph Crewe, see Notes on People and Doc. 67, below.

46 William Webb, quoted in J.P. Earwaker, *East Cheshire Past and Present* (London, 1877), I, 10–11. Sir John Savage's funeral: BL, Harleian MSS 2129. For William Webb, see Notes on People, below.

47 Thomas is described as 'of Lincoln's Inn, esq' in a bond of 28 May 1601: CCALS, CR72/AppendixA/120.

48 Joint stewardship: *CP*, XI, 458. Land settlement: CCALS, DCH/E/302.

49 W.A. Shaw, *The Knights of England* (London, 1905), II, 99. For Mountjoy, see Notes on People, below.

Hugh O'Neill, Earl of Tyrone, were defeated.[50] Thomas's relative Sir Arthur Savage was in an important position in Ireland at the time, and it is possible that the young Thomas was with him or had gained a position through his influence. Shortly after he was knighted Thomas returned to London. A letter from the privy council to Lord Mountjoy written on 22 December 1601 chides him for not sending news of the siege; they had not received any direct communication from Mountjoy since Sir Thomas Savage had arrived back in England five weeks before, having come via Dublin.[51] Five months after this Thomas's marriage settlement was signed, and in May 1602 he and Elizabeth were wed.[52] Thomas's grandmother Jane Allington, from whom he inherited two houses, died shortly afterwards. Thomas was one of the executors of her will; this was probably his first experience as an executor, a role he was to undertake many times.[53]

We have seen that at various stages in their marriage Thomas and Elizabeth inherited lands and property from many family connections, and Elizabeth inherited more from her father after she was widowed.[54] She and her husband also inherited religion – the Savages and the Darcys were both amongst the leading catholic, recusant families of England. Their catholic faith was to be crucially important in their lives, their careers and in the fortunes of their houses.[55]

Early years

Between 1603 and 1630 Elizabeth Savage gave birth to nineteen children; of these twelve were still living when Thomas died in 1635.[56] Henry prince of Wales stood godfather at the baptism of the first, John, who was born shortly before 7 March 1604. The heir to the throne gave a royal gift of a cup and cover of silver gilt.[57] This is evidence of an early connection with the royal court; as Sir John Savage seems to have had little court experience, the links are more likely to have been through the

---

50 For Hugh O'Neill and Sir Arthur Savage, see Notes on People, below. In 1591 Tyrone had an affair with Mabel Bagenal (otherwise Bagnal or Bagnall), sister of Sir John Savage's brother-in-law Sir Henry Bagenal. When Sir Henry died in 1598 Sir John and his brother Edward Savage had to go to Ireland to attempt to sort out the estate, so Thomas's journey to Ireland could relate to this family business.

51 J.R. Dasent (ed.), *Acts of the Privy Council, 1601–04* (London, 1907), p. 437 (22 Dec. 1601).

52 Papers in the earl of Rutland's archive record: 'Given at the marriage of Sir Thomas Savage – Item for a gilt bason and ewer, weight 63 ounces and ¾ at 6s. 8d. £21 5s.', *HMC Fourteenth Report, Appendix I, Rutland IV* (London, 1905), 439.

53 Will of Jane Allington: TNA, PROB 11/103/9.

54 Grants from Thomas Earl Rivers to Elizabeth Savage: ERO, D/Dac/239, D/Dac/241.

55 No relevant records have been found of fines for recusancy in Suffolk or London in this period, but it is highly likely that Thomas was paying regular fines for himself, his family and his servants. When James I came to the throne catholics expected a relaxation in the laws against them. This did not occur and wealthy catholics had to pay more than in the previous reign. The Gunpowder Plot led to a further crack-down; fines were increased and the king empowered to seize two-thirds of the estate of any catholic who refused to attend protestant services. Catholics were forbidden to attend at court, or to remain in London if they had residence elsewhere. These laws were not strictly enforced in the longer term.

56 Funeral certificate, Doc. 57: College of Arms, MS I.8, f. 50r and v.

57 W. Beamont, *A History of the Castle of Halton and the Priory or Abbey of Norton* (Warrington, 1873), p. 108. J. Nichols, *The Progresses, Progressions and Magnificent Festivities of King James the First, his Royal Consort, Family and Court* (London, 1828), i, 604. Nichols says: 'May 16th 1604, Given by the prince his highness to Sir Thomas Savage knight at the christening of his child, one cup and cover of silver gilt, bought of John Williams, 30 oz. 3 qr. di.' We have found no record of John Savage's baptism, but a correspondent of Sir John Manners wrote from London on 7 March 1604, 'Mr Francis Manners' wife is with child and Sir Thomas Savage's lately delivered with a son': *HMC Twelfth Report, Appendix IV, Rutland I* (London, 1888), 387.

Darcy and Lumley families or through Thomas's kinship with the Manners family, earls of Rutland.[58]

By 1605 Thomas was a gentleman of James I's privy chamber; the year before he and his relative Sir Oliver Manners had bought the reversion of the office of clerk to the Star Chamber, after William Mills and Sir Francis Bacon.[59] The clerk to the Star Chamber was the principal officer of that court, with a salary of £36 13s. 4d. a year; two livery gowns were provided, one of damask and the other of wrought velvet. As far as we can tell Thomas never actually took up this office; presumably he sold his right to it at some later date.[60] He may have had other court or legal appointments, but survival of information about court appointments in particular is limited.[61] The Darcy family's links with Prince Henry's household have been mentioned, and a Mr Savage appears as one of the thirty-two 'gentlemen of the privy chamber extraordinary' on one list of that household; which Mr Savage this was we do not know, but he may well have provided another royal link for Thomas.[62] Whatever other roles he had, Thomas's privy chamber role alone would have meant that he had to be at court for at least three months a year; James I spent much of his time in London and at his other homes in the south-east, including Theobalds, his hunting lodge at Royston. If Thomas needed to attend at court, a home in the London area would be essential, and a country home within relatively easy reach of London a great advantage.[63]

Thomas inherited Melford Hall, at Long Melford in south-west Suffolk, when his grandmother died in 1602, and by summer 1604 the legal proceedings necessary for him to take possession seem to have been completed.[64] However Jane Allington's will, or rather what followed from it, had been challenged by her other grandson, Sir Philip Stanhope. He complained to Lord Cecil about Thomas's inheritance of Melford, with some talk of a suit-at-law (Doc. 5). We can find no evidence of this taking place, and the recovery by which Thomas took full legal ownership (Doc. 7) was dated just a few days later. Probably sometime in the interim, the earl of Shrewsbury had written to Robert Lord Cecil on Thomas's behalf (Doc. 6). From

58 In September 1605 Lord Lumley wrote to the earl of Shrewsbury and mentioned that Prince Henry and the duke of York [Prince Charles] were at his house in the country: *HMC Shrewsbury and Talbot Papers, II* (London, 1971), vol. K, f. 115. Elizabeth Lady Lumley wrote to the countess of Shrewsbury, in about 1608, to say she hoped that the visit of Prince [Henry] could be postponed, as her house had recently been infected: *ibid.*, vol. M, f. 412. Elizabeth's brother was a member of the prince's household. Elizabeth was also related to the Manners family, although the connection was more remote.

59 Gentlemen of the privy chamber had to be in at court one month in four; the position gave honour but was unpaid: G. Aylmer, *The King's Servants: the Civil Service of Charles I, 1625–1642* (London, 1961), p. 28.

60 Lease of Frodsham, 1605: CCALS, DCH/F/151. This describes Thomas Savage as of Long Melford, Suffolk, and a gentleman of the privy chamber. Reversion of office of clerk to the star chamber: TNA, SP 38/7. For Sir Oliver Manners, see Notes on People. William Mill held the office of clerk until 1608 and Sir Francis Bacon succeeded him. The next known holder of the office is Thomas May in 1623, but it is not clear whether Sir Francis Bacon officially held the office in all the intervening period. The known holders of the office are listed in J. Southerden, *The Star Chamber* (London, 1870).

61 If Thomas were recognised as a catholic, the law would, in theory, prevent him taking up public appointments.

62 T. Birch, *The Life of Henry Prince of Wales* (London, 1760), p. 449. Thomas Cornwallis also appears on this list, as groom porter. The date of the list is not known. Prince Henry spent a considerable amount of time at Nonsuch Palace.

63 This assumes that Thomas was attending at court and visiting London, both of which were legally denied to him under the laws against catholics. Throughout the reigns of both James I and Charles I the court accommodated more catholics or catholic sympathisers than the House of Commons or the majority of the English population wanted.

64 Details of a recovery in the court of Common Pleas: CCALS, DCH/O/75.

the information we have available, in particular Jane Allington's will (Doc. 4), it seems clear that Thomas had a rightful claim to Melford, but possibly that earlier in her life Jane Allington had arranged a different settlement, which was altered by her will. However in an agreement dated 1606 (Doc. 8) Thomas appears to pay Stanhope for his share of the Melford properties and his half of the High Holborn house, and in return appears to sell various properties in Norfolk to Stanhope, which he would inherit after the death of Dame Mary Savage, Thomas's mother.[65] We do not know if any money changed hands, but Stanhope definitely had the worst of the bargain, for Dame Mary Savage lived another twenty-nine years.[66] Surviving documents indicate other financial settlements being made at this period; one involves Sir George Carey of Cockington, executor to both Jane Allington and her brother Sir William Cordell. In 1607 Thomas was bound to pay George Carey £5000, but was released from the bond in return for releasing Carey from the obligations of these executorships.[67]

Thomas's parents were still alive and active in Cheshire, so he and Elizabeth seem to have settled on Melford as their main country home. By 1605 (and possibly earlier) Thomas was employing William Noye, later to become solicitor general, as his steward. Noye seems to have had responsibilities across Thomas's lands and certainly spent time at Melford (and probably also at Rocksavage) as well as in London.[68] In 1606 Elizabeth Savage's jointure was amended to add income from the Suffolk lands to the Cheshire ones listed in the original marriage agreement.[69] The indenture confirming the addition to the jointure describes Thomas as 'of Melford in Suffolk'. At this time Thomas was considering building work at Melford Hall, possibly major extensions to the house; the plan created then is included in this volume (Pl. 2, p. lxxii) and the extensions are considered in the section on Melford Hall later in this introduction.[70] The new developments extended outside the house, for in 1613 the king granted Thomas a licence to empark, or rather to create a new deer park (Doc. 13); the older park belonging to Melford Hall was a long way from the house and much of it had been converted into arable land in the 1580s. New building and a new hunting park presumably helped Thomas and Elizabeth entertain their friends and others whom they wished to impress, but must have cost a good deal.[71]

With the extensions and the new deer park in place, Thomas may have felt that he had put his stamp on the Melford lands, and that this should be recorded. In 1613 he commissioned a major new map of his lands in Melford and surrounding parishes

---

65 Jane Allington's will (Doc. 4) left the other half of the High Holborn house to Thomas Savage's mother for her life, and then to Thomas.

66 Agreement between Sir Thomas Savage and Sir Philip Stanhope: CCALS, DCH/O/42. For Sir Philip Stanhope, see Notes on People, below.

67 Indenture between Sir George Carey and Sir Thomas Savage: CCALS, DCH/U/37.

68 See Docs 11 and 50. For William Noye, see Notes on People, below. His name is given as Noye or Noy.

69 Increase to jointure: CCALS, DCH/O/29.

70 Thomas may have financed this work by the sale of lands; in 1608 he was finalising the sale of lands in Nottinghamshire and Derbyshire to his uncle Sir John Manners: *HMC, Rutland I*, 413.

71 John Thorpe's plan of the Hall is thought to be from this period; Sir John Summerson identified it as being in the same style as Thorpe's work on the king's house at Theobalds, which was definitely done in 1606. Thorpe drawings: J. Summerson (ed.), *The Book of Architecture of John Thorpe in Sir John Soane's Museum*, Walpole Society (Glasgow, 1966), p. 105. The licence to empark is Doc. 13 in this volume; the original is at Melford Hall. The Salisbury MSS include a docquet dated 17 April, 1612 giving Thomas and Elizabeth licence to empark 400 acres: *HMC Salisbury (Cecil) MSS, XXI, 1609–1612* (London, 1970), 319.

(Pl. VII), along with a detailed survey (Pl. 3); both remain at Melford Hall.[72] The survey shows that 2,960 acres of land were let, at a rental of £1196 2s. 8d. Another 739 acres of park, woods and lands were 'in hand', with no estimated rental value, but it has been estimated that the value of the estate totalled around £1500 a year. Included in the rental is Melford Green which seems always to have belonged to the manor of Melford Hall. Shortly after Thomas inherited the Melford lands, the owership of the Green had been disputed by Sir William Waldegrave, guardian of Sir William Clopton, heir to Kentwell Hall in Melford. The two men 'entered onto the green called Melford Green, which is in controversy between them and Sir Thomas Savage knight, and claimed to hold the same as part of the manor of Monks Melford'.[73]

Jane Allington had left Thomas not only Melford Hall, but also a house near Brentford bridge.[74] Although it was outside London, Thomas and Elizabeth seem to have used this as their family home near London during the first part of their marriage. It was presumably close enough to London for Thomas to be able to see his wife and children reasonably often while being at court. Eight of their children were baptised at All Saints, Isleworth and the church contained a memorial to three of their children who died young.[75] There is a surviving letter from William Noye to 'Mr Savage's house at Brentford', another from Thomas from Brentford in 1609. Elizabeth later wrote of a woman who had been her neighbour for many years at Brentford (Doc. 41).[76] The last of Thomas's and Elizabeth's children to feature in the All Saints' parish register was Dorothy, baptised in 1614. It may be that once they inherited Lumley House on Tower Hill in 1617, Thomas and Elizabeth made less use of the Brentford house and decided to lease it out. In 1635 Thomas's inventory includes the lease of the house near Brentford bridge for, at that stage, thirty-seven years, worth £800. The lease must originally have been to William Noye, for a map of Isleworth dated 1635 shows a house labeled 'Mr Noye' just beside Brentford bridge, backing on the orchard of Syon House and just across the river from Richmond Palace.[77] This would have been well placed for Thomas and later for Noye, who is known to have died in his house at Brentford. Presumably

---

72 The survey has been rediscovered very recently, after having spent over 100 years in a bank vault.

73 Entry onto Melford Green in December 1609: BL, Harleian MS 99/94. The Cloptons held the manor of Monks Melford, which borders the green.

74 The house was on the western side of the bridge, just in the parish of Isleworth. The gardens of the house had formerly been the site of All Angels chapel, which had belonged to the monastery of Sheen. In documents relating to Sheen, a tenant called Walter Sprott is recorded. Lysons (see note 75 below) records that the house was called 'the Sprotts' in ancient records: G.J. Aungier, *The History of Syon Monastery* (London, 1840), p. 225. We are grateful to Gill Clegg for this reference. The 'ancient record' is a list of the possessions of Shene Abbey: BL, Cotton MSS Otho, B.xiv, f. 89.

75 The parish register entries are listed in D. Lysons, *The Environs of London* (London 1796), III, 110. As well as baptisms between 1607 and 1614, there are two burials. Lysons says of All Saints, Isleworth 'In the south east corner is a monument (with corinthian columns, and the effigies of the deceased) to the memory of three children of Sir Thomas Savage, afterwards Viscount Savage. It has no name or date, but the arms and the entries in the parish register sufficiently point out for whom it was intended': Lysons, *ibid.*, 104. He also records that Thomas had placed a stone in memory of a vicar of All Saints near to the monument commemorating the children. All Saints, Isleworth was damaged by fire in 1943 and only the tower survives; presumably the memorial perished at that time.

76 Letter from Noye referring to Thomas Savage's house at Brentford: TNA, SP 15/37/46. Letter from Sir Thomas Savage to his uncle Sir John Manners, 15 October 1609: *HMC Rutland I*, 417. Letter about a neighbour from Brentford: TNA, SP 16/143/44.

77 Map of the hundred of Isleworth by Moses Glover for Algernon Percy, earl of Northumberland, 1635. The map is still at Syon House, London home of the dukes of Northumberland. An 1876 facsimile of the map: BL Maps, 189a.11.

Noye's son bought the house from John Savage when he inherited; it was owned by Humphrey Noye by the civil war and sequestered from him in 1643.[78]

In 1605 a stillborn child of Thomas's and Elizabeth's was buried at St Olave's, Hart Street, the church just yards away from John Lord Lumley's house on Tower Hill.[79] John Lumley died in 1609 after a long illness, and by 1610 his widow and Thomas had come to an agreement about her finances and property (Doc. 10) by which Thomas 'bought' all her household goods.[80] Elizabeth Lumley's will mentions that Thomas had lodgings in the Tower Hill house, so it seems quite likely that at very least he and his family regularly visited the Lumleys at Tower Hill, and that Thomas stayed there at times before Elizabeth Lumley's death.[81] The family might also have used Allington House in High Holborn as a central London base; Thomas's mother had inherited part of this from her mother, and it was to go to Thomas after her death.

Although London and Suffolk may have been the focus of Thomas's life at this period, family affairs would have drawn him back to Cheshire. In 1605 the city council of Chester agreed that he should receive the freedom of that city when he next visited, and in 1607, while his father was mayor of Chester, he was elected an alderman of the city. However he had been elected without his knowledge, and he turned down the office because of other 'occasions'.[82] Whether that related to his need to be in London and Suffolk we do not know, but Thomas was ridding himself of his Derbyshire and Nottinghamshire lands and property at this time; he sold most to his uncle Sir John Manners in 1608. This could have been for financial reasons, or because he wanted to concentrate his interests in Cheshire, Suffolk and London.[83] He presumably returned to Cheshire when a Ralph Bathurst murdered his younger brother John in 1609. Bathurst was arraigned but refused to plead, so was sentenced to the 'peine forte et dure', which means that he was pressed to death.[84] The murder of Thomas's brother was presumably a major family crisis of the period, but in 1612 a family lawsuit involved Thomas, his father Sir John and his uncle Edward Savage versus Sir Richard Trevor, a relative of Sir John Savage's sister Elinor. This may not have been very important in itself, but was probably part of a long running saga which had begun before 1600 involving Elinor's first husband Sir

78 *DNB*. The story of his house is given in C. O'Riordan, 'The Story of a Gentleman's House in the English Revolution', *Trans of the London and Middlesex Archaeological Society*, 38 (1987), 165–7. Noye was buried in Brentford church, just across the river from the house, and considerably nearer than All Saints, Isleworth. His eldest son Edward inherited, but died not long after his father; his brother Humphrey then inherited the house. Humphrey Noye and Elizabeth Savage were joint defendants in a case in the court of requests in 1639: CCALS, DCH/F/931.

79 Parish register transcript held at St Olave's, Hart Street.

80 Letters from John Lord Lumley to the earl of Shrewsbury about his ill health, and commiserating with the earl about his own problems with gout, occur from January 1605 onwards. In a letter written in February 1608 he gives a melancholy account of his illness. He is bereft of the use of legs and one of his arms: *HMC Talbot Papers* (London, 1971), L, f. 147.

81 A letter from Thomas Savage to his uncle Sir John Manners was written in 1609 at Tower Hill (probably on 28 October): *HMC Rutland I*, 418.

82 Freedom of Chester and election as alderman: M. Groombridge (ed.), *Calendar of Chester City Council Minutes, 1603–1642*, Record Society of Lancashire and Cheshire (Blackpool, 1956), pp. 19, 35–6.

83 Sale of lands in Derbyshire and Nottinghamshire to Sir John Manners: *HMC Rutland I*, 413.

84 Beamont, *Halton*, p. 105. If an accused man suffered 'peine forte et dure', his family did not loose all their possessions and privileges, which they would do if he was condemned as a murderer.

Henry Bagenal and the family of her second, Sir Sackville Trevor. There are echoes of this family dispute until at least 1622.[85]

There were other, more positive, family matters. In 1611 Thomas's father became one of the first baronets created by the king. This new rank was introduced expressly to raise money, and like all baronets Sir John Savage had to pay £1095 for the honour. But the purchase meant that Sir John's heirs would succeed to an hereditary honour. Foreign travel was another, presumably new, experience. In May 1613 Elizabeth Lady Lumley was granted a licence for herself, her friends and twenty-four servants to go to Spa to help her improve her health, taking £200 in money with her; the licence was for twelve months. Foreign travel was still worth remarking on, and the English ambassador to Brussels was told by a correspondent that Lord Darcy, his sister and the Savages were on their way to Spa.[86] Unfortunately we have no idea how long they spent away.[87]

Besides family tragedy, family preferment and family holidays, there was also the matter of gaining lands. Back in 1566 the earl of Rutland had obtained a thirty-one-year lease of the manor and lordship of Frodsham from the crown and assigned it to his son-in-law Sir John Savage, Thomas's grandfather. Frodsham is very close to Rocksavage, just across the river Weaver. This Sir John left this lease of Frodsham to his widow, and then to his eldest son.[88] This next Sir John, Thomas's father, inherited other properties and interests in the town directly, some of which he appears to have passed to Thomas by 1603.[89] In 1610 old Sir John's widow (by this time Lady Remington, and widowed again) assigned the lease to Thomas, who then bought the manor and lordship from the crown.[90]

Thomas then began buying property in Frodsham owned by smaller landowners.[91] To quote one local historian, 'This left only the lands in lease, which he called in and re-let at considerably higher rates. Those who would not pay or who queried his exorbitant demands were turned out and the land let to new men.'[92] Thomas also increased the annual charge on the farmers of tithes by some fourteen per cent, which presumably meant that the farmers in turn attempted to get at least as much extra from the landholders. At the same time he denied the right of anyone to hold land in the parish unless they held written proof of their title. Few had, which meant that many in the parish and, in particular the burgesses, were dispos-

85 Answers to a bill of complaint by Sir Richard Trevor, 1612: CCALS, DCH/E/304/5/9.

86 Licence to Elizabeth Lumley to travel, 9 May 1613: TNA, SO 3/5. Letter from John Throckmorten to William Trumbull, English ambassador in Brussels: *HMC Downshire IV* (London, 1940), 117. Spa, now in Belgium, is south-east of Liège. If Elizabeth Lumley and her family took all the allowed servants, they must have made a considerable party. Spa, where the waters have been recognised as therapeutic since Roman times, gave its name to any place of health-giving waters and enjoyment. The wealthy English went in sufficient numbers for Charles I to approve the establishment of an Anglican parish there in 1627.

87 At the end of July 1614 the privy council gave a pass for John Savage gent. to travel for three years, with one man, trunks of apparel and other provisions, with the proviso that he was not to go to Rome. It seems unlikely that this was Thomas's and Elizabeth's son, who was only eleven; it may have been Thomas's illegitimate stepbrother John, or his cousin John, son of his uncle Edward Savage.

88 Frodsham lease left to Elinor Savage, later Remington: CCALS, DCH/F/148.

89 J.P. Dodd, *A History of Frodsham and Helsby* (Frodsham, 1987), p. 53. This seems to have included the tithes of Frodsham, about which an injunction was sought in 1602: CCALS, DCH/F/150.

90 Assignment of lease to Thomas, December 1610: CCALS, DCH/F/153.

91 A grant of 1613 says that Savage paid £1884 2s. 4d. for the manor of Frodsham: TNA, SO 3/3, no. 119. Additional purchases: CCALS, DCH/F/155a, DCH/F/167. The latter refers to lands bought from John Done of Utkinton, one of his friends, in 1616: H.F. Starkey, *Old Runcorn* (Halton, 1991), p. 74. There are hundreds of documents about Frodsham at this period and earlier: CCALS, DCH/F.

92 Dodd, *Frodsham*, p. 54.

sessed on the spot.[93] The Frodsham economy was dependent on access to the marsh; the pasture and meadow elsewhere was said to be insufficient for the inhabitants' livestock.

The inhabitants of Frodsham appealed to James I to save them from Thomas's determination to increase his lands.[94] They accused Thomas of enclosing common lands, thus denying them their ancient rights to grass, turf, fern and stone. The king did not respond, so the inhabitants appealed to Prince Charles, as hereditary lord of the manor. When by 1616 they had received no help from him, they appealed to the privy council. The inhabitants of Frodsham explained that they found it difficult to take Thomas to court because of his power in the county, his many friends amongst those who might form a jury, the fact that he had already threatened them and that they were scared of his power to harm them.[95]

The privy council, which had recently made Thomas a deputy lieutenant of Cheshire, appointed commissioners to hear the arguments. The letter of appointment said that although the council knew Thomas to be a gentleman of worth, and the sort who 'we presume' would not take unjust proceedings against those who petitioned against him, they felt it necessary to get more information about the justness of the complaints.[96] However the people of Frodsham refused to cooperate with the commissioners, because they thought the result a foregone conclusion; Thomas had ties by marriage to four of the commissioners and strong social ties with the others.[97] The privy council continued with their enquiry, while the inhabitants of Frodsham took direct action and physically occupied the marsh meadows. Skirmishes and worse took place; the castle bailiff reported that women and boys with staves were lying under the hedges.[98] Eventually twenty Frodsham inhabitants were summoned to the court of Star Chamber. By the mid 1620s Thomas had enclosed the marsh. Another local historian has commented that while Thomas prospered, life became increasingly difficult for the poor of Frodsham.[99]

At his death Thomas held the castle, manor and borough of Frodsham, 30 messuages, 10 cottages, 20 burgages, a windmill, a dovecot, three water mills and nearly 300 acres of land in the town.[100] The contents of Frodsham castle do not appear in Thomas's inventory because in the mid 1620s he gave it to his eldest son John as his home; presumably all its movable goods belonged to John. Before that, from 1612 onwards, accounts of the castle indicate rebuilding and redecorating.[101] The detail that is available for Frodsham (of which this is just a brief summary), and some of the information we have about Savage's role as Ranger of the Forest of

93 *Ibid.*, pp. 54–5.

94 The story is told in detail in J.P. Dodd, 'Sir Giles Overreach in Cheshire', *Cheshire History*, Autumn 1993, 11–19, and in Dodd, *Frodsham*, pp. 54–8. Petition from Frodsham residents to Thomas, 1614: CCALS, DCH/F/159. Petition from 1616: DCH/F/170.

95 Frodsham inhabitants' appeal to Charles I: *CP*, XI, 458.

96 J.V. Lyle (ed.), *Acts of the Privy Council, 1616–17* (London, 1927), p. 98.

97 The commissioners were Sir George Booth, Sir Ranulph Mainwaring, Sir Thomas Delves, John Done, William Brereton and Ralph Wilbraham. Savage called two of them, Done and Wilbraham, friends with whom he was able to laugh and be merry (Doc. 20).

98 Dodd, *Frodsham*, p. 57.

99 Starkey, *Runcorn*, p. 75. Thomas also owned the nearby manor of Helsby, and it appears that between 1613 and 1617 he increased rents by some 18% and enclosed common land, before renting it back to tenants who had previously had free use of it. One source says he had acquired Helsby in 1612, but the surviving sale documents are dated 1614. The Ireland family had previously owned Helsby. Bargain and sale: CCALS, DCH/F*/26. There were border disputes between Helsby and Frodsham.

100 IPM of Thomas Viscount Savage: TNA, CHES 3/103/12; Doc. 62 in this book.

101 Frodsham Castle accounts: CCALS, DCH/F/158.

Delamere (Docs 43, 49 and 67) highlight the paucity of information about relations between Thomas Savage and his Suffolk tenants. Court rolls for the manor of Melford Hall survive for just four years between 1610 and 1618, and they seem to reflect a continuation of routine business.[102] Quarter sessions records might have provided evidence if there were any particular conflicts, but they do not survive for Suffolk in this period.[103]

Gaining lands and status

When Thomas Baron Darcy of Chiche was left without a male heir, he faced the possibility that his title would die with him and that a large part of his lands would revert to the crown. By October 1613 Darcy and Savage had managed to persuade the king to grant the dignity of Baron Darcy of Chiche to Thomas after the death of his father-in-law.[104] They also found the large amount of money necessary to ensure that at least some of the lands stayed in the family. According to a letter from John Chamberlain to Sir Dudley Carleton, written in November that year, Thomas had paid a large amount to ensure that half Thomas Darcy's lands, and his title, would come to him after his father-in-law's death.[105]

Sir John Savage, Thomas's father, died in the summer of 1615 and was buried in the family chapel at Macclesfield.[106] Thomas became a baronet and finally inherited those Cheshire lands not still held by his mother.[107] He and his father had an earlier agreement about goods at Rocksavage (Doc. 9), and now he made an agreement with his mother about the goods she should keep for herself (Doc. 14); by this he finally gained ownership of lands in the Melford area which he had been renting from his father. Thomas also inherited some of his father's positions in Cheshire; a letter to the privy council in November 1616 says that the earl of Derby wanted Thomas to become a deputy lieutenant of Cheshire in place of his father.[108] This letter was dated just under a month before the privy council appointed the commissioners to investigate the situation in Frodsham. While the Frodsham problems were being investigated, Thomas may have wanted to be in Cheshire. However he would also have needed to be in London in February 1617, when Elizabeth Lady Lumley, died.[109] Although her will left the Tower Hill house to her brother Thomas Darcy, and after his death to her niece Elizabeth Savage and then to Elizabeth's eldest son John, the house seems to have gone straight to Thomas Savage in right of his

102 Manorial rolls, manor of Melford Hall: SROB, Acc. 466.

103 The incursion onto Melford Green mentioned earlier (note 73) may be a one-off incident or part of a much wider schism between the local landowners.

104 Almost all references to Thomas in the Signet Office book spell his surname Savadge or Savedge. Thomas Savage to inherit barony, October 1613: TNA, SO 3/5.

105 'Most of the Lord Darcy's lands by the death of his brother and his son (for want of heirs male) after his decease are to return to the crown, whereupon Sir Thomas Savage that married his daughter has (by the earl of Somerset's means in giving him £24,000 and half the land) compounded for the rest, and for the barony after his father-in-law': TNA, SP 15/75/212.

106 The Savages had been buried at Macclesfield since the late fourteenth century, when the John Savage who married into the Cheshire lands was appointed bailiff of the Forest of Macclesfield: Starkey, *Runcorn*, p. 73. Thomas Savage, archbishop of York, built the Savage chapel in the early sixteenth century.

107 Will of Sir John Savage: CCALS, DCH/E/311.

108 Lyle, *Acts of the Privy Council, 1616–17*, p. 74. Elizabeth Savage was related to the earl of Derby's wife, who was a de Vere, daughter of the earl of Oxford. There was also a relationship through the Kitson family.

109 Thomas and his father-in-law Thomas Darcy, her brother, were executors of her will.

wife.[110] It seems likely that Thomas Darcy gave it to them in a document now missing.

The year 1617 must have been a busy one for Thomas, Elizabeth and their employees. Not only was Elizabeth delivered of a daughter called Ann, in the late spring,[111] but they had to prepare for the visit of James I to Rocksavage in late August on his way back to London from Scotland.[112] During August King James came south via Preston; on 21 August he entered Cheshire and rode to Rocksavage; he had a day of hunting with Thomas and then left for Vale Royal, the Cholmondeley home. He did not spend the night at Rocksavage, but the inventory of 1636 starts with the contents of 'the king's chamber' which presumably recalls that visit.[113]

One of the difficulties of trying to assess Thomas's career at court is to know how able he was. We cannot judge only from the positions he held because if he was known as a catholic he was officially barred from public office. Like his relative the earl of Rutland and other catholics close to the court and linked to the marquis of Buckingham, he did receive some appointments, but as a catholic or suspect catholic he was not going to be appointed to major government office.[114] Does the fact that he was appointed to numerous commissions on financial matters indicate that he had considerable ability in this area, or were the appointments all because of his relationship with Buckingham? Early in 1618 John Chamberlain wrote to Sir Dudley Carleton, following the death of the chancellor of the duchy of Lancaster, Sir John Deckham. He reported that many were seeking the vacant place, including Sir Thomas Savage, Sir Richard Weston and Sir Lionel Cranfield.[115] Other evidence suggests that forty-three men contended for the post, which was in the marquis of Buckingham's gift and expected to cost around £8000, but that these three were amongst the most likely to succeed. In the event the chancellorship went to Sir Humphrey May, whose case had been argued by the lord chamberlain, Lord Pembroke, and the Countess of Bedford. Weston and Cranfield (by then earl of Middlesex) both became Lord Treasurer later in their careers, so Thomas was competing with able men. More evidence comes from the decision of numerous people to make him executor of their wills; someone might be appointed to high

110 Will of Elizabeth Lumley: TNA, PROB 11/129/13. Lady Lumley's death was not the end of the Savage/Lumley link. The Lumley titles and Durham lands had passed from John Lord Lumley to a young cousin, Richard. Richard Lord Lumley was later involved in financial affairs with both Thomas Savage and his son John.

111 Ann was baptised at Melford. We have records of all nineteen of Thomas's and Elizabeth's children: eight were baptised at All Saints, Isleworth, four were baptised at Melford (including two baptised at both Melford and Isleworth), three at St Olave's; the places of baptism of the other six are unknown. We have not been able to find any mention of children of this family in parish registers in the area around Rocksavage.

112 On 29 June 1617 Roger Gray of Northumberland, Thomas Savage of Cheshire and John Caesar were knighted at Edinburgh. *CP* assumes that this was 'our' Sir Thomas, but he had been knighted much earlier and was a baronet by this time. Neither was this his second son being knighted, for that happened several years later.

113 Ormerod includes a description written by William Webb, published originally as *King's Vale Royal*. This and Nichols' *Progresses* provide a description of the visit. These are included in the section on Rocksavage in G. Ormerod, *A History of the County Palatine and City of Chester* (2nd edn, London, 1882), p. 408 and are quoted later in this introduction.

114 R. Lockyer, *The Early Stuarts* (London, 1998), pp. 289–90. It is possible that before 1622 he was acting as a 'church papist', doing the minimum necessary to keep on the side of the law. See below for his confession of his religion to James I in 1622.

115 McClure, *Letters*, II, 133.

office because of the favour of a favourite, but few are likely to appoint as their executor someone whose ability and trustworthiness was in doubt.

Little is known of the family life of Thomas and Elizabeth in this period, although she was still regularly giving birth. However on 9 October 1618 Thomas's mother Dame Mary Savage left Bostock, Cheshire for an extended stay in London. We do not know how long she intended to stay away, but she took all her jewels and gold and silver plate with her, and made her will the day she left.[116] The visit was to cause major family problems. On Dame Mary's return to Cheshire her valuables were sent to Chester in a trunk, but at some point the jewels, gold and silver disappeared. Mary Mainwaring, grand-daughter of Dame Mary and daughter of Thomas's sister Elizabeth, was suspected of taking the goods; that probably split the family. In a court case after Dame Mary's death in 1635, Thomas's two sisters and their husbands were still arguing about this theft, and about pretend wills and codicils. It seems likely that Thomas and Elizabeth were involved in many years worth of family arguments about this business. Thomas would have had a direct interest because at least some of the jewels and plate would have been due to come to him after his mother's death.[117]

Thomas continued to gain positions which brought prestige and income. In 1619 he had been made ranger of Delamere Forest, near Frodsham, and in 1620 his name appears, along with dozens of others of high social status, as one of the commissioners for ecclesiastical causes in the north.[118] He was also closely involved in the affairs of the city of Chester. He was an alderman of Chester at least from 1619, and probably earlier; he was also one of the noblemen regularly called upon to support the city in dealings with the court or privy council, in disputes with other powerful men, or when the city was riven by quarrels amongst the aldermen. The first evidence of this intervention was in the late summer of 1619, when Thomas, the earl of Derby and Sir Peter Warburton, a judge of the Common Pleas, were asked by the city of Chester to resolve a bitter dispute between their mayor and their recorder, which had caused feuding for many months. The chronicler quoted by Catherine Patterson wrote that Warburton and Savage made the warring parties friends; Savage gave each a fat buck on condition that they should give hospitality to each other in their own homes.[119]

This happened with the earl of Derby present, and many other knights and gentlemen. Catherine Patterson comments that the ceremonial feast showed the whole community that the troubles had ended, but the authors of the *VCH* have established that the families of Whitby the recorder, and Gamull the mayor, had been feuding since 1602, that the quarrel continued, and that it had a major impact on the Chester elections in 1627. Aristocratic patronage was not always successful. Council minutes of Chester record other occasions when Thomas was called on to

116 Her will is printed in G.J. Piccope (ed.), *Lancashire and Cheshire Wills and Inventories from the Ecclesiastical Court, the third portion*, Chetham Society, LIV (London, 1861), 185–6. She left almost all her goods to her daughter Elizabeth Manwaring; the phrasing of the will suggests that Mary may have expected opposition from her other children about this.

117 Legal papers about the contested will of Dame Mary Savage: CCALS, Savage, WC 1635. Her daughter Grace Wilbraham took out letters of administration for her mother in May 1636; this was presumably a tactical move at some stage in the contest over her estate.

118 T. Rymer, *Foedera* (The Hague, 1745), VII, pt III, 173.

119 C. Patterson, 'Conflict Resolution and Patronage in Provincial Towns, 1590–1640', *Journal of British Studies*, 37, 1998, 1–25; Groombridge, *Chester Minutes*, pp. 96–108; B.E. Harris (ed.), *A History of the County of Chester* (*VCH*, Oxford, 1979).

provide the city with his patronage or resolve a conflict, some of which are described later.

The limitations of aristocratic patronage were evident again late in 1620, when Thomas proposed John Savage, his step brother, and Sir John Bingley as potential MPs for Chester in the 1621 parliament. His proposals went against the pressure from London, for the government was trying to impose two court candidates, Sir Henry Cary and Sir Thomas Edmondes. Savage and Bingley were well-respected Cheshire men, but there were two other local candidates from Chester itself. Cary was chosen for another seat, so did not stand. On election day, 25 December 1620, the two Chester men, Edmund Whitby and John Ratcliffe, were victorious.[120]

At this period there is no evidence to suggest how much of their time Thomas and Elizabeth were spending in London, Suffolk or Cheshire. Thomas must have been regularly in London for Glyn Redworth says that he was close to Diego Sarmiento de Gondomar, the Spanish ambassador, who had returned to London in 1620. In the spring of 1621 Thomas warned Gondomar to stay at home on Shrove Tuesday, because he might be threatened if he ventured out.[121]

In the history of Stuart government these years are well known for the rise of George Villiers, later duke of Buckingham. By the early 1620s Buckingham was the second most powerful man in England and by many accounts the most unpopular, except to those who depended upon him.[122] Starting as favourite of James I from 1614 onwards, becoming lord high admiral by 1619, Buckingham moved on to become Charles I's principal minister and confidant; his family members and his friends were promoted in many areas of court and government. A group of catholic or crypto-catholic peers benefited particularly from his patronage, Thomas and his relations amongst them. From this point it must be assumed that many of the promotions or positions obtained by Thomas or Elizabeth, or by her father Lord Darcy, were at least partly the result of their being close to Buckingham. The connection was the Manners family, earls of Rutland. Thomas's grandmother had been daughter of the first earl, while Buckingham married Katherine Manners, daughter of Francis, the 6th earl.[123] The only direct correspondence between Savage and Buckingham to survive which is personal rather than about matters of finance or administration is a letter written by Buckingham in September 1622. He had been trying to help Thomas in a family dispute, but reports that his meeting with the woman in question had not gone well. He wrote to Thomas to try to repair any

---

120 J.K. Gruenfelder, 'The Parliamentary Election at Chester, 1621', in *Trans of the Historic Society of Lancashire and Cheshire*, 120, 1969, 35–44. John Savage did serve as MP for Chester in 1624 and 1626.

121 Our thanks to Glyn Redworth for the chance to read extracts from his book 'The Prince and the Infanta' before it was published. He says of Gondomar: 'the envoy normally preferred not to specify who his sources were at any one time, but Thomas Savage and Lord Wooton were particularly close in 1621, the former writing to warn him earlier that year, on the day before Shrove Tuesday, to be on his guard, close all the windows, and not to venture out, on account of English hotheads'. G. Redworth, *The Prince and the Infanta, the Cultural Politics of the Spanish Match* (London, 2003), p. 149. Redworth's reference: AGS, Estado Libro 374, ff. 79–80.

122 R. Lockyer, *Buckingham, the Life and Political Career of George Villiers, first Duke of Buckingham 1592–1628* (London, 1981) provides the most recent detailed examination of Buckingham's career.

123 Only three generations separate the 1st and 7th earls: three of the intervening ones died without a male heir and were succeeded by a brother. The 6th earl and Thomas were both great grandchildren of the 1st earl of Rutland. We have already seen Thomas linked in office-seeking with Oliver Manners, the 6th earl's brother. In February 1620 Sir George Manners (later the 7th earl), Thomas and another knight were granted the reversion of the office of constable and porter of Nottingham Castle, and warden of the forest of Sherwood, after the death of the 6th earl: TNA, SO 3/7, February 1620.

damage which he, Buckingham, may have caused. This is of no great import in itself but provides evidence of close relations between the two men.[124]

Buckingham faced considerable problems in getting the earl of Rutland to agree to his daughter's marriage.[125] Several mediators were needed at various stages. Lockyer, Buckingham's principal recent biographer, says that Lionel Cranfield and Thomas Savage, both friends of Buckingham, worked together and that Cranfield later claimed that they were instrumental in making the marriage possible. The reference is to an unfinished letter drafted years later from Cranfield, by then the earl of Middlesex, to the widowed duchess of Buckingham. Middlesex is reported to have written that the marriage only came about because of his and Thomas Savage's efforts.[126]

Lockyer goes on to suggest that John Williams, one of the king's chaplains, may have been more important in making the marriage (one of his jobs was to attempt to persuade Katherine to forsake her catholicism).[127] However he records that Buckingham and Katherine were married very quietly at Lumley House, near Tower Hill, where Rutland was staying.[128] Another recent author tells us that the marriage was celebrated so quietly that John Chamberlain (normally very well informed), writing eleven days later, could only speak of it as a matter of uncertain report. In fact, only the king himself and the earl of Rutland had been present to witness the nuptials.[129] Because of this secrecy it is impossible to know whether either or both Thomas or Elizabeth were present, in the next room or banished for the occasion.[130]

Royal favour and rural nobility

On 5 July 1621 Thomas's father-in-law, Lord Darcy, was made Viscount Colchester. The reversion of the title after his death went to Sir Thomas Savage, knight and baronet, one of the gentlemen of the chamber. The creation also gave Thomas and Elizabeth the precedence of the eldest son of a viscount, and wife of such an eldest son. John Chamberlain, in a letter written nine days later, said that Thomas procured the promotion.[131] The creation confirms that Thomas was still one of the gentlemen of the chamber, with the attendance at court that the position involved, but we have little other information about his life during these years.[132] Elizabeth was still having children very regularly; the last child whose baptism date is known was

124 Buckingham's letter to Savage: BRO, D/EHY 01/120. The relative in question was a Mrs Bagenal. Thomas's aunt Eleanor Savage had married Sir Henry Bagenal and had nine children, including four sons. She had been widowed in 1598 and later married Sir Sackville Trevor. Bagenal's estate was so confused that the privy council looked into it at Eleanor's request. Whether this Mrs Bagenal was a daughter or daughter-in-law of Eleanor, we cannot tell.

125 The Buckingham/Manners marriage: Lockyer, *Buckingham*, pp. 58–60 and G.P.V. Akrigg, *Jacobean Pageant, or the Court of James I* (London, 1967), p. 220.

126 Lockyer, *Buckingham*, p. 59, referring to *HMC, 4th Report, Earls De La Warre* (London, 1874) p. 290. Middlesex's draft letter to the duchess of Buckingham (in the *HMC* summary) states: '. . . if it had not been for him and Lord Savage she had not been the duke's wife'.

127 Later archbishop of York.

128 Lockyer, *Buckingham*, p. 60.

129 Akrigg, *Jacobean Pageant*, p. 220.

130 The Rutland archive confirms that the earl and his wife stayed with the Savages that May: 'delivered to Mr. Tindall at my lord and lady's journey to the Lord Dacre and Sir Thomas Savage, 2 May, £43 3s. 2d.': *HMC Rutland IV*, 519.

131 Creation, procured by the marquis of Buckingham: TNA, SO 3/7, July 1621. McClure, *Letters*, II, 387.

132 G. Aylmer, *Servants*, p. 152 includes estimates of the time courtiers spent at court.

Richard, baptised at St Olave's Hart Street in February 1622.[133] This birth probably gave her eight children aged under twelve, so she may have spent a good deal of her time out of London. In summer 1622 she was able to get further away from domesticity; John Chamberlain wrote on 13 July that the countess of Rutland and Elizabeth had gone to Spa for their health.[134] Elizabeth may possibly have met her eldest sons while she was away; John and Thomas Savage junior travelled to Florence that summer, as part of their 'grand tour'.[135]

We would probably have known much more about the continental tour of the young Savages had the family not been catholic. Early in 1621 Thomas engaged a young tutor, James Howell, to accompany his sons John and Thomas on their European journey. Howell had already spent several years travelling in Europe, negotiating for glassmakers to come to London.[136] He joined the Savage family at Melford Hall in spring 1621, and also visited Thomas Darcy at St Osyth. He had been introduced to Darcy through Sir James Croft, a family friend.[137] Howell was obviously impressed with life at Melford Hall (Doc. 15) and his letters give us just a glimpse of the way the house was organised. However he eventually went abroad again with another young gentleman. He wrote to his father in May 1622 to say that while he had been with 'a very noble family in the country', he had decided that he was too young to have the charge of the two boys round Europe, and that he differed from them on religion, so he had returned to London and would go to Europe as companion to another gentleman.[138]

Howell, who was to become clerk to the privy council, and later historiographer royal of England, corresponded with a wide variety of people while on his travels, describing both places and people.[139] In 1623 he wrote many letters from Spain when Prince Charles and the duke of Buckingham were there trying to arrange a marriage for Charles with the Spanish king's sister. Both Thomas Savage and Thomas Darcy were among his regular correspondents both then and later; another was John Savage, Thomas's eldest son. Although he had decided he could not keep company with the sons on an extended journey, Howell seems to have had a genuine respect for both Savage and Darcy, and remained a correspondent through both their lives. A later letter related to the death of William Noye, who had become attorney general (Doc. 50).

Thomas's first known court appointment came in 1622, together with his first appearance on a commission for trade.[140] On 16 February Chamberlain wrote that Sir Robert Cary was to become baron of Lepington in Yorkshire and that his job

133 Parish register transcripts kept at St Olave's, Hart Street.

134 McClure, *Letters*, II, 447.

135 Licence to travel for three years for the brothers John and Thomas Savage, sons of Sir Thomas Savage; they could take two servants and fifty pounds: TNA, SO 3/7, 10 February 1620. Licence to travel to the Spa for the Lady Savage, wife of Sir Thomas Savage, for the recovery of her health: TNA, SO 3/7, July 1622. Her health problems may have related to the birth of yet another child earlier in the year.

136 For James Howell, see Notes on People, below.

137 James Howell's first letter to his father mentioning the Darcys or Savages explains that he was introduced to them by Sir James Croft, a friend of both Howell's father and Thomas Darcy: J. Howell, *Familiar Letters on Important Subjects, wrote from the year 1618 to 1650* (10th edn, Aberdeen, 1753), Letter XXXVIII. The first edition was published in 1645. Some editions date these letters to 1619 but the earliest editions and contextual evidence date them to 1621. See the introduction to Doc. 15.

138 J. Howell, *Familiar Letters*, p. 81, letter XLII.

139 A post created expressly for him.

140 Other than being a gentleman of the privy chamber. In 1633 Elizabeth wrote that Thomas had served Charles for nearly twenty years (Doc. 48), but Glyn Redworth makes it clear that Thomas's appointment in 1622 was a new one. Redworth, *Spanish Match*, p. 43.

with Prince Charles was to go to Sir Thomas Savage. Cary had been chamberlain to the prince of Wales.[141] From slightly later that year, manorial documents surviving in Cheshire describe Thomas as one of 'the prince his highness's council'.[142] From evidence in the Spanish archives, Glyn Redworth suggests that he was appointed Prince Charles's chief adviser.[143] This might not appear particularly newsworthy, but Thomas's appointment featured in correspondence between Gondomar, the Spanish ambassador, and Philip IV of Spain. S.R. Gardiner, who wrote ten volumes about the reigns of James I and Charles I, recorded that one of Gondomar's final triumphs before he returned to Spain was to persuade the prince of Wales to appoint Sir Thomas Savage, a catholic, as one of the commissioners to manage his revenue. This was an achievement because not only was Savage a catholic, but also he had 'decidedly' refused to take the oath of allegiance.[144] Glyn Redworth tells us that when offered the appointment, Thomas approached Gondomar for advice about whether to disclose his catholic faith; Gondomar advised him not to take any oaths contrary to his faith and to make his religion clear. Thomas followed this advice; apparently the royal reply was that his honesty made James and Charles more inclined to trust him.[145] Thomas seems to have been Charles's only catholic adviser. When Count Olivares, chief adviser to the Spanish king, was questioning the English commitment to toleration of catholics, he gave as evidence that fact that Thomas Savage was the prince's only catholic councillor, and that he had not been brought to Madrid.[146]

The precise nature of his post is uncertain, but Thomas was head of Charles's commission for his revenues, and long into Charles's own reign he and his fellow commissioners continued dealing with issues relating to lands owned when Charles had been prince of Wales.[147] In 1623 they had to continue managing the financial affairs of the prince of Wales while he and Buckingham were away in Spain. Two letters from Thomas to Buckingham survive; he and Sir Henry Vane, the prince's cofferer, had bound themselves to pay money demanded by Charles that could not be supplied by his estates (Doc. 16).[148]

Elizabeth had been abroad in the summer of 1622 but she was almost certainly back by the end of the year for the wedding of her eldest daughter Jane, the first of her children to marry. Jane married another catholic, John Paulet, later Lord St John, heir of the marquis of Winchester. The marriage was probably celebrated soon after the licence was issued on 18 December.[149] Jane's dowry included the manor of

---

141 Rymer, *Foedera*, VII, pt IV, 23; McClure, *Letters of John Chamberlain*, II, 424.

142 Manorial records, Tarvin: CCALS, DCH/EE/15.

143 Redworth's reference (n. 140 above) is from a letter from Gondomar to Isabella in the Spanish archives. Gondomar to Isabella: 31/21 Jan 1622, RBM, msII-2108, no 119, at d.

144 S.R. Gardiner, *The History of England from the Accession of James I to the Outbreak of the Civil War 1603–1642* (London, 1883–4), IV, 368. The oath of allegiance was proclaimed law in June 1606, part of the reaction to the Gunpowder Plot. It included several statements denying that the pope had any power to depose the king, a matter on which English catholics were divided. There was considerable debate amongst English catholics about whether they should sign; this continued into the 1630s.

145 Glyn Redworth, *Spanish Match*, p. 43.

146 This was during the negotiations in 1623 for a Spanish marriage for Prince Charles. Redworth, *Spanish Match*, pp. 107–8. His reference is from the Spanish archives: MAE, MS 243, ff. 137v–142r.

147 An example from 1631: TNA, SP 16/197/287.

148 Letters from Thomas Savage to Buckingham in Spain: BL, Harleian MSS 1581, f. 258 and f. 282. For Sir Henry Vane, see Notes on People, below.

149 Jane was baptised at Isleworth in 1607, and her age at death confirms this birth year. She was therefore fourteen or fifteen at her marriage. For Lord St John and the marquis of Winchester, see Notes on People, below.

Cheadle Hulme, which had been owned by the Savages for over 250 years.[150] Their second son Thomas was the next of Thomas's and Elizabeth's children to marry, probably in August 1624. This younger Sir Thomas married Bridget née Whitmore, widow of Edward Somerset, fifth son of the earl of Worcester. She was sole heiress (after her mother) to Sir Hugh Beeston of Beeston Castle in Cheshire.[151] Thomas junior eventually established another branch of the Savage family at Beeston.[152] Both Beeston and Whitmore families were catholic.

Correspondence between Thomas Savage senior and William Whitmore, Bridget's father, varied from hard bargaining over money to shared joy when a grandchild was born (Docs 19, 20, 21 and 29).[153] By April 1625 Thomas and Elizabeth had their first grandchild, a girl. Elizabeth Savage was godmother and had the naming of her; however she was not able to write to thank William Whitmore herself because she was ill of a tertian ague (Doc. 20). The same letter tells us that Thomas Savage also had health problems by the mid 1620s. Illness aside, he continued to serve Prince Charles, and Elizabeth took on an administrative role as executrix of Sir James Croft, the friend who had introduced James Howell to the family. Croft's nephew challenged her appointment as executrix, but she was confirmed in the role.[154]

The third child to marry was Thomas's and Elizabeth's eldest son, John, who married in or just before June 1625, the year after he was knighted.[155] His bride was Catherine daughter and co-heir of William Parker, Lord Morley and Monteagle; her mother was daughter of Sir Thomas Tresham; thus this marriage linked the Savages with more prominent catholic families.[156] Catherine brought with her a dowry of £7000. As already mentioned, John and his wife were given Frodsham Castle as their home in 1626, along with Frodsham Park and surrounding meadow. His parents also gave them a considerable amount of furniture and linen from Rocksavage; more went to Thomas junior and his wife.[157]

---

150 The Paulet family owned Cheadle only until 1643, when it was confiscated by Parliament. The Moseleys then purchased the manor. It seems likely that John and Jane St John lived at Hackwood Park, a hunting lodge near Basingstoke. After Basing House was destroyed in the Civil War, the Paulet family extended Hackwood as their new home. In 1625 Jane St John wrote a letter from Hackwood to Secretary Conway 'on the entreaty of her cousin Savage' in support of a candidate for prebend of Winchester: TNA, SP 16/7/16.

151 Thomas had been one of Edward Somerset's executors, along with Richard Lumley and Sir Nicholas Fortesque, sometime before 1622: CCALS DCH/M/35/146. Because Bridget Whitmore's first husband was the son of an earl, and thus of higher rank than her second, she was still called Lady Somerset: letters from Thomas Whitmore to his brother William, UWB, Mostyn Lloyd MSS. Thomas senior had asked Bridget's father to 'make him not less in your opinion than Sir Edward Somerset': UWB, Mostyn Lloyd MSS, 9082/2.

152 The marriage and children of the younger Sir Thomas Savage are recorded in the funeral certificate of Sir Hugh Beeston, 1626, included in J.P. Rylands (ed.), *Lancashire and Cheshire Funeral Certificates, 1600–1678*, Lancs. & Cheshire Record Soc., VI (1882), 13–14. The Thomas Savage knighted at Belvoir on 6 August 1621 was probably this Thomas. We are unlikely ever to know why he was knighted before his elder brother.

153 A descendant of Thomas and Bridget married into the Mostyn family, and the correspondence is now in the Mostyn Lloyd MSS.

154 Will of Sir James Croft: TNA, PROB 11/145.

155 Shaw, *Knights* (London, 1905) p. 186. John was knighted at Belvoir 7 July 1624. The citation says that he was son and heir to Viscount Savage, thus making clear which of several possible John Savages was involved. However he has sometimes been confused with the John Savage knighted at Newmarket on 30 January 1615, whom we have not been able to identify.

156 For William Parker, Lord Morley and Monteagle, see Notes on People, below.

157 At this date John was heir apparent, after his father, to Viscount Colchester; the dowry presumably

In 1626 an account of Thomas's income from the rents of his Cheshire lands shows us that the lands allocated to John and Catherine were worth some £660 a year, some two-thirds of the annual income. Thomas junior was receiving an annuity of £100 a year, and Thomas senior was still paying annuities to several of his aunts. The income from rents was exceeded by expenditure on annuities and other fixed charges.[158] There is no mention of expenditure on food in these accounts, but we know that in one year the kitchen accounts for the summer show over £250 spent.[159] Although rents were not the only income from the Cheshire lands, they would have formed a large part of the total, and it is obvious that expenditure was exceeding income even at this date. A long indenture from 1626 arranges an annual income for the third son, Francis, after his father's death (Doc. 24), with more after the death of his mother and sister-in-law. This is all annual expenditure, but each of their children's marriages was taking capital from Thomas and Elizabeth in the shape of marriage settlements and probably additional expenses afterwards.[160] Doc. 29 suggests that Thomas senior was continuing to pay large sums of money to Bridget Whitmore's family three years after her marriage to his second son.

Thomas mentions his income, or lack of it, in another series of family letters. These date from 1626–8 and relate to Elizabeth Savage's sister Mary, married to a Thomas Maples of Stow Longa in Huntingdonshire. The marriage was obviously an unhappy one, and the Hengrave manuscripts contain letters about it from Thomas to his mother-in-law Countess Rivers, and from Richard Lindall, in attendance on old Lady Kitson, Elizabeth's grandmother. It is possible that Countess Rivers paid Maples off with the promise of her house and lands in Colchester after her death. Maples had died before 1639, but his executor was involved in a court case in Chancery over 'a certain messuage in the parish of Holy Trinity, Colchester'.[161] In this correspondence to his mother-in-law Countess Rivers, Savage stressed his love and concern for her with an insistence which suggests some tension between them. In October 1627 he wrote to her about the legal case, and ended his letter emphasising how much he wanted to be able to help her in any way he could, including helping her with the cost of legal action. He makes it clear that he does not think she realises how much he would do for her.[162]

Working for the queen and the duke – 'the great commissioner'

When James I died in 1625, Sir Thomas Savage was listed as chief of the counsellors and commissioners of the prince's revenue; for the funeral procession he was allocated ten yards of mourning cloth and his servants received another twelve yards.[163] Seventeen men from the commission were listed: nine commissioners, their scribes, doorkeepers, messengers and porters. In the early years of Charles I's reign Thomas continued as a commissioner for Charles's lands owned when he was

reflected this. Indenture relating to Frodsham Castle and mentioning dowry: CCALS, DDX 111. Reference to linen and furniture in accounts: CCALS, DCH/M/35/40.

158 Such as 'wood and fuel, repairs of Rocksavage house, deer houses, pond, conduits, sea-baulks . . . for diet of auditor and bailiff, charges of sturgeons, impaling of the parks, bailiff's wages, [*illeg.*] allowances, liveries for retainers and servants, with what not other subsidies': CCALS, DCH/H/200.

159 Kitchen accounts: CCALS, DCH/K/1/1.

160 Indenture setting up portions for Thomas's and Elizabeth's unmarried daughters: CCALS, DDX 111.

161 Exemplification of an order in the court of Chancery: ERO, D/DH/VID12.

162 Letter to Countess Rivers: CUL, Hengrave 88, II, 115.

163 Accounts of the funeral of King James I: TNA, LC 2/6. At least one source says that catholics were barred from the funeral, but possibly not those of Buckingham's connection.

prince of Wales but he also acquired other positions. In 1625 he became a commissioner for the sale of crown lands (also known as the commission to enhance the king's revenues) and first commissioner for trade.[164] When he was in London he obviously spent no small part of his time in meetings and around Westminster and Whitehall. For example the minutes of the commission for the sale of crown lands show him either to be attending most meetings, or to be away for considerable periods when he was probably out of London. He would have been very familiar with the Inner Chamber at Westminster where most of these meetings appear to have taken place.[165]

Geoffrey Aylmer, who wrote widely on the administrative history of the court of Charles I, expressed concern that Thomas was listed so prominently in the commission to increase the king's revenues. He was surprised that he was named before all the other councillors and holders of financial offices. Aylmer went on to refer to Thomas's catholicism, links to Buckingham and later debts, and suggested critically that his prominence in this matter might characterise early Stuart attempts at reform. He went on to say that there were more reputable figures on the commission.[166] Aylmer may not have appreciated Thomas's previous position as a financial commissioner to the prince of Wales, or have considered the many other commissions which he had held. He did however refer readers to the letters of John Holles, first earl of Clare, who called Thomas 'a useful man'.[167] One way in which he might have been useful is illustrated by a letter from Richard Montagu, an ambitious cleric who in the summer of 1626 wrote to John Cosin (at that stage archdeacon of York and later bishop of Durham) about the vacant bishopric of Exeter. He enclosed a letter for an unnamed 'noble friend' and says that Sir Thomas Savage, if necessary, would combine his influence with that of the earl of Rutland, to persuade the duke of Buckingham to appoint Montagu to the Exeter vacancy.[168] Those forces were not sufficient to get Montagu to Exeter, but he became bishop of Chichester two years later. He and Cosin were both closely associated with Laud's view of Anglicanism.

Thomas also headed the commissioners of the duke of Buckingham's estate and 'admiralty droits', and state papers include several letters to, from or mentioning Thomas in these roles in the period 1625–8. Whether income from prize ships, wrecks and the like was going into the exchequer or into Buckingham's own coffers, the extent of it would need to be assessed and Buckingham's rights to it affirmed.[169]

164 *Foedera*, VIII, pt II, 89, 197, 283; T. Birch (ed. R.F. Williams), *The Court and Times of Charles I* (London, 1848), p. 131.

165 Minutes of the commission for the sale of crown lands from November to early December: CCALS, DCH/X/15/5; minutes from later December to June 1626: TNA, SP 16/69.

166 G. Aylmer, 'Buckingham as an Administrative Reformer', *English Historical Review* (April, 1990), 355–62. The Commissioners included the lord treasurer, chancellor of the exchequer, chancellor of the duchy, Sir John Coke, Sir Walter Pye and Sir Robert Pye.

167 P.R. Seddon (ed.), *Letters of John Holles 1587–1637*, Thoroton Soc. (Nottingham, 1975–85), II, 338. Aylmer may not have realised that Savage and Holles were related in two different ways. Holles' wife was a Stanhope and very probably first cousin to Thomas Savage, and Holles himself was a kinsman of Lord Darcy and Elizabeth Savage. In later times, when Darcy (then Earl Rivers) was ill, Holles says 'I long infinitely to hear how he is, for besides being a kinsman, he is most true friend': Seddon, *Letters*, III, 425.

168 *Correspondence of John Cosin*, Surtees Soc., LII, pt I (1869), letter LXIV, p. 102. Anthony Milton, *Catholic and Reformed: Roman and Protestant Churches in English Protestant Thought 1600–40* (Cambridge, 1995), p. 53, says that Montagu's case was supported at court by catholic peers Lord Savage, the earl of Rutland and the earl of Worcester; he assumes that Savage is 'Edward Baron Savage', but the link with Rutland and this letter make it much more likely to be Thomas Savage. For Montagu, see Notes on People, below.

169 The crown reserved to itself certain properties under the jurisdiction of 'admiralty droits': all 'great

Docs 22 and 34 indicate the detail required from both the captains who took prizes or their superiors and from the duke's collectors, who appear to have been present in all likely ports. Edward Nicholas, the duke's secretary, makes it clear to his collectors that Thomas and the other commissioners want detailed information; the fact that Thomas was head of this body suggests that he was a competent financial administrator.[170]

These administrative skills were to be in increased demand, but there were other duties as well, some of which, on the surface, look a little unlikely. In the autumn of 1625 Charles I decided to re-introduce a scheme to disarm recusants, taking away most of their arms and leaving them with just enough to defend their homes and families.[171] This was an idea which James I had earlier considered, abandoned and then tried to re-introduce shortly before his death.[172] At a time when an aristocrat or gentleman set much store by armour, this was no small matter. A small group of peers was designated by name for disarming; they were excluded from the general action because the king wanted to deal with them separately. Thomas was closely related to three of the fourteen peers in this group who were eventually disarmed, Thomas Lord Darcy, his father-in-law, Lord St John, his son-in-law, and the marquis of Winchester, St John's father.[173] All three were well-known catholic peers and their inclusion is no surprise; even so Jane St John (*née* Savage) wrote to Lord Conway, principal secretary to Charles I, asking for the decision to be reversed. Her letter (Doc. 23) makes it clear that she felt responsible; another letter she wrote the following summer makes it clear that she had been convicted as a recusant.[174]

However Thomas himself has been identified as one of the people doing the disarming at a local level.[175] This might appear unlikely, and is in fact not quite what it seems. His signature appears with others on a letter to the privy council from Chester about William Whitmore, a convicted recusant who had been disarmed but had since died; the letter says that his son, another William, is 'comfortable with the laws of this kingdom' and no recusant, and asks that his arms may be returned to him. Thomas's second son had recently married the younger William Whitmore's daughter, so Savage was attempting to get the arms of his son's father-in-law returned.[176]

In the summer of 1625 Charles I had married the young Henrietta Maria, daughter of Henry IV of France. After she arrived at Dover, she travelled towards

---

fish' found within the beach zone below high-water mark, all beach 'deodands', 'wreck of the sea', 'flotsam' (goods floating on the water), 'jetsam' (goods jettisoned by a crew) and 'lagan' (jettisoned goods tied with buoys).

170 For Edward Nichols, see Notes on People, below.

171 For more information, see B. Quintrell, 'The Practice and Problems of Recusant Disarming', *Recusant History*, 17, 3, May 1985, 208–22.

172 James I's definition of recusants included those who did not ordinarily go to divine service at church, those who had not received communion at least once a year in the last three or four years, those with wives or children who were recusant or non-communicant or 'otherwise popishly affected' and those with any noted or extraordinary number of retainers or tenants who fell into one of these categories.

173 Darcy did not get his arms back until 1633. Quintrell, 'Recusant Disarming', p. 219.

174 Jane's second letter, of August 1626, is written to ask for permission to go to Bath to recover her health as her physicians had advised; as a convicted recusant she was not normally allowed to travel more than five miles from her home. She needed the king's permission for 'as my rank is not ordinary . . . I may receive the mercy of the law only from his majesty': TNA, SP 16/33/37.

175 Quintrell, 'Recusant Disarming', p. 219.

176 William Whitmore snr had been disarmed much earlier, in 1612; a certificate survives which tells us that as a convicted recusant he had surrendered 15 breast plates, 15 back pieces, 5 head pieces and sundry other arms: UWB, Lloyd Mostyn MSS, E688.

Canterbury and was met by a group of courtiers which included Thomas's and Elizabeth's eldest daughter Jane and her husband Lord St John.[177] Henrietta Maria began with an almost entirely French entourage, but a year later many of the French were dismissed by Charles and English replacements appointed. Although the first official mention of Thomas as her chancellor does not come until 1629, his possible appointment is mentioned in a letter of August 1626, which also gives news of Elizabeth's appointment to the bedchamber.[178] It may be that Thomas was proposed for the post in 1626 but for some reason the position was not finally agreed until 1628 (when it was mentioned in a private letter).[179] There are no records of anyone else appointed as Henrietta Maria's chancellor in the intervening period, but the post is mentioned in 1627 and Nathaniel Tomkins was employed by then as the chancellor's registrar.[180]

In contrast to Thomas's appointment, several writers mention Elizabeth Savage's; the most informative account is from Amerigo Salvetti, the representative in England of the dukes of Tuscany. On 2 October 1626 he wrote that the queen appeared to be very happy and cheerful; she was spending most of her time at Denmark House and was accompanied by the duchess of Buckingham, the marchioness of Hamilton, the countesses of Rutland, Buckingham and Denbigh and Madame Savage. Salvetti remarked that the countesses of Rutland and Buckingham and Madame Savage were catholics and were allowed to go to mass with the queen 'in her little oratory'.[181]

We have no earlier evidence of Elizabeth Savage being involved at court, apart from a letter she wrote in 1624 to the duchess of Lennox, asking her to persuade her husband to forward a petition Elizabeth had sent to the king about an old servant of her grandmother, Lady Kitson.[182] The letter suggests that Elizabeth knew the duchess and her husband personally, but how much time she had spent in court circles while Thomas served Prince Charles, we do not know. Her appointment to serve Henrietta Maria has not been found in official sources, but in 1627 she is receiving 'bouge of court', her food and drink, and in her petition of 1633 to Charles (Doc. 48) she says that she has been serving the Queen 'these eight years'.[183] In 1628 Alexander Couler writes in a letter that 'the Jesuits give out that the disposition of the queen's chapel is already theirs through the favour of the countess of Buckingham and Lady Savage'. In a letter of November 1629 Henrietta Maria told the French ambassador that she would enjoy the company of a few French

---

177 Their presence on this occasion caused Lord and Lady St John severe financial problems; see Doc. 23.

178 John Pory wrote to the Revd Joseph Mead in August 1626, 'there are said to be four English papists to attend her, the earl of Rutland, her lord chamberlain; Sir Thomas Savage, her chancellor; the old countess of Buckingham, and the Lady Savage, of her bedchamber': R.F. Williams (ed.), *Court and Times*, p. 131. Pory appears to be regarded as a normally reliable source of information.

179 Seddon, *Letters*, III, 385.

180 Letters patent to queen's council, 1627: TNA, E 156/12.

181 Salvetti's letter (in translation): *HMC Eleventh Report, Appendix I*, Skrine (Salvetti) (London, 1887), p. 85. He was writing somewhat after the appointment of the ladies, for John Pory, writing to Joseph Mead, reported the appointments on 11 August 1626: H. Ellis (ed.), *Original Letters Illustrative of English History* (London, 1824), III, 247; original letter: BL Harleian MSS 383. The queen and her servants were among a very small number of people legally able to attend catholic services in England. The original Somerset House had been renamed Denmark House when it was given to James I's wife, Anne of Denmark.

182 Letter to the countess of Lennox: TNA, SP 16/158/76.

183 Bouge of court: TNA, LS 13/30.

ladies-in-waiting; the countess of Buckingham and Lady Savage were kind ladies, but they were away more often than not.[184]

But the catholicism which was accepted in the queen's court was anathema elsewhere. In summer 1626 the House of Commons sent Charles I a petition about prominent recusants. Many of those named were aristocrats active at court, including Rutland, Lord St John of Basing, Sir Thomas Savage, his wife and children, along with his second son Thomas with his Whitmore and Beeston relations.[185] Thomas senior's religion is only occasionally mentioned or implied in surviving correspondence between his peers, and some of those few references are obscure.[186]

Four months after Elizabeth's appointment at court, on 4 November 1626, Thomas was created Viscount Savage. This was on the same day that his father-in-law Thomas Darcy became Earl Rivers, and Thomas was to have the reversion of the earldom of Rivers after his father-in-law's death.[187] The attendance records of the House of Lords reflect the relative political importance of Thomas, Earl Rivers, the earl of Rutland and the duke of Buckingham. Buckingham is there regularly, Rutland appears on occasion and Thomas and Rivers hardly ever after their first introduction. The earl of Rutland is acting as Thomas's proxy whenever proxies are recorded.[188]

It has been suggested that Buckingham's catholic supporters came to the fore when parliament was not in session.[189] In 1626 Charles I dismissed parliament to protect the duke of Buckingham from attack, but he still had a considerable need for funds. The privy council therefore had to find new ways of raising money and decided on what is now called the 'Forced Loan'.[190] Privy councillors and other senior and trusted men were sent out to each county to encourage the levy and supervise its collection; many of those local gentry and aristocracy who normally collected taxes for the crown chose not to be involved in this loan.[191] Although he was catholic, and not a privy councillor, Thomas was chosen in the winter of 1626–7 to work with the earl of Derby to persuade the subsidy payers of Cheshire and Chester to contribute.[192] There was widespread debate and uncertainty amongst

---

184 Letter from Alexander Couler to William Johnson: TNA, SP 16/68/8. For Queen Henrietta Maria's comment see M.J. Havran, *Catholics in Caroline England* (Stanford, 1962), p. 55.

185 Petition against recusants: J. Rushworth, *Historical Collections of Private Passages of State* (London, 1682), p. 393. A few months earlier Elizabeth's brother-in-law, Sir John Gage, was indicted, presumably as a recusant. An indenture leasing some of Gage's Sussex lands to Thomas Savage survives; on the reverse Sir John Gage wrote, 'This with the rest are of no value but were done when I was first indicted to avoid danger of law': ESRO, SAS/E16/29.

186 In 1628 John Holles, earl of Clare, wrote to Thomas Wentworth, his son-in-law, expressing his concerns about links between Weston, the new lord treasurer, Thomas and the new bishop of London, William Laud, but he did not say what those links were: Seddon, *Letters*, III (1985), 518. Laud had been appointed bishop of London in July 1628 and Weston, who was catholic with Spanish sympathies, was appointed lord treasurer that August, at the same time that Savage became chancellor to the queen. In later years Thomas Wentworth worked closely with William Laud.

187 Creation of Darcy as Earl Rivers and Savage as a viscount, with Savage and his family gaining the privileges and dignities of the eldest son of an earl: TNA, SO 3/8, November 1626. Creation of Savage as a viscount: TNA, SP 39/2; BL, Egerton 2552, Doc. 25.

188 *Journals of the House of Lords, Beginning Anno Decimo Octavo Jacobi Regis, 1620*, III, 685.

189 R. Cust, *The Forced Loan and English Politics, 1626–1628* (Oxford, 1987), pp. 89, 207.

190 Cust, *The Forced Loan*; the introduction and first chapter give a concise summary of the situation.

191 Cust, *The Forced Loan*, chs 3 and 4; R. Cust, 'Politics and the Electorate in the 1620s', in R. Cust and A. Hughes (eds), *Conflict in Early Stuart England* (London, 1989), pp. 154–8.

192 Thomas was also on the list of men to deal with the loan in Suffolk. We assume that he concentrated on the situation in Cheshire. The instructions for raising the forced loan in Middlesex survive and those

those assessed as to whether they should comply. When the city of Chester agreed to pay in February 1627, but the county of Cheshire was still hesitating, Thomas asked Buckingham to arrange for the city to be rewarded and assured of the king's favour. By March the county followed suit and agreed to pay up (Docs 26, 27 and 28).[193] The bishop of Chester, John Bridgeman, was also involved in this commission; Thomas afterwards made sure Bridgeman knew whom he had to thank for reminding the king of the bishop's contribution (Doc. 33).[194] Richard Cust uses Thomas's approach in Cheshire to illustrate one way of persuading people to contribute, which was to 'demonstrate the benefits which followed from being helpful'.

Thomas was in Chester again in mid to late March, so it is at least possible that he had remained in the country rather than return to London. However the housekeeper's accounts for Rocksavage that year include 'paid for the shoeing of the grey mare that my lord had with him from Rocksavage to Melford in February 1627, 16d.' which suggests that he moved south at least to Suffolk after helping to gather the loan in Cheshire.[195] He returned to Chester because of problems between the mayor and aldermen and their new town clerk, Robert Brerewood. This was a continuation of the row between Whitby and Gamull which Thomas had tried to help resolve in 1619. The privy council was trying to deal with this from a distance; by late March they had heard by letter from the city and in person from Thomas, of a public meeting at the town hall in Chester on the issue.[196]

Two months later in May 1627, just as Buckingham was gathering troops and supplies for the expedition to La Rochelle, Thomas heard that old Lady Kitson's sister Mary (known as the countess of Bathon) had died.[197] Richard Lindall, Elizabeth Kitson's man of business, was expecting the news to be hard for her, and wrote to the lady's daughter Countess Rivers that he had been trying to wait for either the lady's physician or Lord Savage to come and break the news, because either would have done it well. Neither were available, and Lady Kitson found out by accident, which had put her into a passion the like of which those about her had never previously seen; however she was now 'well pacified'.[198] Thomas was executor of Mary, countess of Bathon's will, and would receive the residue of the estate, but he was not able to get away from London.[199] According to Richard Lindall, the servants at Thorpe, her home, were expecting Thomas but he would not be permitted to leave London until after the duke of Buckingham had left on his expedition to La Rochelle.[200]

Thomas was presumably looked on favourably by the privy council for having

for Cheshire are likely to have been identical: S.R. Gardiner (ed.), *Constitutional Documents of the Puritan Revolution, 1625–1660* (Oxford, 1906) p. 51.

193 Cust, *The Forced Loan*, pp. 121–2.

194 Thomas's letters to Bridgeman suggest the men were good friends.

195 Housekeeper's account: CCALS, DCH/E/316.

196 J.V. Lyle (ed.), *Acts of the Privy Council, Jan. 1627 – Aug. 1627* (London, 1938), p. 157.

197 Elizabeth Kitson, née Cornwallis, was Elizabeth Savage's grandmother.

198 Letter from Lindall to Countess Rivers: CUL, Hengrave 88, III, 47. 'My Lady of Bathon' was Mary Cornwallis, Lady Kitson's sister. She was also known as Mary Bourchier, countess of Bath. She had been briefly married to the 3rd earl of Bath but the marriage had been annulled amid considerable and long-lasting controversy. See Notes on People, below.

199 In her will Mary described herself as countess of Bathon, of Thorpe, Norfolk: TNA, PROB 11/151/53.

200 Richard Lindall to Countess Rivers: CUL, Hengrave 88, III, 47. The expedition to La Rochelle left in June. Lindall added that there was no more news except that many men planning to travel to London had delayed their journeys, because they were afraid they would be pressed into the navy.

helped with the loan; shortly after this the council spent time on the matter of his father-in-law's barber. Earl Rivers' barber William Giddens had been 'impressed' by the Company of Barber Surgeons to serve the king; this was causing the aged Earl Rivers many problems for Giddens helped him with other personal services. The privy council, in the persons of the lord treasurer, lord president, lord chamberlain, the earl of Salisbury and the chancellor of the exchequer wrote to the barber surgeons to require them to find another barber to serve the king.[201]

However, if this was the privy council returning a favour, they were to find out that the issues in Chester were still not resolved. Robert Brerewood, town clerk, officially known as 'clerk of the pentice', had not been carrying out the job in the way expected by the mayor and aldermen.[202] After the problems earlier in the year both Brerewood and Gamull, one of his main critics, had been summoned to London to 'attend' the privy council.[203] In early December, at a meeting attended by Charles I, the council decided to refer the whole dispute to Thomas to attempt to resolve the matter. Both Brerewood and Gamull agreed to his role as arbiter. Thomas was able to report on his success to the council meeting on 17 December. He had called the parties before him and made proposals to resolve the problem. Brerewood was too busy as a lawyer to properly attend to the demands of the city of Chester, so it was arranged that he surrendered his position voluntarily without losing face.

The privy council was pleased; the report contained both justice and equity, and achieved their intentions. They commended the care and industry Thomas had taken and were pleased to approve and ratify his report. A copy was sent to the corporation of Chester for them to put it into effect. This was by no means the first time Thomas had helped the corporation to resolve a dispute, but it was probably the occasion that did his reputation most good in government circles.[204]

As mentioned earlier, it is likely that Thomas was appointed as the queen's chancellor and keeper of her great seal in 1626, though he first appears on official lists of her household in 1629.[205] In 1628 John Holles, earl of Clare, wrote to Dr Williams, bishop of Lincoln, with the news that at the queen's court Dorset was to be the chamberlain and chief governor of ladies, Savage her chancellor'.[206] If Thomas did not get this appointment until 1628, it came just a few months after being appointed to a commission to examine the queen's revenues. His performance on that commission, and earlier ones, may have paved his way to the position of chancellor. A letter from his steward Thomas Brooke to Countess Rivers speaks of Lord Savage's 'multiplicity of business' at this time (Doc. 36).[207]

That same summer Thomas had to carry out another executorship, that of Lady

---

201 Lyle, *Acts, Jan.–Aug. 1627*, p. 318. Giddens helped Earl Rivers with matters concerning his bodily health, which no one else could do well. The privy council quite frequently involved themselves in personal matters, but presumably it helped if your relations were in good favour with the lords of the council.

202 Otherwise given as 'penthouse'.

203 Calling problem-makers to London made it easier for the privy council to question them; it also took them away from home, allowing matters there to settle down. The participants in this dispute had to spend time in London waiting to be called, away from their businesses. There appears to be a conflict of evidence: the *VCH* says that Gamull defended Brerewood at this time: *VCH Cheshire*, II, 112.

204 At the next election Whitby and his allies won the contests for Chester, but by 1640 Robert Brerewood was recorder of the city: *ibid.*, 112.

205 R.F. Williams (ed.), *Court and Times*, p. 131. Savage is not included on lists of the queen's household written in 1627: TNA L 5/57.

206 Seddon, *Letters*, III, 385.

207 Albert Loomie, in correspondence with Lyn Boothman, has written, 'I believe Savage was the personal choice of Henrietta Maria to be chancellor.'

Kitson (née Cornwallis), his wife's grandmother, who had lived to a great age. She must have been one of relatively few seventeenth-century testators able to leave legacies to their great-great-grandchildren, for three of Thomas and Elizabeth's children had children of their own. In her will Elizabeth Kitson describes herself as 'their grandmother's grandmother'.[208] She had been maintaining a large household at Hengrave, surrounded by servants who kept in close contact with her surviving child, Countess Rivers, and with her granddaughter's husband Thomas. The executorship seems to have caused a number of problems.[209] Richard Lindall, Elizabeth Kitson's man of business, wrote regularly to her daughter. On 19 August 1628, just four days before Buckingham's assassination, Lindall wrote to Countess Rivers about the situation at Hengrave and said that he was praying that the king did not send for Thomas too soon, before the business of the will could be dealt with.[210]

As mentioned earlier, Thomas was chief of the commissioners for the duke of Buckingham's finances, and when the duke was assassinated on 23 August 1628 Thomas was named as one of his executors. The duke's will looks, on the surface, to be fairly straightforward, with a few legacies and the residue to his wife or his son. However the legacies could only be paid once Buckingham's finances had been sorted out, and although he had owned large amounts of property he also died with vast debts. Sorting this out was to be a long and complicated job, which must have taken a large amount of Savage's time, especially in the years immediately after 1628.[211] Joseph Mead reported to Martin Stuteville, 'The duke, before he went his fatal journey to Portsmouth, made a will wherein his executors are Lord Savage, Sir Robert Pye, Mr Oliver and Mr Fotherley, two of his servants. They found his debts to be £61,000 which it is reported the king will pay.'[212] Mead omitted one other executor, Francis earl of Rutland.

Thomas may well have been at Melford when the news of the duke's death arrived. Elizabeth's letter to her mother (Doc. 38) tells us that her husband was summoned straight to London, and presumably had to leave his business with Lady Kitson's will to the other executors. In the next few months Buckingham's executors must have been hard worked. One letter written when they were gathering information is included in this volume (Doc. 40). Buckingham's numerous official positions meant that many people were financially affected by his death. The Signet Office books include, for example, a release to the executors and one of the late duke's servants, of the horses and other goods given to or acquired by the duke in his role of master of the horse.[213] There must also have been many cases similar to that of John Holles, earl of Clare. In 1628 he was sued 'by Hopton's executor' in relation to an agreement made on behalf of Buckingham. In a letter to his son in London,

---

208 Will of Dame Elizabeth Kitson: TNA, PROB 11/154/103. Her will left the music books and instruments at Hengrave as heirlooms of that house. John Wilbye, musician and madrigalist, chose to leave Hengrave at her death, and moved to Colchester to join Countess Rivers' household.

209 The other executors were Sir John Gage, Countess Rivers' other son-in-law, and Thomas Cole, cousin to Elizabeth Kitson.

210 Lindall to Countess Rivers: CUL, Hengrave 88, II, 117. A considerable number of letters in this volume are about business relating to Elizabeth Kitson's death.

211 The duke of Buckingham's will: J.G. Nichols and J. Bruce (eds), *Wills from Doctors' Commons – a Selection from the Wills of Eminent Persons Proved in the Prerogative Court of Canterbury 1495–1695*, Camden Society (London, 1863), p. 90.

212 Ellis, *Original Letters*, p. 247. Original letter: BL Harleian MSS 390. For an example of the correspondence of the executors: TNA SP 16/116/6 (Doc. 40).

213 Release to Buckingham's executors: TNA, SO 3/8, October 1628.

Holles advised it best to speak with Thomas, Sir Robert Pye, or both, and tell them of Holles's problems, and that he felt ill dealt with.[214]

The fact that the king was to pay Buckingham's debts was presumably a great relief to the executors and widow, but an estate of the size of Buckingham's would have taken the executors years to arrange. Some matters were dealt with fairly speedily, for example the king granted the duchess of Buckingham and her trustees the 4000 marks which they, in turn, had to pay to the king for the wardship of the new duke of Buckingham, a minor.[215] There is plentiful evidence that the executors were still working on sales and other arrangements about lands belonging to Lady Buckingham, formerly Katherine Manners, in the early 1630s, and this work continued until 1634, when Thomas and the other executors renounced their role in favour of the Lady Buckingham herself.[216]

Evidence of Thomas's work for the queen, as both chancellor and counsellor, comes largely from surviving letters patent, commissions and similar official documents. He had a salary of £54 a year as her chancellor; this was paid quarterly and collected by one of his senior servants.[217] As chancellor and keeper of her great seal, Thomas had responsibility for all the documents issued in Henrietta Maria's name, and he continued as one of the men commissioned to administer her properties.[218] He was also responsible for the court she was able to hold in relation to those properties, although this does not appear to have been fully operational until shortly before his death.[219]

Alongside these responsibilities at the royal court, Thomas continued his work as executor for the estates of the duke of Buckingham, Lady Kitson and the countess of Bathon; he may have been executor for more estates, but these cannot be identified. Some of these responsibilities involved him in relatively small amounts of money, but Buckingham's estate was on a larger scale. In 1630, for example, the duke's executors were discharged of over £10,755: funds received by Buckingham when he pawned various of the king's jewels in the Low Countries, and £8430 used by him when he was ambassador there.[220] Once more, in 1630, Thomas was called on to help the city of Chester with its problems, when they had a dispute with Sir Ranulph Crewe.[221]

Thomas was still a commissioner for the lands owned by Charles I when prince of Wales, and in early 1630 he bought Halton Park, bordering his Rocksavage lands,

214 Seddon, *Letters of John Holles*, III, 461.

215 Costs of wardship: TNA, SO 3/8, January 1629.

216 As an example: TNA, SP 16/185. The British Library holds some of Katherine Buckingham's accounts, drawn up by Thomas Fotherley; it is likely that he and Oliver did the bulk of the executors' administrative work. Accounts: BL, Add MSS 71601.

217 Payments are recorded in a number of documents including: TNA, E 101/438/11, E 101/438/13 and E 101/438/4.

218 For example: TNA, SP 16/140/10; SP 16/148/56. For information on the queen's court, see N.R.R. Fisher, 'The Queenes Courte in her Councell Chamber at Westminster', *English Historical Review*, CVIII, no. 427 (April 1993), 314–37. We are grateful to Caroline Hibbard for this reference and to N.R.R. Fisher for additional help.

219 The 1634 letters patent re-confirm the establishment of the court. Any six counsellors could set fees or allowances but the six must always include the chancellor or the queen's high steward: Rymer, *Feodera*, pt IV, 75.

220 Discharge of Buckingham's executors: TNA, SO 3/10, February 1631.

221 Groombridge, *Chester Minutes*, p. 161. Correspondence between Savage, Crewe and Chester city corporation: BL Stowe MSS, 812/12, 812/50, 812/58, 812/65. Crewe had been one of Thomas Savage's sponsors when he entered Lincoln's Inn but was to become his opponent (Doc. 67). The dispute was about the right to tolls collected at Eastgate in Chester. Thomas seems to have tried hard to bring the two sides together, and the corporation thanked him for his efforts, but Crewe appears to have won the argument.

from this commission. Halton cost him £100 plus the value of the woods there, which were to be surveyed within six months of the sale agreement.[222] At almost the same time he bought the manor and lordships of Runcorn and the manor and lordship of Moore for £783.[223] This latter purchase set in train a long sequence of legal battles; his son John was still fighting court cases about it in 1640. Thomas bought Runcorn 'allegedly in trust for the tenants'; he agreed to lend his tenants the money 'to pay their share of the first payment'; their copyholds were to be enfranchised and Thomas was to 'reserve only the seignory and the passage of the ferry and fishing'. Apparently some of the richer tenants 'got a great part of the inland of Runcorn into their hands'.[224]

Elizabeth's role is less well documented, but she obviously spent a considerable amount of her time at court, even if Henrietta Maria thought that she was away a lot. Her letter (Doc. 48) to Charles I asking for a continuation of her pension was probably written around 1633, but the implication is that she has been receiving a pension or allowance for some time. By the late 1620s Elizabeth had seen three of her children married, but it likely that she was still to give birth to her last son. In 1629–30 Henrietta Maria was pregnant with the child who was to become Charles II. In a letter written in March 1630, Philip Manwaring wrote that the queen would be moving to Greenwich on the Thursday of Easter week, and had decided to give birth there. Lady Savage had been 'entreated nay commanded' to lie-in at court, with the queen; she looked to be due to give birth three weeks before Henrietta Maria.[225] Elizabeth was pregnant at the same time as her eldest daughter, for Jane marchioness of Winchester gave birth to a healthy boy in January 1630; this was her first child to survive. We do not know whether she had suffered miscarriages, lost previous children in childbirth, or whether she and her husband found it difficult to conceive; the latter is perhaps unlikely for she was pregnant again the next year.[226] There was another grandchild just a few months later, when Thomas Savage junior and his wife Bridget had a healthy son. Thomas senior wrote to his fellow grandfather, William Whitmore, 'I humbly praise God for the great blessing he has bestowed upon us both, in so goodly a grandchild, and I beseech sweet Jesus to bless him with his divine grace, and as he is mine as well as yours, I desire you to give him your name, and I shall account it a favour done unto me.'[227]

The grandchildren both survived to adulthood, but the child born to Thomas and Elizabeth probably died very young, although he was christened and received royal gifts of plate. Elizabeth was by this time at the very least in her mid-forties and several letters in this volume tell us of her health problems. She must have been

---

222 Grant of Halton Park: TNA, SO 3/8, February 1630. Thomas Savage had been keeper of Halton Park since 1598; both he and his father had been paying the annual fee farm of £12 13s. 4d. since at least that point. Many of the crown's land sales at this period were to people who had been renting them previously.

223 Purchase of Runcorn and Moore, 11 February 1630: CCALS, DCH/E/9.

224 Dispute following purchase of Runcorn and Moore: CCALS, DCH/E/10; DCH/E/12; DCH/E/144 and others following.

225 Letter from Philip Manwaring: TNA, SP 16/169/68. However, Henrietta Maria eventually gave birth at St James' Palace because of plague at Greenwich. It is possible that this was Elizabeth's daughter-in-law Catherine but there is no other reference to either her or her husband being at court, so we have concluded that it is probably Elizabeth with a very late last pregnancy. For Philip Manwaring, see Notes on People, below.

226 Birth of a son to Jane marchioness of Winchester: UWB, Mostyn Lloyd MSS 9082/11. For her next pregnancy, see Doc. 45. Given that she was just fourteen or fifteen at her marriage in 1622, it is possible that she did not reached puberty until a little later. It is impossible to be precise about the age of menarche in the early modern period, though informed speculation from demographers suggests fourteen to fifteen.

227 Thomas Savage's letter to William Whitmore: UWB, Mostyn Lloyd MSS 9082/14.

physically strong to survive at least nineteen pregnancies, over a period of nearly thirty years, despite tertian agues and problems with her kidneys and urine.[228] It is more difficult to know what caused Thomas's health problems; in 1625 he is talking of not having the strength to walk well (Doc. 20) and sometime later, probably in 1630, he had a more serious illness. Afterwards he wrote to his brother-in-law William Whitmore to thank him 'for your letter in my great sickness' and described it as his 'great danger'.[229]

Thomas had recovered, but only a year after what must have been Elizabeth's last pregnancy, she and Thomas suffered the first death of one of their adult children. Jane marchioness of Winchester died in the spring of 1631. John Pory wrote:

> The Lady marchioness of Winchester, daughter to the Lord Viscount Savage, had an impostume upon her cheek lanced, the humour fell down her throat, and quickly dispatched her, being big with child, whose death is lamented as well in respect of her virtues as that she was inclining to become a protestant.[230]

Jane's death attracted considerable attention from writers and poets. James Howell wrote briefly of Jane, 'that nature and the graces exhausted all their treasures and skills in framing this exact model of female perfection'.[231] John Milton's 'An Epitaph on the Marchioness of Winchester' has over seventy lines, while Ben Jonson's 'An Elegy on the Lady Jane Paulet, Marchioness of Winton' is longer. There were verses too from William Davenant and William Coleman. Here is just the beginning of Milton's epitaph:

> This rich Marble doth enterr
> The honour'd Wife of Winchester,
> A Vicount's daughter, an Earl's heir,
> Besides what her vertues fair
> Added to her noble birth,
> More then she could own from Earth.
> Summers three times eight save one
> She had told, alas too soon,
> After so short time of breath,
> To house with darknes, and with death . . . [232]

Jonson's elegy is better known, and its opening lines often occur in lists of quotations:

---

228 Gift of '100 ounces of fair gilt plate to be given by the queen at the christening of Lady Savage her child': TNA, LC 5/132, f. 222. The christening was on 4 January 1631.

229 Letter to William Whitmore: UWB, Mostyn Lloyd MSS 9082/13.

230 R.F. Williams (ed.), *Court and Times*, II 106. Katherine Buckingham, writing to her uncle, gives a more intimate picture of the family's distress (Doc. 45).

231 Quoted in the *DNB*, where the reference is 'Collins, volume II, pp. 379–80'.

232 *An Epitaph on the Marchioness of Winchester* is printed in all complete editions of Milton's works. Milton was a student at Cambridge at this period. The poem was not published until 1645. The 'Milton Reading Room' web site suggests that the poem is written in 'rhyming couplets of iambic tetrameter', a style which 'owes much to Ben Jonson'. Jonson was approaching the end of his career when he wrote his Elegy. Other epitaphs are reported to have been written by W. Coleman, Sir John Beaumont and Sir W. Davenant, possibly as part of 'a Cambridge-collection of verses on the death of this accomplished lady': Armstrong, *Savages of Ards*, p. 42. Beaumont's epitaph must have been to an earlier marchioness of Winchester, for it was published in 1629. William Colman's *La Danse Macabre, or Death's Duel* includes 'An elegy on the lady marchioness of Winchester, daughter to the right honorable Thomas Lord Savage'.

What gentle ghost, besprent with April dew,
Hails me so solemnly to yonder yew . . .

He emphasises Jane's merits and her heritage, then goes on to the manner of her death:

How did she leave the world, with what contempt!
Just as she in it lived, and so exempt
From all affection! When they urg'd the cure
Of her disease, how did her soul assure
Her sufferings, as the body had been away!
And to the torturers, her doctors, say
Stick on your cupping-glasses, fear not, put
Your hottest caustics to, burn, lance or cut:
'Tis but a body which you can torment,
And I into the world all soul was sent.
Then comforted her lord, and blest her son,
Cheer'd her fair sisters in her race to run,
With gladness temper'd her sad parents' tears,
Made her friends joys to get above their fears,
And in her last act taught the standers-by
With admiration and applause to die! . . .
Go now, her happy parents, and be sad,
If you not understand what child you had.

Jonson's verse gives the impression that he knew the dead woman, which is possible. He mentions 'her fair sisters' and in the surviving records Jane's death coincides with the first independent mention of Thomas's and Elizabeth's next two daughters, Dorothy and Elizabeth. In 1631 Dorothy was twenty and Elizabeth a year younger; we do not know how long either of them had been at court, but they had obviously established themselves because they both appeared with Queen Henrietta Maria and another dozen aristocratic ladies in Jonson's masque Chloridia. Masques appear to have been less common at Charles's and Henrietta's court than in James's reign, but Elizabeth was to appear once more, again with her sister, in 1635, and Dorothy took part in the last-ever court masque in 1640.[233] These two daughters were very near in age and it is possible that they were particularly close.

Thomas's role as the queen's chancellor and counsellor, and probably generally as a competent administrator who could be trusted with financial matters, continued until his death in November 1635. In 1631 he was one of the men set to check Lord Cottington's vast expense claim of £50,000 for the period eight years earlier when he had accompanied Prince Charles and Buckingham to Spain, and he was also appointed to a commission to sort out a disagreement between the city of London and the officials of the Tower of London, about a 'markstone' on Tower Hill.[234] The

233 Elizabeth and Dorothy were two of three participants who had no title; most of the others were peeresses. For the text of Chloridia, and list of players: D. Lindley, *Court Masques: Jacobean and Caroline Entertainments, 1605–1640* (Oxford, 1995). Ben Jonson wrote many masques, and William Davenant was to become a prominent author of masques in the 1630s. The names of participants and others involved with masques are listed, with some biographical details, on http://shakespeareauthorship. com/bd.

234 Doc. 55 gives us an indication of the way Savage was viewed by some contemporaries. Cottington accounts: TNA, SP 38/15. Tower Hill commission: P.A. Penfold (ed.), *Acts of the Privy Council, 1630–1631* (London, 1964), p. 537.

following year he was one of many men appointed to the commission on fisheries; a letter to Nicholas suggests that he was active on this committee (Doc. 46).[235] Thomas was still having to work on the properties Charles had owned as prince of Wales, and on the queen's properties; in 1632 he was probably closely involved with a major survey of Queen Henrietta Maria's lands.[236]

The early 1630s saw a major dispute amongst catholics in England. Richard Smith, the pope's vicar apostolic to England, had been under threat of arrest, and withdrew from England to Paris in 1631. The secular catholic clergy supported the idea of a bishop in England, but the Jesuits and other 'regulars' opposed this idea. Later that year some twelve catholic peers signed a 'Protestatio Declaratoria' against the bishop, which was sent to the pope. Thomas signed but later repented, 'and sent an archdeacon to testify to this to the bishop'; Earl Rivers and the marquis of Winchester were originally said to have signed but denied doing so. Both the marquis of Winchester and the earl of Rutland were later said to have been patrons of the bishop. In April 1632 a letter opposing the bishop, signed by many leading catholic peers, was reported to have been sent to the king. Thomas was said to have signed this. Although there are only passing references to Thomas in the correspondence surviving about this affair, they confirm his role as one of the leading catholic peers.[237]

Thomas appears always to have been close to his relative and fellow executor of Buckingham's estate, Francis Manners, earl of Rutland. This was confirmed just before the earl's death in late 1632; Doc. 47 describes how the earl summoned his executors and close family to his bedside just two days before his death and allocated tasks.[238] The earl's widow and brother were appointed executors but Thomas Savage and Thomas Lord Coventry were appointed overseers of the will.[239] Katherine Buckingham, his niece, later had disagreements with her uncle, the new earl. In June 1634 she wrote, 'I cannot forbear any longer, for I see you have no disposition to agree to anything unless I give away my father's legacy, which he intended for me absolutely, and my Lord Savage's papers agree to it.'[240]

However, for all Thomas's presumed financial acumen, records suggest that he and Elizabeth were short of money themselves. Two sons and one daughter had married and had received financial settlements, which left less for Thomas and Elizabeth themselves. They had also drawn up settlements for their unmarried daughters, and could expect to have to fund up to nine more marriage settlements.[241] Thomas received as legacy from the earl of Rutland the cancellation of all his debts owed to the earl. The will mentions 'all the bonds, and statutes wherein he stands bound to me . . . and I do by this my will for ever acquit, release and discharge the said Lord Savage of and from the said debts'.[242] Elizabeth, in her petition to King Charles in 1633, said that she and her husband had just £2000 a year, of which

235 The commission was established by July 1632.

236 Survey of Henrietta Maria's lands: TNA, LR 5/57.

237 Our thanks to Michael Questier for material from a forthcoming publication. He quotes references from the Archdiocesan Archives of Westminster (AAW, A XXVI, no. 55, pp. 163–4; AAW, A XXVI, no. 64, pp. 183–4) and T.A. Birrell (ed.), *The Memoirs of Gregorio Panzani* (London, 1970), p. 178.

238 Death of the earl of Rutland: *HMC Rutland I*, 492.

239 Will of Francis Manners, earl of Rutland: TNA, PROB 11/163/18.

240 Letter from the duchess of Buckingham: *HMC Rutland I*, 494.

241 CCALS, DCH/H/200. Thomas's and Elizabeth's second eldest surviving daughter, Elizabeth, married Sir John Thimbleby (or Thimleby) of Irnham, Lincolnshire, before the summer of 1635.

242 William Noye, attorney general, was left £100 in the will, which suggests that he did work for Manners as well as for Savage. Will of Francis Manners, earl of Rutland: TNA, PROB 11/163/18.

around £1200 was spent at court (Doc. 48). Whether or not we believe Elizabeth's arithmetic, the Savages probably moved in a world where many of their friends, acquaintances and fellow royal servants were rather richer than they were, and of higher status.[243]

Whether she needed the money or not, there is evidence from 1633 onwards of Elizabeth asking for royal funds, proposing money-making schemes to the king or trying to get the rights to an appointment she could sell (Docs 48, 51, 52, 53 and 70). Aylmer includes Thomas in a short list of men who appear not to have made as much money from royal service as would have been expected. Either Thomas for some reason did not make the profits other men did, or he made the money, but spent it on his family, his houses, his hunting and his gambling.[244] His religion may also have cost him money, for the penal laws as they stood on paper imposed severe financial penalties on convicted recusants. However it seems clear that most of these laws were either not imposed or that lands were undervalued, so that most catholics paid much less for their faith than the laws would suggest. Those prominent at court are thought to have lost an even lower proportion of their income to recusancy fines.[245]

Documents illustrating Thomas's life give occasional hints of his catholicism and the problems it could cause. A letter written in 1633 gives tantalising mention of something for which we have no other evidence. Henry Cary, Viscount Falkland, wrote to Sir John Coke in September complaining about the short notice he had received (two days) to attend:

> the hearing of Sir Thomas Savage's proofs of his petition referred from his majesty to my lord treasurer and your honour and from you to Mr Attorney. . . . I pray you to persuade my lord treasurer to appoint me a time to be heard, before you make your certificate to his majesty, at what time I shall disclose a very cunning deceit involved in the petition. . . . Add the consideration that it is thus done immediately after my detection of Father Arthur and his apprehension.[246]

We have found nothing more of this petition, and Falkland could not follow through his threat to 'disclose a very cunning deceit'; his letter was written on 10 September but he was buried just fifteen days later, following the amputation of a leg. He had been hunting with the king at Theobalds, had fallen from a standing and broken a leg, so 'that the marrow ran'; it went gangrenous and had to be cut off, and he died

243 Thomas had presumably been paying fines because of his catholic faith. Elizabeth Savage, even as a viscountess, was always the lowest ranking of Henrietta Maria's ladies.

244 Aylmer, *The Kings Servants*, p. 320. Savage's inventory includes 16 'groom porter's tables', which were designed for playing the game of hazard. In hazard, 'the players assemble round a circular table, a space being reserved for the groom-porter, who occupies a somewhat elevated position, and whose duty it is to call the odds and see that the game is played correctly': *Pall Mall Gazette*, 3 September 1869, pp. 10–12.

245 B. Magee, *The English Recusants* (London, 1938), pp. 61–80. Charles I's first parliament had petitioned the new king for the strict enforcement of the penal laws against catholics. Charles issued a proclamation ordering that this should be done, but let it be known that large fines from wealthy laymen, and the imprisonment or transportation of priests, would be more to his liking than the use of the death penalty. From the late 1620s the system of fines was replaced by 'compounding', where the king agreed not to force rich catholics to attend Protestant service on condition that they paid an annual sum to be fixed by his commissioners, according to their means.

246 Letter from Falkland to Coke: *HMC Twelfth Report, Appendix II, Cowper MSS* (London, 1888), p. 30.

the following day.[247] It is not totally clear whether the statement about Father Arthur relates back to the matter of Thomas's petition, but the implication could be that Thomas was somehow involved with this exposure of a catholic priest.[248]

In 1634 Thomas's responsibilities at the queen's law court were probably increasing, for it seems most likely to have been fully functioning from this period. Although there is no surviving evidence, it seems likely that he would have had charge of much of the work of setting up the court, which could only be held when the queen's chancellor and attorney general were present. Once it was established, Thomas would have had its day-to-day working as one of his prime concerns. Earlier, three of the queen's council had been given the power to 'hear, reform, correct, adjudge and punish' according to their discretion in matters relating to the lands which were part of her jointure; her chancellor and attorney general had to be amongst these three.[249] However some responsibilities were waning, in particular the matter of Buckingham's will. In March 1635 the executorship moved to the duke's widow; Frances earl of Rutland had died and the other executors had renounced their responsibilities.[250] The change of executors probably followed a settlement with the crown, which looks to have ended the crown's interest in the estate.[251] However Savage was still becoming involved as executor or trustee for other wills, including that of the countess of Argyle, who died in January 1635. She made him, along with the earl of Denbigh and others, trustees of her estate for the benefit of her daughters.[252]

Religion divided, but aristocrats of all faiths shared a common culture. Thomas must have spent quite a proportion of his income on hunting, as did many men of his status; it is significant that James I hunted in Halton Park on his visit to Rocksavage in 1617. As well as having his hunting parks at Melford and Rocksavage/Halton, Thomas was ranger of Delamere forest in Cheshire and had the right to take some deer from it; Doc. 43 shows both that he was keen to extend this right to his sons, and that he wanted some of the rights and possessions previously held by the forester of Delamere. Doc. 37 gives us more background at a time when Charles I was moved to sell much of the Delamere lands. John Crewe, son of Sir Ranulph Crewe, succeeded as forester after the death of his father-in-law and brother-in-law in the late 1620s.[253] Several pieces of evidence point to problems following Crewe's

247 The facts of Falkland's death are related in several letters, two of which also mention an Irish priest who had been taken: Edward Nicholas to Captain John Pennington: TNA, SP 16/246/85; M.A.E. Green (ed.), *Diary of John Rous*, Camden Society (London, 1856–7), p. 75. It is possible that Falkland's letter was related to one sent to Windebank at Edinburgh on 11 July 1633. There was one letter 'enclosed in Lord Falkland's letter to the Duchess of Richmond, which is to be carefully delivered because it concerns the King's service': TNA, SP 16/242/56.

248 The only listed catholic martyr in England with the first name Arthur was Arthur Bell, from a family connected with Savage's (see Notes on People) but he was not arrested until 1643; the Irish priest was a Dominican named Arthur McGeoghan. See Notes on People, below. Our thanks to Michael Questier for much of the information about McGeoghan.

249 Fisher, *Queenes Court*, pp. 321–5. Letters patent to queen's council, 1627: TNA, E 156/12.

250 Duke of Buckingham's will: Nichols and Bruce, *Doctors' Commons*, p. 90. The work was still going on in 1663 when the 2nd duke of Buckingham took over after his mother's death. The change of executors probably followed a release and discharge (recorded in the Signet Office book) of all sums of money to Buckingham's executors.

251 Settlement: TNA, SO 3/10, March 1635.

252 Countess of Argyle's will: TNA, SP 16/299/86.

253 His father-in-law was Sir John Done, Thomas's friend (Doc. 20). This office had been held by the Done family since the 1350s, according to *VCH Cheshire* (see next note). Sir John died in 1629 and his son John in 1630; John Crewe was married to Sir John's daughter Mary. In 1626 the profits of the office were said by Sir John Done to be £88 16s. 8d. a year.

succession, and the forester's petition (Doc. 49) suggests that Thomas took his rights to their limits.[254] Sir Ranulph Crewe called a petition from Thomas 'exorbitant' (Doc. 67); this must relate to the same or a closely related matter.[255] It is possible that Crewe had right on his side, for in 1639 the then ranger was ordered to take his fee deer according to the seasons and as prescribed by the foresters.[256] As the queen's chancellor Savage was also entitled to receive venison from all Queen Henrietta Maria's hunting parks.[257]

Death and its records

When Thomas died at his house on Tower Hill in November 1635, he was said to have died of 'the running gout'.[258] Anthony Bacon described his own similar case thus:

> a running gout, which held me in my shoulder, my arm and my hand, otherwise in my knee and my foot, in which state I have continued these seven years, sometimes more, sometimes less pained, and yet not lost, God be thanked, the use of any limb nor have got any formed knottiness, but rather a stiffness and weakness in my joints.

This description suggests a disease that might get worse over a period of years.[259] However two contemporary letters giving news of Savage's death (Docs 54 and 55) both suggest that his disease developed speedily. James Howell, writing from Westminster in late November to the lord deputy, Thomas Wentworth, did not comment on the disease but said 'for home matters, there hath been much grief at court lately for the loss of two noble lords, the lord of St Albans and my Lord Savage, especially the latter'.[260] The countess of Devonshire tells us more about the competition for his role as chancellor. 'Lord Savage died of the running gout the day before I came here . . . his place is much desired by my lord marshall and my lord privy seal but it is thought judge Finch will carry it.'[261]

The Savage family chapel was in the parish church at Macclesfield, which had been the family's burial place since the first John Savage of Clifton was buried there

254 The succession to the position of forester was contested: J. Green, in *VCH Cheshire*, pp. 167–87. In 1631, while the office was contended, Thomas, as ranger, was ordered to ensure that subordinate forest officials carried out their duties: CCALS, DAR/A/16.

255 It is not clear which petition Crewe was referring to.

256 Order to ranger: CCALS, DAR/A/3/16.

257 Letter from Thomas Savage to the keeper of the queen's park at Eltham requesting the fee buck he was entitled to in his role as the queen's chancellor: TNA, SP 16/271/45.

258 *CP* gives his date of death as 20 November 1635. This is the date that his entrails were buried, so it is likely that he died slightly earlier. The inventory of the Tower Hill house, where he was living when he died, says that it was taken on 14 November 1635; see Doc. 60. The warrant for Sir Robert Aiton to use the privy seal 'pro tempore' on the death of Viscount Savage, is dated 26 November: O. Ogle and W.H. Bliss (eds), *Clarendon State Papers Preserved in the Bodleian Library* (5 vols, Oxford, 1869–1970), 1, no. 579.

259 Anthony Bacon was brother to Sir Francis Bacon, and worked as secretary to the earl of Essex at the end of Queen Elizabeth's reign. His reference to the running gout comes in a letter to Robert Barker in 1597. Index to the papers of Anthony Bacon (1558–1601): Lambeth Palace Library, MSS 647–662, London 1974. Our thanks to Bill Robinson for this reference.

260 Letter from Howell to Wentworth: W. Knowler (ed.), *The Earle of Strafforde's Letters and Dispatches, with an Essay towards his Life* (London, 1739), I, 489.

261 Countess of Devonshire's letter: *HMC Thirteenth Report, Appendix II, Portland II* (London, 1893), 127.

in 1386. The chapel was built by another Thomas Savage (brother of 'our' Thomas's great-great-grandfather) who had been archbishop of York in the early sixteenth century. Although he died in London, Thomas was also buried at Macclesfield. We do not know whether there was any indecision about this, or whether all Savages would go to any lengths to be buried at Macclesfield, and burial anywhere else was not even considered.

To take a body from London to Macclesfield, in mid-winter, was a considerable undertaking. The records of St Olave's, Hart Street, just yards away from the Tower Hill house, tell us that on 20 November 'the Lord Savage his entrails was buried in the chancel'.[262] Removing the entrails helped preserve the body without too much decay. On 9 December, nearly three weeks after the burial of his entrails, Thomas's funeral procession made its way from Tower Hill to Islington and the road north. By chance a working document about the funeral has survived, created by or for one of the heralds; this fits well with his funeral certificate from the College of Arms (Docs 56 and 57). The certificate notes that the procession consisted of 'his body in an open chariot covered with velvet accompanied with divers lords in their coaches, and his kinsfolk and servants riding before in black'.[263] Recent research has suggested that during the early seventeenth century the number of the grand aristocratic funerals, organised and accompanied by heralds, had declined. The fashion, probably led by religious belief, changed to quieter, more private funerals, often conducted at night. But the earl of Rutland had had a very grand, traditional funeral only three years earlier, and it is possible that catholic families resisted the change in fashion.[264]

The herald noted that the order of the procession would change at Islington. The places of the mainly higher-status people who had carried the banners through London were taken by other men, including William Thornburgh, keeper of Rocksavage park and John Pickering, receiver of Thomas's revenues for Cheshire. The funeral procession left London on 9 December and Thomas was buried at Macclesfield on 16 December. We do not know which route was taken from Islington to Macclesfield, but presumably when travelling with a wagon with the body on it, in December, they went by those roads most likely to be passable. However the procession did pass through Congleton, where Thomas had been high steward of the borough. The body rested 'in the old chapel then standing on the old bridge in Congleton'. The Congleton Corporation records give details of the amount spent at the 'entertainment' of those who accompanied the corpse.[265]

---

262 See p. xiv, note 4.

263 Funeral certificate: College of Arms, MS 1.8, f. 50.

264 R.M. Smuts, *Court Culture and the Origins of a Royalist Tradition in Early Stuart England* (Philadelphia, 1987), p. 200. C. Gittings, *Death, Burial and the Individual in Early Modern England* (London, 1984); R. Houlbrooke, *Death, Religion and the Family in England 1480–1750* (Oxford, 1998). The decline in grand heraldic funerals is still a matter of debate.

265 Stewardship of Congleton: TNA, SP 16/181/444. Congleton Corporation books quoted in Armstrong, *Savage of the Ards*, say that the expenditure included:

Mending Rood Lane against the coming of Lord Savage's corpse	1s. 6d.
Sugar, 6lbs; cloves, 1 oz. at the entertainment	11s. 0d.
Four links to light	5s. 0d.

The Savage archives include a record of expenses for a journey from Beeston in Cheshire to London and back, which details the route taken. The outward journey went via Nantwich and Stableford Bridge, Stone, Middleton, Dunchurch, Daventry, Stony Stratford, Dunstable and St Albans; the return journey went via Dunstable, Daventry, Meriden, Lichfield, Stone and Nantwich. A journey from London to Macclesfield would presumably follow the same route as far as Stone, then turn north to Macclesfield via

Thomas's funeral certificate tells us that 'the greatest part of the nobility and gentry' of Cheshire was 'present and assisting that service'. We do not have any details, but the order of his grandfather's funeral service in the same chapel on 24 January 1598 does survive. It lists the procession in great detail, with all the associated heraldry, symbols of office and details of who bore each banner. The procession included 'his great horse covered with black baise or cloth to the heels with arms thereon on every side and led by the gentle groom of his stable' but the horse was 'but to pass by at the church door'. All were to stand, in order, until the body was taken from the coach; 'gentlemen of blood' carried the coffin into a railed place in the church and the people carrying heraldic banners stood around it. When the sermon ended, the herald took the chief mourner to the communion table and those carrying the heraldic banners delivered them up to the herald; meanwhile the trumpets sounded 'dolefully' and the mourners made obeisance as the banners passed. As the coffin was carried off for burial the choristers sang a requiem; when the body was interred two trumpeters 'sounded up aloud'.[266] Thomas's funeral should have been grander even than this, for heraldic funerals were very much governed by the rank of the deceased person.

Randle Holmes, the deputy herald for Cheshire in the early seventeenth century, appears also to have acted to some extent as an undertaker, and his notes provide information about the proper way to conduct funerals for people of varying status. His notes say that a viscount's hearse was two and a half yards long, a yard and a quarter across and two and a half yards high. Four square banners would be needed for the corners, a long banner for the top. There would be silk pencils about a foot long, plus a velvet valence with a little fringe for the top, and one with a longer fringe for the bottom. The viscount's crown would be laid on a velvet cushion on the table within the hearse.[267] Elsewhere in his notes he lists more fully the items needed; these include many banners, pencils and penons, the arms on silk, the arms in 'metal' embroidery on several cloths, his helm and crest and his viscount's crown and mantle, along with a number of coats of arms, crests and the like in pasteboard and gilt. The total cost Holmes gives as £116 8s. 4d., which included £42 for horses and £30 for three 'officers of arms'. There were other, probably more expensive charges to pay, particularly the cost of black cloth for family and mourners.

At the end of the funeral, immediately before the interment, the York Herald would have pronounced: 'Thus it has pleased Almighty God to take out of this transitory life to his divine goodness and mercy the right honorable Thomas late Viscount Savage chancellor and counsellor to the queen's most excellent majesty. God bless with long life and happiness the right honorable John now Viscount Savage (heir apparent to the honor and earldom of Rivers) with the rest of that right noble family. God save the king.'[268] Thomas's mother, the very long-lived Dame Mary Savage née Allington, was buried at Macclesfield on the same day; presumably many mourners went to both services.

Thomas and his mother were interred in the Savage chapel, but have no memorial

---

Congleton. This route is roughly equivalent to following the A5 out of London as far as Daventry, probably going south and west of Coventry, and following the A51 to Stone. One of Sir John Savage's letters to Lord Cecil, written when he was mayor of Chester, has postal endorsements from Chester, Nantwich, Stone, Lichfield, Coleshill, Coventry, Towcester, ?Bradwell (Bucks), St Albans and Barnet.

266 Sir John Savage's funeral: BL, Harleian MSS 2129.

267 Randle Holmes' notes on funerals: BL, Harleian MSS 2129.

268 Heralds' notes: Bodl., Rawlinson B, 138; Doc. 56 in this volume.

there.[269] The only mention of Thomas in the chapel is on the very grand memorial to Sir John Savage, his grandfather, which Thomas had paid for sometime earlier. At Long Melford the Savage family is now much less well known, but a funeral hatchment has survived, the earliest of its sort in Suffolk. It is thought to be one of the earliest lozenge-shaped hatchments in England, and perhaps the earliest on canvas rather than wood. The shield contains twenty-one quarterings of the Savage family, impaling twelve quarterings of the Darcy family; it has been described as the work of an accomplished herald-painter.[270] The families identified in the quarterings correspond closely to those whose colours were carried at Thomas's funeral (Doc. 56). The hatchment would have been expensive, but is not mentioned separately in Elizabeth's account of her payments as administrator; perhaps it was completed after the summer of 1637, when that account ended. Whether or not this was one of the hatchments carried at the funeral is unknown.

Thomas may have been a practised administrator and 'the great director of other men's estates' (Doc. 55), but for some reason either he did not leave a will or Elizabeth chose not to present one for probate.[271] Elizabeth Savage had to take out letters of administration, which are dated 7 December, two days before the funeral procession.[272] The inventory (Doc. 60) of the movable goods in the Tower Hill house is dated 14 November, which is before the date, 20 November, given for Thomas's death in his funeral certificate. It was not until 12 January that the inventory of Melford Hall was taken, and that of Rocksavage was not completed until 15 February. At the end of the inventory there is a list of Thomas's goods in 'the rooms at court'. It is not clear whether Elizabeth used these rooms as well, or in which royal palace the rooms were; even so this is a rare indication of the furnishing of courtiers' private rooms.[273]

Although the terms of the administration required Elizabeth Savage to pay Thomas's debts and associated charges, and submit her accounts by June 1636, the 'exemplification' of her account is dated a year later than this (Doc. 66). She had paid out over £8700, mainly in debts due but including £1100 owed after court actions in Common Pleas.[274] This was only part of the £14,000 which Garrard (Doc. 55) suggested that Thomas personally owed at his death. Elizabeth was now to live on the income from lands set aside for her jointure (which included the house and park at Melford, although not the wider manor), her pension from the king and support from her father (Doc. 64). Her financial problems seem to have been widely known, as letters written by Sir Frederick Cornwallis to his mother Lady Bacon, and

269 Memorials have to be paid for by those who survive; both Elizabeth and the new viscount died in debt and Sir Thomas Savage, the second eldest son, died while in prison for debt.

270 L. Dow, 'The Savage Hatchment at Long Melford', *PSIA*, 26 (1954), 214–19.

271 There are documents which make arrangements about land 'for the use of his will', and it seems unlikely that a man who had been executor to so many others would have failed to leave a will himself. A will would be very likely to include legacies to others, and if times were hard, Elizabeth may have preferred not to have to pay them. Perhaps Thomas took this decision himself, and decided against leaving a will so that his widow would have more discretion about her use of any money remaining. There were probably settlements relating to the younger children already agreed; we know of those for Francis and for three of the unmarried daughters. If the children's finances were settled, and the descent of the lands agreed with the elder sons, a will may have been less needed.

272 Administration bond: CCALS, DCH/E/324.

273 Inventory: CCALS, DCH/X/15/10.

274 Exemplification: CCALS, DCH/O/27.

by Revd Garrard to Thomas Lord Wentworth (Docs 54 and 55) make clear.[275] Elizabeth's father, Earl Rivers, made a new will in March 1636 leaving all his property to her, excepting certain gifts and legacies which were set down in a separate schedule (now lost).[276] However Earl Rivers lived until 1641, so for the next five years Elizabeth had to find other ways of augmenting her income.

'An impecunious but ingenious courtier'

Elizabeth was very short of money, and she continued to petition Charles I with money-making schemes. She petitioned him to grant her the right to collect money paid in recognizances 'in the City of London by freemen who were working in a trade other than that by which they had obtained their freedom'. The petition was dealt with at Whitehall on 6 December just three days before Thomas's funeral, but it may have been prepared some time earlier (Doc. 53). Seven weeks later a committee of City aldermen recommended that the existing scheme worked well, and that no change was needed (Doc. 59). One of those aldermen was John Cordell, descended from William Cordell's grandfather. Robert Ashton, writing of this petition, called Elizabeth Savage 'an impecunious but ingenious courtier on the make', a judgment with which it is difficult to disagree.[277] She was successful, that same December, in being granted a patent for all minerals, gold and copperas stones found on the seashore.[278]

In the years before his death Elizabeth's father gave her at least two gifts of land in Essex; one indenture states that the gift is 'for the natural love and affection which he bears to the said Elizabeth Viscountess Savage'.[279] Lord Darcy's concern for his daughter is reflected in the letter he wrote to the king shortly before his death (Doc. 64). Charles I seems to have been trying to help even earlier; in May 1636 he wrote to either the earl of Pembroke or the earl of Worcester proposing Elizabeth's eldest unmarried daughter Dorothy (also known as Doll) as a second wife for the earl's son, Lord Herbert (Doc. 63).[280]

Charles's efforts to help Dorothy Savage marry could have been an attempt to discourage a different alliance, for on 10 April 1637 she married Lord Andover, heir of the earl of Berkshire. This marriage was against the wishes of both families, and seems to have caused considerable concern in royal, aristocratic and ecclesiastical circles. In April 1637 Viscount Conway wrote:

> we are here after the old manner, marrying and giving or rather stealing in marriage, for my Lord Andover has lately married Mrs Dorothy Savage contrary to his father's liking and his protestations to him, but *si violandum*

275 Elizabeth's original jointure: CCALS DCH/ H/ 205A (Doc. 3 in this volume); additions to her jointure: CCALS, DCH O/29. Grants from Thomas Earl Rivers to Elizabeth Savage: ERO D/Dac/239, D/Dac/241. Lady Jane Bacon had previously been married to Sir William Cornwallis, Elizabeth Savage's mother's uncle.

276 Will of Earl Rivers: CCALS, DCH/E/325.

277 R. Ashton, *The City and the Court 1603–45* (London, 1979), p. 59.

278 Grant of minerals on the sea shore, February 1636: TNA, SO 3/11. Copperas is a green vitriol or ferrous sulphate, $FeSO_4$, and was used as a mordant, as a dye, to make ink and chlorine, and as a bleaching agent. Copperas was made on a large scale in various parts of southern England. The works at Tankerton Bay, near Whitstable, were recently excavated; for a summary report see www.eng-h.gov.uk/archcom/ projects.

279 Will of Earl Rivers: CCALS, DCH/E/325; grants of lands: ERO, D/Dac/239, 241.

280 Letter from Charles I to Lord Pembroke: Ogle and Bliss, *Clarendon State Papers*, I, no. 729: Bodl., CLSP vol. i, p. 547. See notes to Doc. 63 for the confusion between two earls.

est jus, it was to be done for her; we must leave our father and mother and cleave to our mistress.[281]

The Revd Garrard's more detailed account of the trouble caused by this marriage is in this volume (Doc. 65). It emphasises both the importance of the family's religion to others in the aristocracy, and the importance society placed on obedience to parents from even adult children. The countess of Leicester, writing to her husband, gave a slightly different view of Elizabeth's attitude. She reports the marriage of Miss Doll Savage and Andover, without the parents' knowledge or consent, but writes that while the earl and countess of Berkshire were greatly upset, Elizabeth Savage pretended great displeasure.[282] Whatever the scandal at the time, Dorothy Savage was accepted back into court circles, for she had a role in the last ever court masque, 'Salmacida Spolia', in 1640. This marriage is still mentioned today in art history, as part of the background to Anthony van Dyck's portrait of Dorothy and her younger sister Elizabeth, 'Lady Elizabeth Thimbleby and Dorothy, Viscountess Andover', which is owned by the National Gallery in London and is reproduced in this book (Pl. III).[283] It is supposed that the picture was painted in 1637 to mark Dorothy's wedding; St Dorothy is patron saint of brides and newly weds, and the winged putto with the basket of roses is her attribute. The link with St Dorothy is suggested as referring to her catholicism.[284]

Elizabeth was still attending on the queen and continued to do so at least until 1641. Early in 1637, as a lady of the queen's bedchamber, she was on a relatively short list of people given a key to the new lock at Whitehall; she was also involved in quarrels among catholic ladies at court.[285] Her long attendance on the queen was recognised to some extent in 1639 when she and some colleagues were awarded a monopoly for 'the pre-emption of copperas'. Charles I became the sole merchant for copperas in 1637 and granted this right to Elizabeth and her associates; the grant says that it was partly given 'in consideration of the faithful and acceptable service heretofore done to his dearest consort the queen by the said Lady Elizabeth Viscountess Dowager Savage and at her instance'.[286] However Elizabeth was still looking for more income, investing in fen drainage (Doc. 69) and trying some other petitions relating to the City of London (Doc. 70).[287] Not only was Elizabeth in financial difficulties, but by 1639 her eldest son John had debts totalling over £31,000.[288]

281 Conway's letter to Sir Robert Harvey: *HMC Fourteenth Report, Appendix II, Portland III* (London, 1894), 42. Dorothy Savage married Charles Howard, Lord Andover, later the 2nd earl of Berkshire, on 10 April 1637. For Lord Andover, Viscount Conway and Dorothy Savage, see Notes on People, below.

282 Countess of Leicester's letter: *HMC De L'Isle VI* (London, 1966), 101.

283 Records at the National Portrait Gallery show that the painting was previously thought to be Dorothy with her sister-in-law Catherine Viscountess Savage. It is not known who commissioned the painting.

284 The double portrait by van Dyck has a National Gallery code NG6437; it was in the collection of Sir Peter Lely. A portrait of another of Thomas's and Elizabeth's daughters, Henrietta Maria, probably painted in the early 1660s, hangs at Boughton House (pl. 1).

285 Elizabeth gets a new key: TNA, LC 5/134, p. 145. Quarrels at court, noted in Panzini's correspondence: TNA, 31/9, 10 and BL, Add. 15,390, ff. 95–6. Our thanks to Caroline Hibbard for these references.

286 Copperas award: TNA, E 214/976; BCA, DV 894, 131, 165, 169.

287 Doc. 69: TNA, SP 16/414/72; Doc. 70: TNA, SP 16/439/22.

288 Debts of John Viscount Savage, later Earl Rivers: CCALS, DCH/M/35/1.

Destruction, malignancy and death

In February 1641 John Viscount Savage became Earl Rivers, succeeding his grandfather. But while he was taking his place in the House of Lords, an 'anti-catholic drive' in Cheshire saw the Savage family presented as recusant, malignant and delinquent.[289] They were certainly recusant, and actively catholic. On 7 December 1640 Thomas's and Elizabeth's youngest two sons arrived at Lisbon College with others of the '4th mission'. The college register recorded that Richard Savage, nineteen, had studied humanity to the end of syntax. The records say that he had been sent by 'Leyburn'.[290] His younger brother Charles, aged seventeen, wrote to his grandmother Rivers five months after he arrived (Doc. 71) and implies that the party left England in some haste. Charles took the college habit without oath on 25 July 1641, paid one hundred crowns a year for board, and left for France on 29 April 1643. Richard had not stayed so long. The college register stated that he could not be made to observe college discipline, so was sent away on 2 February 1641.[291]

Meanwhile the House of Commons was hearing a report from its Committee on Monopolies; the members voted to disbar Sir Nicholas Crispe because he had a monopoly 'in the matter of copperas'. In vain, Crispe argued that it was not a monopoly because Elizabeth Viscountess Savage had a patent for the same. Whether Crispe's patent caused Elizabeth and her agents to make less money than had been expected, we do not know.[292]

The spring of 1641 was a period of intense political activity which saw a major push in the Commons to break the circle of catholics within the court, in particular those associated with the queen, along with measures to disarm a much wider range of catholics across the country; there were also concerns about the army in Ireland. These matters were strongly linked to the trial of the earl of Strafford. Members of the Lords objected to interference with the queen's household; the earl of Holland (related to Elizabeth) attempted to find a compromise, and reported that the only two court catholics in office whom the queen wished to protect were her secretary Sir John Winter and Lady Savage.[293] There were arguments in Parliament about Winter, but either Elizabeth was ignored as having a purely domestic position, or any discussion about her role went unreported.[294]

In April 1641 the king created Elizabeth Countess Rivers in her own right, for life. This creation of a female life peer was a very rare honour, which shows the desire of Charles and Henrietta Maria to protect and reward her (Doc. 73).[295] But there were pressures elsewhere as the Savages and their relations were presented yet again in Cheshire as recusant. Elizabeth's second son Sir Thomas Savage and his wife (and her parents) had been presented several times, and in May 1641 their

289 Starkey, *Runcorn*, p. 75.

290 This is possibly John Leyburn, 1615–1702, who was vicar apolistic to England from 1685. However it could also be George Leyburn who was with Charles in 1647 and who later became head of the catholic college at Douai in France.

291 M. Sharratt (ed.), *Lisbon College Register 1628–1813*, Catholic Records Society, 72 (1991), 169. We have no idea of what happened to Richard, but Charles was alive in 1666 and had at least one child.

292 W. Notestein, *The Journal of Sir Simons D'Ewes* (New Haven, 1923).

293 C. Hibbard, *Charles I and the Popish Plot* (Chapel Hill, 1983), p. 191.

294 Notestein, *Simonds D'Ewes*, pp. 486–9.

295 Creation of Elizabeth Savage as the dowager Countess Rivers: TNA, SO 3/12, f. 144v. The only precedents quoted were the creation of Elizabeth Finch as Viscountess Maidstone and then as countess of Winchelsey in the 1620s, and that of Ann Boleyn, who had been made marchioness of Winchester by Henry VIII.

children Elizabeth and Katherine Savage were indicted as recusants but the Cheshire justices were unsure whether they could be convicted, as they were both aged under sixteen.[296]

Elizabeth was now a countess and her children had the precedence of the sons and daughters of an earl, but honours do not make money.[297] She had inherited lands and property from her father, Earl Rivers, but nowhere near enough to meet her debts or those of John Savage, the new earl. In April 1641, the same month that Elizabeth became Countess Rivers, she and her eldest son obtained a licence to develop the site of the Tower Hill house (Doc. 72).[298] Later the same year, on 27 November, Earl Rivers mortgaged Melford Hall, manor and lands for £15,000 to John Cordell, alderman of London, and his son Robert, who were descended from Sir William Cordell's grandfather.[299] The indenture recorded that the estate was free from all incumbrances except that Elizabeth for the rest of her life had rights to the manor house and park of Melford, the deer there and the next presentations to the living of Melford (Doc. 74). John Cordell may have long planned to acquire Melford, but it is possible that only when he sat on the city committee investigating Elizabeth's petition in 1635 did he start thinking about this country estate, with family connections, so suitable for a rising city merchant.[300]

The income from John Cordell would have been welcome, but in 1642 Elizabeth faced increasing troubles relating to her religion alongside her financial problems. In January the high sheriff of Suffolk, Sir William Spring, and Maurice Barrow esquire were ordered by the House of Commons to search the Suffolk house of the Lady Rivers, seize any arms they found and put the arms into safe custody.[301] Hengrave Hall, by this time home of Elizabeth's sister Lady Penelope Gage, was searched in the same month and large quantities of arms removed.[302] Lady Gage, also a prominent catholic, spoke of being daily threatened by the common sort of people. In July Elizabeth was presented as a recusant in Essex.[303]

Earl Rivers, with his mother's agreement, mortgaged Melford Hall and its lands to John Cordell nine months before the eventful summer of 1642. The earl, we presume, moved into Rocksavage after his father's death, and also held Frodsham Castle and the Cheshire lands. In summer 1642 he was in Cheshire working with other leading royalists to recruit soldiers for the king's army; when Charles I visited

296 Note from Cheshire justices: UWB, Lloyd Mostyn MSS, 704.

297 There may have been three Countess Rivers at this period. Elizabeth's mother was still alive, and was presumably the Dowager Countess. Elizabeth was Countess Rivers in her own right, but her daughter-in-law Catherine may still have been alive; if so she, as wife of Earl Rivers, was also Countess Rivers.

298 Licence to build: TNA, SO 3/12, f. 144r.

299 Abstract of Sir John Cordell's title: Guildhall Library, MS 9848; Doc. 74 in this volume is the first part of this document.

300 Cordell already had land outside London; in 1631 he had bought the manor of Henley in Arden, *alias* Beaudesert, in Warwickshire. His son Robert sold it in 1672. Purchase of Henley in Arden in 1631: WCRO, DR 18/1/486. Sale of Henley: WCRO, DR 18/3/7/1.

301 *Journal of the House of Commons*, 2 (London, 1802), 14 January 1642. The *Journal of the House of Commons* and that of the House of Lords can be found at www.british-history.ac.uk. An order by the House of Lords in October 1642 shows that the two Houses had 'not long since' ordered that Elizabeth's arms and ammunition at St Osyth should be seized, that it was currently in the hands of Harbottle Grimston, who no longer wished to care for it, and that the mayor of Colchester was ordered to relieve him of it and keep it safe: HL/PO/JO/10/1/134.

302 J. Walter, *Understanding Popular Violence in the English Revolution, The Colchester Plunderers* (London, 1999), pp. 225–6.

303 Threats from the common people: *ODNB*, vol. 49. Presentation in Essex: ERO, Q/SR 317/34.

Chester, Rivers followed him from the county leading a regiment of foot.[304] His mother Elizabeth appears to have made St Osyth in Essex her base at this period (Doc. 75); it was of course her original family home. Her duties at court must have ended, at the very latest, when Charles I and his family finally left London early in 1642.[305] We do not know whether she regularly or ever visited Melford Hall in these years, or indeed whether it was fully furnished; it is possible that when the lands were mortgaged Elizabeth moved the bulk of her belongings elsewhere. But she still had her rights to Melford Hall for life, as well as other properties which were part of her jointure, and all she had inherited from her father.

The Stour valley disturbances of 1642 have recently been considered in impressive detail by John Walter.[306] The late summer and early autumn of that year saw a series of attacks in Essex and Suffolk; crowds attacked and sacked the houses of catholics and supporters of Charles I and their owners were forced out of the area. The first attacks were in Colchester on 22 August; the next day crowds set off to St Osyth, nine miles to the south-east. Elizabeth was at St Osyth but was forewarned of the approaching crowds and, with members of her family, made her escape and fled to Melford Hall. At St Osyth some of her servants were attacked when the crowd sacked the house. Some of the attackers stayed at St Osyth, others followed Elizabeth and her family to Melford.[307]

On Wednesday 24 August some of the crowd nearly caught up with her; they reached Melford Hall 'before she had fully escaped their sight'; she made her way to Bury St Edmunds and then to London, but behind her the crowd entered Melford Hall and ransacked the house. Elizabeth was quick to respond; her petition to the House of Lords for £50,000 to compensate for her losses is dated 29 August (Doc. 75) as is a draft order to Harbottle Grimston, recorder of Colchester, justices of the peace and others to help her recover her goods and persuade her tenants to pay their rents.[308] The Lords awarded her both compensation and a warrant protecting her from future attack, but she is reported to have believed her life still in danger. On 21 September the *Journal of the House of Lords* recorded that 'the countess of Rivers is now come into this town for her safety'.[309] London may not have been safe enough, for the House of Lords gave Elizabeth leave to 'go beyond the seas' in November 1642. She did not go immediately; in the following January the Lords gave permission for her son and daughter to go with her, and the whole permit was renewed by the Lords in early April 1643, with the addition that 'she shall have liberty to transport a coach and ten horses into France with her'.[310] But she stayed in England for all of April. In the middle of the month the House of Commons reported that 'certain persons, well affected to the countess of Rivers'

304 R.N. Dore, '1642: the Coming of the Civil War to Cheshire: Conflicting Actions and Impressions', *Trans of the Lancashire and Cheshire Antiquarian Society*, 87, Manchester, 1991, pp. 39–63. The House of Commons ordered in July 1642: 'that the Lords be acquainted with the proceedings of Earl Rivers and Cheshire. And that some course may be taken for the speedy apprehending and bringing him to answer the same': *Journal of the House of Commons*, 2, 11 July 1642.

305 Henrietta Maria left England in February 1642, while Charles I headed for York.

306 J. Walter, *Understanding Popular Violence in the English Revolution, The Colchester Plunderers* (London, 1999). John Walter also wrote the entry about Elizabeth in *ODNB*, vol. 49.

307 Walter, *Understanding Popular Violence*, p. 15. Part I of the book describes the events of summer 1642 in the Stour Valley. One of the servants attacked at St Osyth was John Barney, who had been housekeeper at Rocksavage in the 1630s.

308 Petition to the House of Lords and draft order related: HLRO, HL/PO/JO/10/1/132, 29 Aug. 1642 (Doc. 75). A printed order is dated 9 September 1642 (Doc. 76).

309 *Journal of the House of Lords*, 5 (London, 1802), 21 September 1642.

310 *Ibid.*, 11 November 1642, 28 January 1643, 7 April 1643.

had paid £500 for timber in the county of Essex; the committee for sequestration were to investigate. At the end of the month Elizabeth petitioned the House of Lords again about her losses, which were now said to be £100,000; her tenants were still not paying their rents.[311]

The carriage horses gave Elizabeth major problems when she eventually went abroad. On 8 May the *Journal of the House of Commons* records that 'the Lady coming to pass out of the kingdom, six of her horses were taken by Mr Marten: the Lords desire they may be restored'.[312] This Mr Marten was later dubbed the 'Roundhead plunder master-general'. Although the countess obtained from the earl of Essex another warrant for their restoration, on 17 May Mr Marten procured an order from the House of Commons to keep them.[313] The horses and all her other goods which had been licensed to pass by the Lords, and had been allowed by the Custom House, were, after all, seized, and she never recovered any of them.[314]

Although Elizabeth received some compensation for the sack of St Osyth and Melford, and John Walter quotes one source which suggests that she got some of her possessions back, the family's financial situation was getting worse, and there were debts still unpaid from Thomas's lifetime.[315] In 1641, for example, the House of Lords' calendar recorded that the late Lord Savage had been in considerable debt and had conveyed lands in Cheshire and elsewhere to trustees for payment of his debts. Even so his son Earl Rivers had failed to satisfy a decree obtained against him in the court of requests.[316]

Earl Rivers was prominent in the king's army during the civil war, leading a regiment of foot. At the start of the war he put Halton Castle, next to Rocksavage, in a state of defence, but it was attacked by Parliamentarian troops and its defences were dismantled. Rocksavage was looted and made uninhabitable; the roof and some walls were destroyed.[317] The earl's lands in Cheshire and elsewhere were sequestered, and the income was lost to him (these seem to have included part of his mother's property); he was also fined for his allegiance to the Royalist cause.[318] His goods were to be preserved so that when he had paid his fines they would be returned to him. Earl Rivers' first wife Catherine probably died between 1641 and 1644; he had married again before 1647.[319]

Elizabeth may have gained some income after her mother's death in 1644 when she inherited lands in Devon and Dorset, but it is possible that these lands were

311 Petition of April 1643 to the House of Lords: HLRO, HL/PO/JO/10/1/148, 27 April 1643.

312 *Journal of the House of Commons*, 3 (London, 1802), 8 May 1643.

313 *Journal of the House of Commons*, 3, 17 May 1643, 22 May 1643, 12 June 1643.

314 Parker, *History of Long Melford*, p. 336. Mr Marten is most likely to have been Henry Martin; see Notes on People, below. The indictments of some of the individuals captured following the attack on St Osyth survive: ERO, T/A 418/126/5, Q/SR 320/15–16, Q/SR 320/61.

315 Walter, *Understanding Popular Violence*, p. 54.

316 House of Lords Calendar: *HMC Fourth Report I, Appendix* (London, 1874), p. 81. Thomas had owed over £2000 to Edward Wymarke. Wymarke's administrator commenced proceedings in 1639 but the cause was still being fought in 1647, when he petitioned the House of Lords. The petition says that John Viscount Savage (as he had been) had paid £9000 of his father's debts but had not paid the £2000 owed to Wymarke's estate. Petition of John Greene, administrator: HLRO, HL/PO/JO/10/1/203, 8 April 1646.

317 Starkey, *Old Runcorn*, p. 75.

318 The records of the Committee of Compounding catalogue several long-running investigations into John Earl Rivers, and the sequestration of his lands and goods.

319 Death of Catherine Countess Rivers: Doc. 74 includes references to a 1641 indenture where she is included, and a similar one in 1644 where she is not mentioned. Remarriage of Earl Rivers: Mary Countess Rivers, his second wife, petitions the House of Lords in 1647: HLRO, HL/PO/JO/10/1/186, 6 March 1647.

sequestered along with her Essex properties.[320] She attempted to protect her lands by what might now be called 'creative accounting', but was finally obliged to compound for her lands at £16,979 9s.10d.[321] At some point the family moved out of the Tower Hill house; the last evidence of Elizabeth living there is in 1639. After 1642, both St Osyth and Melford Hall were too badly damaged to be occupied, and the Cordell family was already moving into the Melford area.[322]

We do not know how long Elizabeth spent abroad, but she is likely to have been back in England by January 1645, when she once more petitioned the House of Lords.[323] Sequestration documents suggest that Elizabeth was living in Covent Garden by later that year.[324] Her petition in 1646 to be allowed to remain in London (Doc. 80) gives her address as Queen Street; this is highly likely to be Great Queen Street in Covent Garden, where her grandson Earl Rivers was living in 1690.[325] When Elizabeth was assessed to pay £200 towards the support of the Scots army in spring 1645, she appealed and related her reduced financial circumstances to the House of Lords (Doc. 79).[326] When papists and those suspected of supporting the king were commanded to leave London in April 1646, she petitioned the Lords again, stating clearly that she had no other home to go to (Doc. 80).[327] Although both these petitions were successful, she seems to have gone abroad again, for in September 1646 a draft of a House of Lords pass allowed 'the Lady Rivers and her daughter with their servantes and necessaries' to return to England from France, and another adds permission for a grandchild as well.[328]

But family life went on to some extent amidst the financial problems and the civil war. In October 1645, three months after the battle of Naseby, settlements were drawn up concerning the marriage of Henrietta Maria Savage (Pl. 1), Elizabeth's

320 In 1640 Mary Countess Rivers (Elizabeth's mother) appears to settle her manor of Ipplepen and other lands and possessions in Devon on her grandchild, Elizabeth's second son, Sir Thomas Savage of Beeston; he died in 1651 and the lands were sold in 1653 on behalf of Earl Rivers and many others of the family, including this Thomas's widow: DRO: 608 A/PZT/1 and 608 A/PZT/4.

321 Compounding for lands: Parker, *History of Long Melford*, p. 337.

322 Sir Robert Cordell's children were baptised in Melford church from 1643 onwards. Whether he was renting part of Melford Hall (unlikely given a 1649 description of it as being uninhabited), living elsewhere in the area or just bringing his children to Melford for their baptisms is impossible to know.

323 This petition is partially destroyed, but relates to the attainder of the earl of Somerset, who had recently died. Elizabeth was seeking evidences from the records of the Kings Bench, to enable her to 'make her title and defence in the said suit'. We cannot find any evidence of an attainder relating to the earl around the period of his death but there are several references to Elizabeth's need for evidence: *Journal of the House of Lords*, 7, 18 January 1645, 25 January 1645. *Journal of the House of Commons*, 4, 25 January 1645, 5 April 1645.

324 Elizabeth writing from Tower Hill in 1639, Doc. 69: TNA, SP 16/414/72. Evidence that Earl Rivers, owing Sir John Cordell £15,000, conveyed property on Tower Hill and other lands in Essex, Sussex and Cheshire to Richard Lord Lumley and Henry Nevill *alias* Smyth, so that they could raise money to pay the debts: CCALS, DCH/H/506.

325 Elizabeth Savage at Covent Garden: *Calendar of the Committee for Advance of Money* (London, 1888), II, 601. She is assessed as having £3000. Elizabeth at Queen Street: HLRO, HL/PO/JO/10/1/224, 3 April 1646. Earl Rivers at Great Queen Street: D. Keene, P. Earle, C. Spence and J. Barnes, *Metropolitan London in the 1690s* (London, 1992); online at www.british-history.ac.uk

326 Elizabeth's 1645 petition: HLRO, HL/PO/JO/10/1/186, 7 May 1645 (Doc. 79).

327 Elizabeth's 1646 petition: HLRO, HL/PO/JO/10/1/224, 3 April 1646 (Doc. 80). On the same day her daughter Dorothy, Viscountess Andover, also petitioned to be allowed to stay in London. She claims never to have supported the king, that her husband had 'long since submitted himself to parliament' and that her health was too poor to allow any move: HLRO, HL/PO/JO/10/1/203, 3 April 1646.

328 Pass allowing Elizabeth to return to England: HLRO, HL/PO/JO/10/1/213, 10 September 1646. The pass to her grandchild is mentioned in the *Journal of the House of Lords*, 8 (London, 1802) 11 September 1646.

Plate 1. Lady Henrietta Maria Sheldon, attributed to Jacob Huysmans, probably from the late 1650s. Thomas and Elizabeth's youngest daughter. Her sister Anne married the 2nd earl of Cardigan, and the portrait probably belonged to him. It was known to be hanging at Montagu House in Whitehall in the 1770s. *(By kind permission of his Grace the Duke of Buccleuch and Queensberry, K.T., from his collection at Boughton House, Northamptonshire)*

youngest daughter, to Ralph Sheldon of Beoley in Worcestershire. Henrietta had a portion of at least £1500; the settlement gave Ralph lands at Studley, Worcestershire and in Wiltshire.[329] The Sheldons were another catholic family long established in their shire, gentry rather than aristocracy, but with money made from the tapestry-weaving industry as well as from land.[330] The marriage settlement demonstrates continuing links between Elizabeth and others of her family and social network. Viscount Lumley (who had inherited from John Lord Lumley), Richard Croft (brother or nephew of Sir James Croft), Thomas Lord Savage (Elizabeth's grandson, son and heir of Earl Rivers) and Sir John Thimbleby (Elizabeth's son-in-law) were party to the settlement, along with the earls of Bath and Carlisle and Thomas Savage of Worcester, a distant relation. The marriage was to be childless, and Ralph outlived Henrietta Maria by twenty-one years. A friend of his, Anthony à Wood, commented of Henrietta Maria that although 'she was a tall proper and handsome woman, yet she proved not a good wife to him, as being lavish and improvident, to the diminishing of his estate'.[331]

The Savage estate was diminishing very quickly. In 1647 Mary Countess Rivers, the earl's second wife, petitioned the House of Lords about his possessions taken from Halton Castle. Although they should have been preserved and returned to him when he paid his sequestration fines, they had in fact been sold to a William Rudges of London. A month later an agreement had been reached whereby Rudges sold the goods to Sir John Cordell (Docs 81 and 82).[332] Rudges' name appears in relation to the very long list of family linen sold by Earl Rivers to Cordell that year (Doc. 83). In the following spring Elizabeth was ordered to pay her composition for 'two parts of a capitall messuage and parke in Long Melford' and in June 1648 used her business about this as reason to remain in London.[333] But a year later the Melford properties were finally sold to Cordell's son Robert.[334] Earl Rivers and his mother by this time owed Robert Cordell £20,488, so they received just £8511 8s. for the estate with all appurtenant rights, the advowson of Melford church, and the right of the nomination of the warden and brethren of the hospital of the Holy Trinity (Doc. 74).[335]

Even with this financial bonus, both Elizabeth's and her son's financial affairs became 'irretrievably embarrassed'. Sir William Parker tells us that Elizabeth sold large parts of her Essex estates, and some of the evidence survives in documents at the Essex Record Office.[336] Although the family was still the nominal owner of

329 Indenture settling portions for Thomas's younger daughters: CCALS, DDX 111/2.

330 The Sheldons seem to have been at Studley and Weston for generations, but it was Ralph's great grandfather who had introduced tapestry weaving to England. Sheldon tapestries are still renowned. Ralph's paternal grandmother was Ann Sheldon née Throckmorton, whose brother Francis was executed in 1584 for his part in the Throckmorton conspiracy against Elizabeth. One of her sisters was married to a Tresham, another to Sir William Catesby, father of the leader of the Gunpowder plotters, Robert Catesby. Earlier in the sixteenth century a Sheldon daughter married a Savage of Elmley, Worcestershire, a junior branch of the family. For Ralph Sheldon, see Notes on People, below.

331 A. à Wood, *The Life of Anthony à Wood from the Year 1632 to 1672* (Oxford, 1772), p. 330.

332 Petitions of Mary Countess Rivers about her husband's goods: HLRO, HL/PO/JO/10/1/227, 8 April 1647. HL/PO/JO/10/1/230, 15 April 1647. Docs 81 and 82 in this volume.

333 The composition for Melford Hall was recorded by the House of Commons on 22 April 1648: *Journal of the House of Commons*, 5, 22 April 1648. The agreement gave Elizabeth permission to sell the house and park. Elizabeth's 1648 petition to stay in London: HLRO, HL/PO/JO/10/1/263, 19 June 1648.

334 Sir John Cordell had died in the interim.

335 Sale of linen: CCALS DCH/O/13. Sale of property: Guildhall Library MS 9848, Doc. 74 in this volume. Parker, *Long Melford*, p. 337.

336 Sales of property in Essex: ERO, D/DU 207/43, D/DZf/9.

great possessions, Elizabeth had become so impoverished that in early 1650 she was arrested in Middlesex for debt. She pleaded her privilege as a peeress, but the judges decided that not only was it doubtful that she had been properly invested as a countess, but that the rights of peers to escape arrest were now extinct, so her claim was denied.[337] She was imprisoned and died soon after, on 9 March 1651, and was buried at St Osyth, presumably without any of the great show of her husband's funeral.[338] Earl Rivers returned to Cheshire in 1650, and had to live at Frodsham, as Rocksavage was not habitable; he died just four years later, intestate like his father.[339] It was not his wife but a creditor who took out letters of administration for his estate; the papers say that Rivers 'was late a prisoner in the upper bench prison at Southwark co. Surrey'; mother and two sons had been imprisoned for debt.[340]

Elizabeth's daughter had attracted epitaphs by Jonson, Milton and other poets; she herself may have inspired rather more modest verse. A poem 'On the death of the Countesse of Rivers' survives in a volume called 'Tixall Poetry', which includes a number of verses found in the hands of the Aston family, catholics from Staffordshire.[341] Sir Walter Aston of Tixall had been a 'true and fast friend' to the duke of Buckingham. Two of Walter Aston's children married siblings of Sir John Thimbleby, husband of Thomas's and Elizabeth's daughter Elizabeth, whose portrait had been painted by van Dyck. The author of the verse was Herbert Aston, who had married Catherine Thimbleby.[342] The editor of 'Tixall Poetry', writing in 1813, assumed that the countess of Rivers in question was Catherine, first wife of John Earl Rivers, but he appears not to know that her mother-in-law had also been created Countess Rivers. References within the verse include one to the 'courtly stage', which makes it rather more likely that it refers to Elizabeth Countess Rivers:

Heere lyes two miracles in one
Of all our age, and of her owne.
A vertue, durst mentain her prime
When vertues self was growne a crime;
A beauty fell in winter's power.
A vertue, not kept up in a cage
Of some lone cell, or hermetage;
As though her soule, lyke ours, durst try
No goodnesse but necessity:
But, to upbrade our masking age,
A vertue on the courtly stage:
Which had it, formed its sceanes by her,

337 Countess Savage's case is reported in the law reports for the King's Bench court, English Reports, 82ER687, p. 258.

338 Date of death: Parker, *Long Melford*, p. 337. Her second son, Sir Thomas Savage of Beeston, also died in 1651 while in prison, presumably for debt.

339 He died at Frodsham. 'A few hours after the earl's death, with his body still in the castle, a fire completely destroyed the building. With some difficulty the servants rescued the earl's body and carried it to Macclesfield where it was buried without the customary ceremony two days later': Starkey, *Old Runcorn*, p. 75.

340 Earl Rivers' administration: *CP*, XI, 458. His successors in the earldom appear to have recovered the family finances to some extent, before the direct line came to an end in the eighteenth century.

341 Arthur Clifford, *Tixall Poetry* (Edinburgh, 1813), p. 43. There were other family links in later generations; one of Herbert Aston's neices married Sir Edward Gage, Thomas's and Elizabeth's nephew. *Tixall Poetry* includes a verse written for Lady Elizabeth Thimbleby in 1655.

342 The name is given as Thimbleby or Thimelby; the former is used in this volume although *Tixall Poetry* uses the latter.

Had all turn'd vertues theatre.
But malice grew so high, that she
And vertue made one tragedy.
A beauty, both mature and new
Impregnable, yet pregnant too.
So Paradise made Autumn good,
Without the fall of bloome or budd.
Or, as the sun transplants his face
On every planett's looking-glasse,
Yet looses not one glorys ray
In those epitomes of day,
Until, by dead of night opprest,
Himself he must betake to rest,
Leaving those budding lights full blown,
And turned to sunnes now every one:
So she, though printing every yeare,
Coppys of her own caracter,
Left beauty's perfect stamp in all,
Yet was'd not the originall.
Till heaven, in love, contriv'd her second birth
And left thos shining epitaphs on earth.[343]

Melford Hall

Melford Hall and manor were the country home of the abbots of Bury for nearly five hundred years, until the abbey's dissolution in 1539. Earl Aelfric, son of Wihtgar, had given the estate to the abbey before 1065.[344] In Anglo-Saxon times a hall no doubt existed, along with a farmstead or 'grange', but its exact site is not known. Nevertheless, a hall appears to have existed in the present position by the early thirteenth century, at the latest, for Melford's main thoroughfare was known as Hall Street in 1248.[345] The first surviving record specifically mentioning 'Melford Hall' was dated 1305,[346] and the first description of it comes from a rental of 1442. At that time, the site of the manor house, the lord's grange and an associated shepherd's house was given as 17 acres 32½ perches. It was described thus:

> The extent of the land held in the manor revised and measured by the perch of assize, which contains in length five yards and a half. In the twentieth year of the reign of King Henry the sixth and the fourteenth year of lord William Curteys, abbot. The site of the aforesaid manor house with moats, ditches, gardens and pastures lies between the road which leads to the aforesaid manor house on the north side, and the several bank of the abbot's stream on the south, and abuts on the king's highway to the west. And contains by the aforesaid measure 14 acres, 10 perches. Also there is a site of land on which the lord's grange is built, lying between the several way leading to the lord's small

343 Clifford, *Tixall Poetry*, p. 43.
344 C.R. Hart, *The Early Charters of Eastern England* (Leicester, 1966), p. 71.
345 W. Parker, *The History of Melford* (1873), p. 260.
346 *ibid.*, p. 285.

park on the north, and the demesne pasture called Ox Pasture to the south, and it abuts on the site of the manor to the west.[347]

The last abbot of Bury, appointed in 1514, was John Reeve, a Melford man. In 1535 he leased Melford Hall to Dame Frances Pennington.[348] The lease stipulates that the abbot should be liable for repairs to the house, keeping it 'windtight and watertight', but that the lessee should 'at her costs find all manner of clay and straw made and laid ready for the same, and also carry all timber for the said manor for the reparations of the same'. At the dissolution it is likely that the manor was in good repair; 'when the dissolution came, Abbot Reeve was still running an efficient economic machine which could be taken over without a break and operated by its new masters'.[349]

After Bury abbey was dissolved in 1539, its lordship, house and lands at Melford went to the crown. Towards the end of his reign, Henry VIII leased the whole estate to William Cordell, a rising lawyer. Edward VI gave Melford to his sister Princess Mary and in November 1554, as queen, she granted the whole estate to William Cordell, in place of his earlier leases. The letters patent of 1554 mentioned 'the capital messuage of Melford Hall with two closes of land and pasture called Parkfield and Horse Pasture, and two small meadows called Small Meadow and Park Meadow, with all buildings, gardens belonging, etc'.[350] In this grant the site of the manor was estimated at 17 acres, 1 perch. In 1580 Sir William Cordell had a map made of his Melford estate. On it the manor-house and its adjuncts are measured at 17 acres, 1 rood and 3 perches. The map does not show the exact shape of the house, but the disposition of gables indicates four wings around a courtyard.[351] In addition to the main house, several structures are indicated on its southern side: one large building, two others a little further away (stables and granaries), and a building between two of the fishponds. It is significant that the banqueting house does not appear, neither do the turrets which are such a prominent feature of the present building. Cordell's will, written in 1581, describes:

> all that my capital messuage or mansion house, commonly called or known by the name of Melford Hall, situate and built upon the site of my manor of Melford, and all that house commonly called the old house, adjoining to the said capital messuage; and all other houses, barns, stables, brew-houses, dove-houses, and all other edifices and buildings, whatsoever they be, situate and being within the precinct of the said site; and all gardens, orchards, pond yards, and hop garden, enclosed and adjoining unto the said capital messuage or dwelling house.[352]

In a court case a few years later, the description was similar, but added 'certain conduits and conveyances of water for the said capital messuage'.[353] This must have

347 Extent of manor of Melford, 1442, transcribed and translated in SROB, J523. The abbots of Bury were tenth in precedence amongst the twenty-four who ranked as barons.

348 Parker, *History of Melford*, pp. 315–18.

349 R.M. Thomson, *The Archives of the Abbey of Bury St. Edmunds* (SRS, xxi, 1980), p. 40.

350 Parker, *History of Melford*, p. 320. The grant signed by Philip and Mary is still at Melford Hall.

351 The map still hangs in the hall of Melford Hall. The east wing was demolished sometime between 1636 when the inventory was written and 1735 when another plan was drawn.

352 Will of Sir William Cordell: TNA, PROB 11/63/42.

353 Court case between Jane Allington and other executors of William Cordell and Thomasine Gager (William's sister) and others of her family: TNA, C2/Eliz I/C15/60.

been the house that had welcomed Elizabeth I on her East Anglian progress in 1578, for Cordell is unlikely to have undertaken more building in the three years between her visit and his death.[354] Cordell's wife survived him for just three years; after 1584 Melford Hall was owned by his two brothers and then his sister Jane Allington. It is likely that all were absentee owners, for shortly before Jane's death, the author of the 'Chorography of Suffolk' wrote of Melford, 'Here Sir William Cordell, master of the rolls, built a very fair and pleasant house . . . but now it begins to be ruinous'.[355] This was the house inherited by Thomas Savage in 1602, and which he and Elizabeth appear to have made their main country home.

From this summary it is clear that any sixteenth-century building on this site is most likely to have occurred either when Abbot Reeve was in control between 1514 and 1534 or between 1554 and 1577 when Cordell owned the manor and might have been preparing for a royal visit.

How much of the abbots' building survives at Melford and how much was built by Cordell has long been a matter of contention, with fascinating differences of opinion regarding both the dating and building phases of the present house. It has been suggested that the 'old house adjoining' mentioned by Cordell might be the abbot's dwelling, still standing in 1581; this would imply that William Cordell built a new house on the present, neighbouring, site.[356] However the 1442 survey makes it clear that the abbot's grange, or farmstead, was close by the manor house and part of the 17 acre site, and we are convinced that this was the 'old house'.[357]

When Sir William Parker published his *History of Melford* in 1873, he clearly believed that Sir William Cordell had demolished the abbots' manor-house and built most of the structure we see today. This has been the conclusion of several later architectural historians, including those who led a visit to the house for the Suffolk Institute of Archaeology and History in 1992.[358] Clear parallels are drawn with other Suffolk houses of known date and, following a recent re-visit, they remain convinced that the nature of the brickwork, the relation between the bricks and the mortar, the condition of the painted diaper-work decoration and other aspects of the construction confirm that the house is of the mid-sixteenth century, and therefore most likely to have been built by Sir William Cordell.

However other suggestions have been made about the dating of some features in the present building. Again in 1992, David Adshead, the National Trust's architectural historian, and Sir Richard Hyde Parker wrote that an 'inspection of the standing archaeology of the house reveals intriguing anomalies that suggest it may be the product of a complex, and as yet unsatisfactorily elucidated, series of building campaigns'.[359] The authors suggested that there might be more of Abbot Reeve's house remaining than had previously been thought.

The National Trust recently commissioned a detailed computerised survey of Melford Hall using photogrammetry. Although the full report of this survey is not yet available, it has raised the possibility of a more complex history for the present

354 The visit is best described in Dovey, *Progress*, pp. 39–47.

355 D.N.J. MacCulloch (ed.), *The Chorography of Suffolk* (SRS, xix, 1976), pp. 54–5.

356 E. Martin, P. Aitkens, T. Easton and others, 'Excursions 1992, Melford Hall', in *PSIA*, 38, 1993, 105–6.

357 Dr W.D. Wilson suggested to Sir Richard Hyde Parker that if the corners of the existing boundary walls were originally buttressed they would probably have been standing in 1442; if there were no buttresses their stepped style of construction went out of fashion by around 1550.

358 *PSIA*, 38, 1993, 105–6.

359 R. Hyde Parker and D. Adshead, *Archaeological Journal*, 149, 1992 (supplement, 'The Colchester Area').

house.[360] The survey appears to confirm that most of the house above ground-level is from the sixteenth century but, although there are considerable difficulties in distinguishing early-sixteenth-century construction from that of thirty or forty years later, some elements might indicate survivals from the pre-Reformation building. This ambiguity is reflected in the latest edition of the guidebook to Melford Hall, which suggests both that some of Abbot Reeve's house may survive and that the west front and banqueting house are likely to be post-Cordell, probably built for Thomas Savage.[361]

The house inherited by Thomas clearly had four wings enclosing a courtyard. It seems likely that the north wing and parts of the earlier west wing had been built first, and that the south and east wings were later and of one build. The relationship between the west and south wings is uncertain. There are a number of features that may suggest some pre-Reformation survival, although this interpretation is contested in all cases. What follows is a very brief summary of these features.

The 1636 inventory (Doc. 60) mentions a chapel chamber towards the eastern end of the north wing. This would be an obvious location for a chapel if one survived from the pre-Reformation period, and the survey suggests a space here the height of two storeys, with an east-west orientation and an east-facing window. When the north wing was seriously damaged by fire in 1942 the destruction revealed a tall and narrow bricked-up window, facing the courtyard, which rose the whole height of the wing.[362] It had later been blocked by the north-east turret. This location would site the chapel at the private end of the range of state rooms in the north wing. At first-floor level a gallery may have looked into the chapel from another important room (see Appendix I, p. 155). Later a floor was inserted into the chapel, creating two storeys. This eastern end of the north wing carries traces of diaper work unique to the area.[363]

The south-eastern chimney stack has rubbed-brick false crenellations or embattlements which could be of pre-Reformation date, although such features continued to be built well into the later sixteenth century. The east wing no longer exists, but Thorpe's plan shows sockets in the main gateway through it, suggesting a former portcullis.

At some point a previous west wing facing Melford Green appears to have been demolished to the present level of the courtyard. Some earlier cellars survived underneath, although similar spaces under the present kitchen and under the later parlour at the northern end of the west wing were filled in, and the wing rebuilt. The survey suggests that arched ways, thought to be fire-breaks, were inserted between the hall and kitchen area and between the kitchen and the remainder of the south wing. The surveyor has suggested that these are relatively early features. Evidence for these arched ways is clear on the exterior of the south wall and on what would have been the western external wall, but is not clear in the courtyard; this has led to some debate about how effective they might have been against fire, and whether Abbot Reeve or Cordell would have wanted a house with two large holes opening into its courtyard.

360 The surveyor has shared his conclusions to date with the National Trust and Sir Richard Hyde Parker.

361 *Guide to Melford Hall*, National Trust, 2005. Modern scientific techniques may in the future help to resolve the outstanding problems by use of thermoluminescence in dating brickwork, dendrochronology in dating roof-timbers, and the analysis of paint samples.

362 That this area was open to the first floor has been debated, but the evidence convinces us.

363 The brickwork and windows in the eastern end of the north wing have been disturbed, most recently by the post-war fire.

The whole western front of that period (now an internal wall) was faced in large bricks, and the pointing done to receive painted diaper decoration, much of which still survives.[364] It is difficult to date this build. Painted diaper work is not common before 1500, and so the wing may have been the work of Abbot Reeve or of Sir William Cordell after he acquired the Hall in 1554. However, although the diaper work seems to have been painted only once, the paint is still in good condition. This suggests that it was exposed to the elements for at most around thirty years. Some smaller later extensions to the west can be identified, now enclosed by the present frontage.

The 'traditional' view of Melford Hall's architectural history assumes that Sir William Cordell's works included the towers, turrets and additional rooms on the west front facing Melford Green. This build added an additional range of rooms onto the western side of the house and was designed to impress viewers from the main road and Green; it has been thought that the work was done for the visit of Elizabeth I in 1578. However there is now a considerable body of evidence to suggest that Thomas Savage was responsible for the western front as we see it today, by building the central tower, extensions north and south of that tower, the two western turrets and the banqueting house in the north-western corner of the garden. The western turrets, central tower and banqueting house all feature on the map of 1613, but not on that of 1580.[365] They, and the extensions each side of the tower, are all made of a distinctively small brick, and incorporate the earlier extensions added to the painted front.

In the mid-Tudor period, most banqueting houses were either on the roofs of major houses, or much closer to them than the one at Melford. In the later sixteenth and early seventeenth centuries, they began to be constructed further away from houses. At this period they were more frequently used as summer rooms for surveying and admiring gardens, as well as for banqueting.[366]

Turrets were not merely imposing features but had an important function. In earlier times, many servants slept on truckle beds or palliasses on the floor near their work, or near their masters or mistresses. By the early seventeenth century, with the increasing desire for greater privacy, the tendency was more for servants to sleep in the attics of grand houses. Turrets were thus needed to bring servants down from the attics to their masters; in Melford's case access would have been through the long gallery. Another piece of evidence for this shift of sleeping-quarters to attics is that a new shaft was inserted into the earlier garderobe-tower against the south wing, in order to serve the attic.

The turrets on the west front include two garderobes with a plumbing system which was advanced for the early seventeenth century, although there are older garderobes in the central tower. This implies that if the central tower is part of Thomas Savage's additions in the early seventeenth century, it possibly replaced a previous building on this site. The central tower lacks any reception area immediately inside it, and there is no evidence for an approach across the moat from the west. The tower was therefore built for show, something to be seen and admired both from Melford Green and as a backdrop to the new gardens west and north of the house, which are shown on the map of 1613. A commentator at Rocksavage in 1617

364 We are grateful to Timothy Easton for sharing his expertise on painted brickwork.

365 The banqueting house is not mentioned in the records of Queen Elizabeth's visit.

366 Current research on banqueting houses by Christopher Pringle suggests that if the example at Melford was mid-Tudor in date, it would be further away from the main house than any other known example of the period.

was ecstatic about the gardens, and we know that considerable amounts of money were spent on them; similar work at Melford seems likely.[367]

Whatever the sequence of building in the sixteenth century, Thomas and Elizabeth moved into a run-down house, given the comment about it being ruinous at the start of the seventeenth century.[368] If Melford Hall had been little used since the mid 1580s, it is possible that Jane Allington had moved most of the better furniture and fittings to her London home. The Hall may have been empty or just partially furnished when Thomas and Elizabeth took it over, and the layout and any furnishings were likely to have been in the style of the 1570s.

Shortly after taking over legal possession of Melford Hall, Thomas Savage engaged the architect John Thorpe. His plan of the ground-floor survives and can be seen on Pl. 2.[369] It is either a plan of the existing house with some pencilled suggestions for alterations, or, as we think, a proposal for extensions and changes to the west wing, to which later sketches of other possible alterations have been added. We have used Thorpe's plan as a basis for Appendix I (p. 155), which gives our interpretation of the probable layout in 1636. The inventory of January in that year also gives clues as to when the house received most attention. One expert on tapestries and fabrics has commented that rooms were furnished in the style of a generation earlier.[370] We suggest therefore that Thomas and Elizabeth put considerable time and money into the extension and redecoration of Melford Hall in the early years of their marriage, and made few major changes in the following quarter-century. For comparison, the evidence from Rocksavage is of small-scale building work in most years for which accounts survive. After the initial burst of expenditure at Melford, it was probably treated in a similar way with continual small-scale maintenance and improvement. Comparison of the 1636 inventory with that made at Rocksavage in 1615 at his father's death suggests that Thomas spent far more on furnishings and fittings than his parents had done. So perhaps in the years before 1616 the money for building work and redecoration had mainly been spent at Melford.

In 1613 James I granted Thomas a licence to create a hunting park north-east of Melford Hall (Doc. 13). Perhaps it was to celebrate extensions to the house and the creation of a park that Thomas also commissioned a new map of the manor of Melford Hall (Pl. VII) (although two other smaller manors in Melford were also mapped that year).[371] It shows the new hunting park in magnificent detail, as well as the Hall itself, stables, granary and gatehouse, a large building south of the main house, other outbuildings nearby, a building between the ponds which is possibly a dovehouse, and a banqueting house overlooking Melford Green. An unfinished map of 1615 shows only the 'footprint' of the same buildings, although a few details have been drawn in.[372] Apart from the banqueting house, we do not know whether Thomas added to, or altered, the outbuildings around the Hall.[373]

---

367 Payments for work in the garden at Rocksavage are included in the housekeeper's accounts: see p. lxxxi. James I visited Thomas and Elizabeth at Rocksavage, and they may have hoped for a royal visit to Melford.

368 MacCulloch, *Chorography*, pp. 54–5.

369 Plan of Melford Hall by John Thorpe (undated): Sir John Soane's Museum, London, T249, T250.

370 Santina Levey, in private correspondence with Lyn Boothman.

371 Samuel Pierse of Maidstone, Kent, drew his map of Melford Manor in 1613; it still hangs in Melford Hall. Its scale is 16 perches (or 88 yards) to the inch. The manors of Kentwell and Lutons, also in Melford parish, were owned by the Clopton family; a map of both those manors, also dated 1613, belongs to the present owner of Kentwell Hall.

372 The map of 1615 is also at Melford Hall.

373 The rental written for Thomas Savage in 1613 to accompany the map of that year, has recently been rediscovered and is now at Melford Hall.

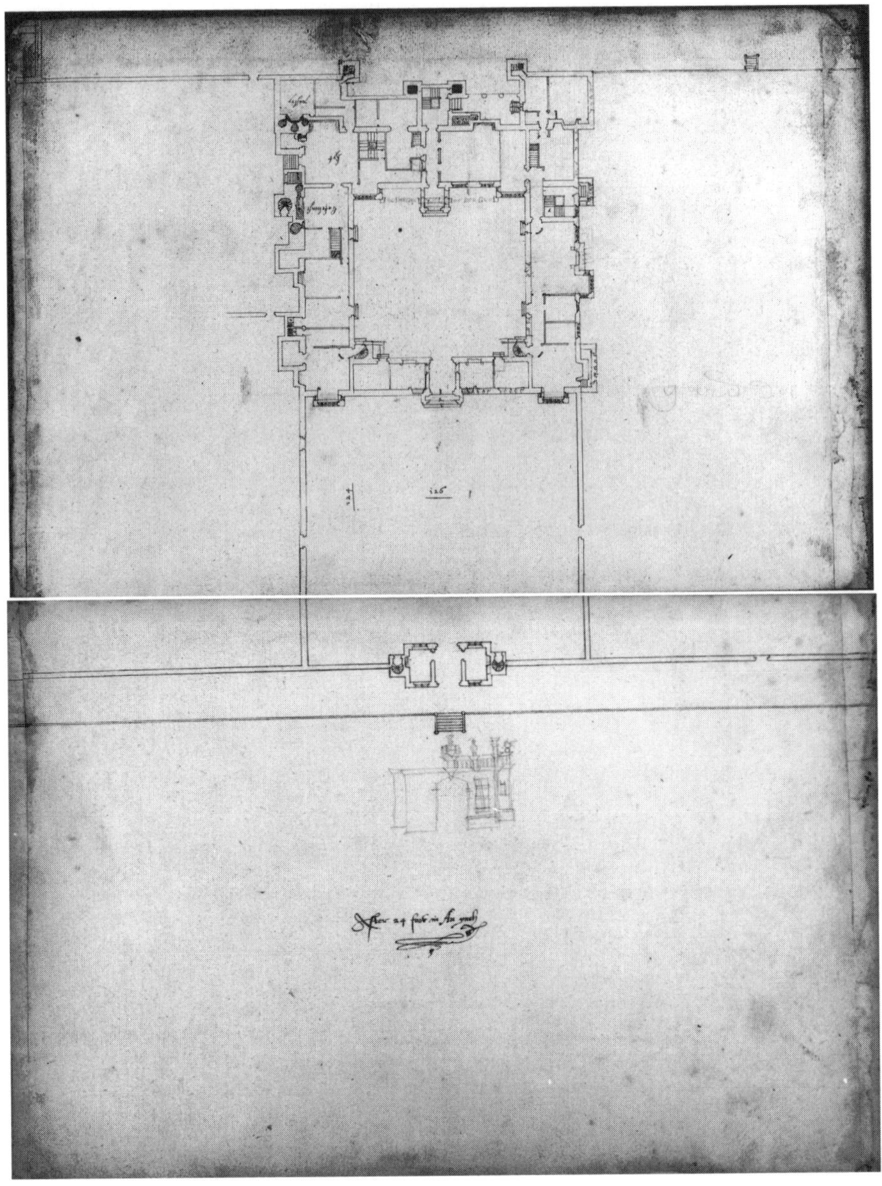

Plate 2. Plan of Melford Hall by John Thorpe, c. 1606. Shows the ground-floor layout in the early seventeenth century with some of Thorpe's proposed alterations. The writing below the plan is a comment on the scale of the original drawing. *(By courtesy of the trustees of Sir John Soane's Museum)*

The inventory of 1636 specified forty-five rooms in the main house, six in the gatehouse, two in the porter's lodge, the granary with a chamber above, the banqueting house, stables with grooms' chamber attached, chambers for the gardener and husbandman which were probably near the stables, and a room called the Pond Chamber, well furnished, with two chambers next to it and two below. These last rooms, and a wing containing a granary with a chamber above, are most likely in the large building immediately to the south of the house, which may have been the old grange.

It is impossible to know how much of their time Thomas and Elizabeth spent at Melford, but the house was certainly in use by the family when the inventory was taken in January 1636. Tapestries, textiles and furniture such as close stools were in the appropriate rooms of the house rather than packed away in store, as was the case at Rocksavage. Of rooms used by the family, only the banqueting house was being used for storage, but banqueting houses were for the summer months and this was January!

Melford Hall after 1636

The next evidence for the state of Melford Hall comes after the sack of August 1642. Elizabeth had been living at St Osyth and, although she still retained the house and park, the bulk of her property at Melford had been mortgaged to John Cordell.[374] Her petition to the House of Lords (Doc. 75) gives a graphic description of the damage at St Osyth, but is much less detailed about Melford Hall, saying just that the multitude had carried away all that was there. However, we have a more helpful description from the diarist John Rous:

> The lady Savage's house was defaced; all glass broken, all iron pulled out, all household stuff gone, all ceilings rent down or spoiled, all likely places where money might be hidden dug up, the gardens defaced, beer and wine consumed and let out (to knee-depth in the cellar), the deer killed and chased out, etc. The lady says the loss is £40,000.[375]

Another description is quoted by Watney:

> The twentieth of August 1642, the king having left Parliament, and thereby a loose rein being put into the mouth of the unruly multitude, many thousands swarmed to the pulling down of Long Melford House [*sic*], a gallant seat belonging to the countess of Rivers, and to the endangering of her person; she being a recusant they made that their pretence, but spoil and plunder was their aim. This fury was not only in the rabble, but many of the better sort behaved themselves as if there had been a dissolution of all government: no man could remain in his own house without fear, nor be abroad with safety.[376]

So Melford Hall went from 'beginning to be ruinous' at the turn of the seventeenth century to being the centre of rural delight described by James Howell in 1621 and the well-furnished house described by the inventory in 1636, to being in ruins just seven years later. In 1649, the same year that Earl Rivers finally sold all

---

374 See p. lxxv, and Doc. 74.

375 Diary of John Rous: BL, Add. MSS 22,989, ff. 85v–86r.

376 Watney, *St Osyth's Priory*, quoting Peck, *Desiderata Curiosa*, ref. XII, 474.

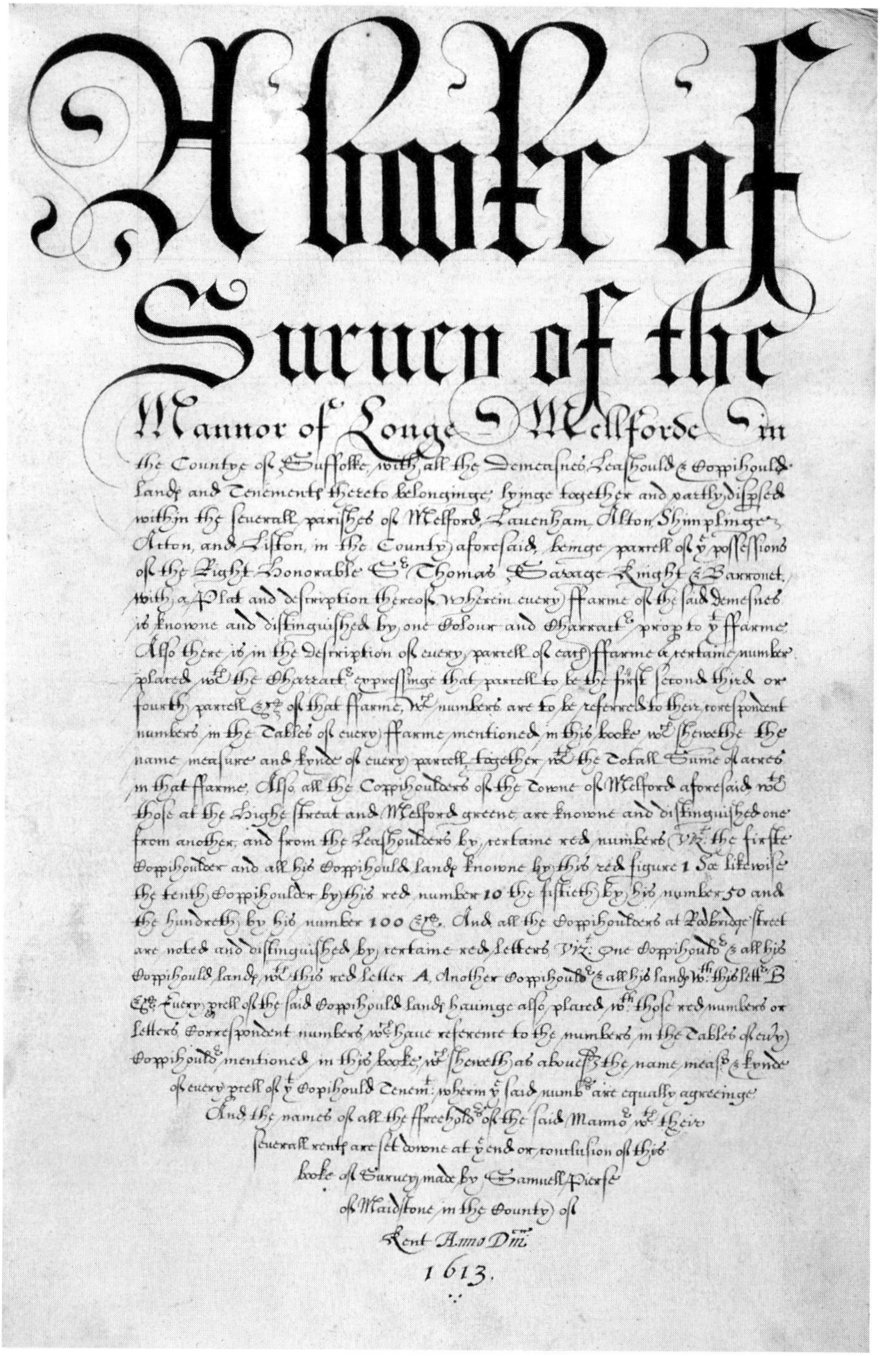

A booke of Survey of the Mannor of Longe Mellforde in the Countye of Suffolke, with all the Demeasnes, Leashoulds & Coppihoulds lands and Tenements thereto belonginge; lyinge together and partly dispersed within the severall parishes of Melford, Lavenham, Alton, Shimplinge, Acton, and Liston, in the County aforesaid, beinge parcell of ye possessions of the Right Honorable Sr Thomas Savage Knight & Barronet, With a Plat and description thereof, wherein every ffarme of the said demesnes is knowne and distinguished by one Colour and Charracter prop to ye ffarme. Also there is in the description of every parcell of each ffarme a certaine number placed wth the Charracter expressinge that parcell to be the first second third or fourth parcell &c of that ffarme, wch numbers are to be referred to their correspondent numbers in the Tables of every ffarme mentioned in this booke wch sheweth the name measure and kynde of every parcell, together wth the totall Sume of acres in that ffarme. Also all the Coppihoulders of the towne of Melford aforesaid wth those at the Highe street and Melford greene are knowne and distinguished one from another, and from the Leashoulders by certaine red numbers Viz. the firste Coppihoulder and all his Coppihould lands knowne by this red figure 1 Soe likewise the tenth Coppihoulder by this red number 10 the fiftieth by his number 50 and the hundreth by his number 100 &c. And all the Coppihoulders at Bridge street are noted and distinguished by certaine red letters Viz. one Coppihoulder & all his Coppihould lands wth this red letter A, Another Coppihoulder & all his lands wth this letter B &c. Every prell of the said Coppihould lands havinge also placed wth those red numbers or letters correspondent numbers wch have reference to the numbers in the Tables of every Coppihoulder mentioned in this booke wch sheweth as aforesaid the name, meas & kynde of every prell of ye Coppihould Tenemt wherin ye said numbers are equally agreeinge. And the names of all the ffreeholders of the said Mannor wth their severall rents are set downe at ye end or conclusion of this booke of Survey made by Samuell Pierse of Maidstone in the County of Kent Anno Dni 1613.

Plate 3. Title-page of the survey of Thomas Savage's Suffolk lands, 1613. The survey must have been carried out shortly before the accompanying map (Pl. VII) was completed, for the symbols used in the survey to indicate tenants are reproduced on the map.
(By courtesy of Sir Richard Hyde Parker, Bt)

the Melford property to Robert Cordell, the Essex clergyman Ralph Josselin noted in his diary that he had passed through Melford: 'I saw a sad divided town; I saw the ruins of that great [house] plundered out, desolate without inhabitant.'[377]

Yet Melford Hall survived and must have been repaired. It remained in the Cordell family until the mid-eighteenth century, when the last heir died without children and the house was sold to Sir Harry Parker. His descendants live there today, and one is co-author of the volume. Apart from the inventory, and seven years' worth of court rolls, no other documents survive about Melford Hall and its manor during the early modern period. It seems very likely that many records were in the Hall in the summer of 1642 and perished when the building was ransacked.[378] However, records were moved between the various family houses. Cheshire Record Office holds a large collection of deeds and related documents about land in Melford, Lavenham, Shimpling and other nearby parishes; these almost all come from William Cordell's time or earlier, and appear to relate to properties which he had bought. They must have survived because they were in Cheshire or London when Melford Hall was sacked.[379]

Rocksavage

Rocksavage stood on the north bank of the river Weaver just outside Halton in Cheshire, and was built by Thomas Savage's grandfather between 1565 and 1568. It lay immediately next to the old hall at Clifton, which was probably built after 1375 when the first John Savage married the heiress of the Danyers family.[380] The Sir John Savage who built Rocksavage had married a daughter of the earl of Rutland, and it is possible that her dowry helped pay for the new house. This Sir John held many high offices and one local historian has said that Rocksavage was built 'because the old family home at Clifton was not now impressive enough for a man of such eminence'. Once Rocksavage was complete, the old hall became outbuildings and a granary.[381]

Rocksavage was well situated at the top of the hill looking south over the valley of the river Weaver, with a prospect over the vale of Chester and the Welsh mountains.[382] The house was brick-built and had extensive gardens. William Webb wrote 'The King's Vale Royal' in the 1620s; his remarks on Rocksavage and Clifton are worth quoting in full:

> And so we next behold the magnificence of Rocksavage, overlooking the waters and goodly marshes round about the skirts of it; and so contrived in the situation, that from the lower meadows there is a fine easy ascent up upon the face of the house, which, as you approach nearer still to it, fills your eye with more delight, as it is in the nature of true beauty; and to see now the late additions of delectable gardens, orchards and walks, would make one say, it longs to be the abode of so honourable a master as it doth service to; but his worth is

---

377 Diary of Ralph Josselin: BL, Harleian MSS, 163, f. 308r.

378 The remaining manorial court rolls are from Thomas Savage's period: SROB, Acc. 466. Surviving records held at Melford Hall date from after the restoration of Charles II.

379 Suffolk records held by the Cheshire Record Office are in DCH/O and DCH/P, along with other records of the Savage and Cholmondeley families relating to property outside Cheshire.

380 Webb, *The Kings Vale-Royall of England*, originally published in 1656, reproduced in Ormerod, *The History of the County Palatine and History of Chester*, i, p. 408.

381 Ormerod, *The History of the County Palatine and History of Chester*, i, p. 525.

382 Nichols, *Progresses*, iii, 400.

Plate 4. Rocksavage, artist unknown, c. 1790. A man born at Rocksavage rode through these ruins while hunting; this story suggests that the decline of the house was unusually rapid. This illustration was published in G. Ormerod, *A History of the County Palatine and City of Chester. (Reproduced by permission of the Syndics of Cambridge University Library)*

likely to have employment, where honour herself cannot give too much attendance. Yet never since the foundation of it was it more graced then when it pleased our gracious sovereign, in anno 1617, to accept the princely entertainment, which there for his majesty, and whole train, was prepared by the honourable Sir Thomas Savage, his royal majesty taking his repast there, and killing a buck in Halton-park, after he was that morning come from Bewsey where his Highness had been at the right worshipful Sir Thomas Ireland's, now vice chamberlain of Chester.

This stately house was built by the grandfather Sir John Savage . . . whose mansion before was Clifton, a seat of great antiquity and of noble resort, the remains of which stand yet at a little distance from this in the park, like an aged matron, well contented to go to her grave, having seen in her lifetime her daughter advanced to such a height of honourable dignity.[383]

A more recent account of Rocksavage makes it sound not unlike Melford Hall; the house is described as quadrangular, entered through a gateway flanked by octagonal towers.[384] The towers are prominent in eighteenth-century illustrations of the ruins. Although today not even the towers survive, another Cheshire house can give us a good idea of Rocksavage's appearance. One of the many Sir William Breretons in Cheshire's history married a daughter of the Sir John Savage who built Rocksavage. He was so impressed by his father-in-law's house that he built his own, Brereton Hall, modelled closely on Rocksavage. William Beamont wrote:

A comparison of Rock Savage with the house at Brereton will leave little doubt that Sir John Savage and his son-in-law Sir William Brereton employed the same architect in the erection of their sumptuous fabrics. The situation of Rocksavage is remarkably fine. Halton Castle rises behind it, at one side is the estuary of the Mersey, and the Weaver, also an estuary, descends in front to its confluence with the first named river. Over the Weaver is a fine view of Frodsham and the Welsh hills – Overton Scar and Helsby Tor closing up one side of the picture while the richness of the Lancashire shore makes a fine contrast on the other.[385]

1615 inventory

Rocksavage is the only one of the three houses to have another detailed inventory to compare with that of 1636. After Sir John Savage, Thomas's father, died in 1615 his goods were inventoried. Again there are inventories for three locations: Rocksavage, Allington House in London and several houses in Chester. Comparing the two inventories for Rocksavage usefully reminds us that an inventory gives only a snapshot of the contents of a house; both the layout and organisation of the house and its contents can change very quickly.[386]

Only four of the twenty-two rooms identified in the 'family' part of Rocksavage (as opposed to the service quarters and servants' rooms) in 1636 have the same name as any room in 1615. The value of goods in the house is also very different. In

383 Webb, *The Kings Vale-Royall*, p. 408.
384 P. de Figueiredo and J. Treuherz, *Cheshire Country Houses* (Chichester, 1988), p. 268.
385 Beamont, *Halton*, p. 108.
386 Sir John Savage's inventories: CCALS, WS1616–18. His goods in Chester were in other people's houses.

1615 the appraisers valued the contents of the entire house and outbuildings at £364; twenty years later the contents were reckoned to be worth £1728. It seems likely that John Savage spent much of his time in Chester and perhaps only fully furnished Rocksavage for the summer months, or when visitors were due. At Thomas's death Rocksavage contained more furniture and far more costly furnishings. Table 1 compares the two inventories.[387]

Table 1. Comparison of two Rocksavage inventories

	1615	*1636*
Bedsteads	21	31
Tables	16	32
Chairs	17	35
Stools and forms	55	120
Cupboards	13	17
Hangings and tapestries	27	84
Value of hangings and tapestries	£104	£496
Carpets	3	45
Value of carpets	16s. 8d.	£60 15s. 0d.

This impression of Thomas and Elizabeth spending far more than his parents on luxury items is reinforced by comparing inventories from each year in relation to jewels, plate and ready money; the totals are given in Table 2.

Table 2. Comparison of the inventories of Sir John Savage and his son Thomas

	1615–17	*1635–6*
Jewels and plate	£337	£1984
Ready money	£3609	£245

Housekeeper's accounts

There are surviving accounts of the housekeeper and park-keeper at Rocksavage for several years in the period 1621–33, and these give us information which complements the inventory.[388] The housekeeper (first Nicholas Squires and later John Barney) appears to have been responsible for building works within the house, on the exterior and in the gardens, and for storage of linens in the house. Some matters relating to the daily care of Rocksavage are mentioned, for example the amount paid for mowing bracken to air the house. The housekeeper also had responsibility for

387 Numbers given are a minimum; in several places the inventory mentions items without specifying an exact number.

388 Household accounts from Rocksavage: CCALS, DCH/H/199 [1624], DCH/E/316 [1627], DCH/M/35/40 [1629], DCH/K/1/1 and DCH/M/1/4 [1633].

gathering hay for use in the parks, for selling hops, for gathering rents from surrounding lands, for buying and selling cattle, for keeping an account of the number of horses in the stable and a number of other tasks which include the costs of cutting up and rendering the occasional porpoise found on the beach!

The accounts suggest that Thomas Savage and possibly his family visited Rocksavage most years, usually during August and early September, and occasionally they were there at other periods. There is certainly evidence of a hurry to get some works finished in July before his lordship arrived.[389]

Most items in the accounts record routine transactions, such as payments to the men who mend the slates each year, those who cleaned the gutters, to the plumber, the locksmith and the glazier for their regular work, along with paying for coal from Lancashire; the payments are balanced by income from selling hops and from pasturing animals belonging to local inhabitants, but every year some new work was being done on the house and in the gardens.

Structural work on the house and gardens

Nicholas Squires' accounts for 1624 tell us of a banqueting house at Rocksavage. As this not mentioned in the inventory, it was presumably empty in February 1636. When it was built we do not know, but in 1624 it needed either new floor boards or its first ones. In 1633 the banqueting house needed re-plastering, and we read of a chamber underneath it, with casement windows. This might suggest that it was in the grounds, as at Melford, rather than on the roof of the house as was relatively common. The 1624 accounts also mention outhouses at Rocksavage, including a barn, old stable and slaughterhouse, which were thatched. Some if not all of these may have been the 'old hall', as in 1629 mention is made of the 'old houses' being re-thatched.

Also in 1624 new bay windows were put into the parlour and Shrewsbury chamber. The major work from January to June had concerned repair of some of the major beams on one side of the house. These accounts also mention a wainscot gallery, and wainscoting in both the parlour and Shrewsbury chamber.

Another major project for 1624 was 'the making and dressing of the new fountain placed in the middle of Rocksavage garden', which cost nearly £35. Squires' accounts say that this was done 'in such sort as it was finished before Sir Thomas Savage came to Rocksavage in August 1624, which work began the 5th of June 1624 and was perfected the last of July 1624'. However the work of putting in the underground pipes to bring water to the fountain had been done in the previous year. But all was not completed by the start of August, for Squires paid out for work on the pipes 'from the 10th of August 1623 on which day Sir Thomas Savage came to his house and gave direction for this new addition and alteration, which was continued and ended the 9th of September 1624 following'. These accounts also confirm that Thomas had two hunting parks close to his house, at Rocksavage and Halton. Building had been going on at Halton Park lodge for the previous few years, the accounts of which were finally cleared in 1624.[390]

The major work in 1627 was 'the making of ten lodging chambers which are made in the upper gallery', but it is difficult to identify these chambers in the inventory made just eight years later. To make the chambers, wainscot had to be taken down and put up again, doors had to be made for each chamber, 'and taking down of the places where as the chimneys are, and windows, and making of it up again'.

389 See below, for the fountain installed in 1624.
390 Rocksavage household accounts: CCALS, DCH/H/199.

The 1627 accounts also tell us about a lantern over the red gallery, where new windows and a door case were needed. A new floor had to be laid 'in the entry by the lantern because the plaster would not be kept whole but was always breaking and it doth make the floor more lighter by taking away the plaster'. Also mentioned is a bay window in the dining chamber, and 'rails and balusters for the side of the house next to the wilderness', which were either on the roof or for a path or walk around the house. The accounts mention getting stone and tell us that the rails and balusters were to 'be done like as the fore part of the house is done'.[391]

The 1629 accounts do not include any major building work in the main house, but do record expenditure on 'what the house which is set up for the keeper doth come unto in the town field'. This house may possibly have been for the keeper of Rocksavage Park.

Interior decoration and repair in the house

In three years the housekeeper paid for the carriage from London to Rocksavage of containers full of pictures, and pictures were being delivered in another couple of years for which we have no accounts. These seem to be new pictures which Thomas had bought in London, rather than some he was moving around the country as he stayed in his various houses, for in the 1629 accounts Nicholas Squires mentions having pictures which had arrived in each year from 1626 onwards.

In 1627 the bedstead in Kendeston chamber (which may be the Kinderton chamber of the inventory) was cut down 'to make it lesser'; it had a new top made and two stools were upholstered with the velvet from the old top of the bed. The following year the red gallery had its matting renewed; the old matting was used for the new chambers in the upper gallery, constructed in 1627.

The 1629 accounts mention my lady's dining chamber and withdrawing chamber. The dining chamber had a window made just outside it, 'where the chests stand'. In 1633 two men were paid for two days 'at taking down the great picture and hanging it up again in my lady her closet'; whatever the picture was it must have been 'great' for that to be four days' labour. More casements were repaired in 'my lady her closet' and new locks and keys provided for the doors of this room. The inventory does not identify Elizabeth's rooms at Rocksavage but these accounts make it plain that she had a suite; it seems most likely that they are in the inventory under other, maybe older, names. The 1633 accounts tell us it took eighty-eight yards of matting to floor 'my ladies closets'; although we do not know how wide the matting was, this gives some indication of the size of her apartments.

There was also redecoration elsewhere in 1633, for the glazier was paid for 'setting up four escutcheons of arms and some other work' and 'for setting up arms in the new room'. It is likely that this 'new room' was built the previous year because the costs of its construction were not mentioned. Repair of the table in the great chamber was done not by local carpenters but by two joiners who came especially from Chester. This year more pictures were being reframed and hung or re-hung, and the carpenter was paid for 'making a frame and timber for . . . the map of Venice'. When the inventory was taken in February 1636 the map of Venice was hanging in the hall.

391 There were also rails and balusters in the 'green court'.

New work in the gardens

The gardens at Rocksavage had excited William Webb, and something of the effort that went into them shines through these accounts. Thomas Peachball the gardener was paid for keeping Rocksavage garden, orchard, wilderness, cook's garden, the green court and the walk before the house. In 1624 trees were brought from London for the new walk; these may have been ash, or the ash may have been in addition to expensive trees brought from the capital. Also in this year the fountain, already mentioned, was built.

The ash trees bought in 1624 were presumably doing well for three years later the accounts mention the 'ash walk'. The 1629 accounts tell us of the terrace walk, with a brick wall at its east end; from the terrace a bridge connected with the park. The brick walls by the terrace were repaired and their copings re-pointed.

The 1633 accounts provide the first mention of a 'pool about the hopyard' which had to be stocked with trout. This year another ten trees came from London for the gardens, and an additional nine from Chester. A 'new garden' is mentioned and six days work 'setting birches in the walks'. There was a new nursery garden this year; sand and dung were brought for it and people paid specially to weed it. This may have replaced an older nursery, for back in 1629 'french roots' were brought from London to Warrington and then on to Rocksavage.

Other matters

The accounts confirm that animals were moved around the country, for there is a reference to oxen bought at Rocksavage which were to go to Melford, and to hay 'spent with Sir Thomas Savage and other strangers' and friends' horses then resorting to, from the 10th of August 1624 until the 16th of September following who went thence for Suffolk'. Goods and supplies were also transported when Sir Thomas and/or his family moved about the country:

Paid 19 August 1624 at Chester		
For right honourable Sir Thomas Savage trunks and boxes weighing 328 pounds at 1d	27s.	4d.
For carriage of 2 hampers with fish and groceries weighing near 200 pounds	14s.	0d.
Summa total paid & [*illeg.*]		
To Robert Malpas to pay	41s.	4d.[392]

Together, these accounts give us an impression of continuous maintenance and piecemeal additions and improvements, rather than major rebuilding. Rocksavage was only around seventy years old, so we might assume that it was in a reasonable state of repair. As mentioned earlier, it was probably only lived in regularly by the Savage family in the summer months; the vast majority of references in the accounts to Thomas Savage being there relate to the summer. Sometimes this would have been with guests, sometimes just with his family and the extra servants who must have arrived when the house was opened up.

Kitchen accounts

Detailed kitchen accounts survive for the weeks between 1 August and 1 October 1633 when the family were in residence. John Barney, who was housekeeper that

392 Rocksavage household accounts: CCALS, DCH/E/314.

year, seems also to have been clerk of the kitchen.[393] The accounts start with £137 10s. 7d. worth of provisions 'received in' at the start of August; the assumption is that the kitchens had not been operational before this date. Table 3 gives the amounts spent on provisions in the following weeks.

Table 3. Example of Rocksavage kitchen accounts

ten days ending 10 August	£49	16s.	10d.
week ending 17 August	£38	2s.	7d.
week ending 24 August	£31	14s.	6d.
week ending 31 August	£26	13s.	6d.
week ending 7 September	£9	5s.	6d.
week ending 14 September	£52	4s.	0d.
week ending 21 September	£6	9s.	0d.
ten days ending 1 October	£41	10s.	1d.

In the accounts for the week ending 7 September, Barney notes 'Your lordship absent 5 days'; the following week he notes 'The Lord Strange and his lady and children here 2 nights besides many other strangers'; and the following week, ending 21 September, 'Your lordship at Vale Royal all the week until Thursday night supper'.[394] When Thomas and his family were present but without visitors, £4–5 a day was spent on their food and for that of their servants. When the family was away, but presumably servants still had to be fed, the average expenditure was around £1 a day. However in the week when Lord Strange and family visited, the average costs rose to over £7 a day. If the visitors stayed for three days, and the expenditure was £5 on other days of the week, around £10 a day was spent while the visitors were at Rocksavage. That summer at Rocksavage, some £255 was spent in the kitchens alone; we have no idea of the amount spent on drink, provision for horses or other expenses.

Fuel was another expense when the family was in residence. That same summer, John Barney paid £25 14s. 8d. for the carriage of 20 tons of coal from Lancashire by sea; this was part of a bill for the cost of provisions 'in preparation for Lord Savage's coming to Rocksavage'.[395] At other times of year, supplies were sent from Cheshire to London; Thomas's sister Lady Grace Wilbraham paid large amounts of money, £19 and more, for cheeses to be bought in Cheshire and carried to London 'for the use of Lord Savage'.[396]

Rocksavage after 1636

When the Rocksavage inventory was taken in February 1636 the house was not in use; many tapestries, carpets and other luxury items were in store and not in the rooms they would furnish when the family was present. We do not know whether the new Viscount Savage moved from Frodsham Castle to Rocksavage straight after his

393 Rocksavage household accounts: CCALS, DCH/K/1/1.
394 For Lord Strange, see Notes on People, below.
395 Payment for coal: CCALS, DCH/F/215c/viii.
396 Payment for cheeses: CCALS, DCH/F/214b; DCH/F/215c/i; DCH/F/215c/vi.

father's death, but it was certainly his home by the start of the Civil War (by which time he was Earl Rivers). Rocksavage was looted during the early years of the war and left uninhabitable, with the roof and some of the walls knocked down.[397] Whether any of its furniture and fittings had been removed first, we do not know. The state of Rocksavage and of his finances meant that when Earl Rivers returned to Cheshire after the war he moved back into Frodsham. When his son Thomas succeeded him in 1654, he lived in London while Rocksavage was still derelict.[398] However in 1660 the estate was returned to him and a little later he moved back into Rocksavage.

The house remained in the family until late in the eighteenth century. It was inherited by the last heiress in the direct line, Lady Penelope Barry, who married Sir James Cholmondeley in 1726, when both were about eighteen. The couple divorced in 1736–7; this was conditional on neither partner remarrying. Sir James, who had become a general, died in 1775 and his ex-wife in 1785. At this point their estates went to the Cholmondelely heir; Rocksavage was no longer needed and it became disused. In 1776 one report tells us that the house was still in good repair, but the description given is basically William Webb's, so the report cannot be trusted.[399]

By the end of the eighteenth century Rocksavage was said to have become a 'picturesque ruin'; one story mentioned by several authors tells us that the house sank so rapidly into decay that a gentleman who had been born in the house followed a pack of hounds through the ruins. The fox, hounds and horsemen are said to have ridden in through the ruined front entrance and out by the back door.

All that remained in 2002 were a few brick garden walls, and a substantial farmhouse said to be built of the remnants of the house.

The house at Tower Hill

Towards the end of the fourteenth century a new mendicant order appeared in England, the Crutched or Crossed, Friars (Friars of St Cross). They requested a house from which to work and were granted land in Aldgate, London. At the Reformation, on 12 November 1538, the house of the Crossed Friars was surrendered to Henry VIII. The land occupied by the friary was used for various purposes. The friars' hall became the site of a glass-maker's and the site of the chapel became a carpenter's yard and a tennis court.[400] Next were fourteen almshouses which had been built earlier in the century.[401] In 1598 John Stow wrote:

397 Starkey, *Old Runcorn*, p. 75.

398 *ibid.*, p. 75.

399 *ibid.*, p. 77. The date of the decline of Rocksavage is not certain. G. Armstrong is sure that General and Lady Cholmondeley both died at Rocksavage. However John Aiken, writing in 1795, says that the decline started soon after the Cholmondeleys' marriage in 1730; he tells the tale of the fox-hunting gentleman and says, 'Part of the stately front, consisting of a fine gateway with a lofty turret on each side, is still standing as well as part of one of the sides. The rest of the pile consists only of foundation walls, broken vaults, and heaps of rubbish overgrown with weeds; the whole surrounded with enclosures of dilapidated walls.' Since another source says that the house was 'used as a quarry', the decline could have happened between 1786 and 1795. J. Aiken, *A Description of the Country from 30 to 40 Miles round Manchester* (London, 1795, Newton Abbot, 1968), p. 415.

400 J. Stow, *A Survey of London, 1603*, ed. C.L. Kingsford (London, 1908), p. 148.

401 It must be a coincidence that these almshouses were built in 1521 by Sir John Milborne, draper, sometime lord mayor of London. Milborne had Long Melford connections and may have been born in the parish. In his will of 1536 he left considerable sums to the poor of Melford.

> Next to these . . . is the Lord Lumleyes house, builded in the time of King Henry the eight by Sir Thomas Wiat the father, upon one plotte of ground of late pertayning to the . . . Crossed Friars, where part of their house stoode: and this is the furthest parte of Ealdgate warde towards the south, and joineth to the Tower hill.[402]

Thomas Wyatt the elder (the poet, father of the rebel leader) would not have had much time to build his new house, for he died in 1541. Some time later, possibly after the execution of Thomas Wyatt the younger, the house was acquired by Henry Fitzalan, 12th earl of Arundel. It seems likely that he bought it with at least some furniture and fittings, for in 1590 Lord Lumley owned a picture of 'old Sir Thomas Wiat' and another of 'the younger Sir Thomas Wiat executed', which are more likely to have come with the house than to have been commissioned by Arundel to commemorate a former owner.[403] We have already seen that Arundel gave the Tower Hill house to his eldest daughter Jane and her husband, Lord Lumley, in 1575. The deed describes 'one capital mese or messuage situate and being upon the Tower Hill within the city of London, wherein Sir John Ratcliff knight deceased lately dwelled and inhabited'.[404] There is evidence that Lumley and his family used the Tower Hill house as their London residence until his death, and he left it to his second wife, Elizabeth Lumley, née Darcy, aunt to Elizabeth Savage. When she died in 1617, Elizabeth Lumley left the house to her brother Lord Darcy and then to Elizabeth and her eldest son.[405]

While Lord Lumley owned the Tower Hill house, he received accounts from his man there, and in 1590 he had an inventory made of its contents, along with inventories of his other homes, Nonsuch Palace and Lumley Castle. Unfortunately what survives is not the individual inventories but a list of the contents of all three houses, without any distinction as to which item was in which house. Over 250 pictures are listed. We might possibly assume that the Holbeins, the Durers and the Raphael were at Nonsuch, and remained there when it was given to Queen Elizabeth, but some others presumably stayed at, or were moved to, Tower Hill when the family left Nonsuch. These include pictures of the great and good of Elizabethan England, including Lumley, both his wives, the earl of Arundel, Thomas, first Lord Darcy of Chiche (drawn by Garlicke), Thomas, third Lord Darcy of Chiche 'done by Hulbert', Lady Darcy of Chiche, and the two portraits of the Wyatts previously mentioned.

Lord Lumley received annual accounts for all his properties, and that for the Tower Hill house survives for 1592. It is not very informative, but tells us that the house had a rentable value of £60 a year (not collected because 'it remains in the lord's hands') and the rent from associated properties (the glasshouse, a tennis court and garden, along with seven tenements) brought in £48 6s. 8d. The keeper of the house had £4 a year.[406]

The only known description of the house is very brief, 'a great mansion with gardens and outhouses' which was built of timber; ironically this comes from

402 J. Stow, *A Survey of London*, p. 148.

403 Milner, *Records of Lumley Castle*, pp. 327–36. For Sir Thomas Wyatt the elder, Sir Thomas the younger, Jane Lady Lumley and the earl of Arundel, see Notes on People, below.

404 Arundel's gift of the Tower Hill house to Lord and Lady Lumley: CCALS, DCH/O/75.

405 Will of Elizabeth Lumley: TNA, PROB 11/129/13.

406 Earl of Scarborough's archives: 'Towerhill house. Account of John Lambton gent. bailiff there for the time aforesaid.'

Doc. 72, the licence to demolish the building. However, because of Lumley House's situation, with its southern wall providing the northern boundary of Tower Hill, it features in the background of many views of London, and is easy to distinguish on maps of the period. Identification of its exact site is confirmed by a plan of the Tower and its surrounds drawn in 1597 as part of a report on the condition of the Tower (Pl. V). At the northern end of Tower Hill is 'The new brick wall', and the land to the north of the wall is labelled 'Lord Lumley's house sometime belonging to Crutched Friars'. There is a gate at one end of the wall and a small tower at the other.[407] The 1635 inventory mentions a chamber 'by the back gate next Tower Hill'. This back wall was one of the boundaries of the liberties of the Tower and its line is today reflected on Tower Hill by the frontage of Trinity House and the building to its immediate west; the two are separated by a road called Savage Gardens. The licence to demolish the property tells us that the land concerned measured 230 feet on the south side facing Tower Hill, 290 feet on the east side towards Crutched Friars, 182 feet on the northern side and 330 feet on the western side. As well as the main house, the plot included 'divers tenements, warehouses and stables' on the northern and western sides; the main house was 'toward Tower Hill'.

A number of illustrations from maps and prospects of London may or may not accurately reflect the buildings on the site in this period. Almost all of them are drawn from the south, across the Thames; in these the wall on the southern boundary is always clear, but that means the illustrator did not have to draw in detail the buildings behind it. The most illustrative are the Agas map of 1560–70 and a sketch of 1615 by Michael van Meer.[408] When Edward VI was crowned in 1547, an unknown artist drew a view of the coronation procession from the Tower to Westminster; this is drawn from the north and very clearly shows a large imposing house inside a rectangular brick wall in the area in question. This view is apparently accepted as accurate in many respects, and could contain a true illustration of the house, but it shows a building of brick, whereas the licence to demolish says that the house is built of timber.[409]

All evidence about this house, apart from the inventory and the description of the site given in Doc. 72, is external, and are maps and illustrations of its site. Of the three houses inventoried after Thomas Savage's death, we know least about the interior of the Tower Hill house. We do however know that this is where Thomas was living at his death.

Tower Hill after 1636

Elizabeth was still living at or visiting the Tower Hill house in 1639, but by spring 1641 she and her son had sought a licence to build on the site (Doc. 72). The plan was to replace the old house with forty-seven new houses including five for 'men of rank and quality'.[410] The original application had been for fifty houses but the eventual permission given was for forty-seven; the sub-committee delegated to approve the development consisted of two aldermen of London and Inigo Jones. The

407 This combined 'bird's eye view' and plan of the Tower is dated 1597. The original is now lost but the Society of Antiquaries have a copy made in 1742; see Pl. V.

408 Ralph Agas, map of London, 1560–70, Guildhall Library; illustration by Michael van Meer, 1615: Edinburgh University Library, MS LaIII 283, f. 346v.

409 Engraving of a destroyed seventeenth-century view of Edward VI's coronation procession from the Tower to Westminster, February 1547, Society of Antiquaries.

410 Licence to demolish and redevelop the site: UHA, DDSQ(3)/18/3 (Doc. 72 in this volume).

application tells us that the buildings on the site were 'very ancient and much decayed and ready to fall down'.

By 1645 Elizabeth was living in Covent Garden, but the new houses were not erected immediately on the Tower Hill site.[411] Earl Rivers owned the house, but by 1648 it was amongst his lands which had been sequestered. In Parliament's hands, it was conveniently sited to act as an overflow from the Tower. The *Journal of the House of Commons* records that persons who were 'fit to be removed out of the Tower' were to be accommodated in the house belonging to the lieutenant of the ordnance, or in 'the sequestered house of the Earl Rivers, a delinquent'.[412]

This use did not last long, for the Easter Rate books of St Olave's parish tell the story from the later 1640s. Here are the relevant extracts:

1648 Lady Savage's house converted into an almshouse or rather a stable
1652 Lord Savage's house void
1654 Lord Savage's house void
1657 Lord Savage's house void
1659 Lord Savage's house
1663 Savage house. Mr Hyde's two brothers 13s
1664 In the new buildings, Ld Savage's house
[*Nine people are named here*]
1666 In the new buildings on the Lord Savage's house
[*Seven people are named here*].[413]

This is the last mention of the Tower Hill house in the rate books. Maps from around 1660 show a number of buildings on the site, mainly houses. A 1666 map of London by Wenceslaus Hollar shows three large houses facing Tower Hill, which may in fact be six 'semi-detached' homes; numerous smaller houses cover the remainder of the site. This fits the terms of the licence granted in 1641.[414] The area just escaped the Great Fire but was presumably affected by the rebuilding work afterwards. A later, very detailed map from 1676 shows a very different plan, with only one house fronting Tower Hill, at the west end of the original wall, but with a new street, Colchester Street, bisecting the plot.[415] By 1720 the current street names were in place, with Savage Gardens going from north to south, Colchester Street east to west. The northern end of Savage Gardens was also called Rivers Street.[416] Pennant says that the site formed part of the Navy Office, which was later replaced by a great East India Company warehouse, but this must have been true only for the north-western part of the site.[417] Today Savage Gardens is lined with office blocks but the frontage of Trinity House and adjacent buildings on the north side of Tower Hill follow the line of Thomas' and Elizabeth's back garden wall.

---

411 Elizabeth at Covent Garden: see note 325.

412 *Journal of the House of Commons*, 5 (London, 1802), 15 April 1648.

413 Poor Rate records of St Olave's, Hart Street: Guildhall Library, MS 872/1–7.

414 Map drawn by Thomas Porter 'c. 1660' but thought to be 1655: London Topographical Society, 1898, Sheet 2. 1666 map of London by Wenceslaus Hollar.

415 'A large and accurate map of the City of London, 1676' by John Ogilby and William Morgan.

416 First known reference to Savage Gardens: Strype (ed.), *Survey of London by John Stow* (London, 1720).

417 T. Pennant, *Some Account of London* (2nd edn, London, 1791), p. 273.

EDITORIAL METHODS

Insertions in the original documents are shown between oblique lines, thus \. . ./
Deletions which can be read are shown in angled brackets, thus <. . .>
Illegible words are shown thus [*illeg.*]
Words or passages made illegible by damage to the original are shown thus [*damaged*]
Where uncertainty exists about a word or number, it is shown thus [*?*]xxx

Original spelling has been retained, with certain exceptions: j has replaced i where modern usage demands it. Obvious abbreviations have been extended without comment.

Light punctuation has been added where it will aid the reader, but never where it might impose a questionable reading. The use of capital letters has been modernised and minimised. Most of the numbers used in the documents were in arabic; where a number was originally given in roman it has been changed to arabic. In sums of money the abbreviation 'li' has been modernised as '£', but the abbreviations 's.' and 'd.' have been retained. The dates quoted in original documents are retained, but in titles and introductory remarks dates between 1 January and 25 March have been given in new style: 25 February 1630, for example, is given as 25 February 1631. The original layout of the documents has not been retained. Quotations in the introduction have been modernised in spelling, capitalisation and grammar, except for extracts of poetry.

Each document in the collection has been numbered, and all cross-references and mentions in the introduction use these numbers.

It was not possible to carry out final checks on transcriptions of documents in the Hengrave MSS as they had been temporarily withdrawn from Cambridge University Library; some inaccuracies might therefore survive.

Plate I. The hatchment of Thomas Viscount Savage which hangs in the church of the Holy Trinity, Long Melford, c. 1636; from a modern painting by Stefan Oliver. The female figure comes from the Darcy arms. (*By courtesy of the artist*)

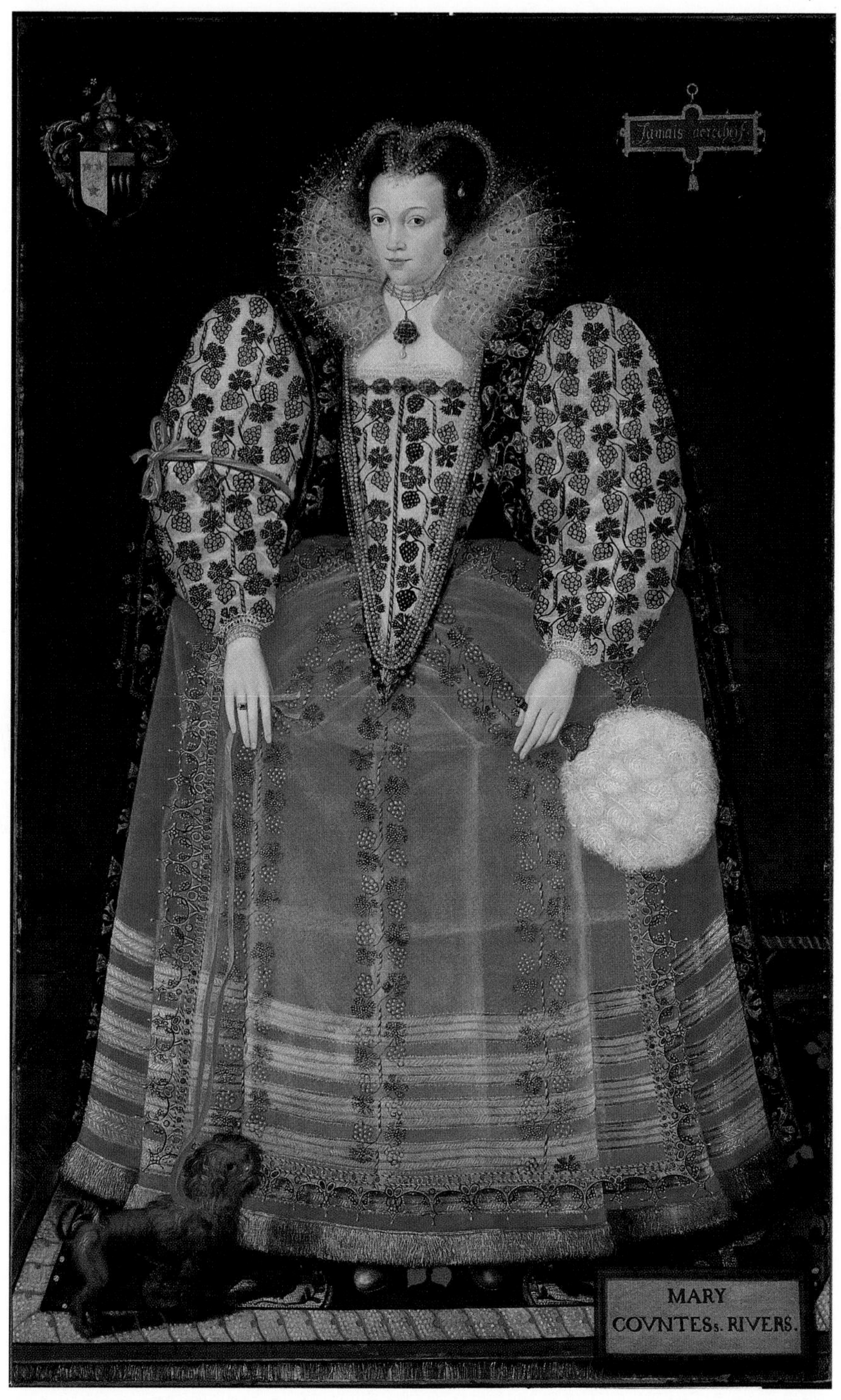

Plate II. Mary Kytson, Lady Darcy of Chiche, later Lady Rivers, c. 1590s, English school. The grandest of several surviving portraits of Elizabeth's mother; the others show her later in life as a small plump lady. *(Held in a private collection, reproduced by courtesy of the owner)*

Plate III. Lady Elizabeth Thimbleby and Viscountess Andover, by Anthony Van Dyck, c. 1637. Elizabeth and Dorothy Savage, second and third daughters of Thomas and Elizabeth, as married women. The National Gallery bought it from Earl Spencer in 1977. The winged putto bearing roses is thought to represent St Dorothy, the patroness of newly weds. *(By courtesy of the National Gallery)*

Plate IV. The procession at the funeral of Lady Lumley, 1577. Jane Lumley was the first wife of John Lord Lumley; they received the Tower Hill house as a gift from her father, Henry Fitzalan, earl of Arundel. There are four heralds; Thomas's funeral procession would have had two. *(By courtesy of the British Library)*

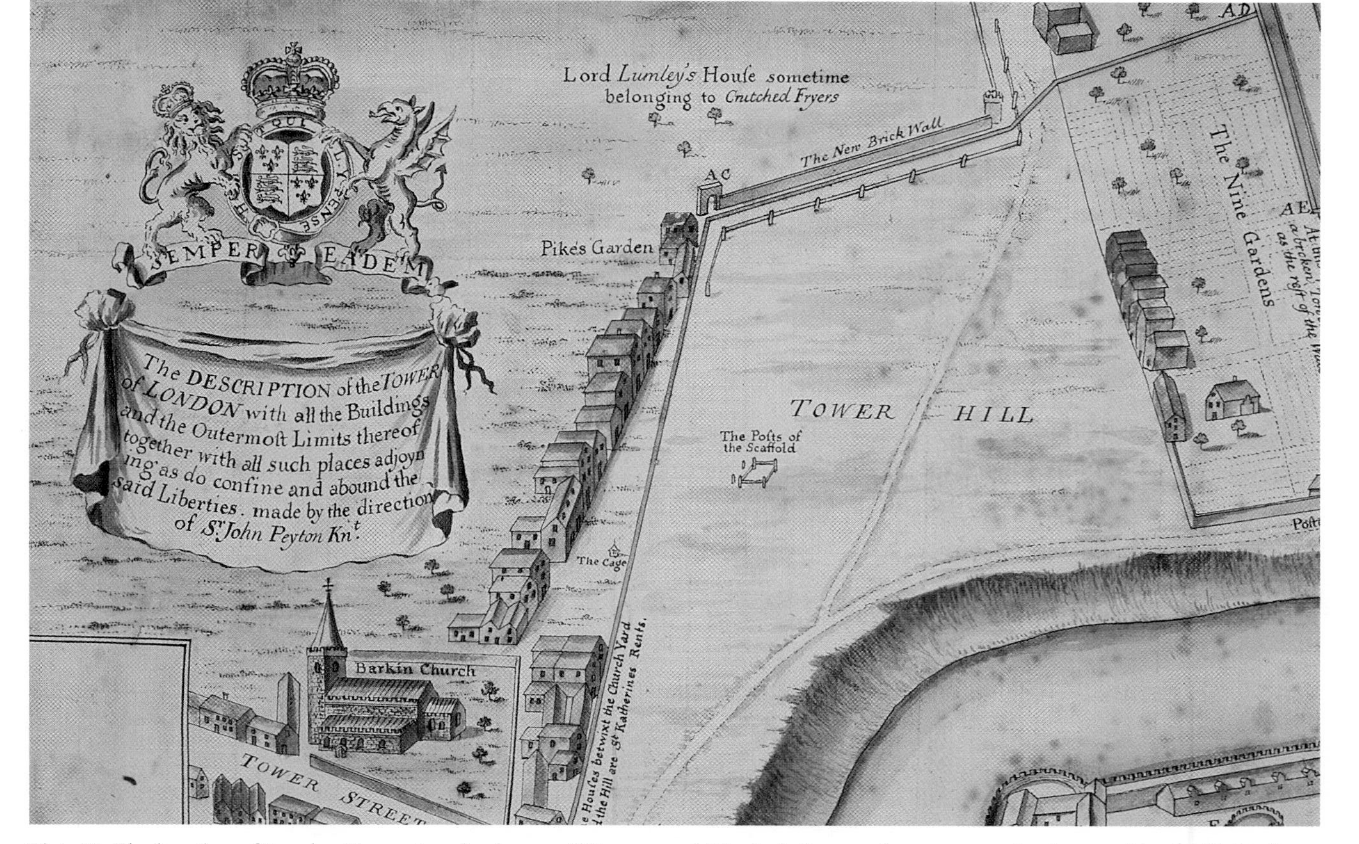

Plate V. The location of Lumley House, London home of Thomas and Elizabeth Savage, from a copy of a plan combined with bird's-eye view of the Tower of London, produced in 1597. The original is now lost. The line of the back wall of Lumley House was maintained in later development of the site; today it is the frontage of the Trinity House building and adjacent office blocks. *(By courtesy of the Society of Antiquaries)*

Plate VI. Melford Hall, watercolour by Michael Angelo Rooker, 1796. View at the entrance from Melford Green with the banqueting house on the right. The flat roof of the west wing can be seen clearly. The second-floor room of the north-west corner was the purple bed chamber in 1635.
(By courtesy of Sir Richard Hyde Parker, Bt)

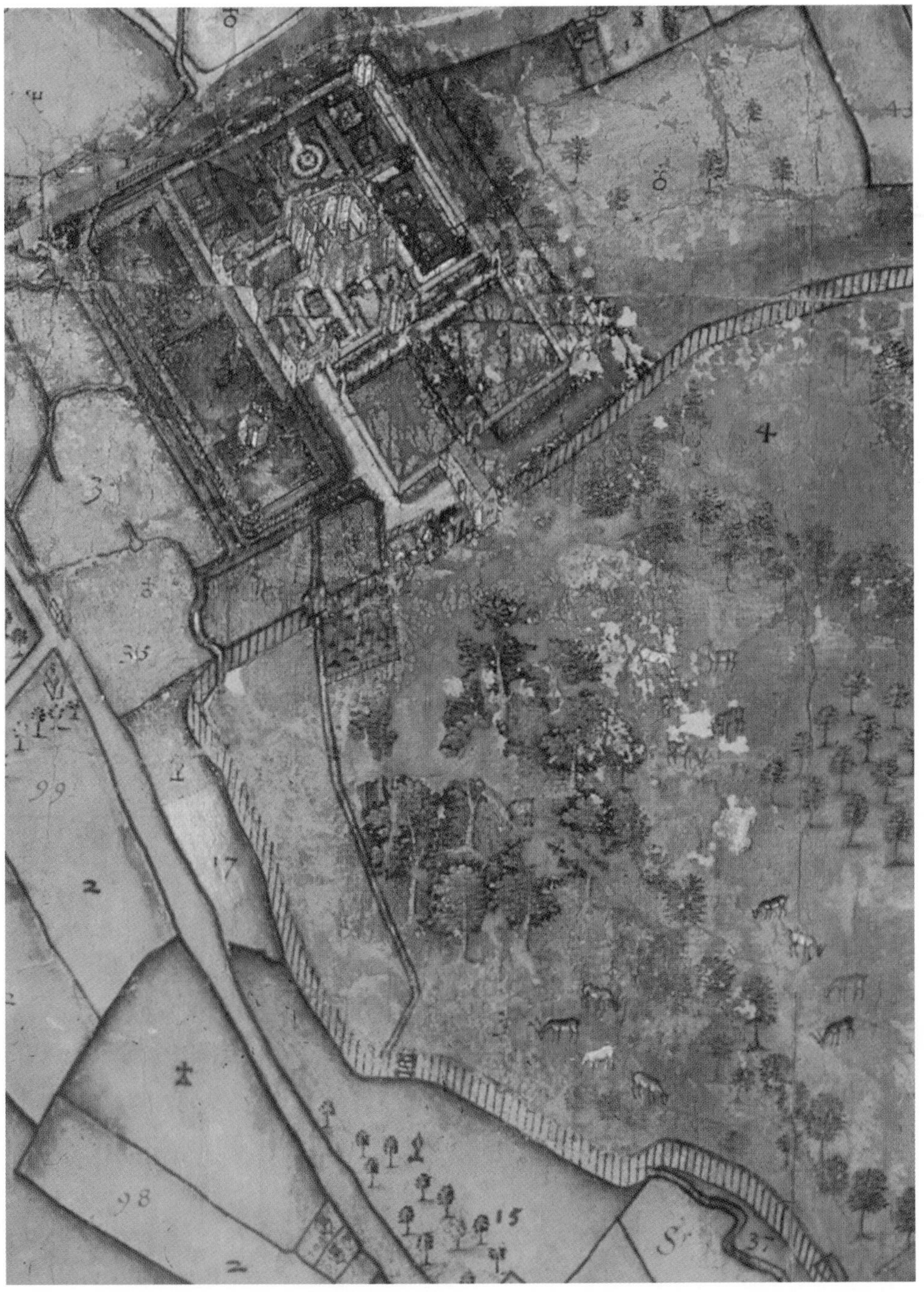

Plate VII. Melford Hall and some of the deer park, from a map drawn by Samuel Pierse in 1613. This map was accompanied by a survey of Thomas Savage's Suffolk lands (pl. 3). The map has been damaged and unfortunately some of the repairs are around the representation of Melford Hall. This is the only illustration of the east wing, demolished some time before the 1730s. For more detail see n. 371 on p. lxxi. *(By courtesy of Sir Richard Hyde Parker, Bt)*

Plate VIII. Melford Hall today, as seen from the east. The east wing was demolished between 1635 and 1735. *(By courtesy of the National Trust)*

DOCUMENTS RELATING TO THE LIVES AND HOUSES OF THOMAS AND ELIZABETH SAVAGE AND THEIR FAMILIES

1635–7: Death and after

1638–47: Grandeur and penury

Doc. 1. Pre-nuptial settlement relating to the marriage of Thomas Savage and Elizabeth Darcy, 26 March 1602. [CCALS: DCH/E/302, pp. 15–20. The damaged original: CCALS: DCH/O/16]

This is a long, dense legal document mentioning lands in Cheshire, Nottinghamshire and Derbyshire. Though not the most interesting document in this collection for many readers, it exemplifies what happens when families with considerable lands were making alliances. The lands to be settled on the couple had to be defined to the lawyers' satisfaction, for the settlement acted as a legal conveyance of lands from Sir John Savage to his son. Almost all marriages amongst gentry and aristocratic families would have involved such settlements, with their associated records. This example is transcribed from a later seventeenth-century copy of the original, which exists but is considerably damaged. The copy is in a bound collection of settlements and similar documents, mainly concerning Thomas Savage. The copyist added his own comments in the margins, but as these merely summarise the original they are not included in this transcription.

This indenture made the sixe and twentith day of March, in the foure and fortieth yere of the raigne of our soveraigne lady Elizabeth by the grace of God queene of England, Fraunce and Ireland, defendor of the faith etc., betweene Sir John Savage of Rocksavage in the county of Chester knight, and Sir Thomas Savage knight, sonne and heire apparant of the said Sir John Savage on thone parte, and the right honorable John Lumley knight, lord Lumley, and the right honorable Thomas lord Darcy of Chech on thother parte.[1]

Witnesseth that whereas it is entended that by the permission of God a mariage shalbe shortly had and solemnyzed betweene the said Sir Thomas Savage and Elizabeth Darcy, daughter of the said right honorable Thomas Lord Darcy, now (in consideracion of the said mariage so to be had & solemnyzed and for parte of the joincture of the said Elizabeth (if shee fortune to survyve and overlyve the said Sir Thomas Savage) and for the preferment and advauncement of the said Sir Thomas Savage and Elizabeth, and the heires males of the body of the said Sir Thomas Savage upon the body of the said Elizabeth laufully to be begotten, and other the heires males of the body of the said Sir Thomas laufully to be begotten, and for thestablishment and setling of the mannors, landes, tenementes and heredytamentes hereafter mencioned to such person and persons, and to such uses, ententes and purposes, and in such manner and forme, as hereafter in and by these presentes is mencioned and expressed, and for dyverse other good causes, and reasonable consideracions, the said Sir John Savage and Sir Thomas Savage thereunto especially moving).

The said Sir Thomas Savage for him and his heires, doth covenant, promise and graunt to and with the said John lord Lumley, and Thomas lord Darcy, their heires and assignes by these presentes, that he the said Sir Thomas Savage, and his heires, and all and every other person and persons, and their heires, clayming or having any estate by, from or under the said Sir Thomas shall and will ymediatly, from and after thensealing and delyvery of these presentes, stand and be seized of and in the mannors or lordshipps of Greseley and Kymberley, in the county of Nottingham, with their and either of their rightes, members, liberties, and appurtenances whatsoever.[2] And of and in the mannor or lordshipp of Macclesffield parck *alias* Maxefield

1 Note John Lord Lumley's involvement. He appears to have been involved with Lord Darcy in many legal and family matters.

2 Gresley and Kimberley were given by Henry VII to the Sir John Savage who helped him win the battle

parck,[3] in the said county of Chester, with the rightes, members, liberties, & appurtenances thereof, and of and in all and singuler mesuages, landes, tenementes, meadowes, leasowes, pastures, woodes, underwoodes, rentes, revercions, services and hereditamentes whatsoever, to the said mannors or lordshipps, or any of them, belonging or appurteyning, and now or att any tyme heretofore esteemed, reputed, taken, used, occupyed, demysed, letten or enjoyed, as any parte, parcell or member or belonging, of, with or to the said mannors, or lordshipps, or any of them, and heretofore the inherytance of the said Sir John Savage knight, or of Sir John Savage knight deceased father of the said Sir John Savage, and graundfather of the said Sir Thomas Savage, or any of them, and of and in all and singuler other the mannors, mesuages, landes, tenementes, meadowes, pastures, milnes, woodes, waters, fishinges, moores, waste, marshes, rentes, revercions, advousons, patronages of churches, chappelles and vicaradges, rectories, tythes, courtes, leetes, hundredes, customes, franchesies, liberties, proffettes, commodities and heredytamentes whatsoever, with all and singuler thappurtenances, & whereof or wherein the said Sir Thomas Savage now hath or att any tyme heretofore had, or whereof the said Sir John Savage at any tyme heretofore had, any estate of inherytance, scytuat, lying, beyng, happening, growing, renewing or comyng, in the tounes, fieldes, hamlettes, parishes or places, of Greseley, Kymberley and Macclesfield parck *alias* Maxefield parke aforesaid, and in every or any of them, and now or late in the respectyve tenures, houldinges or occupacions of the said Sir Thomas Savage knight, his undertennantes, assignee or assignes or of somme of them (except the mynes of cole, and other mynes in the said mannors of Greseley and Kymberley,[4] aswell not opened as opened, and all services, boones and averages, of all the tenantes of the said mannors of Greseley and Kymberley, and all the tymber trees, woodes and underwoodes now growing or beyng, or hereafter to growe or be, in or upon the said mannors of Greseley and Kymberley, or in or upon any parte thereof).

To the severall uses, ententes and purposes, hereafter mencionned and expressed, and to noe other uses, ententes or purposes, nor to any other use, entent or purpose whatsoever (that is to say) to the use and behoof of the said Sir Thomas Savage, and his heires, untill the said mariage shalbe had and solemnyzed, and afterward to the use and behoof of the said Sir Thomas and Elizabeth and the heires males of the body of the said Sir Thomas Savage upon the body of the said Elizabeth laufully to be begotten. And for defaulte of such issue, then to the use and behoof of the heires males of the body of the said Sir Thomas Savage, laufully to be begotten, and for default of such issue, then to the use of the said Sir John Savage knight, father of the said Sir Thomas Savage knight and the heires males of the body of the said Sir John Savage laufully begotten, and for default of such heires males, then to the use and behoof of the said Sir John Savage, father of the said Sir Thomas Savage and his heires forever.

And whereas Sir Robert Remyngton knight and Dame Elianor his wief,[5] as in the right of the said Dame Elyanor, are laufully seized in their demesne as of freehold for terme of the naturall lyef of the said Dame Elyanor, with remaynder to the said

of Bosworth; this John Savage was also made a knight of the garter. The manors are very near Ilkeston, in Derbyshire, which was also given to this Sir John. Thomas Savage sold Ilkeston to one of his Manners relatives in 1609; that family still held the lands in the 1890s.

3 The Savages had had an interest in Macclesfield since the late fourteenth century.

4 There was a coalmine in Kimberley in 1880, but it appears to have gone out of use before 1908, according to lists published by the Coal History Resource Centre on www.cmhrc.pwp.blueyonder.co.uk

5 Dame Eleanor Remington was Thomas Savage's grandfather's second wife, and widow, who had later married Sir Robert Remington. These manors were part of her jointure.

Sir Thomas Savage, and in the heires males of his body, with remaynder to the said Sir John Savage, and the heires males of his body, the revercion or remaynder being in the said Sir John and his heires, of and in all the mannors, landes, tenementes and hereditamentes, in Shipbrooke and Mynshall Vernon or either of them, in the said county of Chester, with their and either of their rightes, members, liberties and appurtenances whatsoever.[6]

Now the said Sir John Savage and Sir Thomas Savage (for the consideracions, reasons and respectes aforesaid) doe and either of them doth, for them their heires and assignes, covenant, promise and graunt to and with the said John lord Lumley and Thomas lord Darcy, their heires and assignes, that they the said Sir John Savage and Sir Thomas Savage, before the feast of the natyvity of St John Baptist next ensewing, by fyne or fynes in due form of lawe to be levyed, with proclamacions before the queenes majesties' justices of Chester, according to the lawes and statutes of this realme in such case provyded, betweene the said John lord Lumley and Thomas lord Darcy plaintifes, and the said Sir John Savage and Sir Thomas Savage deforcyantes, shall and will at the request, costes and charges in the lawe of the said Thomas lord Darcy, and so as the said Sir John Savage travell not out out of the county of Chester for the doyng thereof, recognyze, and acknowledge all the said mannors, landes, tenementes and heredytamentes in Shipbrooke, and Mynshall Vernon aforesaid, or either of them, with their and either of their rightes, members, liberties and appurtenances in Shipbrooke and Mynshall Vernon aforesaid. And the revercion and revercions of the same, and all landes, tenementes, meadowes, feedinges, pastures, woodes, underwoodes, rentes, revercions, services, comons, proffettes, commodities, easementes, hereditamentes and appurtenances whatsoever, to the said mannors, landes, tenementes and hereditamentes in Shipbrooke and Mynshall Vernon, or either of them, belonging, or in anywyse apperteyning, or with them or any of them now or heretofore lett, or occupyed, or accepted, reputed or taken as parte, parcell or member of them or any of them, in Shipbrooke and Mynshall Vernon aforesaid or either of them.

And all other the landes, tenementes and heredytamentes of the said Sir John Savage and Sir Thomas Savage, or of either of them, scituat, lying, being, happenyng, growing, renewing or coming in the townes, fieldes, hamlettes, parishes or places of Shipbrooke & Mynshall Vernon aforesaid, in Shipbrooke and Mynshall Vernon aforesaid, [*sic*] or in either of them (except all and every the groundes, pastures, woodes and heredytamentes whatsoever, comonly called Mynshall parke, Whelkley parke and Milne Heyes, scituat, lying and being in Mynshall Vernon aforesaid) to be the right of the said John lord Lumley, as those which the said John lord Lumley and Thomas lord Darcy shall have of the guift of the said Sir John Savage and Sir Thomas Savage, and the same by the said fyne, shall remyse and quyte clayme from them and their heires to the said John lord Lumley, and Thomas lord Darcy, and the heires of the said John lord Lumley forever.

And further the said Sir John Savage and Sir Thomas, by the said fyne shall severally graunt for them and their heires, that they shall severally and respectively warrant, and defend the premysses with thappurtenances, unto the said John lord Lumley and Thomas lord Darcy, and the heires of the said John lord Lumley against them the said Sir John and Sir Thomas and their heires forever. And yt is further declared, witnessed, covenaunted, concluded and fully agreed by and betweene the

6 The wife of the John Savage who fought at Bosworth was a Vernon and it is likely that she brought the manors of Shipbrook and Minshull Vernon to the Savage family. The Vernons were another family who came with William the Conqueror and the first generation was described as 'of Shipbrooke'.

said parties to these presentes and their heires, that the said fyne so to be had, and levyed as aforesaid, and all other fynes, recoveries, conveyances and assurances whatsover, had, levyed, suffered, knowledged or executed, or to be had, levyed, knowledged, suffered or executed, by or betweene the said parties or any of them, of the said mannors, landes, tenementes and heredytamentes in Shipbrooke and Mynshall Vernon or either of them, and of all other the premysses last before mencioned in Shipbrooke and Mynshall Vernon aforesaid, or either of them, or any parte thereof, by the names aforesaid or by any other names whatsoever, and the full execucion of them, and every of them shalbe and shalbe adjudged, and taken to be, to the uses, ententes and purposes, hereafter in these presentes lymited, mencioned and expressed, and to noe other use, purpose or entent.

That is to say, to the use and behoof of the said Sir Thomas Savage and his heires, untill the said mariage had and solempnyzed, and after to the use and behoof of the said Sir Thomas and Elizabeth, and the heires males of the body of the said Sir Thomas Savage upon the body of the said Elizabeth, laufully to be begotten. And for default of such yssue, to the use and behoof of the heires males of the body of the said Sir Thomas Savage laufully to be begotten, and for default of such yssue, to the use and behoof of the said Sir John Savage father of the said Sir Thomas Savage, and of the heires males of the body of the said Sir John Savage laufully begotten, and for default of such heires males, then to the use and behoof of the said Sir John Savage and his heires forever.

And the said Sir John Savage for hym his heires, executors and administrators and for every of them doth covenaunt, promyse and graunt to and with the said John lord Lumley and Thomas lord Darcy, their heires and assignes by these presentes, that the said mannors or lordshippes of Greseley and Kymberley, now are and be, and hereafter at all tymes (not withstanding any act or thing, made, done, comytted or willingly and wyttingly suffered, or to be made, done, comitted or willingly and wyttingley suffered by the said Sir John Savage to the contrary) shall continue, remayne and be to the severall person and persons before mencioned, according to the true entent and meanyng of the lymittacions before specyfyed, of the cleare yerely value of nyne poundes by yere of ould rent of assyze, over and above all charges and repryses, and that the said mannores, landes, tenementes & heredytamentes in Shipbrooke and Mynshall Vernon aforesaid, now are and be and att all tymes hereafter (notwithstanding any act or thing made, done, comytted or willingly and wyttingly suffered, or to be made, done, comitted or willingly and wittingly suffered, by the said Sir John Savage to the contrary) shall continue, remayne and be to the severall person and persons before mencioned, according to the true entent & meaning of the lymittacions before specyfied of the cleare yerely value of forty foure poundes three shillinges sixe pence, and the said mannor or lordshipp of Macclesfyeld parke *alias* Maxefield parke of the cleare yerely value of forty poundes and tenn shillinges by yere, of ould rent of assyze over and above all chardges and repryzes.

And moreover that the mannors, landes, tenementes, heredytamentes and premisses, before by these presentes mencioned with thappurtenances and every parte and parcell thereof, now are and be and hereafter at all tymes and from tyme, to tyme forevermore, shall remayne and contynue to the severall uses, lymittacions and ententes in these presentes mencioned, and according to the true entent and meaning of these presentes, free and clear, and freely and clearly acquyted and dischardged, or from tyme to tyme well and sufficiently saved and kept harmlesse, by the said Sir John Savage, his heires, executors and administrators of and from all and all manner of former or other bargaynes, sales, guifts, grauntes, statutes marchant and of the staple, recognyzances, joynctors, dowres, fynes, willes, yssues, seizures, forfeytures, liveries, ouster le maynes, fynes for alienacions without lycence, and of and from all other tytles, troubles, and incombrances whatsoever, had, made, done or wittingly and willingly suffered, or to be had, made, done or wyttingly and willingly suffered, by the said Sir John Savage (all leases made of the premysses, or any parte thereof, for one, two or three lyves, or twenty and one yeres or under, whereupon the old and accustomed rentes or more are reserved, and shalbe dew and payable during the contynuance of such severall leasees, to the persons aforesaid, according to their estates, and the true meanyng of these presentes, and thestate for lief of the said Dame Elyoner Remyngton, of and in the said mannors, landes, tenementes & hereditamentes in Shipbrooke and Mynshall Vernon aforesaid, only excepted).

And further that the said Elizabeth and her assignes, during her naturall lief, according to the true entent and meaning of these presentes, shall and may peaceably and quyetly have, hold, occupy, possesse and enjoye the said mannors, mesuages, landes, tenementes, heredytamentes and other the premysses, before by these presentes mencioned, with thappurtenances according to the lymittacions aforesaid, and the true entent and meanyng of these presentes (as a parte of her joincture) without lett, suyte, trouble, entry, vexacion, eviccion, contradiccion or interrupcion of the said Sir John Savage, his heires or assignes, or of any other person or persons, laufully clayming, or which shall or may laufully clayme from, by or under the said Sir John Savage (all lessees claymyng only by or under such estates, as are before excepted, and thestate for lyef of the said Dame Elyoner Remyngton) only excepted and forepryzed.

And moreover that the said Sir John Savage, and all and every other person and persons now having, clayming, or pretending to have, or which of right ought to have, clayme or pretend to have, any estate, right, tytle, interest, use, possession, revercion, inheritance or demaund of, in or to the said mannors, landes, tenementes, hereditamentes and premysses, or any parte thereof, by from or under the said Sir John Savage, the said lessees before mencioned, for and in respect only of such estates as are before specifyed.

And the said Sir Robert Remyngton and Dame Elyoner, for and in respect of her estate before mencioned, only excepted, shall and will hereafter at all tymes, and from tyme to tyme during the space of seaven yeres next ensewing the date hereof, at the reasonable request, costes and chardges in the lawe of the said Thomas Lord Darcy, his heires or assignes, or of the said Elizabeth or her assignes doe cause, acknowledge, procure and suffer to be done, knowledged and executed, all and every such further laufull and reasonable act and actes, thing and thinges, devyse and devyses whatsoever, for the further, more, better and perfecter assurance, suerty and sure making and conveying of the premysses and every parte and parcell thereof, to the severall uses, ententes and purposes before mencioned, and according to the true entent and meanyng of these presentes. As by the said John lord Lumley and Thomas lord Darcy, their heires or assignes, or the servyvor of them, or by the said Elizabeth or her assignes or her, their or any of their counsaill lerned in the lawes, shalbe reasonably devysed or advysed, and requyred (so as the said Sir John Savage be not requyred nor compelled to travell for the doyng therof furth of the county of Chester).

And the said Sir Thomas Savage, etc. The like covenantes from Sir Thomas as the former from Sir John (mutatis mutandis), saving only that Sir John doth covenant only for his owne actes, and Sir Thomas doth covenant for the actes of himself and of the said Sir John his father.

In wytnes etc.

That parte of the indenture which is under the handes & seales of Sir John Savage & Sir Thomas Savage is remayning with my Lord Darcy. And the said indenture was sealed and delivered in the presence of Sir Richard Lewkenor, Thomas Aston, Thomas Ireland, John Maynwaring, J. Jeffreys, Wy Ottley and William Alcock, as by an indorsement upon the said indenture under their handes may appeare.[7]

Doc. 2. Jane Allington gives an annuity to her grandson Thomas Savage, 12 May 1602. [CCALS: DCH/E/302, pp. 49–50]

This is a transcription of a later seventeenth-century copy of the original document, which is lost or in an unknown archive. In her lifetime Jane Allington gives Thomas and Elizabeth some of the income from lands that they will eventually inherit from her. The copy is in the same bound collection of settlements and similar documents, mainly concerning Thomas Savage, as Doc. 1. Again the copyist added his own comments, which have not been reproduced below.

To all Christian people, to whom this presente wryting shall comme, Jane Allyngton of Highe Holborne, in the county of Middlesex, wydowe late the wief of Richard Allyngton esquyer deceased, sendeth greeting in our lord God everlasting.[8] Knowe yee me the said Jane Alyngton for the great love and affeccion which I beare to Sir Thomas Savage knight, sonne and heire apparant of Sir John Savage knight, my graundchylde, and to Elizabeth Darcy, daughter to the right honorable Thomas lord Darcy of Chech,[9] whom the said Sir Thomas Savage entendeth by Godes permyssion shortly to take to wyef, and for the better mayntenance of the said Sir Thomas Savage and the said Elizabeth Darcy, and for the advauncement, and encrease of the joynture of the said Elizabeth, yf shee happen to servyve the said Sir Thomas, to have given and graunted and by these presentes doe give and graunt unto the said Sir Thomas Savage my said graundchylde, and to the said Elizabeth Darcy, one anuytie or yerely rent chardg of one hundreth poundes of laufull money of England, yssewing and goyng furth and yerely to be perceived, and taken out of the mannor of Melford in the county of Suffolck.[10]

To have, hold, receive, perceive and take the said annuytie, or yerely rent charge of one hundreth poundes of laufull money of England, to the said Sir Thomas Savage and Elizabeth Darcy for terme of their lyves, & the lyef of the longest lyver of them, at the feast of St Michaell thearchangell & thannunciacion of our lady by even porcions, the first payment thereof to be had and paid at the first of the said feastes that shall next happen after thensealing and delyvery hereof. Provyded \alwaies/ that yf yt shall happen, the said anuyty or yerely rent chardg of one hundreth poundes or any parte or parcell thereof to be behynd and unpaide, in parte or in all by the space of one quarter of a yere, next after any of the said feastes being laufully demaunded, that then yt shall and may be laufull to & for the said Sir Thomas, and the said Elizabeth Darcy, into all and every parte of the said mannor of Melford, to enter and distreyne, and the distresse and distresses, then and there found, to lead dryve and ympound, and in pound detayne, untill the said Sir Thomas

7 For anything known of the witnesses to this document, see Notes on People below.

8 Jane Allington inherited this property from her brother Sir William Cordell.

9 Chiche was the original name of the place later known as St Osyth, after the priory built there. It is just west of present-day Clacton, in Essex.

10 Melford or Long Melford is in south-western Suffolk, just north of Sudbury.

Savage and the said Elizabeth Darcy shalbe fully satisfyed, contented and paid of the arrerage of the said rent, yf any shalbe.

And the said Jane Allyngton doth for her self, her heires, executors and assignes covenant, promyse and graunt to and with the said Sir Thomas Savage and the said Elizabeth Darcy their and every of their executors, administrators and assignes by these presents, that the said mannor of Melford is and soe shall contynew, remayne and be during the lyves of the said Sir Thomas and Elizabeth, sufficyent, overt and lyable, to and for the entry and distresse of the said Sir Thomas and Elizabeth and of either of them, their and either of their assignee and assignes, for the said rent and tharrearage thereof, and of every parte and parcell thereof, when and so often as the same or any parte thereof, shall happen to be behynd and unpaid.

In witnes whereof I the said Jane Alyngton have hereunto sett my hand and seale, geoven the twelveth day of May in the foure and fortieth yere of the raigne of our soveraigne lady Elizabeth by the grace of God, queene of England Fraunce and Ireland, defendor of the faith etc., 1602

Jane Allyngton, signed sealed & delyvered in the presence of those whose names are hereunder written, Oliver Manners, Ry Reynelle, Nicholas Ducke, John Lumley, Christofer Osmond.[11]

Memorandum that this rent chardg is remaynyng with Sir Thomas Savage.

Doc. 3. Elizabeth Savage's jointure, ?1602. [CCALS: DCH/H/205A]

This lists the lands from which Elizabeth Savage would receive income after the death of her husband, according to the terms of their marriage settlement. It is undated and it has been placed here because of the links with Docs 1 and 2. In a later document, which survives but is very damaged [CCALS, DCH/O/29], Thomas added his Melford lands to Elizabeth's jointure.

Landes assigned to the Lady Elizabeth Savage, wife of Sir Thomas Savage for her joincture

The present joincture after Sir Thomas Savages death			£200
Nottingham	Gresley and Kymberley	£9 ould[12]	
Cester	Macklesfield parke	£40 10s. ould	
Derbyshire	Rent out of Ilston[13]	£50 10s.	
	Mrs Allingtons annuity[14]	£100	
More after the death of the Lady Remington (albeit Sir John shalbe then living)[15]			£244 3s. 6d.
Cester	Shipbrooke & Minshulvernon	£44 3s. 6d. ould	

11 For Oliver Manners, John Lumley, see Notes on People below.

12 'Ould', we think, means 'old rent of assize', see Glossary below.

13 Ilkeston, Derbyshire.

14 Jane Allington's annuity is Doc. 2. The lands in Gresley, Kimberley, Ilkeston and Macclesfield Park along with those in Shipbrook and Minshull Vernon are mentioned in Doc. 1, the pre-nuptial settlement made before Thomas's and Elizabeth's marriage.

15 Lady Remington was Thomas Savage's grandfather's widow by his second marriage. Sir John was Thomas's father, Sir John Savage.

More after the death of Sir John Savage (albeit the Lady Remington survive him).			£445 13s. 6d.
Derbyshire	Ilston (being £52 ould) so there will come more then <then> the annuity 30s., for the annuity wilbe suspended & the mannor will come in possession being £52 ould rent & so encreased.	30s.	And £52 ould
	Cole mynes there	£200	
More after the death of the survivor of the Lady Remington and Sir John Savage.			£531 13s. 6d.
Cester	Kingesley, Bradley iuxta Frodsham & Bradley Orchard[16]	£48 ould.	
	The herbage of the medowing wich and wich wood	£38	

So as the joincture is in present	£200
And after the Lady Remingtons death (albeit Sir John live)	£244 3s. 6d.
And after Sir John Savages death (albeit the Lady Remington live)	£401 10s.
And after Sir John and the Lady Remington are both dead	£531 13s. 6d.

Doc. 4. Will of Jane Allington, 15 July 1602. [TNA: PROB 11/103/9]

Thomas inherited most of his Suffolk property and more in London from Jane Allington, his grandmother. She uses the term 'nephew' for her male grandchildren throughout this will.

In the name of God amen. I Jane Allington late the wief of Richard Allington esquier decessed beinge at this presente (thankes be to God) of good and perfect remembrans, and understandinge the instabilitie of this <lief> my naturall lief, doe make and ordaine this my last will and testament in manner and fourme followinge, revokinge & adnihilatinge all former wills whatsoever.

Firste I commytte my sowle into the handes of our saviour Jhesus Christe, throughe the merrittes of whose bitter passion I firmelie and stedfastlie beleve to be one of the partakers of his celestiall kingdome; beseechinge all good people and especiallie all those my lovinge freindes to have me in theire remembrances in theire devoute prayers to the celestiall father in heaven.

Item my will is that my bodie maye be buried in the Chappell of the Rolles of the same vaulte that my late welbeloved husband Mr Allington nowe liethe buried in.[17]

Item I give to the poore to praie for me the somme of thirtene poundes sixe shillinges and eighte pence, whereof five poundes to be distributed to the poore people in London, fyve poundes at Melforde in Suffolk and the other three poundes

16 Kingesley is probably Kingsley, Cheshire, south-east of Frodsham. Bradley is just outside Frodsham, again to the south-east. Frodsham is immediately south of Runcorn, just across the river Weaver from Rocksavage.

17 Sir Richard Allington died in 1561. His memorial remains in this chapel, which was until recently part of the Public Record Office, and is now part of King's College, London. It is likely that her brother, Master of the Rolls, arranged for Jane Allington to bury her husband in the Rolls Chapel; he was not, as far as we know, associated with the Rolls office.

sixe shillings \&/ eighte pence at Horseth in Cambridgeshire to suche poore people as to my executor shall seeme moste needefull.[18]

Item I give to the poore prysoners remayninge in Newgate, Ludgate, the Fleete, the Kinges Benche, the Marshalsey, the Red Lyon and the Gatehowse at Westminster the somme of twentie poundes equallie to be distributed amongest them by the discrecion of my executors.

Item I give to fower and twentie poore women to eache of them a blacke gowne.

Item my will is that all suche debtes as I of righte or in conscience doe or shall happen to owe unto any person or persons be well and trulie contented and paide by my executors as soone as possiblye it maye be.

Item whereas my late husband Mr Allington did by his laste will and testament give and bequeathe fower hundred markes to be ymployed and bestowed for the mayntenanse and relief of suche poore and needie persons as to the discretion of certaine his faithefull freindes named in his saide laste will and testament shoulde seeme moste best and convenient, I doe likewise give and bequeathe for the better maintenaunce and reliefe of suche poore and needie persons as to the discrecion of my executors shalbe thoughte moste meetest, best and convenient, the somme of two hundred markes more, which in the whole amounteth to the somme of sixe hundreth markes. And my will is that for and duringe the terme of eighte yeeres ymmediatelie after my decesse there shoulde be weekelie given and distributed to seaven poore folkes to everie of them eighte pence in monye, and yeerelie to everie one of them one good fryze gowne readie made, to be given unto them alwayes the three and twentithe daie of November; excepte the foresaid somme of sixe hundred marckes as is aforesaid, beinge my late husbandes bequest and myne, be <bestowed> in the meane tyme bestowed to those good and godlie uses for the relievinge of the poore in manner and fourme as before rehearsed, or as to my executors shalbe thoughte moste meete and best.

And my will is that my children or childers children or anie other in theire behalf which are to receive anie legacie or benefytte by this my will, that they nor anie of them shall molest or trouble my executors or either of them by accion of accompte or otherwise, which they shall seeme to pretende due unto them or either of them from my self either as executor unto Mr Allington their late father or as gardian unto them or either of them. For thoughe I protest before the almightie that I have expendyd asmuche and farre more in theire bringinge up then ever I receyved as any way due \un/to them, yett because I am desirous to avoide trouble and suite in lawe unto my executors, whoe I knowe muste be inforced to take a greate dealle of paines to see this my presente will executed, and to performe some other thinges commytted to theire charge.[19]

My will and meaninge is that the guyftes and legacyes hereafter given or bequeathed unto my saide children shalbe conditionall soe as they and either of them shall sufficientlie releasse or otherwise cleerelie discharge my saide executors and either of them of all suche accomptes or demaundes which they or either of them shall or maye pretende ageinste them or either of them by reason of any pretendyd demaunde they maye or shall make from me. And yf any refuse soe to doe then my will is that all suche guyftes, legacyes and bequestes hereafter expressyd in this my testament and last will shalbe utterlie voide to such and soe

[18] The Allington family home was at Horseheath, Cambridgeshire.

[19] Jane Allington had faced at least two court cases when she acted as one of the executors of her brother Sir William Cordell.

manie of them as shall soe refuse and not releasse or discharge my saide executors as aforesaid.

Item I give and bequeathe unto my daughter the Ladie Marie Savage wief of Sir John Savage (with Godes blessinge and myne) uppon the condicion aforesaid, my jewell of the storie of Suzanna and my border and alsoe my cusshion clothe and pillowbeare wroughte with carnation silke and one sweete bagge of crymosin satten imbrothered over with goulde and sylver, prayenge and requestinge my daughter Savage that shee will give and bestowe the said jewell after hir decesse to my nephewe Sir Thomas Savage hir eldest sonne yf he be then lyvynge or on hir next heire male.[20]

Item I give and bequeathe unto the Ladye Elizabeth Savadge wief of my said nephewe Sir Thomas Savadge my jewell of aggott sett with diamondes and the appendante of diamondes hanginge thereat and my chaine of aggaton and pearle.[21]

And whereas I have alredie given and delyvered to my nephewe Phillippe Stanhope one crosse of dyamondes I doe nowe hereby will, devise and bequethe unto him the somme of one hundred poundes to make him a cheine, and also one peece of goulde of sixe poundes thirtene shillinges \&/ fower pence as a speciall remembranse to him from me.[22] To be paide and delyvered unto him when he shall accomplishe the age of twentie and one yeeres. And I beseeche God to blesse him with all happie fortune.

Item I give to my godsonne and nephewe John Savage, second sonne unto my daughter the Ladie Savage, the somme of one hundred marckes to make him a cheine to be delyvered unto him at his age of twentie and one yeeres, beseechinge God to blesse him and make him his servaunte.[23]

Item I give to my neece Elizabeth Savage, my daughter Savages eldest daughter, the somme of seaven hundred poundes to be paide unto hir the daie of hir marriadge (except shee be married in my lief tyme), beseechinge God to blesse hir with all happines.[24] The same seaven hundred poundes to be perceived and taken owte of the rentes, revenewes and proffittes of my landes in sorte as hereafter followeth.

Item I give and bequeathe unto Mr Richard Wilbraham esquier and Grace his wief[25] (my graunde childe) to either of them twentie poundes a peece and Godes blessinge and myne. And suche quantitie of my lynnen as to my executors shall seeme expedient.

Item I give unto my daughter Savages younger sonne William the somme of one hundred marckes to make him a cheine to be delyvered unto him at his age of twentie and one yeeres.[26]

---

20 Mary Savage was buried on the same day in 1635 as her son Thomas Viscount Savage. Her will left most of the goods that she was free to bequeath to her daughter Elizabeth.

21 These would not be Elizabeth's only pearls. Her long triple string of pearls, shown in her portrait, are rumoured to have been thrown into the fishponds as she was escaping from Melford Hall in 1642. That string had matching earrings.

22 For Philip Stanhope, see Notes on People below.

23 This is Thomas's younger brother, who was murdered by Ralph Bathurst in 1609. Bathurst was arraigned for the murder and refused to plead, so was sentenced to *peine forte et dure* and was pressed to death: William Beamont, *A History of the Castle of Halton and the Priory or Abbey of Norton* (Warrington, 1873), p. 105.

24 Elizabeth Savage first married Thomas Manwaring and later Sir Ralph Done.

25 Grace was the second daughter of Sir John Savage and his wife Mary. She survived her husband and died in Chester in 1662. For Sir Richard Wilbraham, see Notes on People below.

26 This William is thought to have moved to Taunton, Somerset. His eldest son has been suggested to be the Thomas Savage who founded the Massachusetts branch of the Savage family.

Item I give to my sonne Sir John Savadge knighte the somme of fourtie poundes to buye him a bason and ewer, and to my sonne John Stanhope fourtie poundes.[27]

Item I give to my nephewe Doctor Gager forty poundes in monye.[28]

Item I give to my brother Mr William Allington a ringe of goulde to the valewe of fourtie shillinges.

Item I give to my verie good frende Mr Richarde Carie the somme of tenn poundes.

Item I give to my good frende Mr Thomas Carie of Graies Inne a ringe of goulde of fourtie shillinges.

Item I give to Anne Edgecombe wief of Richard Edgecombe thirtie poundes.

Item I give to Jane Carie daughter of Sir George Carie knighte the somme of twentie poundes.

Item I give to Johane Dethicke, yf shee be my servaunte at the tyme of my deathe, tenne poundes over and above hir wages due unto hir at that tyme.

Item I give and bequeathe unto Grace my servaunte the somme of five poundes.

Item I give unto my servauntes Thomas Paddon, Edwarde Salter and Nicholas Squire to everie of them the somme of five marckes a peece over and above theire wages.[29]

And to all the residue of my servauntes I give the somme of fourtie shillinges a peece.

Item I give to my cosen Mr Standen the somme of fortie shillinges.

Item I give unto my cosynne Mrs Margarett Webb the somme of tenn poundes.

Item I give unto my verie speciall good freinde Sir George Carie of Cockington knighte my blacke talbott of goulde, my bracelette of goulde which I usuallie weare and likewise I give unto him the same guilte standinge cuppe with his cover that my good brother the late Master of the Rolles gave me in his last will and testament.[30]

And my will, full meaninge and intent is, and thereuppon doe charge my executors, that all my hangings, waynscott, beddes, tables, fourmes, chayers, stooles and other like implementes of howshold which shalbe in my howse in Highe Holborne at the tyme of my deathe shall not be soulde or disposed awaye, but shall remaine as heire loomes in the saide howse for the use and commoditie of such persons unto whome I have assured and conveighed or shall by this my will conveighe and assure the said howse, willinge and charginge my executors to take suche assurances as the lawe dothe requier of those unto whome I have conveyed the interest in the said howse that the same maye remaine from heire to heire soe longe as they shall contynewe.

Except all suche hanginges, howshold stuffe, implementes, goodes, furniture, utensilles and thinges whatsoever which nowe or moste usuallie have bene accustomed to be used or to remaine within those three chambers and a clossett and twoe wardrobes lyenge over the said three chambers, being parte and parcell of my saide howse in Highe Holborne aforesaid or in anie of them, which three chambers, clossett and twoe wardrobes I have latelie demised unto the said Sir Thomas Savage; all which hanginges, howshold stuffe, implementes, goodes, furniture, utensilles

27 These are Jane Allington's sons-in-law. For Sir John Stanhope, see Notes on People below.

28 For Dr William Gager, see Notes on People below.

29 This is presumably the Nicholas Squire who was housekeeper at Rocksavage until at least the late 1620s.

30 For Sir George Carie, see Notes on People below. He and Jane Allington had been executors of Sir William Cordell's will of 1581.

and thinges soe excepted I doe freelie and whollie give and bequeathe unto my nephewe Sir Thomas Savadge to his owne proper use and behooffe.[31]

Item I give and bequeathe all my estate, righte, title and interest of in and to all my messuage or tenement with the appurtenances in Brandford in the countie of Middlesex, and of in & to all other my landes, tenements, rentes, revercions, services and hereditamentes in Brandford and Thistleworthe and in either of them in the saide countie of Middlesex,[32] and alsoe the somme of one hundred poundes to make a cheine and alsoe one peece of golde of twentie nobles and alsoe all the rest and residue of my jewells, plate, redie monie and all other my goodes, cattells & chattells whatsoever in the [sic] my clossettes in Branford and Holborne or elsewhere wheresoever, unto the said Sir Thomas Savage my nephewe to his owne proper use and behooff and God in heaven blesse him with longe lief and happie fortune.

And concerninge the disposicion of such landes, tenementes and hereditamentes whereof I am seised of an estate in fee simple, I devise the same as followeth:

Imprimis I give, devise and bequeathe that all my messuadge or tenement called Melford howse scituate in Longe Melford in the countie of Suffolk and all landes, tenementes and hereditamentes <in the said countie of Suffolk> thereunto belonginge and all other my fee simple landes, tenementes and hereditamentes in the said countie of Suffolk, to the said Sir Thomas Savage my nephewe, to have and to houlde to the said Sir Thomas Savadge, his heires and assignes for ever.

And alsoe I give and bequeathe the moytye or one half of all that my capitall messuage in Highe Holborne and the moyetie or one half of all howses, buyldinges, landes, tenementes & hereditamentes thereunto belonginge or therewith lett or occupied, and the moyetie or one half of all other my fee simple landes within the realme of England, unto my daughter Savage for and duringe the terme of hir naturall lief. And after hir deceasse I give and bequeathe the same unto the said Sir Thomas Savage, his heires and assignes forever. And the other moyetie or one half of the saide capitall messuadge in Highe Holborne and of the saide howses, buyldinges, landes, tenementes and hereditamentes thereunto belonginge or therewith lett or occupied, and the other moyetie or one half of all other my fee simple landes within the realme of England, I give and bequeathe unto my nephewe Phillippe Stanhope (sonne and heire apparant of John Stanhope esquier and of Cordell his wief my late daughter) and to the heires and assignes of the said Phillippe Stanhope forever.

And for the executinge and performinge of this my last will and testament I doe hereby constitute, ordaine and appointe my said trustie and assured good frende Sir George Carie of Cockington in the countie of Devon knighte and my saide lovinge nephewe Sir Thomas Savadge knighte to be my executors of this my last will and testament willinge, charginge and requyringe my saide executors by the hartie good will and perfect frendshippe that hath bene allwayes betwene us to see this my testament to the uttermoste of their powers to be executed and performed in suche sorte

---

[31] Sir John Savage had property in the house at High Holborn when he died in 1615. Thomas and his mother were buried on the same day, and he would never have inherited the part of the High Holborn house left to her. However he bought the half left to his cousin Philip Stanhope (Doc. 8). This was not included in his inventory; the whole house may have been sold or Thomas may have given his part to one of this children.

[32] This is the house by Brentford Bridge used by Thomas Savage and later rented by William Noye and his son. Thisleworth is Isleworth, Middlesex.

as I have willed the same, and that my poore children after my deathe maye finde them both friendlie aidinge & assistinge unto them.[33]

And I doe constitute and ordaine my especiall good freindes my sonne Sir John Savage knighte and my sonne John Stanhope esquier the overseers of this my presente last will and testament.

And I doe expresselie lymytte and appointe, and my full intent will and meaninge is, that all my said debtes, legacies and bequestes before mencyoned (except only the jewells and howshold stuff before mencioned) shalbe levied, perceived, taken, collected & gathered owte of the rentes, revenewes, yssues and proffites of all my landes, tenementes and hereditamentes which, by any conveighances or assurances by me heretofore made, I have charged or appointed to be subject, liable or chargeable to for or with the payment thereof.

And yf the sayde legacies before mencyoned or any of them shall not be satisfied and payde accordinge to the true intent and meaninge hereof, then I doe will, lymytte and appointe that it shall and maye be lawfull to and for everie person and persons to whome I have given any of the legacies and bequestes before mencyoned within one yeere after the said legacie shall growe due to enter into all the said landes, tenementes and hereditamentes and to distreine for the same.

In witnes whereof to this my present last will and testament I have putte my hande and sealle the fiftenthe daie of Julie, Anno domini one thowsand sixe hundred and <three> twoe, and in the fower and fourtithe yeere of the reigne of our sovereigne ladie Elizabeth by the grace of God queene of England, Fraunce and Ireland, defender of the faithe etc. Jane Allington.

By [*per*] Warmarden John Ardern, George Cary sealed subscribed and pronounced by the within named Mrs Jane Allington for hir last will and testament the verie daye and yeere within specified in the presence of us whoe have hereunto subscribed our names, that is namely [*vizt*] B. Langley, William Newport, J. Leigh.

The will written above was proved at London before Master Henry Fletcher clerk, surrogate of the venerable man of God John Gibson knight doctor of laws, master keeper commisary of the prerogative court of Canterbury lawfully constituted on the seventh day of January in the year of our lord according to the computation of the church of England one thousand six hundred and three, by the oath of Thomas Ward, notary public, procurator of Sir George Carye and Sir Thomas Savage, knights, executors of this will to whom administration was granted of all and singular goods chattels and credits of the deceased, they having been first sworn well and faithfully to administer the holy gospel of God.

Doc. 5. Petition to Robert Lord Cecil from Philip Stanhope, 19 June 1604.[34]

[Marquess of Salisbury, Hatfield House: Petitions 1607]

Stanhope's petition conflicts with Jane Allington's will (Doc. 4), although it may possibly reflect arrangements she had made earlier in her life and later revoked. Doc. 7 shows that Savage got legal recognition of his claim just a few days after this petition was written, but the settlement in Doc. 8 suggests that Stanhope's claim may have had some justice to it.

33 Cockington is now part of Torquay, Devon.

34 For Cary, Stanhope and Cecil, see Notes on People below.

To the right honorable the Lord Cecill Baron of Essenden, principall secretary to his majestie and master of his highnes most honorable courte of wardes and liveries.

The humble peticion of Phillip Stanhope esquire, sonne and heire apparant of Sir John Stanhope knight and one of the coheires of Jane Allington widdowe deceased.

The peticoner humbly sheweth that the said Jane Allington did in her life tyme convey all her lands to certen feofees, till her will, and Sir William Cordell's will were performed; and then to Sir George Cary knight Lord Deputie of Ireland till he had levied 2 ?thousand [?M]markes. And that then the feofees should stand seyzed of one moytie of her landes during the lyves of Sir John Savage and Dame Mary his wife, one of the daughters and coheires of the said Jane Allington and after to the use of Sir Thomas Savage knight sonne and heire apparant of the said Sir John Savage and Dame Mary with divers remainders over to the rest of Sir John Savage his children, and for want of such issue to your orator Phillip Stanhope, leaving the fee simple in her the said Jane.

And that the feofees should stand seised of the other moytie of the lands to the use of this peticioner Phillip Stanhope untill he should accomplishe the age of 21tie yeares, and then to the said Phillip and the heires of his body with like remainders over, and that the feofees should then be accomptable for the issues and profitts they should receave during his nonage.

After the said Jane Allington made her will and dyed aboute Christmas last (this peticoner being then and yett under age). And by her will maketh Sir George Cary (now absent in Ireland) and the said Sir Thomas Savage her executors, and giveth her lands to them till debtes and legacies be paid and the said wills performed. In the absence of Sir George Cary the said Sir Thomas Savage hath entered uppon the mannor of Melford and other lands in Suffolke to the valew of £1000 by yeare as executor but now claymeth the inheritance of the whole <after the will performed> both from his mother and your honors said peticioner.

Whereupon this peticioners councell in Ester tearme last drew a bill in to his majesties most honorable courte of wards and lyveries, and when the same was ready to be put in to the courte the said Sir Thomas Savage moved that there might be a freindly conferrence by councell without suite in lawe which of all sides was agreed. And at a meeting of the two councellors for this peticioner, 2 for Sir John Savage, and 2 for the said Sir Thomas Savage, it was in Ester tearme last amongst other thinges then agreed that for the title of the landes in question all the said councell should this Trinity tearme agree of a case, and that if the said councell could not satisfie one the other touching the said parties theire rightes in lawe, then they should chose certen judges to determin thereof for them, and in the meane tyme nothing to be done.

Now this peticioner humbly sheweth that since this agreement and before this tearme the said Sir Thomas Savage being in possession but only as executor hath kepte a courte, taken attorneyment of tenantes and surrendors of coppy houlders and hath made feofmentes to straingers as well to defeate the wills for payement of debtes and legascies and to defraude his father and mother of theire estates for life, as also for ever to disinheritt this peticoner Phillipe Stanhope his majesties warde.

And is now in passing a recoverie to confirme this his practice, where of this peticoner having had but 2 daies knowledge hath labored what in him laie to staie theis proceedings, yett on fridaie last the said Sir Thomas Savage caused the said recovery to be suffered in the common place and prosecuteth the same with all vehemency which wilbe perfected uppon Wednesdaie next if staie be not made in the meane tyme. For which his undue proceedinges your honores said peticoner hath now preferred his bill into the said most honorable courte of wards and lyveries against the said Sir Thomas Savage and others, but cannot have any releese by injunction or otherwise by the ordinary course of that courte untill they have answered, before which tyme he will have perfected his recovery to the utter disinheritting of this peticoner being his majesties ward.

Therefore his humble suite is that your good Lordship would be pleased to write your honorable letters to the Lord Andersone and the rest of his majesties justices of the Common <pease> pleas to make present staie of the proceeding in the said recoverie untill further order shalbe taken therein by your Lordship in the said most honorable court of wardes and liveries. And your peticioner shall praie for your good Lordship in all health and honor long to continew.

[*on the reverse*]

19 June 1604

The humble peticion of Phillipp Stanhope his majesties ward.

Doc. 6. Letter from earl of Shrewsbury to Robert Lord Cecil c. 1604.[35]

[Marquess of Salisbury, Hatfield House, CP109/32]

This document is undated, but written before 20 August 1604. It is likely to have been written in June, shortly after Doc. 5, Stanhope's petition, and before Doc. 7, the recovery in the court of common pleas. Gilbert Talbot, earl of Shrewsbury was related to Thomas Savage through the Manners family – Shrewsbury's mother and Thomas's grandmother were sisters. The references to Nonsuch must relate to John and Elizabeth Lumley; the implication is that Savage was at Nonsuch and petitioned Shrewsbury there.

My Lord, I am so earnestly intreated by my cosen Sir Thomas Savage to move you for your favore unto him in not crossynge his course of conveyance, which is common (as he sayth) to all good subjectes, lawfully to take, as I may not refuse him therin. He tells me, that he heres of the wayes of cowrte that are sought agaynst him, beynge only to delay the busyness he goes aboute, untill this tearme be past, but he hopes confidently that you will meane him no wrong <neyther in respect of frend> for \any/ foes mediation <for him or> agaynst him, because you love justice above all, and in this he desyres nothynge else.

I was laden yesternight with commendacions to you from Nonsuche, and for theyr sakes their (besydes myne) I hope you will holde no harde or straynable hande over this gentleman, as he doth not say you doe, but knowes you may doe, yet assuredly hopes you will not doe. So untill anon that we meete, I will byd you good morrow, this thorsday morninge goynge to a committie.

Your most assured & affectionate

Gilbert Shrewsbury

[*on the reverse*]

To the right honorable and my very good lord the Lord Cecill

35 For the earl of Shrewsbury, see Notes on People below. There was a well-known and long standing quarrel between Earl Gilbert and the Stanhope family.

Doc. 7. Record of a recovery in the court of Common Pleas relating to Thomas Savage's inheritance of Melford, 30 June 1604. [CCALS: DCH/O/75]

This records Thomas Savage taking full legal ownership of Melford Hall and its associated property after his grandmother's death, and gives a measure of the lands he inherited directly from her. A common recovery was a 'fictitious legal action' which was used to break an entail and convey the entailed land. The recovery itself is in the Common Plea rolls at the TNA but adds nothing to our knowledge of the lands involved.

This indenture tripartite made the laste day of June in the seconde yeare of the raigne of our soveraigne lorde James by the grace of God kinge of Englande Fraunce and Ireland defendor of the faithe etc. and of his raigne of Scotlande the seaven and thirtith betwene Sir Fraunces Fane of Badsell in the county of Kente knighte, and Edwarde Savage of Bradley in the county of Southampton esquire on the first parte, William Holte of Graies Inne in the county of Middlesex esquier on the seconde parte, and Sir Thomas Savage of London knighte on the thirde parte.[36]

Whereas in Trynety terme now laste paste a common recovery was had by the saide Sir Frauncis Fane and Edwarde Savage againste the saide Willliam Holte in the kinges majesties courte of common pleas att Westminster of all that the mannor or lordeshipp of Melforde *alias* Longe Melforde in the county of Suffolk with all and singular the rightes members and appurtenances thereunto belonginge or there-with or with any parte therof used occupied or enjoyed, and also of all and singular the mannors, messuages, landes, tenementes, rentes, revercions, services and hereditaments with all and singular theire appurtenances whatsoever scituate, lyinge and beinge within the parishes, townes, feildes and hamlettes of Melforde *alias* Longe Melford, Shimplinge, Lavenham, Acton and Alpheton or elsewhere within the saide county of Suffolk, which sometymes were the inheritance of Sir William Cordell knighte deceased or the landes tenementes and hereditamentes of Jane Allingeton widdowe deceased or otherwise, and all and every parte and parcell therof. And the advowsons of the churches of Stansteed and Alpheton with theire appurtenances in the saide county of Suffolk.[37] By the names of the mannor of Melford *alias* Longe Melford with thappurtenances and of twenty and five messuages, twenty and fower toftes, twenty and five gardens, three hundred and threescore acres of lande, three hundred and ten acres of meadowe, three hundred and twenty acres acres [*sic*] of pasture, \two hundred & twenty acres of wood,/ two hundred acres of furse and bruerye, and two hundred acres of moore with thappurtenances in Melforde *alias* Longe Melforde, Shimplinge, Lavenham, Acton, and Alpheton, and also of the advowsons of the churches of Melforde *alias* Longe Melforde, Stansteede and Alpheton, as in and by the same recovery more att large itt dothe \and may/ appeare.

Now this indenture wittnessethe that the true intente and meaninge of the saide recovery and of all the parties to the same att the tyme of the saide recovery suffred was and is, that the same recovery and all and every other recovery and recoveries heeretofore suffered or heereafter to be suffered by the saide William Holte to the saide Sir FraunCis Fane knighte and Edwarde Savage esquire of the premisses before mencioned to be comprised in the saide recovery as aforesaide or any parte thereof, should be and shall be and inure, and be adjudged, deemed, construed and taken to be.

---

36 For Sir Francis Fane, Edward Savage, Thomas Brook and William Holt, see Notes on People below.

37 Stansted, Shimpling, Lavenham, Acton and Alpheton all border Long Melford, Suffolk.

And that the saide Sir Frauncis Fane and Edwarde Savage and theire heires should and shall stande and be of all and singular the saide premises, and of every parte and parcell thereof with theire and every of theire appurtenances, seised. To the only use and behoofe of the saide Sir Thomas Savage, his heires and assignes forever, and to no other use intente or purpose. In witnes whereof to one parte of theis presente indentures remaininge with the saide Sir Thomas Savage, the saide Sir Frauncis Fane, Edwarde Savage and William Holte have sett theire handes and seales.

To an other parte therof remaininge with the saide Sir Frauncis Fane and Edward Savage, the saide Sir Thomas Savage and William Holte have sett theire handes and seales, and to thother parte thereof remaininge with the saide William Holte, the saide Sir Thomas Savage, Sir Frauncis Fane and Edward Savage have sett theire handes and seales the day and yeare firste above written, 1604.

[Signature and seales of Thomas Savage and William Holte]

[*on the reverse*]

Sealed and delivered in the presence of John Arderne, Thomas Brooke, Edward Adilton.[38]

Doc. 8. Settlement between Sir Thomas Savage and Sir Philip Stanhope, 12 February 1606.[39] [CCALS: DCH/O/42]

Stanhope, in return for an unknown payment, confirms his cousin Savage's ownership of the Melford lands, and sells to him that part of part of the house in High Holborn which he, Stanhope, inherited from Jane Allington. Philip Stanhope settles for lands in Norfolk after the death of Dame Mary Savage, Thomas's mother. In the event she lived another twenty-nine years. However we do not know if any money changed hands, or how much, so it is impossible to be sure of the real effect of this agreement. Indentures like these are normally summarised when printed, because of the immensely repetitive nature of the text. We feel that publishing this document in full may be of assistance to other local historians faced with similar evidence. Only by transcribing the whole document can one be sure that no important matters of land holdings or lordship have been overlooked.

This indenture made the twelvth daie of February in the yeeare of the reigne of our soveraigne lord James by the grace of God kinge of England, Fraunce and Ireland, defendor of the faith etc. the third and of Scotland the nyne and thirtith, betweene Sir Thomas Savage of Long Melford in the county of Suffolk knight of the one parte and Sir Phillop Stanhop knight, sonne & heire apparant of Sir John Stanhop of Elveaston in the county of Darby knight of thother parte.

Witnesseth that the said Sir Phillip Stanhop for & in consideracion of a competent some of money, and for divers other causes and consideracions him movinge, dooth by theis presentes bargaine, sell, release & confirme unto the said Sir Thomas Savage and his heires, all \that/ moiety of the mannor of Melford *alias* Longe Melford in the county of Suffolk with all & singuler his rightes, members and appurtenances, and of the advowson of the parrish church of Melford, and of one

38 For Fane, Brook and Edward Savage, see Notes on People below.

39 For Stanhope, see Notes on People below.

chappell in Melford aforesaid called our Lady Chappell,[40] and of all other the landes, tenementes, rentes, revercions, services & hereditamentes in Melford, Lavenham, Akton *alias* Acton, Alpheton *alias* Alton, Shimplinge and Gleynsford in the said county of Suffolk, which were the inheritance of Jane Allington deceased, and of the advowsons of the parrish churches of Alpheton *alias* Alton and Stansted in the said county of Suffolk, and all his right, title, interest, clayme & demaund in and to all and singuler the premisses & every parte, parcell and member thereof, and all other mannors, landes, tenementes and hereditamentes in the said county of Suffolk, late the inheritance of the said Jane Allington.[41]

And the said Sir Phillipp dooth alsoe for the consideracion aforesaid bargaine, sell, release and confirme unto the said Sir Thomas Savage and his heires, all the moyety of one capitall messuage which lately was the inheritaunce of the said Jane, scituate, lyeinge and beinge in High Holborne in the county of Middlesex, and of all courtes, yardes, gardens, easementes, and backsides to the same belonginge or therewith used, occupied or enjoyed, together with all and all manner deeds, charters, wrytinges, munimentes and evidences concerninge the premisses only, or only any parte or parcell thereof .

To have and to hold the said moyety of the said manner of Melford and of all and singuler the premisses in Melford, Lavenham, Aketon *alias* Acton, Alpheton *alias* Alton, Shimplinge and Gleynsford and the said advowsons in the said county of Suffolk, and of the said capitall messuage in High Holborne aforesaid, and all and singuler the premises in the said counties of Suffolk and Middlesex, to the said Sir Thomas Savage his heires and assignes forever, to his & their only proper use and behoofe.

And the said Sir Phillip Stanhopp for him his heires, executores & administrators & every of them, dooth covenaunte & graunte to and with the said Sir Thomas Savage, his heires, executors, administrators & assignes & every of them, that he the said Sir Thomas Savage, his heires and assignes shall or may have, holde & enjoy all and singuler the premisses by theis presentes bargained, sold, releassed or confirmed or mencioned to be bargained, solde, released or confirmed by the said Sir Phillipp Stanhopp unto the said Sir Thomas Savage, discharged or otherwise upon reasonable request, saved harmeles of and from all and all manner charges, titles, interestes, incumbrances and demaundes had, made, doone or willingly or wittingly suffred by the said Sir Phillip Stanhop or any other person or persons lawfully clayminge in, by, from or under him the said Sir Phillip Stanhopp.

And the said Sir Phillip Stanhopp for him his heires, executors and administrators, and every of them, dooth covenaunte and graunte to and with the said Sir Thomas Savage his heires, executors, administrators & assignes, and every of them, that he the said Sir Phillip Stanhopp and his heires, & all & every person or persons that lawfully shall or may clayme, all or any of the premisses or any clayme, title, interest or demaund into or out of the same & a<r>ny part thereof by, from or under the said Sir Phillip Stanhop, shall & will at all tymes within the space of seaven yeeres next ensueinge the date hereof, when and as often as hee, they or any of them shalbe hereunto requested, at the proper costes & charges of the said Sir Thomas Savage or his heires, shall doe, suffer, acknowledge & execute all & every such acte & actes whatsoever for the more suer and better establishinge, settlinge & assuringe

40 The Holy Trinity church of Long Melford has a Lady Chapel attached to its east end, and is said to be the only parish church in England to have a chapel in this position. Entry to the chapel was gained by an internal door from the vestry, and by an external south door.

41 'Gleynsford' is presumably Glemsford, which also adjoins Melford.

of all & every the premisses to the said Sir Thomas Savage, his heires and assignes, as by the said Sir Thomas Savage, his heires or assignes shalbe reasonably devised & required.

Be it by fyne with proclamacions, recovery with double or single voucher or vouchers, or by all or any of them, or by such other waies or meanes & soe often as by the said Sir Thomas, his heires or assignes within the said space of seaven yeeres, he, they or any of them shalbe thereunto required, soe as the same conteyne noe other or further warranty but only against the said Sir Phillip Stanhopp and his heires. And soe as for the doeinge & executinge thereof, he nor they be inforced to travell from the place of their aboad at the tyme of such request made. And that all and every conveyance & assurance hereafter to be had and made or that sithence the last day of this present terme of St Hillary hath byn had, made, acknowledged, suffered, doone or executed of all or any the premisses, shalbe to the use of the said Sir Thomas Savage his heires & assignes forever.

In consideracion whereof as alsoe for a certeyne somme of money paid, the said Sir Thomas Savage dooth bargaine, sell, release & confirme unto the said Sir Phillipp Stanhopp & to his heires all those the mannors of Foxley, Bawdeswell & Sparham with all and singuler their & every of their rightes, members & appurtenances whatsoever in the county of Norfolk.[42] And the advowsons & patronages of the churches of Foxley, Bawdeswell and Sparham in the same county of Norfolk, and all those messuages, landes, tenementes, woods, underwoods, millnes, meadowes, moores, heath, furzes, commons, wast groundes, rentes, reversions, services, fraunchesies, commodities & hereditamentes to the same mannors or any of them belonginge or in any wise appurteyninge or reputed, taken or lett as any parte, parcell or member of the said landes, and all other the landes, tenementes & hereditaments of the said Sir Thomas Savage in possession, revercion, remainder or in use in the townes, parishes, hamblettes or feildes of Foxley, Bawdeswell and Sparham aforesaid or elswhere in the county of Norfolk, which were or were reputed to be the inheritaunce of the said Jane Allington, & the revercion & revercions of all that the full & entier moiety of the said mannors of Foxley, Bawdeswell & Sparham and of the advowsons & patronage of the churches of Foxley, Bawdeswell & Sparham and of all other the messuages, landes, tenementes and hereditamentes with all & singuler the premisses in the county of Norfolk, sometymes the inheritaunce of the said Jane Allington, imediately expectant upon the death of Dame Mary Savage mother of the said Sir Thomas; and all manner deeds, charters, mynimentes [*sic*] and evidences touchinge & concerninge only the premisses in the said county of Norfolk or only any parte or parcell thereof, and all the estate, right, title, interest, challenge and demaund of the said Sir Thomas Savage of, in, unto & out of the said mannors and premisses in the said county of Norfolk, which the said Sir Thomas Savage shall or can challenge by force and vertue of the last will and testament of the said Jane Allington deceased or by any other waies or meanes whatsoever.

To have and to hold the said mannors, messuages, landes, tenementes and hereditamentes, deedes, evidences and all and singuler the said premisses in the said county of Norfolk and the <the> revercion of the said moitie to the said Sir Phillip

42 These three parishes are small villages in mid-Norfolk, approximately halfway between Norwich and Fakenham. They were presumably part of the 'moyetie or one half of all other my fee simple landes within the realm of England' which Jane Allington's will left 'unto my daughter Savage for and duringe the terme of hir naturall lief. And after her deceasse I give and bequeathe the same unto the said Sir Thomas Savage, his heires and assignes for ever'.

Stanhopp, his heires and assignes to the sole & only use & behoofe of the said Sir Phillip Stanhopp his heires and assignes forever. And the said Sir Thomas Savage for him, his heires, executors and administrators & every of them, dooth covenaunte and graunt unto & with the said Sir Phillip Stanhopp, his heires, executors, administrators & assignes & every of them, that he the said Sir Thomas Savage at the tyme of the sealinge & deliverye \of/ theis presentes, is seised of the revercion of the said moiety as of fee & right to him and his heires of an absolute estate in fee simple imediately expectant after the death of the said Dame Mare Savage his mother without any condicion or lymitacion of use or uses to alter, change or determine the same. And that the said Sir Phillip Stanhopp, his heires and assignes shall or may at all tymes and from tyme to tyme to tyme [*sic*] forever hereafter have, holde and enjoye all the premisses in the said county of Norfolk for and duringe such estate and interest as he the said Sir Thomas Savage and Sir George Cary knight or either of them have, hath or had in the premisses without the lett, denyall, disturbance, interupcion or incumbrance of him the said Sir Thomas Savage or his heires or of the said Sir George Cary, his executors or administrators or any person or persons havinge or lawfully clayminge the same or any parte thereof, in, by, from or under them or either of them, their or either of their title or estate, or by their or any of their assent, consent, meanes or procurement.

And the said Sir Thomas Savage dooth further covenante, promise & graunte for him, his heires, executors & administrators, and every of them, to and with the said Sir Phillip Stanhopp, his heires, executors, administrators & assignes, and every of them, by theis presentes, that immediately from and after the death of the said Dame Mary Savage, he the said Sir Phillipp Stanhopp, his heires and assignes shall or may at all tymes and from tyme to tyme forever then after, lawfully have, holde, occupie and enjoye that one moiety of all the premisses in the said county of Norfolke, without the lett, denyall, disturbance, interuption, eviccion, expulsion or incumbrance of him the said Sir Thomas Savage & his heires or of the said Sir George Cary his executors or administrators and without the lawfull lett, denyall, disturbance, interupcion, eviccon or incumbrance of any other person or persons havinge or lawfully clayminge all or any of the premisses in the said county of Norfolk, from by or under the said Sir Thomas Savage, Sir George Cary or Dame Mary Savage or any of them or by their or any of their assent, consent, meanes or procurement.[43]

And the said Sir Thomas Savage for him, his heires, executors and administrators dooth covenante & graunt to and with the said Sir Phillipp Stanhopp, his \heires/, executors & assignes, that if after the death of the said Dame Mary Savage the said moyety of the premisses in the said county of Norfolk or any parte or parcell thereof shall happen to be evicted from the said Sir Phillip Stanhopp, his heires or assignes by [?]accion or lawfull entry of any person or persons clayminge by, from or under the said Sir Thomas Savage or the said Dame Mary or the heires of them or either of them, that then the said Sir Thomas Savage & his heires shall & will within fower monethes after notice given to him or them, of such eviccon & of the value of the land soe evicted, convey and assure or cause to be conveyed & assured to the said Sir Phillip Stanhop, his heires & assignes at the proper costes & charges of the said Sir Thomas or his heires, or the landes, tenementes or hereditamentes of a good & perfect estate in fee simple of as great yeerely value as the said landes, tenementes or hereditamentes soe evicted shall amount unto, discharged, or from tyme to tyme

43 Sir George Carie and Sir Thomas Savage were executors of Jane Allington's will.

to be saved & kepte harmeles of and from all interestes, titles and incumbrances whatsoever.

And the said Sir Thomas Savage, for him, his heires, executors & administrators, dooth further covenaunte and graunte to and with the said Sir Philip Stanhopp, his heires and assignes that he the said Sir Thomas Savage and his heires, & all & every person & persons that lawfully shall or may clayme all or any of the premisses or make any clayme, title, interest or demaunde into or out of the saide bargained premisses in the said county of Norfolk, or any parte thereof, by, from or under the said Sir Thomas Savage, shall & will at all tymes & from tyme to tyme within the space of seaven yeeres next ensueinge the date hereof, and within the space of three yeeres next after the death of the said Dame Mary Savage, when and as often as he, they or any of them shalbe thereunto requested at the proper costes & charges of the said Sir Phillip & his heires, doe suffer, acknowledge and execute all and every such act & actes whatsoever for the more suer & better establishinge, settlinge & assuringe of the said mannors, landes, tenementes & hereditamentes in the said county of Norfolk, and of the said moiety of the said premisses in the said county of Norfolk, to the said Sir Phillipp Stanhop, his heires & assignes to the sole & only use & behoofe of the said Sir Phillip, his heires & assignes, or to such person or persons as he the said Sir Phillipp, his heires or assignes shall thereunto appoint or assigne, or by his or their learned counsell in the lawe be reasonably advised, devised & required, be it by fyne with proclamacion, recovery with single or double voucher or vouchers, or by all or any of these or by such other waies or meanes, and soe often as by the said Sir Phillipp Stanhop, his heires or assignes, or any of them, within the said space of seaven yeeres & three yeeres, hee, they or any of them shalbe thereunto required, soe as the same conteyne noe other or further warranty then against the said Sir Thomas Savage & his heires. And so as for the doeinge & executinge of the same, hee nor they bee inforced to travell from his or their place of aboad at the tyme of such request made. And that all & every such conveyance & assurance hereafter to be had or made, or that sithence the first daie of this present terme of St Hillary hath beene had, made, acknowledged, suffred or executed of the said moitie or any part or parcell thereof, shalbe to the use of the said Sir Phillip Stanhop his heires and assignes forever.

And the said Sir Philip Stanhop for him and his heires dooth further covenaunte & graunt to and with the said Sir Thomas Savage & his heires, that he the said Sir Phillip or his heires shall or will before the feast of Pentecost next ensueinge the date hereof, at the costes & charges of the said Sir Thomas Savage or his heires, convey and assure to the said Sir Thomas Savage & his heires by such reasonable assurance as by the said Sir Thomas or his heires shalbe devised & required, the moyty or one halfe of all such landes, tenementes and hereditaments \in the said county of Suffolk/ as at the tyme of the death of the said Jane Allington were holden by coppie of court rowle, and whereof the said Jane Allington was at the tyme of her death seised of any estate of inheritance \by coppie of court rolle/, savinge alwaies that for the conveyinge & assuring of the said coppie holde landes the said Sir Phillip shall not be compelled to travell further then his owne place of dwellinge.

And the said Sir Phillip Stanhop for him & his heires dooth further covenaunte and graunte to and with the said Sir Thomas Savage and his heires, that he the said Sir Thomas and his heires shall or may lawfully, peacably & quietly have, holde & enjoye all and singuler the said landes, tenementes & hereditamentes holden by coppie of court rowle against him the said Sir Phillipp Stanhop & his heires and the severall lordes of the mannors of whome the said landes, tenementes and hereditamentes are holden by coppie of court rowle and all and every other person

& persons cleered & discharged of all titles, interestes and incumbrances, any acte or thinge whatsoever by the said Sir Phillip had, doone or willingly suffered or hereafter to be had, doone or willingly suffered by him the said Sir Phillipp not withstandinge one lease made by the said Sir Phillipp of certeyne coppiehold landes, parcell of the mannor of Laneham, to one Anthony Smyth by the lycence of the lord of the said mannor for the terme of seaven yeers only excepted & forprised.[44]

In witnes whereof the parties above named to the present indentures interchangeably have sett their handes and seales the day and yeeres [*sic*] first above written. 1605.

Examined in the presence of me, Mathew Carew knight, Master in Chancery [Latin]

[*on the reverse*]
Written on the dorse of a close roll of the King's chancery, 14 February of the year underwritten, by John Lewes; Stanhope Knight and Savage Knight. [Latin]

Indenture between Sir Thomas Savage and Sir Phillip Stanhop concerninge Mrs Allington's lands, 12 February, 3 James.

Sealed and delivered in the presence of George Carey, Willliam Noye.

Doc. 9. Thomas Savage's agreement with his father about furniture at Rocksavage, 30 April 1607. [CCALS: DCH/M/34/81r]

We do not know why this agreement was made, but its reverse was used later for Doc. 14, Thomas's agreement with his mother about the furniture she could have from Rocksavage after Sir John Savage's death. The plate inherited from Sir William Cordell was not specified in his will, but Jane Allington received the residue of Sir William's estate and presumably gave them to her daughter and son-in-law.

To all men to whome these presentes shall come, I Sir John Savage of Rocksavage in the county of Chester, knight, send greetings. Knowe yea, that for the love I beare unto Sir Thomas Savage knight, my sonne, & unto John Savage my graundchild, sonne of the said Sir Thomas, and in [*?*]recompence of kyndnesses done me by my said sonne, I doe by these presents ded, geve, graunte, bargayn, assure & confirme unto my said sonne these parcelles of goodes and howshold stuff hereafter mencioned, nowe being in my howse at Rocksavage, namely [*vizt*] all the wainscott in the howse be the same fixed or not, item all the tables and court cubbords in the howse, item all the bedsteedes in the hows havinge testers of wainscott, and all bedsteedes for servinge men having no covers at all, item one sute of hanginges used in the great dyning chamber, item the hangings, bedd and all other furniture used in one chamber within the said howse, called Derby chamber, item all my brewing vesselles and leades in the bruehowse and one peece of plate namely [*vizt.*] a standing cupp with a cover fashion like a peare.

To have and to hold to my said sonne Sir Thomas Savage, his heires and assignes forever, provided that my said sonne shall permitt them to remayne and to be used as nowe they are during my lief. And further knowe yee that I have in like manner geven, graunted, assured and confirmed and by these presentes doe geve, graunt,

44 There is a Langham in Suffolk, north-east of Bury St Edmunds, but this is likely to be Lavenham, which is adjacent to Long Melford; the manor of Melford extended into the parish of Lavenham.

assure and confirmme unto my said grandchild John Savage these parcelles of my plate following, which sometyme were the plate of Sir William Cordell knight: namely [*vizt.*] one great bason & ewer embosted, two flaggons or [*?*] Indy pottes & three bowles embosted with a cover. To have and to hould to my said grandchilde, his heires and assignes forever, provided ever that my said graundchild shall after my decease permitt Dame Mary nowe my wief to have the use of the said parcelles of plate during her lief, upon securitie for delivery of them back at her deathe to my said grandchilde or his heires.[45]

And also that after the decease of my said wife, my said graundchild shall permitt my said sonne Sir Thomas to have the use of them during his lief upon like securitie for delivery of them back at his deathe. In witness whereof I have hereunto put my hand & seale the last daie of Aprill in the yeare of the raigne of our soveraigne lord king James by the grace of God over England Fraunce and Ireland the fifte and over Scotland the fortithe etc., 1607.

Doc. 10. Agreement between Thomas Savage and Elizabeth Lumley about her finances and debts, 22 May 1610. [CCALS: DCH/O/13]

This agreement, made shortly after the death of John, Lord Lumley, is the last in this series relating to Thomas as he came into his various properties and lands. Sir James Croft and Thomas Lord Darcy were executors of Lord Lumley's will. Although Elizabeth Lumley's surviving will is dated November 1616, it is possible that Thomas Lord Darcy and Sir Thomas Savage had already been appointed her executors.

This indenture made the twoe and twentith daye of May and in the yeere of the raigne of our most graciouse soveraigne lord James, by the grace of God of England, Scotland, Fraunce and Ireland, defendor of the faithe etc., that is to say of England, Fraunce and Ireland the eight and of Scotland the three and fortith, betweene the right honorable Elizabeth Lady Lumley, late wiefe of the right honorable John Lumley knight, Lord Lumley, deceased of thone parte and Sir Thomas Savage knight of thother parte.

Whereas the said Sir Thomas Savage together with the said Elizabeth Lady Lumley and for her debt standes bound to diverse persons in sondry great sommes of money, and likewise by himself alone standes bound to diverse other persons in other great sommes of money for mony which was procuered for her the said Elizabeth Lady Lumley and ymployed to her use, and whereas alsoe the said Elizabeth Lady Lumley is indebted in diverse great sommes of money to the said Sir Thomas Savage, and whereas the said Elizabeth Lady Lumley is desirous that the said Sir Thomas Savage should [*damaged*] and kept harmelesse of and from all the said severall obligacions or ells be satisfied and recompenced of and for all such losses, damages and sommes of money as he shall sustayne, beare and paie by reason or meanes of the said obligacions or of any of them, and be satisfied and paid of all such debtes as are or shalbe owinge unto him by the said Elizabeth Lady Lumley.

This indenture witnesseth that the said Elizabeth Lady Lumley aswell for the consideracion aforesaid, as in consideracion of other competent sommes of money paide unto her by the said Sir Thomas Savage and other consideracions, hath given,

[45] John Savage's grandmother lived until 1635, so presumably held this plate until her death, but it could well have been amongst the plate and jewels stolen from her in 1618 (see Introduction above, p. xxxi).

graunted, bargayned and sould, and by theise presentes doth give, grant, bargayne and sell, unto the said Sir Thomas Savage, his executors, administrators and assignes all her hanginges, beddinge, furniture of howse and howsehould stuffe and all other her goodes and chattelles, whatsoever and wheresoever in the realme of England (all her money and her wearinge apparrell and all her plate and jewells, the bedd wherin she usually lieth with the furniture therunto belonginge, her coach and coach mares, and all her horses and gueldinges only excepted and foreprysed).

To have and to houlde the same to the said Sir Thomas Savage, his executors, administrators and assignes, to his and theire owne proper use and behoofe without any condicion, and without any accompte or other thinge to be therfore yielded, rendered or payd to her the said Elizabeth Lady Lumley, her executors, administrators and assignes or any of them for the same or any part thereof.

And this indenture further witnesseth that the said Elizabeth Lady Lumley in consideracion of the somme of twoe thowsand and seaven hundred poundes in hand paid to her by the said Sir Thomas Savage, and in recompense of the paynes and travaill which the said Sir Thomas Savage hath taken and is still likelie to take for her the said Elizabeth Lady Lumley and on her behalfe, hath graunted, bargayned and sould and by theise presentes doth graunte, bargaine and sell unto the said Sir Thomas Savage all those lordshipps, mannors, hundreds, rectories, messuages, forestes, parkes, chases, landes, tenementes, tithes, liberties, franchises and hereditamentes whatsoever with theire and everye of theire rightes, members and appurtenances scituate, lyeinge and beinge, comminge, happeninge, renewinge or growinge in the counties of Sussex, Surrey, Yorke, Durham and Sadbergh or any of them, or ells where wheresoever, which late were any parte of the inheritance of the said John Lumley knight, Lord Lumley, deceased and were conveyed and assuered to or for the use of the said Elizabeth Lady Lumley for her liefe or for the jointure of the said Elizabeth Lady Lumley or in liewe or recompence of her dower, together with the revercion and revercions of the same premysses and every part therof.

To have and to houlde all and singuler the said lordshipps, mannors, hundredes, rectoryes, mesuages, forestes, parkes, chases, landes, tenementes, tithes, liberties, francheses and hereditamentes together with the revercion and revercions thereof and of every parte thereof, to the said Sir Thomas Savage, his executors, administrators and assignes from the feast of the annunciacion of the blessed Virgine Marye last past before the date of theise presentes, for and duringe the terme of forty yeeres from thence next ensuinge fully to be compleate and ended yf she the said Elizabethe Lady Lumley shall lyve so longe.

Yeildinge and payeing therfore yeerelie duringe the said terme to the said Elizabeth Lady Lumley the somme of three hundred powndes of lawfull mony of England uppon the feastes of St Michaell the Archangell and the annunciacion of the blessed Virgine Mary, at the now dwellinge house of the said Elizabeth Lady Lumley scituate neere Tower Hill in the parrishe of St Olave *alias* St Olaff in Hart Street in the cyttie of London, by equall porcions to be paide.

And whereas Thomas Lord Darcye and Sir James Crofte knight by vertue of a conveyaunce or assuerance hertofore made by the said John Lumley knight, Lord Lumley, doe stand possessed of and in the castle and mannor of Lumley in the countye Pallatine of Durham and of and in the castle and mannor of Wytton, otherwise called Wytton uppon the water, in the countie of Northumberland and of and in diverse other mannors, messuages, landes, tenementes and hereditamentes which sometymes were the inheritance of the said John Lumley knight, Lord Lumley, and were not assuered or convayed for the joynture of the said Elizabeth Lady Lumley nor in liewe or recompence of her dower, and of and in the revercion of the lordshipps, mannors, hundredes, rectoryes, mesuages, forestes, parkes, chases, landes, tithes, liberties, francheses and hereditaments the which were convayed [*damaged*] the use of her the said Elizabeth Lady Lumley for her lief or for her jointure for [*damaged*] yeeres unexpired, uppon trust neverthelesse that the same should be and remayne to the use of the said Elizabeth Lady Lumley and that the rents, yssues, revenewes and proffittes therof should be ymployed and bestowed in such sorte as she the said Elizabeth Lady Lumley should from time to time lymitt and appoynt.[46]

Nowe this indenture witnesseth that the said Elizabeth Lady Lumley hath limitted and appoynted, and by theise presentes doth lymitt and appoynte, that from henceforth the said Sir Thomas Savage, his executors and administrators shall and may from tyme to tyme take, retayne and keepe all the rentes, yssues, revenues and proffittes of all the premysses conveyed or assured unto them the said Thomas Lord Darcy and Sir James Croftes as aforesaid, and converte and ymploye the same to his and theire owne use, proffitt and behooffe without anye accompte to be therfore rendered to the sayde Elizabeth Lady Lumley, her executors, administrators or assignes or any of them.

And that the sayde Thomas Lord Darcye and Sir James Croft, their executors, administrators or assignes shall convey and assure the same premysses unto the said Sir Thomas Savage, his executors or administrators when they or anye of them shall be therunto requyred by the said Sir Thomas Savage, his executors, administrators or anye of them.

In witnes whereof the parties abovesaid to theise presentes interchangeablye have sett theire hands and seales geoven the daye and yeere first above written.
[Signed T. Savage and sealed]
[*on the reverse*]
Sealed and delivered in the presence of William Noye, Christopher Hopper[47]

Doc. 11. Grant to William Noye by Thomas Savage, 15 September 1610.
[TNA: SP 14/57/59]

The first surviving record of a link between Sir Thomas Savage and William Noye dates from 1605. This document appears to be a legal retainer. Noye seems to have acted for Sir Thomas Savage as a legal adviser and to some extent as steward, while also being MP for Grampound in Cornwall from 1603.

To all christian people to whome this present writeing shall come, Sir Thomas Savage knight sendeth greetinge in our lord God everlasting. Knowe yee that I the said Sir Thomas Savage for me & my heires doe by theis presentes give and graunte unto William Noye of Lincolnes Inn gent, for his councell hereafter to be given to me and my heires, one annuetie or yearelie rent of fyve powndes of lawfull mony of England yssueinge out of my mannor of Melforde and out of all other my landes, tenementes and hereditamentes in Melforde in the countie of Suffolk, to be paid yearelie on the Mundaye next after the feaste of the Holie Trinetie.[48] To have and percyve [*sic*] the same to the said William dureing the terme of his naturall life. And

46 Lumley is south-east of Chester-le-Street in Co. Durham; Whitton is immediately south of Rothbury in Northumberland.
47 For Sir James Croftes, William Noye, Christopher Hopper, see Notes on People below.
48 Long Melford parish church is dedicated to the Holy Trinity, and its feast day was often used for dating annual payments.

if the said annuetie or yearelie rent or any part thereof happen to be behinde & unpaide, at any daye wherein the same ought to be paid, that then and so often as the same shall be so unpaid, it shall and may be lawfull for the said William into the said mannor & premisses to enter, and there to distrayne for the same. And to retayne the distresse untill he shall be, of the said rent and the arrerages thereof, if any shall be, satisfied & paid.

In witnes whereof I have hereunto sett my hand and seale, dated the fifteenth daie of September in the yeare of the raigne of our soveraigne Lord James by the grace of God kinge of England, Scotland, Fraunce and Ireland, defendor of the faith etc., that is to saie of England, Fraunce & Ireland the eight & of Scotland the fower and fortith, 1610.

Doc. 12. Elizabeth Lady Lumley to Robert Cecil, earl of Salisbury, 9 June 1611.[49] [TNA: SP 14/64/21]

This letter is included partly as evidence that Thomas and Elizabeth Savage moved in the highest social circles, and partly to show the way in which the network of social relationships and obligations was maintained.[50] *The letter tells us that the writer's brother Thomas Lord Darcy was in Italy in 1611; during Elizabeth's reign Italy had been forbidden to English travellers and barriers were only removed in 1604; Darcy was among a small group to have travelled in Italy at this period.*

My lord I have lately reseved letters out of Italy from my lord my brother in which he remembers his love & sarves to your lord & hath sent unto your lord a marble table with a head of Fardenando late duke of Tusken, & althowgh he sayth it be not worthy the presenting to your lord, yet he presumeth of your noble acseptans, it coming from one that supplyeth the meannes thar of, with his affecsinat well wyshing to your lord, <being> who can never forget the many favors that himself & his frends have reseved from your lord. Sir Thomas Savage hath ordar from my brother to see them delyvered whar your lord please to apoynt them. I wyll not troble your lord ani further that am fast bound unto you.[51]
Elizabeth Lumley
this present Sunday

Doc. 13. Licence for Thomas Savage to empark, 6 May 1612. [HPP]

In Cheshire Thomas had access to the hunting parks of Halton and Rocksavage, in addition to his rights in relation to the Forest of Delamere. In Melford the 'old' park had been enclosed at some point in the 1580s; it was in the north of the parish, a considerable way from Melford Hall. This licence gave Thomas and Elizabeth permission to empark an area closer to their house.

A perpetuity granted to Sir Thomas Savage knight and the Lady Elizabeth his wife, [*signed*] Cartwright. For Melford Park [*in later hand*].

---

49 The archivist at Hatfield House has reported to the authors that such a table has not survived in the Salisbury collections.
50 Lady Lumley had sent other gifts to the earl after her husband's death in 1609. The Hatfield accounts mention a picture of the 'queene mother of Scotland' and 'pictures which was given . . . as a legacye': Marquess of Salisbury, Hatfield House, Accounts 160/1.
51 For Ferdinand, duke of Tuscany, see Notes on People below.

James by the grace of God king of England, Scotland, France and Ireland, defender of the faith etc. To all to whom the present letters come, greetings. Since our beloved and faithful subject Thomas Savage knight and Lady Elizabeth his wife, hold to themselves and to the heires of the said Thomas Savage certain lands, meadows, pastures and woods containing in total by estimation three hundred and forty acres or thereabouts, now enclosed by pales, ditches and hedges [*paleis fossatis et sepibus*] lying in Melford and Acton or either of them in our county of Suffolk, near the mansion house of the same Thomas in Melford in the aforesaid county of Suffolk, and being parcel of the desmesne lands of the same Thomas Savage.

And since the same Thomas humbly prayed that we deem it worthy to grant our royal and free licence and legal power and authority to the same Thomas Savage knight his heirs and assigns, the same Thomas Savage knight and Lady Elizabeth his wife and the heirs and assigns of the said Thomas Savage knight are empowered to hold the aforesaid lands, meadows, pastures and woods, enclosed as mentioned before, from henceforth in perpetuity, enclosed and gathered in severalty, to make of it a park for game and to keep and maintain wild animals and deer [*pro feris et damis*] in the same park from time to time. Be it known therefore that, graciously approving the humble petition of the aforesaid Thomas Savage knight, from our special grace and from certain knowledge and pure intent, and by these presents for us, our heirs and successors, we grant free licence and legal power and authority to the aforesaid Thomas Savage knight and Dame Elizabeth his wife and the heirs and assigns of the said Thomas, that they the aforesaid Thomas Savage knight and Lady Elizabeth and the heirs of the aforesaid Thomas may hold and enjoy the lands, meadows, pastures and woods with their appurtenances. And they are empowered to hold and enjoy any part or parcel of the same, not exceeding in total the number of four hundred acres, enclosed as previously said with pales, ditches and hedges and restored to severalty, and hereafter to make one whole park of these premises there to pasture, maintain and conserve deer and other beasts.

And this without the exercise of ploughing or agriculture called husbandry [*et hoc absque exercicio aratri sive agriculture vocat* husbandry] while the same lands, meadows, pastures or woods or any of them be not within the metes of our forest, to have use and exercise to the aforesaid Thomas Savage knight and lady Elizabeth his wife and the heirs and assigns of the same Thomas Savage in the form foresaid and for the use aforesaid, any statute, act, ordnance or provision to the contrary notwithstanding. And further we wish more fully by our special grace, certain knowledge and pure intent, and by these presents for us our heirs and successors we give and grant free licence and legal power and authority to the aforesaid Thomas Savage knight and lady Elizabeth and the heirs and assigns of the said Thomas, that the aforesaid lands, meadows, pastures and woods with their appurtenances, and whatever or any part of it, enclosed as aforesaid, be henceforth and in posterity a free and legitimate park to pasture, maintain and conserve deer and other beasts there, any statute, act, ordnance or provision to the contrary notwithstanding, and further we wish of our ample and special grace and from certain knowledge and pure intent and by these presents for us, our heirs and successors, we grant to the same Thomas Savage knight and lady Elizabeth and the heirs and assigns of the same Thomas Savage that the aforesaid Thomas Savage knight and lady Elizabeth and the heirs and assigns of the same Thomas may have free warren [*liberam warrennam*] in all the aforesaid lands, meadows, pastures and woods enclosed as aforesaid, and whatever part or parcel of it, any statute, act, ordnance or provision to the contrary notwithstanding.

Therefore we wish, and by these presents for us, our heirs and successors firmly order, that the holdings [*tenementa*] aforesaid, enclosed as aforesaid, from henceforth in perpetuity be a park and free warren. And that the aforesaid Thomas Savage knight and lady Elizabeth and the heirs and assigns of the said Thomas shall have and hold freely, lawfully, well and quietly the aforesaid lands, meadows pastures and woods with their appurtenances, enclosed as aforesaid, and whatever parts of them, as a free and legitimate park and free warren in the same lands; they can have, hold, use and enjoy the aforesaid lands freely, legally, well and quietly in perpetuity, together with all and singular liberties, privileges and commodities which pertain to a free park and free warren; while however all and singular lands, meadows, pastures and woods, or any parcel of them, are not within the metes and bounds of our forests.

We wish moreover and command that no one may enter or presume to enter the park and warren aforesaid or any part of it, to drive, hunt and hawk deer or wild beasts [*ferras*], there to take, chase or disturb or otherwise take anything which belongs or ought to belong to a park or warren of this kind, nor make or do anything in the same park or warren which is or might be to the loss, damage or prejudice of the park or warren aforesaid, or the liberties of the same park or warren, or the wish and licence of the aforesaid Thomas Savage knight and Dame Elizabeth and the heirs and assigns of the same Thomas Savage, under penalty in statute and ordnance of this our kingdom of England for conserving parks and free warrens, under penalty of forfeiting ten pounds.

However providing always that if any person or persons have or ought to have any common pasture in the aforesaid lands, meadows, pastures, woods, enclosed as aforesaid, or in any part of them, that then these our letters patent with respect to the aforesaid lands, meadows, pastures, woods and other premises in which any other person or persons has or claims to have any common pasture, shall be wholly annulled and of no effect in law, and for the rest shall nevertheless stand good and sufficient in law, anything in these presents to the contrary notwithstanding – because express mention is very little made in these presents of the true annual value, or of the certainty of those things mentioned before, or any of them, or of other gifts or grants by us or by any of our progenitors to the aforesaid Thomas Savage knight and Dame Elizabeth his wife. By any statute, act, ordnance, provision, proclamation or restriction to the contrary before this made, or any other thing, cause or matter notwithstanding. In testimony of which we make these our letters patent in my presence at Westminster the sixth day of May in the tenth year of our reign of England, France and Ireland and of Scotland forty five.
By a writ of the privy seal, etc.

Doc. 14. Agreement between Thomas Savage and his mother following his father's death, 15 September 1615. [CCALS: DCH/M/34/81v]

Written on the reverse of Doc. 9. This is included as additional evidence of the re-arrangements made after Sir John Savage's death. By the time of her own death in 1635 Dame Mary Savage was living at Bostock in Cheshire; she had moved there by 1618 when she wrote her will, so she may have lived at Bostock for most of her widowhood.

15 September 1615
Memorandum that it was this daie fullie agreed and concluded upon betwene the Lady Savage on the one parte and Sir Thomas Savage knight and baronett her sonne on the other part, in fourme followinge:

Imprimis it is agreed, and the said Sir Thomas hath freelye geven to the said ladie his mother, all such goodes and howsholde stuffe as were remayneinge at his fathers deathe in the two lower stoore howses, and in the clossett at the staire heade, her ladyship to take all or what she pleaseth there. In liewe whereof her ladyship was fullie agreed and promised to afford and contynewe her motherlye love to her said sonne, and not by sutes in lawe to impeache any leases made by Sir John Savage her late husbande as the said Sir John desired in his last will, but tak such composicion as her tennth by agrement will geve her.

Item it was then also agreed and the said Ladie did freelye and absolutely geve, graunt, release and surrender to the said Sir Thomas all such landes and tenementes in or neere Melford, for which landes the same Sir Thomas paid to the said Sir John his father in his lief tyme the yerelye rent of thirtie poundes.[52] And the said ladie agreed to assure the same to the said Sir Thomas and his heires as he shoulde pleas; in liewe of which the said Sir Thomas did freelie geve to the said ladie the hangings, beddinge and furniture in her chamber at Rocksavage and two paire of pillabeares wrought and two cusshion clothes sutable to the same, and all his parte of the peeces of lynon clothe at Rocksavage not cutt out or shaped, and all the brasse and pewter in the kitchin there. Witnesses to this agrement wee whose names are hereunto subscribed.

Thomas Mallory Deane of Chester and executor of the last will and testament of Sir John Savage knight and baronett, Thomas Manwaringe, Robert Gwynn, John Glegge, Thomas Brooke.[53]

Doc. 15. Letters from James Howell at Melford Hall. [James Howell, *Epistolae Ho-Elianae. Familiar Letters Domestic and Forren*, 2nd edition, 1650, section II, pp. 8–9]

Many of James Howell's letters appear to have been written with a view to eventual publication, and the Cambridge History *suggests that perhaps they were written only for publication, never sent, and that some were written long after the dates given. Howell's* Familiar Letters *went through many editions; the editors took these from the second edition of 1650.*[54] *These letters are dated 1621 in this edition, but 1619 in later editions. A letter Howell wrote to his father about his coming visit to Melford is dated March 1621 in the second edition, but it mentions the recent death of Queen Anne of Denmark; she died in 1619. Howell's other correspondence shows that he was abroad from 1618 until early 1621. It is likely that the letter to his father is a confection which Howell wrote or revised later, and that he muddled events in two separate years.*

1. To Dan Caldwall, Esq. from the Lord Savage's house in Long Melford[55]
My dear Dan,
Though considering my former condition of life I may now be called a

52 These lands were very likely to have been given to Sir John Savage by his mother-in-law, Jane Allington. They are not given in her will, so may have been gifted earlier in her life.

53 For Thomas Manwaringe, Thomas Mallory, John Glegge, Robert Gwynn, Thomas Brooke see Notes on People below.

54 *The Cambridge History of English and American Literature*, 7, *Cavalier and Puritan* (1907–21). chs 11 and 12. J. Howell, *Epistolae Ho-Elianae. Familiar Letters Domestic and Forren, divided into sundry sections, partly historicall, politicall, philosophicall, upon emergent occasions*: by J.H. Esq., 2nd edn, . . . with an addition of a third volume of new letters (London, 1650).

55 For Daniel Caldwell, see Notes on People below.

countreyman, yet you cannot call me a rustic (as you would imply in your letter) as long as I live in so civill and noble a family, as long as I lodg in so vertuous and regular a house as any I beleeve in the land, both for oeconomicall government and the choice company, for I never saw yet such a dainty race of children in all my life together. I never saw yet such an orderly and punctuall attendance of servants, nor a great house so neatly kept; here one shall see nor dog, nor cat, nor cage to cause any nastines within the body of the house; the kitchin and gutters and other offices of noise and drudgery are at the fag end; ther's a back gate for beggars and the meaner sort of swains to come in at. The stables butt upon the park, which for a chearfull rising ground, for groves and browsings for the deer, for rivulets of water may compare with any for its bignes in the whole land; it is opposite to the front of the great house, whence from the gallery one may see much of the game when they are a hunting.[56]

Now for the gardning and costly choice flowers, for ponds, for stately large walks green and gravelly, for orchards and choice fruits of all sorts, ther are few the like in England. Here you have your *bon cristien pear* and *bergamott* in perfection, your *muscadell grapes* in such plenty that ther are som bottles of wine sent every year to the king. And one Mr Daniel, a worthy gentleman hard by, who hath bin long abroad, makes good store in his vintage.[57] Truly this house of Long Melford, though it be not so great, yet it is so wel compacted and contrived with such dainty conveniences every way, that if you saw the landskip of it, you would be mightily taken with it, and it would serve for a choice pattern to build and contrive a house by. If you come this summer to your mannor of Sheriff in Essex, you will not be far off hence; if your occasions will permit, it will be worth your while coming hither, though it be only to see him, who would think it a short journey to go from Saint Davids head to Dover cliffs to see and serve you, were ther occasion: if you would know who the same is, 'tis

Your J. H.

20 March 1621

2. To Robert Brown Esqr

[*The first part of this letter relates to business in Europe*]

. . . Dear Sir, I pray make me happy still with your letters, it is a mightie pleasure for us countrey folks to hear how matters passe in London and abroad; you know I have not the opportunity to correspond with you in like kind, but may happily here after when the tables are turn'd, when I am in London, and you in the west. Wheras you are desirous to hear how it fares with me, I pray know that I live in one of the noblest houses and best air of England: ther is a daintie park adjoyning, wher I often wander up and down, and I have my severall walks, I make one to represent the Royall Exchange, the other the middle isle of Pauls, another, Westminster Hall; and when I passe through the herd of deer methinks I am in Cheapside.[58] So with a full return of the same measure of love, as you pleasd to send me, I rest

Yours J.H.

24 March 1621

56 This reference had been understood to indicate a gallery on the east side of the house in the wing since demolished. For the latest thinking on Melford Hall at this period, see the Introduction, pp. lxviii–xxi above.

57 This is almost definitely Mr Daniell of Acton Hall. The Daniells of Acton were among the prominent recusant gentry in west Suffolk, along with the Martyns of Melford. See Francis Daniell, Notes on People below.

58 All these places in London were well-known locations for meeting people.

Doc. 16. Thomas Savage writes to the marquis of Buckingham about Prince Charles's finances, 30 March 1623. [BL: Harleian MS 1581, f. 258]

In 1622 Thomas had started to serve as one of the financial commissioners to Charles, prince of Wales; by 1625 he was head of this commission and he may already have been in that position when he wrote these letters (this and Doc. 18). These letters to Buckingham are the only records we have found relating to Thomas's responsibilities for Charles's finances as prince of Wales. This first letter is misleading in that Thomas made a mistake with the date; the original letter is dated 30 March 1622, when it should have been 1623.[59] *The mistake is important because Prince Charles and Buckingham had left for Madrid in February 1623 to negotiate a marriage between Charles and the Infanta of Spain. The word 'Madrid' in this letter is very badly written and could be interpreted in other ways, so there is nothing absolutely definite to tell us of the error. However the following letter in the Harleian collection is from Sir Henry Vane, Prince Charles's cofferer, writing to the prince about the same £5000, and that is clearly written to Spain.*[60] *It seems likely that Thomas and his colleague, having had instructions which were difficult to fulfil, decided that if one of them wrote to the prince and the other to Buckingham, they might succeed in convincing the prince of his financial difficulties. Savage's ending suggests that he was writing regularly to Buckingham at this period.*

Most honored lord
Noe heartt can joye more then my self to heare of my master his highness safe arrivall att [*?*]Madrill, where and every \where/ I beseech sweet Jesus eternally to bless you both.

Itt hath pleased his highness lately to derect a letter unto us his commissioners, to provyde to have fyve thousand pound made ready for him, when his highness should derect bills of exchange unto us, upon which wee tooke veiw of his exchequor, butt there was butt two thousand pound [*deleted*] to be had; therupon wee derected his highness receivors to take \a/ care that sutch a somme should be made ready for his highness, when \he/ commanded, in which they protested they had labored butt there creaditt would nott doe itt, unless Sir Thomas Savage would be bound; his readines to doe his highness servyce, I hope your lord doubtes nott, and itt is done, allthough withoutt the least meanes to service him, as allsoe Sir Henry Fane is bound and wee onely stand bound with they receivors, his highness hath nott sentt soe mutch as a pryvy seale unto us, I thought good to address my self to your lord, my onely piller, and humbly beseech your lord to advyce his highness to some sutch course as he may nott upon his bills be desappoynted, for his highness estate will nott supportt this extrenordenary charge, and his highness shall fynd few men that will engage themselves with outt better warrentt, then wee <w> have done. <itt upon>. I beseech your lord to pardon me that my letters doe thus dayly follow your lord butt your noablenes to me hath caused this your lord's trouble, for as I must still flye unto your lord upon all occasion, soe I hope I shall one daye have that happines,

59 This is dating in the old style, with the year starting on 25 March.

60 Vane's letter to Prince Charles, BL Harleian 1581, f. 259. It begins: 'In the first place, give me leave to congratulate youre safe arrival in the court of Spain' and continues later, 'we receaved youre highnesses letter of the 10 of Marche . . . commandinge us to have always £5000 in banke . . .' Vane goes on to say that the money had been made available, but that his estate would not bear any more being spent, and suggests that Charles applies to his father for additional funds 'to defray the charges of these public ceremonies . . .'

to be employed by your lord, whose most humble and faythfull servantt I am to serve you.
Tho Savage
This 30 of March 1622

Doc. 17. Thomas Savage writes to the justices of the peace for Cheshire, 24 April 1623.[61] [CCALS: Quarter Sessions, microfilm 212/84, f. 198]

Thomas Savage was probably writing from the home of his sister Grace who had married Sir Richard Wilbraham of Woodhey.[62]

After my very hartie commendations
Forasmuch as at my late being at my house of Rocksavage, great companies of poore people from the townes of Halton and Runcorne resorted to mee complayninge for wante of releefe. I shall hereby comend theire miserable estates to your consideracions, desiringe you will in this tyme of scarcitye directe some corse for theire releefe as the statute requireth. The complainte is that manye of the best wealth in that quarter wante charitye to yeeld helpe to the poore accordinge to their abillities, and that manie charitable minds want meanes to yeeld such releefe as they would. The remedey that I can conceyve is by taxacion, as the lawe requireth, to lay the burthen equallye, I knowinge I shall nott need to use persuasions to soe good a worke of mercye and pyetye. I leave it to your wisdomes [*and*] can rest.
Your verie lovinge frend Thomas Savage
from Woodhay Aprill the 24th 1623
[*on the reverse*]
To the right honorable Sir George Booth knight and barronet and to the rest of his majesties justices of the peace at the quarter sessions holden at Knottesford these deliver.[63]

Doc. 18. Thomas Savage to the marquis of Buckingham, 2 May 1623. [BL: Harleian MS 1581, f. 282]

Savage and his fellow commissioners were continuing to receive communications from the prince of Wales which were difficult to respond to (see also Doc.16).

Most honored lord
I humbly thank your lord for your noable remembrance of me in these tymes of your soe great employmentts, for all which I have nothinge \to/ render butt a heartt which is allready yours, and a body that is ever ready to attend your lords commands.

Itt hath pleased his highness of late to send us a comfortt by his highness generall letter unto us of his commission for revennue, all I can saye for one is, that when I may know itt is, [*deleted*] his highness pleasure I shall engage lyfe, as well as creaditt in my estate, itt is all I have, and less I cannott offer to soe gracious a work,

61 In Cheshire Savage lived in a county where the Elizabethan poor law had not yet been properly implemented; in Suffolk he lived in a parish with records of organised collection of relief for the poor since the mid 1500s; perhaps his comments to the Cheshire justices should be seen in the light of his Suffolk experience.
62 Woodhey is in southern Cheshire, near Cholmondeley Castle. The house was eventually inherited by one of the earls of Dysart but was later demolished.
63 For Booth, see Notes on People below.

on whome I beseech the father of heaven to power his dayly blessinges, and to make your lord ever happy in his favor, and to whose devyne provydence I humbly recommend your lord, beinge for ever
Your lords most bounden servantt, Thomas Savage
This 2 of Maye 1623

Doc. 19. William Whitmore to Thomas Savage, 6 July 1624. [UWB: Mostyn 9082/1]

In 1624 Thomas's and Elizabeth's second son, also Thomas, married Bridget Somerset née Whitmore, widow of Edward Somerset, the fifth son of the earl of Worcester, and daughter of William and Margaret Whitmore.[64] *The Whitmores were a long established and prominent catholic family in Cheshire; Margaret Whitmore was daughter and heir to Sir Hugh Beeston of Beeston Hall and Castle. Thomas Savage's correspondence with William Whitmore is the only set of personal letters we have found concerning the finances surrounding the marriage of any of Thomas's and Elizabeth's children. In some cases references in the letters are obscure, but the down-to-earth nature of the financial negotiations is clear.*

<Right honorable> Honorable Sir

I had \[*deleted*]/ returned answeare to your letter and paper which long since I receaved from Sir Richard Wilbraham;[65] but that \I was/ informed, nay assured, you would be in Cheshire this sommer, and now lerrning you are otherwise resolved, cann noe longer forbeare to expres my dislike of the <lands there proposed> \propositions/ in your particular. To answeare every thinge therin particularly weare needles, because you have my resolution by my last letter; which yf you be not pleased to accept I am sorry; and must indevor to releive my poore estate by other meanes, and not trust longer to the uncertainty of delayes, having now for the space of three yeares expected a supply from you and after all that time and trety am [*illeg.*] to beginn then at first. I thought my [*deleted*] \demandes/ had not bine soe unreasonable, but had deserved your money without repayment, and, what els (for ought I heere) you intend for the present preferment <for> of your sonne, being but a possibility farr of after many lives. Neyther did I thinke that in the conclusion yt would have bine required that myself and my wyf should be tyed to passe away the estate of Beeston landes for and on consideracion of £2000 \[*deleted*]/ for I ever thought my owne landes had well deserved that somme (in such maner as I have offerd to assure yt) but since yt is not soe valued by you, I have little reason to expect your money, and you as little to looke my landes should be estated on your sonne. And wheras you are pleased to say that yf it should soe fale out that I did not like of your propositions, you hopt I would take care for my daughter as you would doe for your sonne, whereto I answere, yf my daughter had committed her self to my care or followed my counsell, in all reason I must then have provided for her, but shee hath rejected me and committed hir self to their care, that I hope will not see her waul. Thus being unwilling to prosecute further a subject so unpleasing, with

64 It is possible that Sir Thomas Savage senior was one of the executors of Bridget's first husband; CCALS, DCH/M/35/146 relates to Thomas Savage, Richard Lumley and one other dealing with the debts of Edward Somerset in 1622, after his death. For William Whitmore and Sir Hugh Beeston, see Notes on People below.

65 For Richard Wilbraham, see Notes on People below.

my best respect to your honor, and my service to your honorable lady I doe rest ever ready to serve you

W. Whitmore

Leighton the 6 of July 1624

Doc. 20. Sir Thomas Savage to William Whitmore, 21 April 1625. [UWB: Mostyn 9082/3]

This letter and the next are some of the most personal we have found relating to this family. If Bridget Whitmore was not pregnant at the altar, she and Thomas Savage junior must have married in late July or early August 1624, not long after Doc. 19 was written. The newly born child was almost definitely Thomas's and Elizabeth's first grandchild to survive infancy, and possibly the first born.[66] *This letter gives the earliest indication we have of ill-health in both Thomas and Elizabeth.*

My good brother Whittmore
I rejoyce with you for the delivery of our good daughter and I shall heartely pray for her strength and that God will bless and preserve her and our little gerle, which as you wryte I hope wilbe the cause to settle all questions for the good of ours and our great comfortts, after our daughter is stronge. Iff all thinges may nott be done to settle them in Chesheere I shalbe glad to receive her at Mellford when please you. For your desire to the earle of Shrewsbury I have sentt unto him, and I looke for an answere every daye from him, I writt very effectually. I pray God itt may fall outt to your content, and as in this, soe in all, I shallbe ready to serve you as a brother. My wyfe takes itt very kindly your choyce of her for a godmother, the name she would have to be Margett or Elizabeth, which of them you please.[67]

I pray commend me to my brother Wilbraham whoe I presume you will see this asize, and when you two are aloane with Sir John Done wish me with you, for I thanke God I am able to laugh and be merry with my frends allthough I wantt my strenght to walk.[68] My wyfe hath had severall fitts of a tertion ague butt I thanke God this last fitt was nott soe very ill as the others, soe that I hope itt will awaye. Iff she had bine well she would have writt her owne thankes, and therefore I must doe itt for her, that you affect soe mutch her name, and from us both I send you thanks for your noable usage of my sonne. I pray God bless you longe with them.

I will not trouble with more, beinge allmost tyred with wrytinge, butt will conclude <bea> beseechinge sweet Jesus to be your protector in all your courses, and will ever rest your most affectionate lovinge brother to command
Thomas Savage
This 21 of Aprill 1625

---

66 Thomas's and Elizabeth's eldest daughter Jane had married John Paulet in 1622, but she was very young and none of the genealogies show any surviving children before her son Charles, later duke of Bolton, was born in late 1629 or early 1630.

67 If this daughter was named Elizabeth, she married Sir Marmaduke Langdale. Her great grandchild, Sir Hugh Smithson, married Lady Elizabeth Seymour heiress of the Percys, dukes of Northumberland. When Elizabeth Seymour's father died, an act of Parliament was passed to allow her and her husband to assume the surname and arms of Percy; from them descend the present dukes of Northumberland.

68 For Sir Richard Wilbraham and Sir John Done, see Notes on People below.

Doc. 21. Thomas Savage to William Whitmore, 6 May 1625. [UWB: Mostyn 9082/4]

My good brother
I am very sorry any message of myne or my absence from London butt for a few dayes should hinder your intention of comminge uppe to soe good a purpose, [*deleted*] I am now goinge uppe and I shalbe glad to see you there when you please, and in all places you shalbe most wellcome unto me. My sonne Thomas wrytes unto me that he is most bound unto you for your noable and free entertaymentt of him att your house; I wish he were soe seviceable to you as that he might ever give you contentt.

Your usage of him hath made him declare to me a greater affection to a countrey lyfe then [*deleted*] ever I conceived afore, of which I am soe glad as to continue him in that desire, I have offered a preposition to Sir Hugh Beston to board him, and iff itt lyke nott him I wish itt did you, iff neyther they shalbe wellcome to me.[69]

For your business \to/ <of> my lord Shrewsbury, he hath promised me a reasonable answere assoone as he shall come downe to advyce with his servanttes, which as yett I have nott received butt assoone as I shall, I shall give you an accountt of itt.[70] As in this soe in any thinge, I pray command me, for as God hath made us neere by alliance, soe I will ever express \myself/ to be your most affectionate lovinge brother
Thomas Savage
Maye this 6 <of> 1625

Doc. 22. Instructions from Thomas Savage and others to the vice-admirals, 16 August 1625. [TNA: SP 16/521/134]

In one of his official roles at national level, Thomas Savage was financial commissioner to the duke of Buckingham as Lord High Admiral. This is an extract from a letter to various vice-admirals based around the English south coast. Buckingham had a right to a financial share in any prizes (ships and their cargoes) seized, and the admiralty droits, and his financial commissioners wanted to ensure that he received his full entitlements.[71] *Along with Doc. 34, this gives an indication of Thomas insisting on careful administration and record keeping.*

Instruccions for the vice admiralls
You are to give speedy notice unto the lord admirall of all passages, seisures, forfeytures or other [*illeg.*] whatsoever hapining or accureing within your viceadmiralty, setting downe all such thinges as shalbe seised, or come into the hands of your, or any of your, officers by waie of inventory, wherein you are to expresse the burthen, weight, measure, quantitie and qualitie of such shippes, theire tackling and furniture, peces of ordnance or murthdies (whither iron or brasse),

69 Thomas's eldest son John was to have Frodsham Castle, and so there seemed to be some problem settling Thomas and Bridget. However Sir Hugh Beeston must have accepted the proposition to board them, and Bridget, as his granddaughter, was his only heir.

70 We have been unable to find out what this business might have been, but in the light of Doc. 29 it may have related to the debts of Edward Somerset, Bridget's first husband.

71 The crown reserved to itself certain properties under the jurisdiction of 'admiralty droits': all 'great fish' found on beaches below the high-water mark; all beach 'deodands'; wreck of the sea; flotsam (goods floating on the water) and jetsam (goods jettisoned by a crew) and 'lagan' (jettisoned goods tied with buoys).

anchores, cables, goods or merchandises whatsoever, which shalbe by you seised in the right of the lord admirall, declaring the time when they were seised, the place where, of what country they are, in whose handes you founde them, and for what cause you seised them, and any other considerable circumstances which may give satisfaccion and expresse a true and faire dealing.

You are to take care that such thinges as are apprized at leser value then they are worthe, be sold and accompted for by you to the lord admirall according to the true value, which may be easily understood if your inventories be made according as is before directed, and that you expresse the time of sale, and with whose assistance, and by whome and to whome solde. And that you may the better justify your proceedinges herein, you are to take care that no sale be made of any thinge by yourself or your deputies alone, but that (if there be not some joyned in commission with you or them), that you call unto you for your assistance some 2 or 3 of the cheife officers or men of worthe adjoyning, especially if the shippe or goodes to be solde be of any greate value, & such commissioners and assistants are to subscribe your inventorie or aprize it together with yourself.

When goodes taken by pyrats, or otherwise brought into any parte of your viceadmiraltie, are seised by you or any of your officers, being claymed by proprietors, are adjudged by the courte to be restored, you are not to deliver the same untill his lordship (being by the judge made acquainted there with) shall send his speciall direccions, to the ende that just payment may be made of such chardges and salvage as shalbe due and fitt according to the adventures and hazard undergon in the redeeming whereof . . . [*continues on other business*]
Thomas Savage, John Suckling, Robert Pye, George Paule[72]
16 Aug 1625

Doc. 23. Lady Jane St John to Lord Conway, 24 November 1625. [TNA: SP 16/10/23]

Jane St John was Thomas's and Elizabeth's eldest daughter. This letter was written when her husband and her father-in-law were expected to be disarmed, a great dishonour; this was because of their religion, for they were both catholic. Jane obviously felt that her own catholic beliefs contributed to their dishonour.[73] *Conway was the king's principal secretary at the time. Overall the sense is clear, if the sentence structure is not.*

My very good lord
It is come unto my lord's eare that my lord his father's armes shallbe taken from him; I confesse, my lord, itt is a great greife unto me to heare itt and the more that the suspition growes from me, as it is conceaved, who doth not desire life longer to me and myne then I shalbe faithfull to his majesty and his. To have the armes taken away weare such a disgrace as never happened to a famely that hath preserved itt to doe service for his countrye.

But my lord if it shall not in pointe of state be held fitt for my lord to keepe it, I beseech your lord to be our meanes that we may sell it towards the payment of our

72 For Suckling, Pye and Paule, see Notes on People below.

73 The bishop of Winchester was deputed to disarm the marquis of Winchester and Lord St John. He returned the letters on the matter to the king, saying that he was too ill to undertake the task, and asked Charles to find someone else: Quintrell, *Recusant Disarming*, p. 218. The marquis and his son were eventually disarmed in spring 1626.

debtes which have much encreased by my lord and my owne adtendance on the king and the queene to Dover, for my lord to support so great a dignity hath a very small living.[74] It was our desire to doe service drew us to itt and not our fortune, but when his majesty commands we shall never leave to hazard all to serve him.

Now my good lord, your professions have bin such unto me that I presume by you to present this \[*deleted*]/my humble suite unto his majesty, to preserve my lord from so great a marke of disgrace. You in doing itt shall but add to the care you have of ladies, and binde me to acknoledge your lordship's great favour to her that as longe as God shall give life will never faile to praye for his \majesty's/ long and most happy raigne over us, ever remaining your lordships most affectionate and obliged friend,

Jane St John

Hackwood, the 24 of November 1625[75]

Doc. 24. Indenture about the future income of Francis Savage, 1 May 1626.[76]
[ERO: D/DHF/T192]

Thomas's and Elizabeth's third son, Francis, was provided with an income after his father's death. Such documents indicate the way that major landowners arranged for their childrens' future, but they can sometimes also give useful information about acreages and names of local lands, boundaries and uses. A court case in the 1660s tells us that Thomas Savage had also settled an annuity on his youngest son Charles. Other financial arrangements made at this time include the pre-nuptial settlement for Sir John Savage, his eldest son, and the indenture providing financially for the three youngest daughters.[77]

This indenture made the first day of May in the second yeare of the raigne of our most gracious soveraigne lord Charles by the grace of God of of England, Scotland, France and Ireland kinge defendor of the faith etc., betweene the honorable Sir Thomas Savage of Rocksavage in the county of Chester knight and baronett on thone part and Francis Savage gentleman one of the younger sonnes of him the said Sir Thomas Savage on thother part, witnesseth that the said Sir Thomas Savage for the naturall love and affection which hee beareth unto the said Francis Savage and for the preferment and advancement of the said Francis Savage, and by vertue of the power and authoritie that hee hath in that behalfe limited or reserved unto him in & by certaine indentures quadripartite bearinge date the eighteenth day of June in the first yeare of the raigne of our said soveraigne lord the kinge, made betweene the said Sir Thomas Savage & the lady Elizabeth his wyfe of the first part, the right honorable Elizabeth Lady Morley widowe, late wyfe of William Lord Morley and Monteagle deceassed, and Henry nowe Lord Morley and Monteagle of the second part, Sir John Savage knight, eldest sonne and heire apparent of the said Sir Thomas

74 Henrietta Maria arrived at Dover late on 12 June 1626. The next morning Charles arrived from Canterbury, where he and a group of courtiers had been waiting. Later that day the royal couple journeyed towards Canterbury, and were greeted by the waiting courtiers *en route*.

75 For Hackwood, see above, Introduction, p. xxxvi, note 150.

76 Doc. 77 tells us that Francis Savage was in Paris in winter 1642/3, and we do not know whether he returned to England soon afterwards or stayed away until after the Restoration; he was living in Acton, a parish neighbouring Melford, in 1663.

77 Income for Charles Savage: TNA, C 10/106/42, C5/182/2. One of Charles Savage's sons sued Robert Cordell, trying to get an annuity out of the Melford estate. Financial provision for Thomas's and Elizabeth's daughters and marriage settlement of Sir John Savage, their eldest son: CCALS, DDX 111/2.

Savage and Dame Katheryn nowe the wyfe of the said Sir John Savage by the name of Katherine Parker of the third part, and the right honorable Francis earle of Rutland, William Noy of Lincolnes Inne in the countie of Middlesex esquier, John Minshall of Minshall in the said countie of Chester esquier, and William Alcocke gentleman of the fowerth part.[78]

Hath granted, limited & appoynted and by theise presentes doth grant, limitt & appoynt unto the said Francis Savage one annuytie or yearely rent charge of threescore powndes of lawfull money of England to bee issuinge and goinge out of all that the mannor of Rocksavage *alias* Clifton and out of all that the castle, mannor and lordshipp of Frodesham with theire rightes, members, liberties and appurtenances in the said countie of Chester, and out of the burrough of Frodesham in the said countie of Chester, and out of all those the mannors and lordshipps of Hellesbie and Huxley with theire and every of theire rightes, members, liberties and appurtanences in the said county of Chester, and out of the third part of the mannor of Over Ronkhorne with the appurtanences in the said countie of Chester,[79] and out of all those three water corne millnes in Frodesham affouresaid called Frodesham Myllnes with theire appurtenances, and out of all those twoe closes, inclosures or woody growndes in Cattenhall called Cattenhall woodes with the appurentances in the said county of Chester, and out of all those demaine landes of Bradley orchard called Pykes and Williamsons farmes lyinge in Bradley within the lordshipp or parish of Frodesham in the said countie of Chester withall and singuler their appurtenances, and out of all other the castles, mannors, messuages, myllnes, landes, tenementes and hereditaments whatsoever nowe or late of him the said Sir Thomas Savage set, lyinge or beinge in Rocksavage, Clifton, Frodesham, Netherton, Overton, Woodhowses, Bradley, Over Ronkhorne, Nether Ronkhorne, Halton, Halton Parke, Hellesbie, Huxley, Cattenhall woodes and in the towne and burrough of Macclesfeild and in every or any of them in the said county of Chester (except the landes and tenamentes which the said Sir Thomas Savage doth hould by coppie of court rowle or by the rod as the will of the lord) imediately from and after the decease of the said Sir Thomas Savage.[80]

And from and after the decease of the said Sir Thomas Savage, the Ladie Elizabeth his wyffe and the Ladie Katherin the wyfe of Sir John Savage knight, then alsoe out of all that the the mannor of Melford *alias* Longe Melford with the rightes, members, liberties and appurtenances theire of in the county of Suffolke, and out of all mannors, messuages, landes, tenamentes and hereditamentes whatsoever nowe or late of the said Sir Thomas Savage set, lyinge or beinge in Melford *alias* Longe Melford in the said countie of Suffolke, and out of all that parcell of meadowe conteyninge bye estimacion fower acres lyinge in a place called Ree Meadowe *alias* Ray Meadowe in Aketon in the said county of Suffolke nowe or late in the tenure or occupacion of Francis Daniell esquier (except all that wood or wood grownd called Lynnage wood conteyninge bye estimacion one hundreth and twentie acres with the appurtanences theireof).[81]

To have, receive, perceive, take and enjoy the said annuitie or yearelie rent charge

78 Sir John Savage's wife Katherine was Elizabeth Lady Morley's daughter, and some of these lands were included in her jointure.

79 Helsby is immediately south-west of Frodsham. Huxley, Cheshire, is south-east of Chester. Over Rowthorne is probably Rowton, Cheshire, immediately south-east of Chester. The only Rowthorne in modern gazetteers is in Derbyshire.

80 Netherton, Overton and Woodhouses are part of Frodsham lordship.

81 Acton borders Melford to the east. Lineage Wood still survives to the north of Melford Hall.

of threescore powndes unto the said Francis Savage and his assignes imediatelie from and after the death of the said Sir Thomas Savage for and duringe the naturall lyfe of the said Francis Savage to bee paid yearelie at the feast daies of the nativitie of St John Baptist and of St Martin the bishopp in winter.[82] And the first payment theireof to bee made at such of the said feastes as shall next happen after the death of the said Sir Thomas Savage.

And if it shall happen the said annuitie or yearelie rent of threescore powndes or anie part theireof to bee behynd and unpaid after anie of the said daies limitted and appoynted for the payment theireof, that then and soe often it shall and may bee lawfull to and for the said Francis Savage and his assignes imediatelie from and after the decease of the said Sir Thomas Savage to enter into all and singuler the said mannors, messuages, landes, tenementes and all the premisses in the countie of Chester, and after the decease of the said Sir Thomas Savage, the Lady Elizabeth hys wyfe and the said Ladie Katherin into all the premises in the said countie of Suffolke (except before excepted) heireby ment or intended to bee charged with the said annuitie or yearelie rent of threescore powndes or into anie part theireof, and theire to distraine for the said annuitie or yearelie rent and all arrerages theireof if anie bee. And the distressee and distresses theire fownd to take, leade, drive, cary away and impownd, and the same impownd to detaine and keep untill the said annuitie or yearelie rent and all arrerages theireof, if anie bee, shalbee unto the said Francis Savage or his assignes fullie satisfied and paid.

And this indenture further witnesseth that the said Sir Thomas Savage for the consideracions before mencioned and by vertue of the lyke power and authoritie which hee hath, to him limitted or reserved in and by the said indentures quadripertyte hath granted, limitted and appointed, and by theise presentes doth grant, limitt and appoint unto the said Francis Savage one other annuitie or yearelie rent charge of fowertie powndes of lawfull money of England to bee issuinge and goinge out of all the before mencioned mannors, messuages, milnes, landes, tenementes and hereditamentes in the said counties of Chester and Suffolk (except the said wood grownd called Lynnage wood with thappurtenances), to have, receive, perceive, take and enjoy the said annuitie or yearelie rent charge of fowertie powndes unto the said Francis Savage and his assignes imediatelie from and after the deathes of the said Sir Thomas Savage, Ladie Elizabeth his wife and of Dame Katherin nowe wyffe of the said Sir John Savage knight, sonne and heire apparent of the said Sir Thomas Savage, for and duringe the naturall lyffe of the said Francis Savage to be paid yearelie at the said feastes of the nativitie of St John Baptist and of St Martin the bishopp in winter by even porcions, and the first payment theireof to bee made as such of the said feastes as shall next happen after the deathes of the said Sir Thomas Savage, Ladie Elizabeth his wyffe and Dame Katherin.

And if it shall happen the said annuitie or yearelie rent of fowertie powndes or an parte theireof to bee behynd and unpaid after the said daies limited and appoynted for payment theireof or after anie of them, then and soe often it shall and may bee lawfull to and for the said Francis Savage and his assignes to enter into all and singuler the said mannors, messuages, landes, tenementes and other the premisses here by ment or intended to bee charged with the said annuitie or yearelie rent of fowertie powndes or into anie part theireof, and theire to distraine for the said annuitie or yearlie rent of fowertie powndes and all arrerages theireof, if anie bee,

82 The feast of St Martin of Tours (Martinmas), 11 November, was one of the quarter days in the north of England.

and the distresse and distresses theire found to take, leade, drive, cart away and impownd, and the same impownd to detaine and keepe untill the said annuitie or yearelie rent of fowertie powndes, and all arrerages theireof, if anie bee, shalbee unto the said Francis Savage or his assignes fully satisfyed and paid.

And the said Sir Thomas Savage doth declare, limitt and appoint all those to whom anie conveyance or assurance of the premisses or anie part theireof hath beene made, by vertue of the said indentures quadripertite accordinge to the agreementes theirein conteyned, and theire heires shall theireof stand and bee seysed. To the intent and purpose that the said Francis Savage and his assignes duringe the tearme of his lyffe shall have and perceive out of the same the said yearelie rentes and somes of money in such manner and forme as the same are before granted, limitted and appointed. Provided allwaies that if the said Sir Thomas Savage shall at anie tyme declare by wrytinge wheireunto hee shall subscrybe his name with his owne hand and which shalbee sealed with his seale, that the said yearlie rentes or either of them shall cease, determin or bee void, then the said yearelie rentes or such of them as shalbee soe declared to cease, determin or bee void, shall cease, determin and bee utterlie void. In witness whereof the parties affowresaid to theise present indentures interchangeablie have put theire handes and seales the day and yeare first above written.
Thomas Savage [*signature and seal*]

Doc. 25. Thomas Savage created a viscount, 27 October 1626. [BL: Egerton 2552]

This document has a marginal note to say that it is a copy; it was probably made at the time of the creation. The official patent for the creation is in State Papers: TNA, SP 38/13.

Warrant for Vicount Colchester to be earle of [*blank*] & Sir T. Savage to be Vicount Savage
CR
Trusty and welbeloved wee greete you well. Our will & pleasure is that you forthwith prepare a <book> \bill/ in due & usuall forme fitt for our signature, conteyning our graunt of the honour & dignity of earle of Rivers unto the now Vicount Colchester & the heyres males of his body, & after his decease for want of such issue the same honour & dignity to descend to Sir Thomas Savage knight & baronet & the heyres males of his body, who is to take the same place of the earle of Rivers as if he were now created earle.[83] The creacion money for this to be out of our great old custome within our portes of Colchester & Harwich. And our further will & pleasure is that the same booke conteyne likewise our graunt of the honour & dignity of Vicount Savage unto the said Sir Thomas Savage & the heyres males of his body with the ordinary allowance of creacion money out of the issues of our county of Chester and all preheminences due to the honour & dignity of vicount. For which this shalbe your sufficient warrant. Given att our court att Whitehall this 27th day of October in the second yeere of our raigne, etc.

To our trusty & welbeloved Sir Robert Heath knight, our attorney generall.[84]

83 Thomas Lord Darcy had been created Viscount Colchester on 5 July 1621.
84 For Sir Robert Heath, see Notes on People below.

Doc. 26. Thomas Savage to the duke of Buckingham about the Forced Loan in Chester and Cheshire, 4 February 1627. [TNA: SP 16/53/17]

Thomas Savage acted for the privy council in 1627, working to persuade the subsidymen of Chester and Cheshire to pay what is now called the Forced Loan. The city of Chester had paid up, but the county was causing more problems.

May it please your grace
Wee the grave aldermen of Chester presentt unto your grace a letter of our servyce, and iff I might presume to advyse your grace, iff you would retorne an answere to us how well his majesty [*deleted*] doth acceptt of itt, itt would doe mutch good to the servyce of the adjacentt countreye, for I assure your grace, I fynd a Northampton and Warwicksheere infection which I hope I shall cure in this countrye, the cyttye havinge allready [*deleted*] subscribed all butt one man, butt all hath payd there money \before mee/ and \it/ is [*illeg.*], and an entrance is made into the countrye which I shall prosecute with the same diligence to gett in the money, for itt may be elce [*deleted*] they may be slow in paymentt when I am gone.

I shall in this as in all thinges advance his majesties endes whylest I live, I beseech your grace to excuse me iff his majestie should expect my retorne, for this servyce to proceade and to bringe in the money must be a work of some tyme, and I hope itt well done with that alacritye of his majesties subjectes heere that will give good contentt to his majestie and be good example to other countreys. I will nott trouble your grace with [*?*]advice att this tyme butt whylest I live I am your graces most faythfull and humble servantt.
Savage
This 4 of Feb 1626
[*on the reverse*]
9 Feb 1626
Lord Savage to the duke concerning the loanes in the citty of Chester

Doc. 27. Thomas Savage to the duke of Buckingham about a favour for some Chester merchants, 6 February 1627. [TNA: SP 16/53/39]

One of Savage's tactics to get the 'countrye' to loan their money was to show what the city of Chester gained from being loyal. The Chester merchants referred to here had their goods impounded in a French ship at Beaumaris in north Wales.[85] *This letter to the duke was inclosed in another to Edward Nicholas, which is Doc. 28 below.*

May itt please your grace,
Some marchentts of this cyttye of Chester intendinge to petitcion your grace, desire to have there petitcion recommended to your grace by me, the which as a member of that cytty myself, I doe most humbly presume to presentt, and I beseech your <gracious> grace to cast an eye upon itt as from a body that will ever be ready to serve your grace, itt beinge a cyttye nott ritch, butt in all thinges most ready to there uttermost to obeye <serve> his majestie and to advance his pious ends.

Thus in all humilitye, I seeke your gracious favor for them, that ever wilbe your graces most humble servantt, Savage

85 Cust, *Forced Loan*, p. 121.

Chester this 6 of Feb, 1626
[*on the reverse*]
For the duke of Buckingham his grace

Doc. 28. Thomas Savage to Edward Nicholas, on the same matter, 6 February 1627. [TNA: SP 16/53/41]

Thomas presumably did not want to ask a favour of the duke if it was not needed, so asked Nicholas, the duke's secretary, to pass the letter on if the goods had not been released by the time the letter was received.

Mr Nicholas,
I am entreated to recommend a petition unto the duke from some younge merchentts of Chester; a letter to that purpose and the petition I send you heerinclosed, the which I pray you to peruse before you deliver itt. And iff in course the shippe may be descharged, I pray you to procure itt them and to detayne my letter, iff nott I pray deliver my letter, for I am willinge to afforth them all the curtesye I may, and I desire you to doe them all the good you can. In this remoate place I should be glad to see a letter from you, for I am your faythfull freind.
Chester Savage
this 6 of February, 1626
[*on the reverse*]
To his assured frend Mr Nicholas secretarie to the lord duke \of Buckingham/ his grace at court.

Doc. 29. Thomas Savage to William Whitmore, 28 February 1627.
[UWB: Mostyn 9082/6]

It is difficult to discern exactly what this letter is about, but possibly William Whitmore was being very difficult about accepting a final settlement for his daughter (now married to Thomas Savage junior) in relation to her first marriage to Edward Somerset. The letter is included here as an example of family correspondence which while informative on some matters, only hints tantalizingly at others of a disturbing and emotional kind. This suggests that Thomas Viscount Savage was paying out £3500 over and above the sum or lands he had settled on his second son at his marriage. Note that Whitmore is addressed as 'Sir', rather than 'my good brother' of earlier letters; in later letters Savage addresses him as 'Brother Whitmore'.

Sir
I am now gone more amazed att your nature then I did from Lyme, for allthough you held my sonne fitt to be then havinge noe issue to be bound in fetters, yett that now you havinge meanes offered you to paye your debtes, a portion for your daughter, and an oportunitye offered of the settlinge your \other/ daughter and her issue in \an/ estate that you have seemed longe to desire, and nothinge will satisfye you butt that which is beyond my power.[86] Iff you conceive me to be a christian you would beleive me, butt itt is your will <butt> must onely governe you and nott chyld or freind can move you; I am sorry for itt, and I pray God you may embrace those councells

[86] Lyme was presumably Lyme Park in Cheshire, home of the Legh family.

which may turne to the good of yours, for I confess I feare little is intended to myne, that you cannott be contented for to settle an estate \for landes/ which stands dangerous by contingencye, for iff your wyfe were certeyne of her lyfe to survyve you.

I cannott be jealous that neyther father nor mother holds there <my> daughter Sommersett worthy eyther there fortunes, nor to take money to settle itt to free your self. I pray you to remember that for a Chesheere man to give a younger sonne what I have done and to give you now one thousand fyve hundred pound for to settle your and your wyfes estate is a fayre portion, your self to have the money and to partt with nothinge, and Sir \Hugh/ Beston to have two thousand pound, with which the land stands charged, these are considerations sufficient to settle a great deale of land more then in your power, on your eldest daughter and an heyre, and sutch daughter as I know nott her fellow, and as lyke your selfe as a woman can be to a man; iff these considerations move nott, I know nott what can doe.

I will conclude with this. I leave all to God, and I beseech him that the course you hold with your daughter teach me nott to forgett my sonne, butt I will promise you, use me as ill as you will, I will use you ever as a brother, and nott [*damaged*] as those that have gone before that by conteninge you have gotten your whole estate to them and theres, as wittnes a bond of ten thousand pownd. Commend my servyce to your wyfe and I pray God to bless both you, yours and myne, and iff please you, you may command what is in the power of
Savage
This 28 of February, 1626

Doc. 30. Thomas Savage to John Bridgeman, bishop of Chester, 28 February 1627.[87] [SRO: Bradford Papers: D1287/18/2, part]

Written on the same day as the last, this letter is very different in tone; perhaps Thomas was catching up with correspondence before leaving Cheshire. He appears to have been a good friend of John Bridgeman, who had been bishop of Chester since 1619 (see also Docs 33 and 37). Thomas's religion seems not to have stopped him contributing to worthy local causes.The south transept of the cathedral was at this period used as the parish church of St Oswald.

My very good lord,
I am now goinge outt of the countrey and therefore my lord, I must bidd you farewell with a promise ever to be ready to serve you.

For the wyndow in the cathedrall church I have taken order with my servantt Alhock to paye for itt when your lordship shall command itt; the stoary I desire is the birth of our saviour, that by his humilitye itt maye teach our spiritts how to humble our selves.[88] I presume the <pryse> \charge/ wilbe \betweene/ £20 and £30,

87 For John Bridgeman, see Notes on People below.

88 Alhock was probably William Alcock; see Notes on People below. All the stained glass in Chester cathedral was destroyed during the civil war. Although the published accounts for 1626–8 mention work done by glaziers, no record of an entire window being inserted in this period exists; in 1631 however, £6 9s. 4d. was paid to a glazier for the great window 'in the south side of the parish church'. Accounts quoted in R.A.H. Burne, *Chester Cathedral* (London, 1958), p. 110. However, a separate document about Bridgeman's work in the cathedral says 'he glazed the east window with the story of the Annunciation, Nativity, Circumcision and Presentation of our Saviour' and also 'whereas the stone windows of the church were so eaten out with antiquity and weather as most of them were in danger of falling and one of them did fall down directly over the pulpit in the choir . . . he made new stone windows almost all about

which I shall most willingly contrebute hopinge that others will follow itt, and I must recommend \to his majesty/ your lordship's great care to repayre that mother church of Chesheere to her anchiantt rights, and I shall pray for a happy peace betweene your lordship and our poore cyttye.[89]

I beseech your lordship to commend my servyce to your good wyfe, and my best wish shall attend both you and yours, and I give your lordship a free power to command
Savage
This 28 of Feb, 1626
[*on the reverse*]
To the right revered father in God and my very good lord the lord busshop of Chester geve these.
Letter of Lord Savage that he would glasse one of the cathedral windowes.

Doc. 31. Thomas Savage to Countess Rivers, his mother-in-law, 15 March 1627.
[CUL: Hengrave 88, III, f. 46]

This and some succeeding letters from the Hengrave MSS, along with the Whitmore correspondence, are the bulk of family letters in this collection. Elizabeth Savage's sister Mary had married a Thomas Maples of Stow Longa in Huntingdonshire, and the marriage had run into serious problems. Thomas Savage's handwriting here can best be described as a scrawl.

Madam
My lord Rivers hath layd his command upon letter to me to attend him to London, soe that I shall nott be able to performe that charge to your lady I desired by makinge render of myne owne servyce to your lady, and therefore as I desire this letter may doe itt for me. Soe I beseech your lady lett me understand how things stand for my poore sister Maples that I may the better [*?*]soilicett your commands, butt I hope he wilbe soe wyse as to bringe her to you, and that you may despose of all things in peace to both your comfortt.

But howsoever I shall apply my self to your commands in this as in all thinges, for I have nott frazes to express my self in, butt you as shall ever fynd a practical heartt to serve you with all, and iff I had a fortune equall my charge, your lady should fynd that noe wants of yours should ever have beene unsupplyed, and wheresoever I have mett with the meanes to serve you, or yours, I have not bene wantinge in any thinge, and soe I beseech your lady to conceave I never wilbe, howsoever I have beene subject to censure, butt my obedience with patience I hope by God his permission will overcome all difficultyes, for my ends upon all the world shalbe censeer and honest, and I hope [*illeg.*] that badge God will send me to my grave.

Tomorrow wee goe towards London and I beseech your lady to send me by this bearer your resolution and derections, which I shall both with my best councell and

---

that choir'. This latter reference is to the south transept of the cathedral. If Bridgeman paid for these himself, the cost would not appear in the cathedral accounts. CUL, Baker MSS, 'The estate of the diocese of Chester in the time of . . . John Bridgeman, Lord Bishop of Chester'.

89 The mayor and the bishop were disputing where each should sit in the parish church within Chester cathedral, which services and events should take place in the south transept, and which in the body of the cathedral. Our thanks to Nick Fry of Chester cathedral for this information; more detail can be found in Burne, *Chester Cathedral*, pp. 104–5.

uttermost endevors follow, as itt doth becom a sonne, that will pray for your \ladys/ lyfe, and be ever ready to serve your lady.
Savage
this 15 of March, 1626
[*on the reverse*]
To the right honorable my very good lady the Countess Ryvers geve theis.

Doc. 32. Richard Lindall to Countess Rivers, 19 March 1627.[90] [CUL: Hengrave 88, III, f. 51]

Lindall appears to have been steward or man of business to Elizabeth Lady Kitson, mother of the Countess Rivers and grandmother of Elizabeth Savage. Lady Kitson was probably in her eighties at this point.

Right honorable,
After my humble dutye remembered unto your honorable good ladyship. My ladye receaved your honors lettres sent by my fellowe Soames, which lettre was verye welcome to her ladyship, because it brought with it tydinges of your honors good health.

My lady is in good hope that my Lord Savage will be to your honor & to your ladyships daughter the lady Marye, a true, loving & carefull friende, and I am one that can trulye witnes in his lordships behalfe. He was so much perplexed to heare me relate the unworthie behavior towardes the lady Marye that in the next morning, before I did thinke his lordship had beene awake, he sent to have me come to his lordship, & to tell \him/ of the matter againe, which when I had done, his lordship speach was this, 'I thinke the man is madd, & voyde of all understanding, doe he thinke to have my lady Rivers goodwill, when he abuseth her daughter in this manner'. My lady desyred his lordship to take care of the lady Marye your honors daughter, & to doe for her what his lordship coulde, which he faythfully promissed, & I am verye confident his lordship will trulye performe it.

My ladye have (as it is feared) gotten an ague by eating fish, when your phisition prescrybed that her ladyship shoulde eate flesh, & on Frydaye last her ladyship had a verye tedious fitt, another yesterdaye, but nothing soe violent as the former, the third she expecteth to take her ladyship to morrowe, which I will hartilye praye to God to deliver her from. And thus I doe most humblye take my leave, & will be ever at your honors commandment.
Richard Lindall
Burye St Edmunds
March 19th, 1627
[*on the reverse*]
To the right honorable my verie good ladye the Countesse Rivers at her house in Colchester be these delivered.

90 He signed himself Lyndall or Lindall; the name has been given as Lindall throughout this volume.

Doc. 33. Thomas Savage to John Bridgeman, bishop of Chester, 26 March 1627. [SRO: Bradford Papers, D1287/18/2, part]

Thomas Savage dated this letter 26 March 1626. This would have been at the very start of the new year, which began on 25 March. However, its reference to the bishop's service on a commission almost certainly applies to the forced loan, on which Bridgeman served.[91] *The activities of that commission began in the summer of 1626 and were coming to an end in the following February (Docs 26, 27). It is most likely that the letter was written on 26 March 1627 and that Savage dated it in the previous year by mistake. The first paragraph here is the most direct evidence we have of Thomas's access to King Charles.*

My very good lord,
I have acquaynted his majesty with your lordship's great zeale to his servyce, the which he takes most graciously att your hands, and when your lordship shall see him his majesty wil lett you know as mutch. In the meane tyme he hath commanded the lords of the councell to wryte a letter unto my lord of Derby and your lordship and to the rest of the commissioners, to lett you understand how graciously he doth acceptt of your servyces.

And my lord for my self lett me thanke you, and assure you that in the place I live I will serve your lordship as a faythfull freind, and I pray commend my servyce to your good wife and my best love to your good sonne. And soe in hast I end (meaninge shortely to visitt your lordship with a letter, of sutch newes as the presentt tyme bringes forth) butt ever to remayne your lordships most affectionate and faythfull freind
Savage
This 26 of March, 1626
[*on the reverse*]
To the right reverende father in God and my very good lorde, the lord busshop of Chester geve these.

Doc. 34. Edward Nicholas to John Drake, collector of prizes, requiring accounts, 20 July 1627.[92] [TNA: SP 14/215/23]

This is just one of a group of letters from Edward Nicholas, Buckingham's secretary, to naval captains and others about the commissioners' desire for full and complete records.

[*Marginal note*] John Drake to make exacte account of his collectorship and vice-admiralty

Noble Sir,
I have received direccions from my Lord Savage and the rest of his graces commissioners for his estate to desire you forthwith to prepare and make upp particuler true and exacte accomptes of all such tenthes as you have received for my lordes use since the time of your first enteringe into that office of collector of the tenths of prizes.[93] Wherein you are to sett downe the particulers you have received out of

91 Letter from commissioners to the duke of Buckingham: TNA, SP 16/56/72.

92 For Edward Nicholas, see Notes on People below.

93 The duke of Buckingham, as Lord High Admiral, was entitled to one tenth of the value of all prizes taken.

every prize a parte, what parte thereof you have sold, and for money, and what parte is yett unsold, how much money you have paid in for the same and to whome, & how much is still <deleted> in your handes or due to be paid for the same, by whome and when. And you are to sett downe in your said accompte anie thinge else that may make the same cleere in all pointes.

I have herewith sent you the forme of an accompte that you may the better know how to forme one for that the commissioners are verie earnest to receive formall and exacte accountes from you, and all other the collectors of my lordes tenthes. I am likewise to desire you to prepare against Michaelmas an accompte of all the profittes of the vice admiralty of Devon. I here there are prizes brought into Milton by one captaine Bryan. I pray quicken all your deputies in every porte to looke out dilligently, for otherwise in this generall time of takeing of shippes there wilbe much concealed to my lords disadvantage.[94] I have herewith likewise sent you a letter from my lord Savage and the rest of his commissioners concerninge the colleccion at Bristoll. We heare not as yet anie newes from my good lord but doe expecte some every day, I pray God send it may be good, and answere to his noble harte.[95]

I write in greate haste and rest

EN

20 July, 1627

Doc. 35. Commission to examine Queen Henrietta Maria's revenues, 18 October 1627. [TNA: LR 5/57, ff. 9–10]

This is the first of three official documents relating to Thomas's role in the queen's court. It dates from October 1627, well before our first conclusive evidence that he had been appointed chancellor, which comes eighteen months later, in April 1629. As noted in the Introduction, it is possible that he was appointed in 1626; alternatively it is at least possible that his performance on this commission led to his appointment.

A comission granted to Henry earle of Holland[96] and others her majesties commissioners to examine the state of her revenues & to comptroll unreasonable debtes and not to exceed her revenue in expences. [*marginal note*]

Henriette Marie by the grace of God of England, Scotland, France and Ireland queene, to our right trusty and \right/ wellbeloved cozens Henrie earle of Holland and George earle of Totnes, our treasurer and receavour generall, and to our right trusty and and [*sic*] welbeloved cozen Thomas Lord Visc\o/unt Savage, and to our right trusty and welbeloved Aliernoon Lord Percey, Sir Georg Goring knight and baronett our vicechamberlayne, Sir Robert Ayton knight our principall secretarie, Sir Ralph Freeman knight one of the masters of requestes in ordinary to our dearest lord and husband the king, Sir Thomas Stafford knight gentleman usher of our privie chamber, Sir John Tonstall knight our gentleman usher daylie wayter, and Sir John Finch knight our attorney generall, greeting.[97]

94 If this place is in Devon, the most likely candidates are South Milton near Kingsbridge or Milton Combe near Plymouth. It could also be Milton in Hampshire.

95 Buckingham was leading the expedition to relieve La Rochelle; his forces were comprehensively beaten and were forced to withdraw.

96 The earl of Holland was Henry Rich, second cousin to Elizabeth Savage.

97 Aliernoon is Algernon.

Knowe yee that wee for our better informacion of the state of our revenues and debtes, and for the better ordering of our said revenues for the tyme to come, trusting in your fidelities and approved wisdomes have chosen assigned and appointed, and by these presentes doe choose, assigne and appoinnt, you to be our commissioners, and doe by these presentes give unto you or any fowre of you full power and authority from tyme to tyme and at all tymes hereafter, untill our pleasure signified to the contrary, to examine the state of all our revenues, and of all matters therein touching, concerning any of our honores, lordshippes, mannors, parkes, forrestes, liberties, possessions, feefarme rentes, landes, tenementes and hereditamentes and the issues and profittes of every of them. And to examine diligently how, in what sorte and by whome the same hath beene heretofore issued. And allsoe to examine and controll such debtes as have beene unreasonably chardged upon us. And withall to settle such a constant and certayne course that expences hereafter may not exceed the proporcion of our said revenues.

And wee doe by theis presentes give you or any fower of you full power and authority from tyme to tyme and at all tymes hereafter, till our pleasure signified to the contrary, to doe and execute all thinges that may the better enable you to performe our said will and pleasure in the premisses or in any of them. And therefore our will and pleasure is and wee doe by theis presentes charge and comand you carefully and diligently to [?]intend the premisses with effect. Given under our signett at Whithall the eighteenth day of October in the third of the raigne of our dearest Lord Charles by the grace of God king of England, Scotland, France and Ireland defendor of the faith etc.
John Finch, Robert Ayton

Doc. 36. Thomas Brooke to Countess Rivers, 18 January 1628. [CUL: Hengrave 88, III, f. 52]

Thomas Brooke was steward or man of business to Thomas Savage for many years. He was probably one of the Brookes of Norton, a gentry family who lived close to Rocksavage.

Madam,
I was comaunded by my lord to send unto your lady by the townes carrier a large pye with woodcock in it, which was sent unto his lord from a verie noble friend of his out of the countrye; which is hoped is better condicioned than the former was, which as I hard, proved not so well as it was desired, or ment. And for that these baked comodities maie prove ill, and that the charge of the carriadge to your lady maie exceed the thinge, to prevent & ease that, by my lords derection, the carrier is agreed withall and paid for his carriadge. And so upon your lady sendinge to him for the pye which is parcell well upp, and layd betwene two bordes, with a derection written on a paper, fastened to the same, I hope without further demaund will deliver it to anye your lady wilbe pleased to requier the same from him. If not, and the same not cominge saff and free, I beeseche your lady to heare thereof the next week.

My lord, who ment to write to your lady, for multiplicitie of busyness att this tyme, desireth to be excused, who remembereth his humble dutie and service to your lady, who is, I thank God, in reasonable good helthe. But my lady Savage, your daughter, beinge a [?]head attendant and waiter on the quene, with distemperatures & goinge abroad with her majestie in these cold seasons, the last night was muche troubled with a stitche & other paynes in her bodye, that she appointed Docter

Gifford to be with her earely this morning to geve her lady some thing to evacuate and ease the same. For the rest of theirs are in helthe [*damaged*], keepe cloase by good fiers, which as theis tymes are, is groen scarce, and deare beyond measure.

I sawe Mr Foster yesterdaie, who told me that your lady's mother was reasonable well. And so cravinge pardon for troublinge your lady with my tedious lynes, with the humble rememberance of my bounden dutie and service to your lady, doe in all humble manner take my leave and rest as your ladys humble servant to comaund,
Thomas Brooke
Towerhill, this 18th of January, 1627
[*on the reverse*]
To the right honorable my verie good lady the Countesse Ryvers att her howse in Colchester geve these.

Doc. 37. Thomas Savage to John Bridgeman, bishop of Chester, about Delamere Forest, 11 August 1628. [SRO: Bradford Papers, D1287/18/2, part]

This is the earliest document about changes afoot in the forest of Delamere. In another letter from the same collection Thomas suggests that Bridgeman wanted the land 'to make you a seate'; that letter tells us that the king was to have some nine thousand statute acres.[98]

My very good lord,
Whereas your lordship was desirous to have layd outt some money upon the forrest of Dalameere longe sythence, and to that effect you writt unto me, I <told> did assure you that when tyme was fitt, I would acquayntt your lordship. Now my good lord, the latter end of this moneth a commission is comminge downe for the agreeinge with the charterers and then the kinge shall know what his demeane is, soe that you may then know what is to buye, and the kinge know what to sell, and noe doubtt a great purchase is to be had iff itt be pursued.

Sir Thomas Fainshow is to bringe downe the commission, and I know wilbe ready to advance your desire as farre as a faythfull servantt may doe unto his masters servyce.[99] My lord I have had mutch a doe to bringe itt to this, wherby his majesty's profitt and the good of the countrey may be preferred, but noe man's greatnes shall make me afrayd to doe what is fitt for me to doe, and now accordinge to your desire and my promise, I have certefyed your lordship how the state of that forrest doth stand, and noe doubtt iff money come of roundly, butt your lordship may have as good precedentye in the bergeyne as any man.

Soe with my best wishes to your good wyfe and all yours, I rest for ever your lordship's most affectionate freind to serve you,
This 11 of August, 1628 Savage

[*on the reverse*]
To the right reverende father in God and my very good lorde the lord busshop of Chester deliver these.

98 It seems unlikely that Bridgeman was successful in buying the land for a family seat, for in 1629 he bought Lever Hall in Great Lever, near Bolton, which was to remain in the ownership of the Bridgeman family until the 1930s.
99 For Sir Thomas Fanshawe, see Notes on People below.

Doc. 38. Elizabeth Savage to her mother, Countess Rivers, August 1628. [CUL: Hengrave 88/2, f. 132]

Although this letter is undated, it must have been written in late August 1628. This and Doc. 39 are the only letters from Elizabeth Savage found in the Hengrave collection.

Madam,
I humble besiech your lady to pardon me that I have not waited of you all this while, for \if/ my ill health had not bene the cause nothinge els coulde have hindred me, but indede ever since I was with your lady I can not say that ever I was an howre well, <but> \for/ I am afrade I have the stone in the bladder and withall a greate sharpnes of urin, soe that I am in perpetuall torment with that; and besieds I have lost so worthy a friend by the death of my lord duke that I am unfitt for any company.[100] But I have presumed to present your lady with this halfe stack which, because I saw it soe good, I hoped your lady wold eccept of it, and if you wolde be pleased to commaunde any thinge in my powre than I shoulde beleive that your lady loved me, which none shall more strive to deserve than myselfe, and if you wolde favor me with any of your commaunds I shoulde thinke myselfe most happie in obaieng them.[101] Tomorrow my lord goes to London being sent for by the king as I thinke it is about taking care of my lady duckes and my lord dukes estaiete; but I hope I shall be soe happie as to waite of your lady eare it is long, for I hope you are confident that you have noe childe that more honors your lady then my selfe, and whielst I breath I will ever be your ladys most affectionate and obedient daughter till death.[102]
Elizabeth Savage
I besiech your lady send Dockter Duke to me as sonne as you can get him to come, for I am very ill.
[*on the reverse*]
To the right honorable my very deare mother the <lady> Countes Rivers give these, at Collchester.

Doc 39. Elizabeth Savage to her mother, Countess Rivers. [CUL: Hengrave 88/2, f. 133]

This letter is undated, but as it survives in the same archive as Doc. 38, it may have been written at around the same time. It could have been written earlier, for we know from Doc. 36 that Elizabeth was ill in January 1628. It is possible that these two letters are all that survives of what may have been a regular, long-term correspondence between mother and daughter.

Madam,
I am now come to London with my infirmed body and must to morrow morning goe to Winsor[103] with the quene. I am extreame ill of my owlde deseases, cheifly the paine in my kidnies and the sharpness of urin which trobles me very much. I have send your lady your goune which I hope is very fitt for it hath not wanted any care, and I desire it may like your lady as I hope it will. I have sent allsoe a role to weare

100 The duke of Buckingham was assassinated at Portsmouth on 23 August 1628, aged thirty-six.
101 'Stack' means 'stag'.
102 Thomas was one of the duke of Buckingham's executors.
103 Windsor, Berks.

with\it/, such a one as I weare my selfe, and have lined it with tafity, for calicoe is unfitt for your lady to weare; therefore I besiech your lady to weare it as it is <made> made for I hope it is fitt. Thus humble craving your ladys blessing, besieching swete Jesus to send you health and long life and all other happiness, with my humble duty I rest, your ladys most affectionate and obedient daughter.
Elizabeth Savage
[*on the reverse*]
To the right honorable my verie loving mother the Countes Rivers give these at her house at Colchester.

Doc. 40. Letter from Thomas Savage and the other executors of the duke of Buckingham to Captain Pennington, 1 September 1628.[104] [TNA: SP 16/116/6]

Thomas Savage was working on the estate of the duke of Buckingham until at least 1633, but this letter marks an early stage in the process.

After our harty comendacions. Whereas it hath pleased almightie God to take to his mercy our late good lord the duke of Buckingham his grace, and by direccion as present care is to be taken of his estate for the good of his noble lady and children, whose afflictions are nowe such as shee is not able to looke into it and hath desired us to doe it, whome it hath pleased his lordship to name to be executors. In regard whereof wee are to give an account presently to his majesty and the better to understand howe the estate standes to be undertaken. Wee out of theis consederacion doe ernestly intreate you to send us a breife account in writinge under your hand with as much speede as you can, of such somme or sommes of money as yow have receaved from his grace, his servantes or agents by his direccions and for what service it was intended and hath bene issued by you. Whereby wee may give full satisfaccion to his majesty and see how [*illeg.*] may be for execucion of his will. And so wee rest, your verie loveinge frends F. Rutland, Savage, Robert Pye, Richard Oliver, Thomas Fotherley, 1628[105]

Savoy this firste day of September 1628
[*on the reverse*]
To Captain Pennington

Doc. 41. Elizabeth Savage petitions Viscount Dorchester for the life of a convicted man, May 1629. [TNA: SP 16/143/44]

This is the earliest of several documents in this volume which Elizabeth Savage wrote to petition for favours; most of the others are on her own behalf. It seems unlikely that the petition would have succeeded without the name of the man in question.

My Lord,
Since I had the honor last night to se your lord ther was a poore woman which was my neibor many years at Brandford that hath bene with me and made lamentable mone for her husband which is condemned and is to be hanged on Saterday

104 For Captain Pennington, see Notes on People below.
105 For Rutland, Pye, Oliver and Fotherley, see Notes on People below.

morning, and he swears that he is wrongfully acused and is <in> not gilltie but only taken upon susspecion; if your lord wolde be pleased to procure his pardon of the king I should thinge myselfe much bound to your lord and will be ready to serve you in any thing wherin I may doe you service, and for this favor will ever be your lords affectionate frinde and servant.[106]
Elizabeth Savage
[*on the reverse*]
to the right honorable the lord Vicecount Dorchester principall seacretary to his majestie and one of his majesties most honorable privy councell give these.[107]
Endorsed: May 1629
My Ladie Savage to the lord Viscount Dorchester.

Doc. 42. Appointment of the commission for leasing Queen Henrietta Maria's lands, 31 October 1629. [CCALS: DCH/U/13]

The second of three 'official' commissions from Henrietta Maria included in this collection. Although more survive they add little to our picture of the work involved. By this time, Thomas had been working for some years on the commission for sale of the lands which Charles I had owned as prince of Wales, and for eighteen months on the commission examining the queen's revenues. The piece number at Chester Record Office includes a number of documents; one is a copy of this document in Latin, another the translation printed here.

Henriette Marie by the grace of God queene of England, Scotland, Fraunce and Irelande. To our right trusty and right welbeloved cozen and councellor Thomas Viscount Savage, our chancellor and keeper of our great seale, greetinges. Wee will and commaund that under our said great seale yow cause these our lettres to bee made patente in forme followinge:

Henriette Marie by the grace of God queene of England, Scotland, Fraunce and Ireland: to our right trustie and right welbeloved Richard Lord Weston lord high treasurer of England and to our right trustie and right welbeloved cozens and councellors Henrie earl of Holland high steward of our revenues, Edward earle of Dorsett lord chamberlaine of our howshould and Thomas Viscount Savage our chancellor and keeper of our great seale. And to our right trustie and welbeloved councellors Sir Robert Aiton knight our secretarie, Sir Richard Winne knight and baronett our treasurer and receaver generall, Sir Thomas Hatton knight our surveyor generall and Sir John Finch knight our atturney generall, greetinges.[108]

Know yee that wee for the better preservacion and increase of our revenues and treasure, trusting in your fidelities and approved wisedomes, have constituted, assigned and appointed, and doe by these presents constitute, assigne and appointe you to be our commissioners for the letting of all our houses, mannors, landes, tenements and hereditamentes; and do hereby authorise and appointe you or anie fower of you (whereof you the said Thomas Viscount Savage allwaies to bee one) from time to time and at all times hereafter to direct, order, appoint and give warrant for the making of all such leases, estates and grants of anie our said houses, mannors,

106 'Brandford' is Brentford, Middlesex. Thomas Savage inherited his house at Brentford from his grandmother Jane Allington; see above, Introduction and Doc. 4.
107 For Viscount Dorchester, formerly Dudley Carleton, see Notes on People below.
108 See Notes on People, below, for information about these men.

landes, tenementes and hereditamentes as you in your wisedome shall thinke fitt and convenient.

Provided allwaies that the said leases or estates so to bee granted do not exceed the terme of one and twentie yeares in possession or revercion, or the number of sixtie yeares in possession or revercion determinable upon one, two or three lives. And that upon such leases or estates so to bee graunted there bee reserved for the benefitt of us and our assignes during our naturall life, and after for the benefitt of our dearest lord the kings majestie, his heires and sucessors, the auncient and accustomed yearelie rent or more, and where no such ancient rent hath beene reserved, then so much rent as to yow shall seeme most just and convenient.

And for the better enabling of yow from time to time to make such leases, estates and grauntes according to our direccion aforesaid, wee do further by these presentes give to you or anie fower of yow (whereof yow the said Viscount Savage allwaies to bee one) full power and authorities from time to time and at all times hereafter for and in our behalfe, and to our use to take anie grant or grantes, surrender or surrenders of anie estate or lease, and of anie estates or leases for lyfe, lyves or years of anie our honors, lordships, mesuages, howses, landes, meadows, pastures, marshes, groundes or anie other profites, commodities, emolumentes or hereditamentes whatsoever heretofore leased, or which hereafter shalbe leased or graunted unto anie person or persons whatsoever. And upon those grauntes or surrenders to make or cause to be made such leases, estates and grantes as aforesaid, as also for us and in our behalfe from time to time, and at all times hereafter, to nominate the life or lyves upon which the said terme of sixtie yeares in anie the said leases so to bee made as aforesaid shalbe determinable, and to assesse and sett downe anie such fyne or fynes, summes of money or other valuable consideracion to bee given or paid in hand or at daies to come to our use for the leasing of the premisses or of anie of them or anie parte of them in manner aforesaid.

And likewise to sett downe or cause to be sett downe all such covenants, articles and agreements as well on our parte as on the leassees parte concerning the premisses or anie of them or anie parte of them to bee performed as in the wisedom and discrecions of you or anie fower of yow (whereof yow the said Viscount Savage allwaies to bee one) shall seeme best. In witnes etc.

Roger Aiton secretary
Approved the last day of October 1629

Doc. 43. Thomas Savage petitions Charles I for the lease of herbage and pannage of the forest of Delamere, ?1630. [TNA: SP 16/531/83]

This is the only document we have found in which Thomas petitions for something to his own advantage, whereas we have several examples of Elizabeth doing the same. The imbalance may be a matter of chance survival or Thomas may have been genuinely more reticent in these matters. Sir Ranulph Crewe refers to his 'exorbitant patent' in Doc. 67, so possibly the former is more likely. This document is not dated, but has been listed by the editors of State Papers as 1630, which is when John Done junior died.

To the kings most exellent majestie, the humble peticion of the Lord Viscount Savage
May it please your majestie,
John Done esquier lately deceased did hold of your majestie the herbage, pannage

etc. of the forrest of Delamere in Cheshier for three lives, and also the hundred of Edisbury within the said forrest for the like tearme, the said herbage and pannage etc. is yet in being for one life, but the hundred of Edisbury, by his death, is fallen into your majesties hands.[109] It is humbly desired by your peticioner that under the same rent the said John Done paid, your majesty wilbe graciouslie pleased to bestow a lease for threscoore yeares in reversion of the said herbage, pannage etc. and the like terme of threscore yeares of the hundred of Edisbury, withall such other profitts as the said John Done had by vertue of the said leases.

And whereas your majesties peticioner doth hold for his owne life the place of Rainger of that forrest, he doth most humbly beseech your majesty to add two of his sonns lives thereunto with the fee of one bucke and one doe yearly out of every walke.[110] Humbly beeseeching your majestie if it be your gracious pleasure to conferr theis upon him, that your majesty wilbe graciouslie pleased to signifie your pleasure to your attorny gennerall to draw up a booke accordinglie.[111]

[*on the reverse*]
Viscount Savage

Doc. 44. Thomas Savage and others re-appointed to administer Queen Henrietta Maria's properties and lands, 10 January 1631. [CCALS: DCH/O/42]

A long official document, which with Docs 35 and 42, illustrates the records which can survive for appointments relating to the royal court. Doc. 42 gave named men the power to make leases of Henrietta Maria's properties, whereas this one gave wider powers over matters relating to her lands.

Henriette-Marie by the grace of God queene of England, Scotland, Fraunce and Ireland: to our right trustie and right welbeloved cozen Thomas Viscount Savage our chancellor and keeper of our great seale, greeting: wee will and require you that under our great seale remayninge in your custody you cause theis our letteres to be made pattente in forme following:

Henriette-Marie etc. to our right trustie and right welbeloved Richard Lord Weston, lord high treasurer of England, and to our right trustie and right welbeloved cozens Henry earle of Holland high steward of our revenewes, Edward earle of Dorsett lord chamberlayne of our howshould, Henry earle of Danby and Thomas Viscount Savage our chancellor and keeper of our great seale; and to our right trustie and right welbeloved George Lord Goreing master of our horse, Sir Thomas Edmonds knight treasurer of the howshould to our dearest lord the king, Sir Thomas Jermyn knight vicechamberlen of the howshold to our dearest lord the king, and Sir Francis Cottington baronett chancellor of the exchequer to our dearest lord the king: and to our trustie and welbeloved Sir Robert Killigrew knight vicechamberlen of our

109 The Done family had been Foresters of Delamere since the 1350s; Sir John Done had died in 1629, and this John Done esquire was his son. After his death the office passed to his brother-in-law, John Crewe, son of Sir Randulph Crewe; see Docs 49 and 67. An entry in the Signet Office book in April 1631 suggests that this petition was at least partially successful: TNA, SO 3/10. For Sir John Done and John Crewe, see Notes on People below. Doc. 20 tells us that Sir John Done had been one of Thomas Savage's old friends.

110 See Doc. 49.

111 William Noye was attorney general at this point. In April 1631 Charles confirmed Thomas's position of Ranger of Delamere with the addition of what was asked for here: TNA, SO 3/10, April 1631.

howshould, Sir Robert Aiton knight our secretarie, Sir Richard Wynn knight and baronett our treasurer and receavor generall, Sir Thomas Hatton knight our surveyor generall, Sir Ralphe Freeman knight one of the masters of requests to our dearest lord the king, Sir John Finch knight our attorney generall and Thomas Mallett esquire our sollicitor generall, greeting.[112]

Knowe yee that wee out of the great trust and confidence which wee doe repose in your great care, industry and discrecions, have chosen, assigned, ordayned and appointed, and by theis presentes doe choose, assigne, ordayne and appoint you and every of you to be our councellors and specially of our councell dureing our pleasure, for the faithfull and provident councelling and advising of us in all thinges that doe or may anie way concerne anie honors, castles, lordshipps, mannors, parkes, forrestes, liberties, possessions, feefarme rentes, landes, tenementes, anuyties, pencions and hereditamentes whatsoever heretofore granted or belonging unto us, or which hereafter at any tyme shall happen to be granted or to be belonging unto us, and as it shalbe expedient from tyme to tyme truely and faithfully to enforme and certifie us of your knowledges and judgementes in and concerning the premisses and faithfully, providently and carefully to doe and performe in and concerning the premisses all thinges which doe or may therein appertayne to the duety place and office of our faithfull councellors.

And furthermore wee have assigned, constituted and appointed, and by theis presentes doe assigne, constitute and appoint and speciall authoritie, power and trust give, grant and committ to you and anie five or more of you (whereof our will and pleasure be that one of you the said Richard Lord Weston lord high treasurer of England, Henry earle of Holland, Edward earle of Dorsett, Henry earle of Danby, Thomas Viscount Savage, George Lord Goreing, Sir Thomas Edmonds, Sir Thomas Jermyn, Sir Frauncis Cottington, Sir Robert Killigrew and Sir Robert Aiton shall allwaies be one) well, providently and carefully to oversee, rule, governe, direct and order our said honors, castles, lordshipps, mannors, parkes, forrestes, liberties, possessions, feefarme rentes, landes, tenementes, anuyties, pencions and hereditamentes and all and singuler the premisses.

And to consult advise and deliberate of the estate and setling of our revenewe which wee now have, in or by reason of any the premisses, or which hereafter wee shall or may have in any honors, castles, lordshipps, mannors, parkes, forrestes, liberties, possessions, feefarme rentes, landes, tenementes, anuities, pencions or hereditamentes whatsoever. And alsoe to heare and determyne all causes, controversies and differences which shall depend, arise or growe amongst anie of our tennantes or which may anie wayes concerne our said revenewe or any of the premisses.

And further from tyme to tyme to examyne all and singuler the debtes nowe oweing or which hereafter shalbe oweing by us, and as you shall see cause and finde convenient to controule them and every of them, and to take order for the satisfaccion of all and singuler our said debtes as to you shall seeme fitt and necessarie; and alsoe to settle such a certaine and constant course in the premisses that hereafter our expences may not exceed the proporcion of our revenewe.

And further wee doe by theis presentes give power and authoritie to yow or any five \or more/ of yow (where of our will and pleasure is that one of you the said Richard Lord Weston lord high treasurer of England, Henry earle of Holland, Edward earle of Dorsett; Henry earle of Danby; Thomas Viscount Savage; George

112 See Notes on People, below, for details of these men.

Lord Goreing, Sir Thomas Edmonds, Sir Thomas Jermyn, Sir Francis Cottington, Sir Robert Killigrew and Sir Robert Aiton shall alwayes be one) to nominate, assigne, appointe and authorize any fowre of our councellors above named from tyme to tyme and at all tymes which they shall thinke convenient to heare receave and take a true and perfect accompt of our said treasurer and receavor generall, and of every other our treasurer and receavor generall for the tyme being, and of all others to whome the care and chardge of any accompt hath bin or at any tyme hereafter shalbe committed by us for or concerning all our treasure and revenewe already come or hereafter to come into his or their handes and possession, and for and concerning every other thing belonging or in any wise apperteyning to his or their offices, or wherewith he or they have bin or hereafter shalbe charged and entrusted by us, or which have or hereafter shalbe committed to his or their care and chardge and for which they or anie of them stand accomptable unto us.

And to allowe or disallowe unto him or them and to every of them upon their said severall accomptes all just and reasonable peticions and allowances that our said fowre councellors, soe to be nominated, appointed, assigned and authorized as aforesaid, shall in their wisedomes thinke fitt and convenient. For which purpose our will and pleasure is that our treasurer and receavor generall for the tyme being and all others to whome itt shall appertayne to give us anie accompt as aforesaid, doe prepare their severall accomptes, and perfect the same in such sort as whensoever our said fowre councellors, soe to be nominated, appointed, assigned and authorized as aforesaid, shall call for the same, the said accomptes may be presented unto them and by them be allowed or disallowed as aforesaid.

And for your better furtherance in the premisses wee doe hereby straightly charge and command all our officers, ministers and servantes from tyme to tyme to be attendant uppon yow and ayding and assisting unto yow as you shall have occasion to direct; and therefore our will and pleasure is and wee doe hereby command and require yow, carefully and diligently to intend the premisses with effect. In witnes whereof etc. Given under our privy seale at the court at Whitehall the nynth daie of January in the sixth yeare of the raigne of our deare lord and husband King Charles.

Robert Aiton

Approved 10 January 1630

Doc. 45. Letter from Katherine duchess of Buckingham to her father the earl of Rutland, 16 April 1631. [In print: *HMC Rutland*, vol. 1, p. 490. The Rutland archives are not open to researchers.]

This letter from a daughter in London to her parents at Belvoir[113] *is brief but full of news, typical of many family letters of the period. The death of Jane marchioness of Winchester, née Savage, attracted considerable attention at the time from poets; see the Introduction to this volume, pp. xlvii–viii.*

April 16. Buckingham House

My lord, I have made your excuse to both their majesties for your not being at ther first coming to Grinwiche, which thaye do excuse.[114] This night they both supted att the gatthowse with my Lady Buckingham, where they hade a great supper. Your

113 Belvoir Castle, Leicestershire, was the home of the earls of Rutland.

114 Charles had given Greenwich Palace to Queen Henrietta Maria.

lordship will to sonne here the great lose my Lord and Lady Savage has had in the death of my Lady Marques who dyed with an impostome in her checke, and the extreemety of that putt her in a fever.[115] Shee was delivered before shee died of a deed boye.[116] It was a great lose to her father and mother who takes it very hevelye. Mr Mountague has come out of France. The queene mother is wher shee was, and the younge queene in great creedit with the kinge; she was never so well in her life. Our kinge, queene and prince ar very well and so all yours. So humbly craving your blesing for us all, I take my leve.
Your lordships most obedient unfortunat daughter K. Buckingham
I beseech you present my humble servis to my lady. Signet.

Doc. 46. Letter from Thomas Savage to Edward Nicholas concerning the commission for fisheries, 25 September 1632. [TNA: SP 16/223/47]

A mundane letter about the date of the next meeting of a committee survives presumably only because its recipient was an administrator who kept his correspondence, however routine. It tells us that Thomas Savage was back from Cheshire and Belvoir, where he seems to have spent most summers, ready to resume his administrative business.

Good Mr Nicholas,
I send these lynes to wellcome your retorne outt of the countrey, and to give you thanks for the <two> letter I received from you before you went outt of London. I pray you to send me word iff there be any intention of the meetinge of the commissioners for the fishinge, and when.[117] This place afforths noe newes, therefore I shall breifly tell you that I will ever assure you, and yours, a most faythfull and constantt freind of
Savage
Mellford, this 25 of September, 1632
[*on the reverse*]
To my most assured freind Mr Nicholas at his house in Kingston

Doc. 47. Francis Manners earl of Rutland's instructions from his deathbed, 15 December 1632. [In print, *HMC Rutland*, I, p. 492.]

Here follows the bulk of a document written by George Manners, who succeeded his brother Francis as earl of Rutland. He describes Francis's instructions from his deathbed; the earl had called together his daughter (the duchess of Buckingham), his wife ('my sister of Rutland'), Thomas Savage and his brother. The Manners brothers and Savage had a common great-grandparent; although this was enough for them to recognise each other as kin, it was not so close a relationship that successive earls of Rutland had to involve Thomas Savage in their affairs. It seems

115 Jane, marchioness of Winchester, Thomas's and Elizabeth's eldest daughter.
116 She had already had one son, who survived to become the first duke of Bolton.
117 The Commission for Fisheries was set up in 1632; its members included many of the great and good of Britain. Thomas Savage was present at what may have been the first meeting in June 1632. A meeting in July 1632, when Thomas Savage was one of eight men who attended, appointed Edward Nicholas as one of the two clerks to the 'councell of the societie of the fishing of greate Britaine and Ireland'. TNA, SP 16/294 includes evidence given to commission/council but there are no further minutes or notes of meetings.

clear therefore that the long association of Savage with the earl of Rutland was based on more than family loyalties. The earl died on 17 December 1632, two days after these events. This is another document which infers that Thomas had direct access to the king.

1632, December 15
It pleased my lord to call my lady dutchess, my sister of Rutland, my Lord Savidge, and myselfe, and to use theise speeches unto us.

Sweete hart give mee your hand,[118] now I pray God blisse you and your children. It greeves me I shall see none of them before I die, but I leave them my blessinge. You know there was a match wished by your housband betweene my lord chamberline's sonn and Mall, which I desier may go on.[119]

That hee gave his best heroners to his majestie, and that Mr Robert Terrett the kinges querey might goe to his lordship's stable and chewes either his best huntinge horsse for the hare or his best buck hunter, which his majestie showld make choyce of, and that I showld present them unto his majestie.

That my lord Savidge wowld present his humble service to his majestie leting him know that never kinge had a more faithfull servant or a more loyall subject than myselfe, nor never subjecte had a more gracious soveraigne, acknowledginge himselfe infinightly bound to his majesty for his ever gracious favoures unto him.

That his lordshippe desiered there might bee no difference betwixt my sister of Rutland and myselfe in the execution of his will; and I desier you my lord Savidge, if there bee any, to deside it, but if you cannot, then I pray you to commend my love unto my lord keeper,[120] and my desier is that your two lordshippes showld deside it.

That there was a thowsand pounds in his iron chest at London, and five hundred pounds in his servant Robert Cooks custody, and desiered us his executors to put to it five hundred pounds more, and pay it to Sir John Ayres whom he ought two thousand pounds.

His lordshipp is pleased to give Mr Doctor Litster fifty pounds for the care he hath taken of him in this his sicknesse.

For my funerall I wowld have it such as my auncestors have had, which will bee no greate charge, for that my toombe is allreddy made, and I wowld have my bodie so soone as it is embalmed to bee removed forth of the Inn.[121]

Theise directions weare by his lordship delivered unto us, hee beeinge in perfitt memory after his will was made, this 15th day of December 1632.

[*Endorsed in Sir George Manners' hand*] My brother's speache to my lady Rutland and myselfe at Storford.

---

118 This must be the duchess of Buckingham.

119 Mall was Mary, Buckingham's daughter, who did marry Charles, Lord Herbert of Shurland, third and eldest surviving son of the lord chamberlain, the earl of Pembroke. Charles died in 1635.

120 Thomas Coventry, later Lord Coventry, was the lord chancellor and keeper of the great seal from 1625 to 1639.

121 The earl was given an expensive heraldic funeral costing £3544 (given in R. Houlbrooke, *Death, Religion and the Family, 1480–1750* (Oxford, 1998), p. 274).

Doc. 48. Petition from Elizabeth Savage to Charles I, concerning her pension and finances, undated. [TNA: SP 16/257/76]

The first of several documents in this collection which provide evidence of Elizabeth Savage's attempts to bolster her finances. It is undated but was placed among the State Papers in 1633.

I have had the honor to know and love your majesty with my whole hartt ever since your infantie. I have served your majestie and my gratious mistris this eight yeares, my lord hath served your majestie nere twenty yeares, wherin he hath bene deligent and fathfull, and he my selffe or children have upon all occations presented our service both at the reception of our most gratious mistris, and upon all the occations of charge we have never absented our selves. I have twelve chilldren and I live here at a great charge, and without helps from any friend. My lord and his sonne are both intebted [*sic*], and to maintaine all our charge I protest unto your majestie we have not tow thousand pounds a yeare, and of that small fortune I spende twelve hundred pounde a yeare here. All this I lay at your majesties feete, besechinge you not to make me the only example of a servant that am not worthy neither diett nor other entertainement, therfore I besich your majestie to continue your pention to me that I may therby be the more able to attende the service of my mistris, and not apeare less deservinge in your majesties favor then I have bene in the eyes of my husband and my owne friends.

[Indorsed by secretary Windebank] Lady Savage

Doc. 49. Petition of the chief forester of Delamere to Charles I, undated.[122] [TNA: SP 16/257/46]

Elements of this petition remind us of Thomas Savage's high-handed dealings with the population of Frodsham (see Introduction, pp. xxvii–viii) but John Crewe, son of Sir Randulph Crewe, had married into the Done family; he was a powerful man in his own right within Cheshire. This petition suggests that Thomas Savage's earlier petition (Doc. 43) was successful at least in part. See also Doc. 67 which relates in some way to this one.

To the kings most excellent majestie
The humble peticion of John Crew esq, cheife forester of your majesties forrest of Delamere in the county of Chester.[123]
Sheweth that whereas your royall majestie was graciously pleased the last sommer to grant & command a restreynt from killing any deere in that forrest for the space of three yeeres then next following, because the game was greately decayed; yet the Lord Viscount Savage, ranger of that forrest, who claymed a buck and a doe of the season in every walke, which amount to twenty yeerely, whereas the rangers anciently had but fowre, did not forbeare after knowledge given hym of the restrainte made by your majestie to kill his fee deere, pretending to have obteyned libertie from your majestie for killing the same after the restreynt made by your majestie, which hee being required to shewe unto the forester refused to doe.

122 Delamere became a royal forest soon after the Norman Conquest. It was officially enclosed in 1812 but survives today, owned and run by the Forestry Commission. It comprises a mixture of deciduous and coniferous woodland, the ages varying from old mature forest to new plantings.
123 For John Crewe, see Notes on People below.

And did not onely hunt deere in that forest without any notice thereof first given unto the forester, as he ought to doe by the auncient custome of that forrest and the usage of other rangers before hym, but also if any walke did not afford deere to his liking he would supply his number out of the rest, allthough out of some of them he had taken his fee deere before. And when a fee deere was killed the said Lord Savage did take away the deere without giving the accustomed fees to the underkeepers. And some deere by reason of this hunting being driven into the lands of the Lord Savage adioyning to the forest wherein hee claymes a pourliew, hee nor his under officers did not rechase them into the said forrest, according to the dutie of his & their place, but permytted them quietly to rest in that purliewe and the underkeepers were prohibited to hunt them into the said forrest when they attempted in defaulte of hym and his under officers soe to doe. In which said purliewe the deere finding better foode then in the forrest continue there, and so ar in danger to be killed at pleasure of the Lord Savage.

Now forasmuch as the forester being thus neglected, and the fee of the underkeepers taken from them, the number of deere greatly decayed and many suffred to continue in the aforesaid purleiw, the residue, if the Lord Savage shalbe permytted to take his twenty fee deere yeerely, are like in short tyme to bee destroyed, if your majestie according to your great wisdome doe not give due and seasonable remedy for the prevencion thereof.

This peticioner being desirous to preserve the game & state of the said forrest humbly beseecheth your roiall majestie to continue the restrainte for killyng of deare, within the said forrest, against the said Lord Savage for the terme aforesaid. And that your majestie will also be pleased to comand & declare that the said lord & his deputies shall not hunt in the said forrest for his fee deere without knowledge by hym, or his deputies at all tymes first given to the forrester, and that if hee have taken his fee deere out of any walke hee may not resorte to the same for more, and that the underkeepers upon the killing of every deere may have their auncient fees and be permytted to rechase the deere out of the purliewes of the said Lord Savage in defaulte of the said Lord Savage, his deputies & under officers. By which meanes the honor of the forrest, which is your roiall majesties, may be preserved. Wherein this peticioner shall ymploy his care and best endevour.

(And as in duty bound) he shall daily pray for your majesties long & happie raigne.

Doc. 50. Extract from letter from James Howell to Thomas Savage about the death of William Noye, ?1634. [Howell: *Familiar Letters*, 2nd edn, 1650, section 6, pp. 204–5]

James Howell continued his correspondence with both Thomas Savage and Thomas Lord Darcy for many years after his short stay at Melford, or at the very least later wrote letters suggesting a correspondence. Most of the letters are about foreign affairs, written while Howell was abroad, but this one returns to domestic matters. This letter is dated October 1635, but Noye died on 9 August 1634. It is possible, although unlikely, that the letter was written in 1634 and sent with the wrong date at the time; alternatively it could have been written and dated 1634, with the error made when it was put in print, or possibly it was not written until later in Howell's life, and the error occurred then. It has been placed here as if it was written in 1634.

To the right honorable the Lord Vicount Savage at Long Melford
My lord, the old steward of your courts, master attorney generall Noy is lately dead,

nor could Tunbridg waters do him any good: though he had good matter in his brain, he had, it seems, ill materialls in his body; for his heart was shrivelled like a leather peny-purse when he was dissected, nor were his lungs found.[124]

Being such a great clerk in the law, all the world wonders he left such an odd will, which is short, and in Latin. The substance of it is, that having bequeathed a few legacies, and left his second son 100 marks a year and 500 pounds in money, enough to bring him up in his father's profession, he concludes, *reliqua meorum omnia progenito meo Edoardo, dissipanda (nec melius unquam speravi) lego*; I leave the rest of all my goods to my first-born Edward, to be consum'd or scatterd (for I never hoped better.)[125] A strange and scarce a Christian will, in my opinion, for it argues uncharitablenes. Nor doth the world wonder less, that he should leave no legacie to som of your lordship's children, considering what deep obligations he had to your lordship, for I am confident he had never bin attorney generall els.

The vintners drink carowses of joy that he is gon, for now they are in hopes to dress meat again, and sell tobacco, beer, sugar and fagots, which by a sullen *capricio* of his, he would have restraind them from.[126] He had his humors, as other men, but certainely he was a solid rational man; and though no great orator, yet a profound lawyer, and no man better versd in the records of the Tower. I heard your lordship often say, with what infinit pains and indefatigable study he came to this knowledge. And I never heard a more pertinent anagram then was made of his name, William Noye, I moyle in law . . .

Your lordshipps most humble and obliged servitor,
J.H.
Westminster 1 October 1635.[127]

Doc. 51. Elizabeth Savage and Mary Hamiliton petition for income from a duty on the import of brass, 24 January 1635.[128] [TNA: SP 16/282/80]

The earliest, as far as we know, of Elizabeth Savage's 'business' petitions. Whether she got the original ideas, or whether one of her trustees (see Doc. 61) or business partners found the possibilities, we do not know. We cannot find any further reference to this petition.

To the kings most excellent majestie, the humble peticion of Dame Mary Hamilton and Dame Elizabeth Savage.

Whereas your majesties loyall subjects with great charge & industry have in this your highnes realme severall brass works, & are attained to perfeccion in the manufactures thereof, whereby the plentie of calamy myne here lately found may have fuller vent, & both honor & profit accrew to your majesties dominions and subjects.

---

124 For William Noye, see Notes on People below. The health-giving quality of the spring at Tunbridge, Kent, was discovered by Lord North in 1606. Queen Henrietta Maria had visited in 1630 after the birth of Prince Charles.

125 'Progenito' is given as 'primogenito' in the 1673 edition. Edward Noye died in a duel two years later, and the estate then passed to Humfrey Noye, the second son; it included the lease of Savage's house at Brentford Bridge. It was Humfrey who was living in that house when it was sequestered in 1643; he had failed to pay the fines for supporting the royalist cause. Whether he was still renting the house from Earl Rivers (as John Savage was by then) or whether he had bought the property, we do not know. Christopher O'Riordan, 'The Story of a Gentleman's House in the English Revolution', *Trans of the London and Middlesex Archaeological Soc.*, 38, 1987, 165–7.

126 Noye had been about to introduce laws restricting the work a vintner could do.

127 See introduction to the document for a note about the date.

128 For Dame Mary Hamilton, see Notes on People below.

The Dutch & German marchants to suppress the undertakers herein, & to beat the English out of this trade, have for some yeares past ingrossed into their hands the Sweden copper (being a principall materiall for the making of brass), & for their owne ends, have raised & lessned the prices thereof, & imported into this your majesties realme great quantities of brass, & their manufactures thereof, which they have sould at low & meane rates, intending (as may be presumed) to enhance the same at their owne wills, thereby impoverishing your majesties subjects & inforcing them to leave off this trade.

For redress wherein, & the rather in respect it is by the letters pattents of your late father of happy memory, & by his speciall comaundement published in print & declared to be reasonable, that manufacture of other nations should be charged with imposicions; and for that the poundage & impost inwards, now payed to your highnes for battery & other manufactures of brass (according to the rates the same are in these times usually sould at) exceede not in the whole the proporcion due to your majestie for poundage onely. May it therefore please your majestie, at the humble suite of your peticioners to lay a new impost of 3s. 4d. upon the hundred waight of all mannor of brass \battery/ & manufactures of brass, which shall here after be imported into this realme. And that in compensacion of the yearely pencion by your highnes given to your peticoner the Lady Savage whereof a £1000 is arreare, & also in reward of the long service by both your peticioners done to your majestie & your dearest consort their most gracious mistress, to graunt to your peticioners, or to such persons as they shall nominate, the said new impost of 3s. 4d. for the terme of 21 yeares upon the yearely rent of £100 to bee reserved to your majestie, for whose prosperous raigne (as in dutie bound) they shall ever pray.

At the court at Whitehall 24th January 1634.

His majestie referreth the consideration of this petition to the committees for trade, who are to report to his majestie what they thinke fitt for his service and the publiques good.

John Coke[129]

52. Elizabeth Savage's petition to the king about a legal appointment, 1635. [TNA: SP 16/306/1]

This petition is undated, but has been placed in 1635 by the organisers of State Papers. It was presumably written before Thomas Savage's death, because Elizabeth then became the Dowager Viscountess. It is included here as additional evidence of Elizabeth's quest for income. Whoever became chief prothonotary would have a considerable income from the post, and would be willing to pay well for it.[130] *Elizabeth is asking for the right to make the appointment and thus receive that payment.*

To the kings most sacred majestie, the humble petition of Elizabeth Vicecountes Savage

Most humble shewing

That it hath bene your petitioners great happines for many yeares to attend the royall parson of your most excellent consort the quenes majestie, wherin as your petitioner doth in all humblenes acknowledge your majesties gratious acceptance of her

129 For John Coke, see Notes on People below.

130 The *DNB* suggests that the holder, Richard Brownloe, made an annual profit of £6000 a year on this post, which he held from 1591 until his death in 1638.

service in your royall favors towards her, soe for the better ennablinge your petitioner to doe her majestie service, your petitioner is a most humble sutor.

That your majestie will be gratiously pleased to grant to your petitioner the next donation and disspotition off the place or office of Richard Brownloe now one of the prothonotaries of your majesties court of common pleas<s>, and care shall be taken to present a fitt and able parson for execution of the sade office, and accordinge to her most bounden duty daly pray for your majesties longe and most glorious raigne.[131]

Doc. 53. Elizabeth Savage's petition to the king relating to income from those granted the freedom of the City of London, autumn 1635. [TNA: SP 16/303/65]

Another petition probably delivered sometime before Thomas Savage's death. However, it was dealt with in Whitehall in the period between his death and funeral. This is the only one of Elizabeth's business efforts where both petition and result survive. Doc. 59 is the response.

To the kings moste excellent majesty, the humble petition of Elizabeth Viscountesse Savage your majesties servant.

Where your moste honorable cittie of London, your majesties chamber, hath beene from ancient tymes the seminary of trade and merchandize, wherein for the moste part freedome hath beene obtained by apprentices from theire maisters by full instructions, paines and faithfull service. And although yearely some few as a priviledge to the present [*illeg.*] have beene admitted to theire freedomes by redemption of money, yet that hath beene with especiall caution that the parties soe made free should not exercise anie other trade than that of the company they were admitted unto uppon the purchase of theire freedome. And to such purpose the persons made free have with twoe sureties a peece entered into bond to the chamberleyn of London, or to some other pryme officer trusted for the publique good of the cittie, in the penaltie of an hundred markes conditioned in effect that they should not use anie other trade then that of which they were made free. Soe it is, may it please your majestie, that of late yeares divers and sundry persons have neverthelesse contrary to theire saide securities, they have and doe use other trades then what they were made free of, to the greate damage and prejudice of your majesties poore subjectes the poore tradesmen of the saide cittie, and being persons of abilitie, doe soe use the matter as theire saide bondes are not put in suite, to the deludeing of the government of the saide cittie.

Forasmuch as the saide penalty being neglected, doe justly belong to your majestie and ought to bee put in suite and receaved for your majesties use, your majestie being the supreme governor of the saide cittie, and therefore to supply by your highnesses prerogative the breach of trust in your subordinate officers, may it please your majestie to graunt unto such persons as this petitioner shall nominate and trust the penalities of such of the saide securities as shall bee proved to bee broken, and to give direction and comaund unto the lord maior under your majesties privie signett that the same may bee recovered with all convenientt speede at this petitioners instance and charge in the names of the obligees, by which course the obligors shall but justly suffer and persons of the like condicion bee discouraged to incurre the future breach of the like securities.

131 For Richard Brownloe, see Notes on People below.

And your petitioner (as in all dutie bound) shall ever pray for your majesties long and happie raigne over us.
[*on the reverse*] reference to Lord Cottington and Secretary Windebank who, calling to them the Attorney General and some aldermen of London, are to certify their opinions.[132] Whitehall, 6th December, 1635.

Doc. 54. Letter of Sir Frederick Cornwallis recording Sir Thomas Savage's death, 26 November 1635. [*The Private Correspondence of Lady Jane Cornwallis, 1613–1644* (London 1842), Letter CLXXXVII, p. 280]

Elizabeth Savage's grandmother was a Cornwallis; this is an extract from a longer letter.

My deare mother,
I hope your ladyship was pleased to receive my wiefe's excuse, & so to pardon mee that I had not the honor to write to your ladyship the last weeke, for, just as I was aboute it, the king sent mee in a greate deale of haste to my Lorde Sauvage, whoo, for all my speede, I founde deade before I came. Hee hath leafte noe will, and they say that his debts are a greate deale more then his fortune will bee after my Lord Rivers his death, especially if he should die before my ladie . . .[133]
Theobalds, November 26, 1635

Doc. 55. Letter from Revd G. Garrard to the Lord Deputy of Ireland (Thomas Wentworth, later earl of Strafford), December 1635. [*The Earle of Strafforde's Letters and Dispatches, with an Essay towards his Life*, ed. W. Knowler (London 1739), I, 489]

This is the most graphic account we have of Thomas Savage's disease, extracted from a much longer letter; it also gives an interesting description of him, along with a contemporary summary of his financial problems.

May it please your lordship,
. . . The great commissioner, the great director in other men's estates is dead, the Lord Savage, who had a universal gout took him all over his body, which put him into a strong fever, which in less than ten days ended him. His estate is £2500 a year clogg'd with a debt of £30,000 contracted by himself, his eldest son, and his own wife; his proper debts £14,000, his son £10,000 and his wife the rest. The Lord Rivers is their hope, who is rich both in land and money, and cannot by reason of his great age long keep it from them; that now is their greatest comfort . . .
Your humblest servant, G. Garrard
December 1635

132 For Lords Cottingham and Windebank, see Notes on People below.
133 'My ladie' here must refer to Lady Rivers, Elizabeth Savage's mother. If Lord Rivers died after his wife, her jointure would not have to come out of the remaining estate.

Doc. 56. Herald's account of Thomas Savage's funeral, 9 December 1635 and after. [Bodl.: Rawlinson B 138, f. 20]

These working notes of one of the heralds should be read alongside the photograph of the first two pages of the original, which appear in Pl. 5.

Wed the 9 of December, 1635

The proceeding through London with the corps of my Lord Savage from his house at Tower hill to Islington and so to his buriall place \Macclesfield church/ in Cheshire on horse back as followeth:

Two conductors with blacke staves
Servantes to gentlemen and esquires
Servantes to knights
Servantes to knights of the Bath
Servantes to barronetts
Servantes to barons, viscountes and earles younger sonnes
2 trumpeters
The standard borne by Mr Edward Savage[134]
Servantes to the defunct
Groomes & yeomen
Gentlemen servantes to the defunct & others
Esquiers
Knightes
Knightes of the Bath
Barronettes
Barrons, vicounts, younger sonns of earles
Comptrouler steward

<Mr [*deleted*] > Mr Hopper with white staves
Mr Spencer
The great banner borne by Sir <Edward> \Robert/ Needham, Mr Dutton <illeg.>
<Rougedragon> healme and creast
<Yorke coate of armes and targett>
\Rouge dragon/[135]
<Yorke> sworde and targett
Yorke[136]

Mr Mannering gent esqr bare on the left hand	Coate of armes <and crowne> <Yorke>	Mr Fletcher with the [*illeg.*] on the right hand <bare headed on the left hand>

The corps drawne in an open chariot with 6 horses [*?*]trapt and adorned with escuchions

Savage & Vernon	Savag and Bostwick
Mr [*illeg.*]	Mr Danyell

134 For Edward Savage and all other individuals mentioned in this document, see Notes on People below.
135 Rouge Dragon was Thomas Thompson; see Notes on People.
136 York Herald was George Owen; see Notes on People.

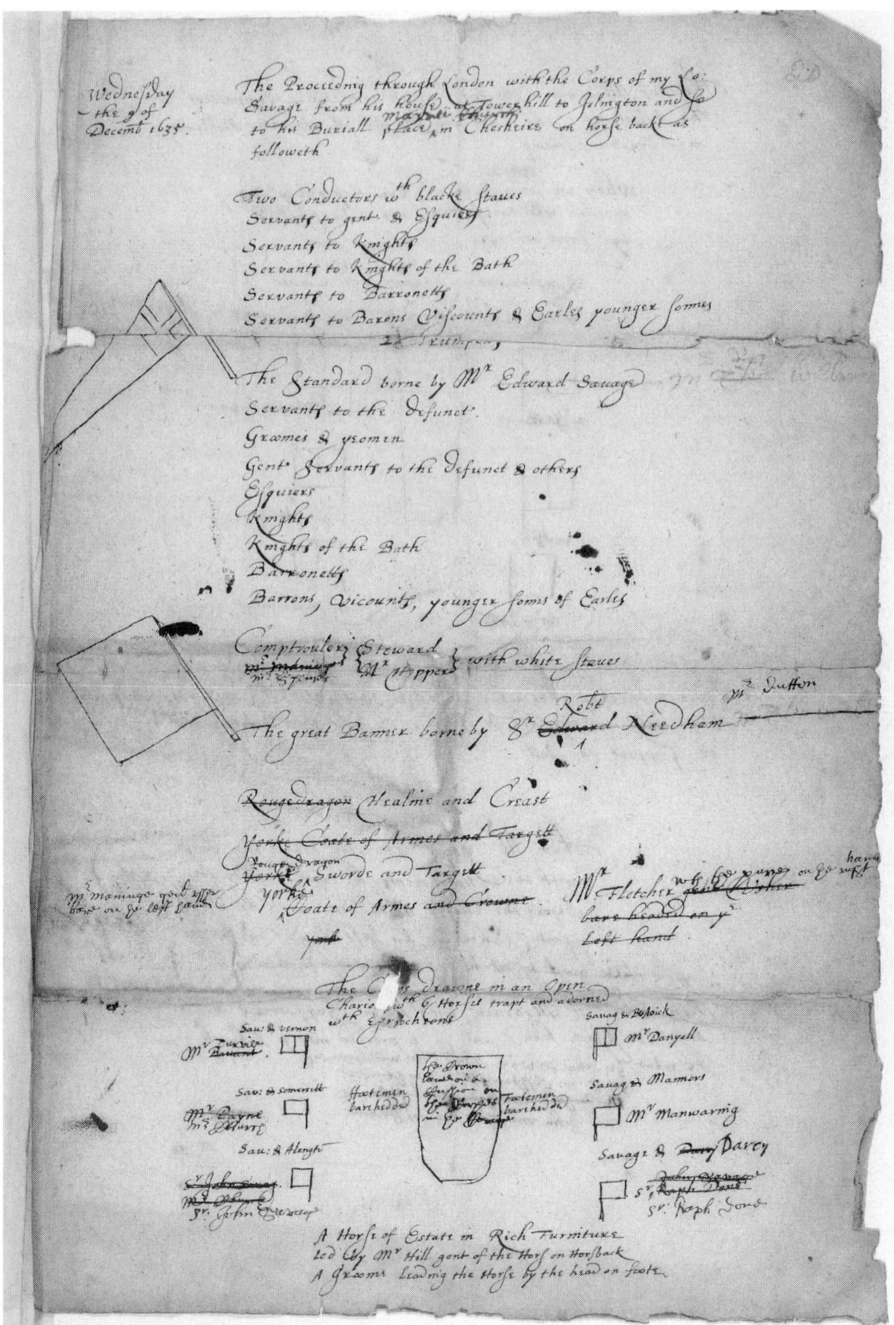

Plate 5. A herald's working notes describing the funeral procession of Thomas Viscount Savage, 1635. The notes include a list of the nobility present at the funeral. This shows the first two pages of four; the text is fully transcribed in Doc. 56. *(By courtesy of the Bodleian Library)*

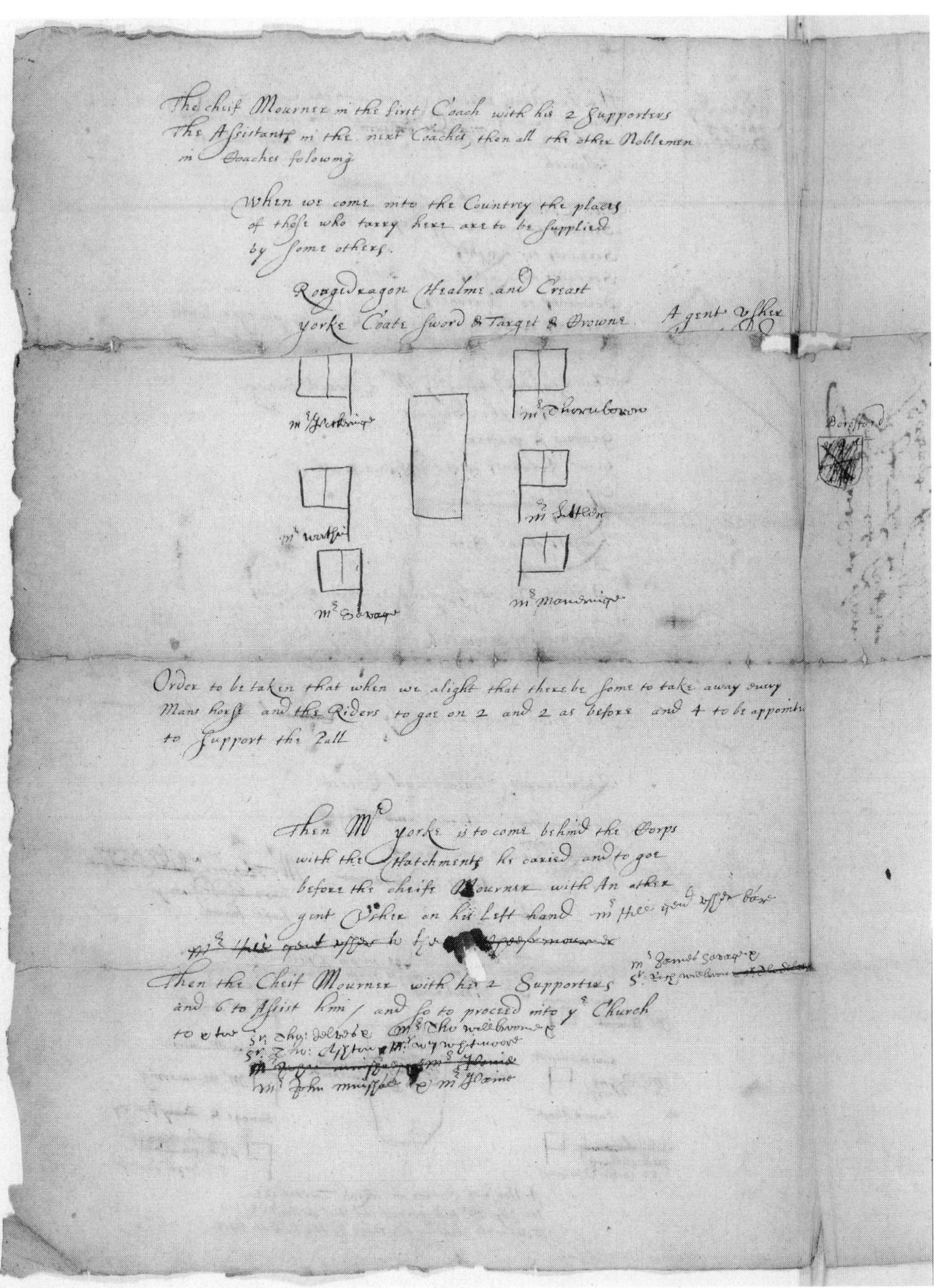

The cheif Mourner in the first Coach with his 2 Supporters
The Assistants in the next Coaches, then all the other Noblemen
in Coaches folowing

When we come into the Country the places
of those who tarry here are to be supplied
by some others.

Rougedragon Healme and Creast
Yorke Coate Sword & Target & Crowne   A gent Usher

Order to be taken that when we alight that there be some to take away every
Mans horse and the Riders to goe on 2 and 2 as before and 4 to be appointed
to Support the Pall

Then Mr Yorke is to come behind the Corps
with the Hatchments he caried and to goe
before the cheife Mourner with An other
gent Usher on his left hand Mr Hill gent Usher [illegible]
~~Mr Hill gent Usher to the [illegible] mourner~~

Then the Cheif Mourner with his 2 Supporters   Mr Daniel Savage &
and 6 to Assist him / and so to proceed into ye Church   Sr Rog: Wilbraham ~~[illegible]~~
to wit   Sr Thy: Delves & Mr Tho Wilbrome &
Sr Tho: Aston & Mr Wm Whitmoore
~~Mr [illegible] [illegible] & Mr [illegible]~~
Mr John Mainwaring & Mr [illegible]

Savage & Somersett		The crown		Savag and Mannors
	footimen	laid on a	footimen	
<Mr Payne>	barehedded	cushion on	barehedded	Mr Manwaring
Mr Church		the corpes		
		in the carriage		
Savage & Alington				Savage and Darcy
<Sir John Savage>				<John Savage>
<Mr Church>				<Sir Raph Dant>
Sir John Savage				Sir Raph Done

A horse of estate in rich furniture led by Mr Hill
gentleman of the hors on horsback
A groome leading the horse by the head on foote

The chief mourner in the first coach with his 2 supporters. The assistantes in the next coaches, then all the other noblemen in coaches folowing.

When we come into the countrey the places of those who tarry here are to be supplied by some others.

Rougedragon healme and creast
Yorke coate sword & target & crowne   a gent usher

Mr Pickeringe	Mr Thornborow
Mr Worthin	Mr Littler
Mr Savage	Mr Maneringe

Order to be taken that when we alight that therebe some to take away every mans horse, and the riders to goe on 2 and 2 as before, and 4 to be appointed to support the pall.

Then Mr Yorke is to come behind the corps with the hatchmentes he caried, and to goe before the cheife mourner with an other gent usher on his left hand.

Mr Hill gent usher bare

<Mr Hill gent usher to the Cheefe mourner>

Mr James Savage

Then the chief mourner with hir [*sic*] 2 supporters   Sir Richard Wilbraham
<deleted>

and 6 to assist him, and so to proceed into the church, to and too.[137]

Sir Thomas Delves &	Mr Thomas Wilbroome &
Sir Thomas Ashton	Mr William Whitmore
<Mr John Minshall	Mr Paine>
Mr John Minshall &	Mr Paine

137 'Hir' in reference to the chief mourner is probably an error. At heraldic funerals the mourners were all of the same sex as the deceased person, so the chief mourner here would have been John Viscount Savage.

The Viscount Savages armes and quarterings used at his funerall

1 Savage
2 Walkington
3 Danyers
4 Chedle
5 Stockport
8 Vernon
9 Lacy
6 Swinerton
7 Becks
10 Bostock

Berefford

11 Chester
12 Venables
13 Dutton
18 Minshall
19 Alington
<16 Argentine>
Fitz trake
23 Midleton
24 Cordall

14 Thornton
15 Kingsley
16 Helsby
17 Hutton
20 Berefford
21 Argentine

Darcy Earl Rivers
his armes and quartered coats

1 Darcy
2 Harleston
3 Bradwell
<damaged>
5 Fitz Langley
6 Kidson
7 Donengton
8 Pye
9 Darcy

The escuchion of presedence
1 Darcy
2 Harleston
< Wanteen>
3 <Bradwell> [*?*]Wanteen
4 Kydson

1 Viscount Kylmorey
2 Viscount Cholmley
3 Viscount Molenaux

The stile pronownced per Yorke (deputy to Mr Garter) \instantly/ after the parson had done the internment:

Thus it hath pleased allmighty God to take out of this transitory life (to his divine goodnesse and mercy) the right honorable Thomas late Viscount Savage, chauncellor and counsailor to the Queens most excellent majestie.

God blesse with longe life & happinesse the right honorable John now Viscount Savage (heire apparent to the honour and erledom of Rivers) with the rest of that right noble family.

God save the Kinge.

[*on the reverse*]
The preceding through London with the corps of <hen> Thomas Viscount Savage from his house on Tower hill to Islington & soe to his buriall place Macclesfield church in Cheshire.

The goeing thorow London was the 9th day of December 1635

The composition for the funerall was threscore and ten pound for 3 officers, £30 for Mr Garter, <and> £20 for Mr Owen Yorke and £20 for Mr Thomson Rougedragon (it beeinge theire turne). It was after agreed that Yorke and Rougedragon should goe to Cheshire with the corpes & to solempnise the funerall there for which they had transportance allowed them: to York as deputy to Garter after the rate, 14^{d} per every mile outward and homeward, and to Rouge dragon as a herald <for Yorke> allowed [*deleted*] 10^{d} per the mile (which came <to between them both> to £28) to bee devided between them, les their £20 before mencioned.

Doc. 57. Funeral certificate of Thomas Viscount Savage, December 1635. [College of Arms: MS I.8, f. 50]

The College of Arms issued a funeral certificate whenever an individual died who had the right to bear arms.

The right honourable Thomas Viscount Savage, chauncellor and counsailer to the queenes majesty and heire apparent to the earledome of Rivers, departed this mortall life the 20th day of November 1635 at the house at Towerhill, from whence his body in an open chariot covered with velvet accompaned [*sic*] with dyvers lords in their coaches, and his kinsfolk and servants riding before in black, was honourably conveighed through the city of London unto Maxfeild[138] in Cheshire where he was solemplie enterred with other of his noble auncestors, the greatest part of the nobility and gentrie of that county being present and assisting that service.

He maried Elizabeth daughter and coheire of the foresaid Thomas Earle Rivers, by whom he had yssue 11 sonnes and 8 daughters, whereof 10 [*sic*] were lyving at the tyme of his decease, namely John his eldest sonne now Viscount Savage who maried Katherin, 2d daughter [*sic*] of Henry Lord Morley and Monteagle, by whom he has yssue two sonnes and 3 daughters, namely Thomas eldest sonne, John 2d sonne, Elizabeth, Jane and Katherin.[139] The 2d sonne of the defunct is Thomas Savage who maried Briget one of the daughters and coheires of William Whitmore of Leighton in the county of Chester Esq, which Briget was likewise heire to her mother Margaret, daughter and heire to Sir Hugh Beeston of Beeston Castle in the county of Chester.[140] The 3d sonne to the defunct is Frances Savage, the 4th James, the 5th William, the 6th Richard, the 7th Charles.

The eldest daughter to the defunct was Jane Savage who married John Lord Marquest of Winchester who deceased in the life tyme of his [*sic*] father,[141] the 2nd daughter is Dorothy, the 3d Elizabeth who married Sir John Thymbleby[142] of [*blank*] in ye county of Lincolne, kt, the 4th daughter is Anne,[143] the 5th Katherin

138 The Savage family had been burying their dead at Macclesfield for over two hundred years, long before their family chapel was built there in the early sixteenth century.

139 From this marriage are descended, amongst many other people, Sarah Ferguson, former wife of Prince Andrew, Alfred Lord Tennyson, General Curzon, Sir Francis Galton, Bertrand Russell and numerous aristocratic families. For Lord Morley and Monteagle, see Notes on People below.

140 From this marriage are descended, amongst others, the Percy family, dukes of Northumberland. Another descendant married into the Mostyn family. For Sir Hugh Beeston and the Whitmore family, see Notes on People below.

141 From this marriage are descended the dukes of Bolton and thus many other aristocratic families including the dukes of Bridgewater. For the marquis of Winchester, see Notes on People below.

142 Anthony van Dyck's portrait of Elizabeth Thimbleby with her sister Dorothy, by then Viscountess Andover, is reproduced in this volume, Pl. III. For Sir John Thimbleby, see Notes on People below. This was another catholic gentry family, whose principal lands were in Irnham, Lincolnshire, south-east of Grantham.

143 Anne Savage later married Robert Brudenell, 2nd earl of Cardigan. From them are descended both

and the 6 is Henritta Maria.[144] The whole proceeding and ceremonyes were ordered by Garter Principall King of Armes, and the officers that attended were George Owen Yorke herauld, Thomas Thomson Rougedragon and William Ryley Blewmantle Pursuivant of Armes.[145]
Savage

58. Lord Paulet to the duchess of Richmond and Lennox, 26 January 1636. [TNA: SP 16/312/44]

This was presumably written by Thomas's and Elizabeth's son-in-law, who had been married to their daughter Jane. There is an indication elsewhere that Thomas had served the duchess of Lennox, but we have found no direct evidence of his role.[146]

Madam,
I have receaved the letter you did me the honor to write to me, by which I find the continuance of your favor and good afecion, which I shall strive to meritt by all the wayes possiblye I can serve you. I am sorrye for the death of my lord Savage, the more for that your excellencye hath lost a very able and [*deleted*] \humble/ servant. I intend to waite one you this terme, if I have health to carrye me out of the countrye, otherwise I must stay till it be fairer weather. Whilest I was uppon the seas in his majesties employmentes, the lord cheefe justice Finch did me very great curtesyes and favors in some businesse of mine which weare in disorder by my absince: if it please your excellencye to let him knowe that you take notice of it, and doe give him thanks in my behalfe, and will be the meanes that his majesty shall \know/ the care he took of my affaires, whilest I was in his service, you will acquite a great part of my obligation to him and by the same meanes putt still more obligation uppon your excellencyes most humble servant,[147]
Poulet[148]
26th Jan
[*on the reverse*]
For her excellencye the dutchesse of Richmound and Lanex.[149]
Lord Poulet to E duchesse of Richmond, delivered by his [*?*]man, 23 Febr 1635.

Doc. 59. The City of London's reply to Elizabeth Savage's petition, 28 January 1636. [TNA: SP 16/312/58]

The city worthies who dealt with Elizabeth's petition acted speedily, either because it was taken seriously and needed robust action, or because it was of little account and could be rapidly rebutted.

Prince William (by his mother's Spencer line) and Camilla Shand, now the duchess of Cornwall. Charles James Fox and the vanished Lord Lucan were other descendents of this couple.

144 A portrait of Lady Henrietta Maria Sheldon, attributed to Jacob Huysmans and in the style of Peter Lely, hangs at Boughton House in Northamptonshire and is reproduced in this volume, Pl. 1, p. lxiii. It is probably there through a family connection with the Brudenells, earls of Cardigan.

145 For the heralds, see Notes on People below.

146 The duchess, in a letter to the king, mentions Thomas over a problem with some merchants: TNA, SP 16/292/27.

147 For chief justice Finch, see Notes on People below.

148 For Lord Paulet, see Notes on People below.

149 For the duchess of Richmond and Lennox, see Notes on People below.

Clitherow Manor — Thursday 28th January, 1635
The 11th year of King Charles

This day Sir Hugh Hamersley, Sir Morris Abbott knighte & aldermen, Mr Alderman Gurney, Mr Alderman Cordell, Mr Stone & Mr Phesant, comittees formerly appointed to consider of the matters to them referred by order of this corte of the 11th of this instant January touching a peticion exhibited to the kinges majestie by the righte honorable Elizabeth Viscountesse Savage, did deliver into this corte a reporte in writing under their handes how they said the same & their opinions, the tenor whereof is as followeth namely:[150]

To the right honorable the lord maior of the citty of London & corte of aldermen.

According to an order of this honorable corte of the eleaventh of this instant January, wee have considered of the matters referred unto us conteyned in the peticion lately exhibited to the kinges majestie by the righ[*sic*] honorable Elizabeth Viscountesse Savage, whereby she desiereth the graunt of the penalties of such recognizances thereby pretended to be forfeited by diverse persons whoe have acknowledged the same to the chamberlenn of this citty, upon their admittances unto the freedome by redempcion togeather with their suerties. And wee finde:

1. That such persons whoe are admitted into the freedome of this citty by redempcion by order of the corte of aldermen doe before their admittances enter into a recognizance with their sureties, namely the principall in one hundredd marks and the suerties in twenty pound a peeice to the chamberlenn of this citty for the use of the citty and not to the kinge.

2. That the persons soe admitted into the freedome doe enter into recognizances as aforesaid, especially & principally to occupie the craft or mistery wherof he is then admitted, more then any other craft which he shall occupie or happen to occupie, and that theire is noe such caution therein that the parties soe made free should not exercise any other trade absolutely as in the peticion of the Lady Savage is mencioned or otherwise then before is expressed.

3. That from tyme to tyme upon complaintes of the breach of such recognizances, the persons offending have bine put in suite in the lord maiors corte in the chamberlenns name & thereupon have bine punished and disfranchised.

4. Wee are informed that most of those whoe are admitted freemen by redempcion are recomended by the right honorable the lords of his majesties most honorable privie councell and other persons of greate qualitie, and admitted by the grace and favor of this corte, payeing only a small fine unto the chamber of London to the citties use.

5. That noe private benefitt att all doeth by such admittances into the freedom accrew to the governors of this citty to their private use, as is pretended in the peticion.

All which nevertheles wee leave to the grave consideracion of this honorable corte, this 28th of January 1635,
Hugh Hamersley, Morris Abbott, Richard Gurney, John Cordell, John Stone, Peter Phesant.[151]

The which reporte was here openly read & it was thought fitt & ordered that the right honorable the lords to whome it hath pleased his majestie to referre that peticion be forthwith attendend with a coppie of the said reporte.

150 For these men, see Notes on People below. Note that Sir John Cordell was one of the aldermen on the committee.

151 For these men, see Notes on People below.

by Robt Michel[152]
common clerk to the city of London
[*on the reverse*]
Report of Hugh Hamersley & Maurice Abbot to the lord mayor and court of aldermen concerning the Lady Savage's business, 28 January 1635.

Doc. 60. Inventory of the moveable goods and chattels of Thomas Viscount Savage, at Rocksavage in Cheshire, Melford Hall in Suffolk and Tower Hill in the City of London, 1635/6. [CCALS: DCH/X/15/10]

The three inventories which make up this document were taken at different times by different groups of men. Later, presumably for Elizabeth Savage's administration, a scribe copied the three on one roll; apart from the very end, the roll is in almost perfect condition. In the Melford part of the inventory we have added, after the name of each room, our suggestion of its location; the letter relates to the floor, the number to those inserted on our version of John Thorpe's plan of c. 1606, included in this volume (Pl. 7, p. 86).[153] *Thus G15: the room numbered 15, on the ground floor. Since the Thorpe plan is only of the ground floor, the numbers on the other floors (first F, second S and cellars C) can only give an approximate location.*

An inventorie indented of all the goodes & chattells, creditts & moveables of the right honorable Thomas late Viscount Savage deceased; and first of those goodes and chattells at hys mansion house called Rockesavage in the county of Chester, taken, veiwed & apprised the fifteenth day of February in the yeare of our lord God one thowsand sixe hundreth & thirtiey five, by Thomas Cheshire gent, Hugh Wicksted citizen & marchant of Chester, William Hough of London uphoulster, Thomas Cheshire & John Pearson, Hugh Birch, Robert Cooper & Richard Kinge,[154] **as followeth**

	£	s.	d.
In the kinges chamber[155]			
Inprimis five peeces of tapistrye hangeinges	60	15	0
Item one bedstead, the testar, headcloth, five curtaines, double valence of watched damaske, laced & fringed with gould & silver	80	0	0
Item one downe bedd, boulster & two pillows, one fustian quilt, two blankettes & a canvas mattres	19	0	0
Item two great Turkie carpettes, two watchett velvett carpettes & two damaske window curtaines	60	15	0
Item one great chaire, two blacke stooles & foure other stooles & a callico lyneing for the bedd	15	0	0
Item brasse andirons, fire shovell, tonges & bellowes, one cupbord, one groome porters table, two canvas curtaines & a rodd for the windowe	2	6	0

152 For Robert Mitchel, see Notes on People below.
153 Thorpe's plan: Pl. 2, p. lxxii.
154 For as much is as known of the appraisers of the inventory, see Notes on People below.
155 The name of this room presumably related to King James I's visit to Rocksavage in 1617. The king did not spend the night at Rocksavage, but may have rested here before or after hunting in the park.

	£	s.	d.
In the inner chamber			
Item one feild bedstead with three roddes, one feather bedd, one boulster, one pillowe, one rugge, two blankettes, testar, headcloth, vallence, three curtaines & a counterpointe of taffetie sarsnett with one court cupbord & one old chaire	7	15	0
In the gallerie[156]			
Item one high chaire, five folding chaires, one scrowlebacke chaire, sixe high & two lowe stooles of crimson velvett	10	0	0
Item one taffatie traverse curtaine & a rodd & seaven cushions of crimson velvett	16	0	0
Item one couch of tawney cloth with a cover, one carpett, foure window clothes	18	10	0
Item one pair of old virginalls	1	10	0
In the kinges withdraweing chamber			
Item five peeces of tapistry hangeing & three windowe curtains & rodds	21	10	6
Item one high chaire, twelve high stooles, five lowe stooles & two longe cushions of Irish stitch	11	6	8
Item one table, one cabinett of China worke, a paire of copper andirons, fire shovell, tonges & bellowes	6	13	4
In the great dineing chamber[157]			
Item seaven peeces of tapistrye hangeinges	144	16	0
Item twentie foure Turkie carpettes of severall sizes, nine Persian carpettes, foure long cushions, foure square cushions of tentestitch & nedle workes	98	10	0
Item three high chaires, twentie high stooles, foure lowe stooles of tawney velvett with covers	13	6	8
Item foure tables, three court cupbordes, one paire of copper andirons, one fireforke, one fire shovell & a paire of bellowes	7	15	0

156 As this is the only gallery mentioned at Rocksavage, it is likely to be the one included in the 1615 inventory. It then contained pictures, one table, 'one payre of andayrons' and 'one cubbord at the dyninge chamber doore'. This could be the 'wainscot gallery' mentioned in the Rocksavage accounts of 1624. Nicholas Squires, then housekeeper, records spending '2s for mendinge of the glasse taken downe of the wyndowes in the wainscott gallery & setting it upp agayne', and '53s 8d to one Williamson a joyner for taking downe of wainscott in the wainscott gallery, Shrewsbury chamber & the parlour, and for making of some newe that wanted': CCALS, DCH/H/199. However the accounts of 1627 tell us that the upper gallery was that year converted into ten lodging chambers, and part of that operation was 'takinge dowen of the waynskott and makinge of itt feett for the chambers, and setten of itt upe ageane', so two galleries may have originally existed: the upper one having wainscot and the lower one being that listed in the inventory of 1636: CCALS, DCH/E/316. But the 1615 inventory again includes only one gallery, so we are left in some confusion. The ten lodging chambers made in 1627 do not seem to appear on this inventory. It is possible that they were empty when the inventory was made. Sir John Savage's inventories: CCALS, WS1616–18.

157 The Rocksavage accounts for 1627 record, 'payd for 7 lettell crassinges of Iaron to fasten the stones over the baye wendowe of the dininge Chamber': CCALS, DCH/E/316.

	£	s.	d.
In Shrewesbury chamber[158]			
Item five peeces of tapistrye hangeinges & one Turkey carpett & foure window curtaines of greene taffatie	26	13	4
Item one bedstead, testar, headcloth, valence, five curtains & counterpointe of greene taffate	20	0	0
Item one downe bedd & boulster, one holland quilt, one rugge & one paire of blankettes	19	10	0
Item three high chaires, one high stoole & one other stoole of stuffe fringed, one paire of copper andirons, fire shovell, tonges & bellowes with one groome porters table & a court cupboard	13	6	8
In the inner chamber			
Item one feather bedd & boulster, two blankettes & one rugge	5	10	0
Item one liverye bedstead, a table & two stooles	0	12	0
In Darbie chamber[159]			
Item sixe peeces of tapistrye hangeinges	44	10	0
Item two downe beddes, two bolsters & one pillowe	16	10	0
Item foure featherbeddes, 4 boulsters, three paire of pillowes, foure rugges, foure paire of blankettes, one holland quilt & one canvas mattresse	22	4	0
Item sixe bedsteads, whereof three liverye ones, one tester & valence of blew velvett with five taffate curtaines, one valence & testar & three old curtaines of blacke & white damaske & one other testar valence & curtaines of redd saye	8	10	0
Item two high chaires & one lowe stoole of blewe velvett, three groome porters tables & one cupboard	2	6	8
Item two paire of copper andirons with fire shovells & tonges, foure paire of iron andirons with fire shovells & tonges & three paire of bellowes	5	12	0

158 The Shrewsbury Chamber was not mentioned by name in the 1615 inventory but may have been the room called 'Weinscott chamber'. The Rocksavage accounts of 1624 mention the wainscot in the Shrewsbury Chamber (see note 156 above). They also record a payment for taking away rubbish 'which happened upon settinge up of the baye wyndowes by the parler and the Shrewsbury chambers' and another 'iii li to a painter of Chester to painte the wyndowes in the parlour and all the wainscott in Shrewsbury Chamber and lyinge the wyndowes with white lead and oyle'.

159 The Darbie (Derby) Chamber is one of the few rooms with the same name on the 1615 and 1636 inventories (assuming that it is the same room). In 1615 the inventory lists its contents as follows: one bedstead, mat and mattress (30s.), one featherbed, one boulster two pillows (£7), one silk covering, quilted (40s.), two blankets and two fustians (26s. 8d.), one cupboard with one covering (20s.), one velvet chair, one velvet cushion, one other cushion, two low stools (£4), curtains and covering over the bed and hangings at the bed's head with the fringe (£6), five pieces of hangings (£24). In Derby back chamber: one bedstead, one mattress (10s.), two feather beds, one boulster (40s.), one caddoue, two blankets (10s.). The value of the goods in 1615 in the Darby chamber alone comes to £46 16s. 8d.; this is the second most costly furnished room in the house and by far the most expensively furnished bedchamber; the dining chamber is more expensively furnished only because of the value of the hangings. By 1636 the value of the room's contents has more than doubled to £99 12s. 8d., but it is only the fourth most expensively furnished room at Rocksavage.

	£	s.	d.
In Sir James Croftes chamber[160]			
Item one feather bedd & boulster, one rugge, one paire of blankettes & one greene carpett	6	1	8
Item one French bedstead, one testar headcloth, valence of cloth, five taffate curtaines & one old quilt	5	0	0
Item one high chaire, one high stoole & one long cushion of old velvett, one groome porters table, andirons, fireshovell & tonges	1	16	0
In the inner chamber to it			
Item one liverye bedstead, one feather bedd & bolster, one rugge & a paire of blankettes	2	16	0
In Buckley chamber[161]			
Item one feild bedstead, topp valence, curtaines & bases of damaske & a scarlett counterpointe	9	5	0
Item one bedd, boulster & two pillowes of downe, one rugg and an old holland quilt & one paire of blankettes & a canvas mattres	14	8	0
Item one folding chaire & two lowe stooles of redd satten, one groome porters table, a court cupbord, andirons, fire shovell and tonges	1	13	4
In the inner chamber to it			
Item two feather beddes, two bolsters, two rugges, two paire of blankettes, two bedsteades & an old cupbord	8	10	0
In the Lord Savages chamber[162]			
Item a velvett gowne	10	0	0
Item seaven peeces of tapistrye hangeinges	61	4	0
Item one bedstead, testar, headcloth, valence & five curtains of scarlett	6	13	4
Item one downe bedd & boulster, two pillowes, one counterpointe of crimson figg satten, one rugge, two blankettes, one wooll bedd & one mattras	24	0	0
Item two high chaires & two high stooles of scarlett, one groome porters table & a cupbord	1	10	0
In the inner chamber to it			
Item one bedstead, one featherbedd & boulster, one rugge, two blankettes & a table	4	11	0
In the withdraweing chamber to it			
Item five peeces of tapistrie hangeinges	56	14	0
Item foure backe chaires, tenn high stooles with two lowe stooles & one cushion imbroidered & one groome porters table	5	0	0

160 For Sir James Crofts, see Notes on People below.

161 Buckley Chamber is another room with the same name in 1615 and 1636. When Sir John Savage died the contents of the room and its related chamber were valued at £1 0s. 8d.: one bedstead (10s.), one cupboard (6s. 8d.). Near Buckley Chamber, one bedstead (4s.). In this inventory, twenty years later, the contents of this room and its inner chamber are valued at £33 16s. 4d.

162 The 1615 inventory did not identify any room as Sir John Savage's chamber, although Lady Savage's chambers are named as such.

	£	s.	d.
In my Lords little dineing roome			
Item five peeces of tapestrye hangeinges	36	7	6
Item eleaven brasill stooles, two other little stooles, two high bedsteades, two little tables, one cupbord & one great standard in the entrye	6	13	4
In the closett by the skreene			
Item glasses & glasse plates, china dishes & two china voiders, three covering baskettes, twentie seaven knives, a paire of tables, one old carpett, two stands & some other trifeling thinges	10	0	0
In the wardrope			
Item fifteene peeces of tapistrye hangeing	33	15	0
Item twentie foure peeces of verders	8	16	0
Item one downe bedd, twentie sixe feather beddes & twentie sixe bolsters, seaven downe pillowes, fourteene feather pillowes & one holland wooll bedd	92	7	8
Item thirteene rugges, some of them very old, fifteene fustian blankettes, thirtie one woollen blankettes, some of them very old, quiltes & counterpointes of satten & taffatie, five	33	6	8
Item long cushions & others of cloth of tissue, velvett satten cloth, tenn	15	16	0
Item one sparver of white satten, one sparver of cloth of tissue with valence & five yellow curtaines, one East Indian canopie with a counterpointe of nedleworke, one slope bedd with curtaines, valence & counterpointe of tinsell, one testar & valence with five curtaines of cloth of gould, one testar, headcloth, valence & curtaines of crimson velvet, one testar, valence, curtaines & counterpointe of blew cloth & one valence with five curtaines of striped stuffe	70	0	0
Item one taffate travers, sixe windowe curtaines, foure greene cloth carpettes & one purple velvett carpett	9	17	0
Item threescore and tenn yardes of old greene cloth, two peeces of greene kersey & tenn yardes of redd cloth	10	0	0
Item high chaires of severall sortes, two of them old, five high stooles & two lowe stooles, seaven liverye bedsteades, three groome porters tables, twentie close stooll cases of severall stuffes, twelve close stoole pannes, thirtie seaven chamber pottes, nine brasse perfumeing pannes & 23 dozen of trenchers	16	10	0
Item one bible, one lookeing glasse, foure hundred curtaine ringes, two brasse warmeing pannes, two paire of bellowes, one paire of tables, one groome porters table, one Cipresse chest & an old standard	2	6	8
In the armorie			
Item some armours but out of fashion, with match & halberdes & other trifeling lumber	3	6	8
Item twentie tunnes of coles	6	0	0

	£	s.	d.
In the parlour			
Item two tables & one cupbord, one high chaire, three backe chaires & fifteene stooles of tawney leather, one mappe of the world & one paire of copper andirons	5	6	8
In the great roome			
Item two paire of andirons & one paire of bellowes	0	6	8
In the hall			
Item two longe tables & two lesser tables with formes to three of them, one mapp of Venice,[163] one paire of andirons & a fireforke	1	5	0
In the pantry & chamber to it			
Item one broad bynn, one table, two formes, one old bedstead & an old chest	0	10	0
In the two sellars			
Item beere twentie sixe hoggesheades, eleven stallages for beere & wine, other emptie vessells and some old borded bedsteades	18	6	0
In Kinderton chamber			
Item foure cupbordes & three bedsteades all old	0	8	6
In the kitchin			
Item in brasse & copper stuffe	10	5	0
Item in pewter	31	8	0
Item in iron	8	0	0
Item in lead	4	3	8
In Mr Barneys keepeing[164]			
Item one hoggeshead of sacke	12	0	0
Item fourteene sugar loves	3	10	0
Item in old and new hoppes[165]	4	0	0
In the laundry			
Item in woodden vessells, two old tables, one cisterne & a cheese presse	5	15	0
In the clocke house[166]			
Item one clocke & two bells fastened to the house	0		

163 The Rocksavage accounts for 1633 include: 'paid to Thomas Harper and his man at hanging pictures and putting them in frames, one day 2s . . . Paid to them more for making a frame and tymber for the same for the mapp of Venice 5s': CCALS, DCH/M/1/4.

164 John Barney was housekeeper at Rocksavage.

165 The housekeeper's accounts for Rocksavage regularly show the sale of hops.

166 Because the clock is fastened to the building, it is not a moveable and not therefore valued.

	£	s.	d.
In the storehouse & Mr Barneys chamber			
Item blacke jackes jugges, bottles, baskettes, trayes, trenchers, chestes, barrells, chaires & other implementes	1	2	0
Item linnen in sundry trunkes & chestes	220	0	0
Item divers pictures,[167] three marble tables & one great lookeing glasse	32	0	0
Item one silver boale weighing 26 oz at 4s 11d	6	7	10
In the court house at Frodsham[168]			
Item one bedstead, one feather bedd & boulster, one rugge, three blankettes, one paire of sheetes, all very old & overworne	2	6	8
Item in other old implementes & lumber	2	0	0
In the out roomes & abroad			
Item geldinges, mares & coltes, nineteene	57	3	4
Item one bull, two heifers & eight oxen	50	0	0
Item in corne	153	13	0
Item in hay	10	0	0
Item in cartes, plowes, harrowes & other implementes	14	3	10
Item in brewing vessells	4	0	0
Item debtes, credittes & arrerages of rent	0	0	0
Item one lease of the herbage & turbarie in the forrest of Delamer for thirtie yeares in reversion after Sir Richard Wilbrams life,[169] the turbarie being the cheifest commoditie & much exhausted	150	0	0
Item one lease of the waifes & strayes & deodandes of Holton for nine yeares & an halfe,[170] the casualties not answereing the rent & charge, average annually, as alsoe the lease of Eddisbury hundred[171]	10	0	0
The totall somme of the goodes & chattells at Rocke Savage	2163	0	8

An inventorie of the goodes, chattells, credittes and moveables of the right honorable Thomas late Lord Viscount Savage deceased taken & made at the late mansion house of the said viscount called Melford Hall in Melford in the countie of Suffolk, the twelveth day of January in the yeare of our lord god one

167 In most years the Rocksavage accounts contain references to paying for the transport of pictures from London to Rocksavage. In the 1629 accounts Nicholas Squires, John Barney's predecessor as housekeeper, mentions the arrival of pictures each year from 1626 onwards.

168 Sir Thomas Savage's relationship with the manor of Frodsham has been mentioned in the Introduction. The castle does not feature in this inventory because it had been given to Thomas's and Elizabeth's eldest son and his wife in 1626, but this item indicates that Thomas still had the Court House.

169 For Sir Richard Wilbraham, see Notes on People below.

170 In 1631 William Thornborough, keeper of Rocksavage Park, accounted for 'one waife stear, two fatt cows, two waife naggs, one waife stear, one waife heffer, 16 waife sheepe' which Sir Thomas Savage had gained in the previous year as lessee of the right to take waifs and strays. Their value is included in a larger total which includes heriot animals and totals over £16: CCALS, DCH/M/35/1. The same year, Thornborough recorded that he paid out '£3 6s. 8d. payd to his majesties receyvor of the duchy of Lancashire for the rent of felon's goods, wayves, Estrayes etc. due for one whole yeare ended att the feast of St Michaell tharkangell last 1633': CCALS DCH/E/322.

171 Eddisbury Hundred was one of the eight hundreds of Cheshire, and covered the south-west of the county.

An Inventorie of the Goods
Chattells Creditts & moveables of the right hoble
Thomas late Lord Viscount Savage deceased
taken & made at the late mansion house of the
said Viscount called Melford hall in Melford
in the Countie of Suffk the twelveth day of
January in the yeare of or Lord God One
Thousand Sixe hundreth & Thirtie five
viewed and apprised by Robert Warren
Doctor of Divinitie Roger Aggas Edward
Paynell Francis Johnson & Andrew Byatt
as followeth

	li	s	d
Imprimis in the hall three long Tables foure formes one square Table one chest wth some old decayed halls one paire of Andirons & a firefork	3	0	0
In the Armorye			
Item old Armes for three horsemen some other old Armes [illegible], browne Bills five Pistolls & some other lumber	1	10	0
In the Armorie Chamber			
Item one long Table one forme & one livery bedstead	0	10	0
In the Wardrope			
Item three old bedsteads one old Standard & and some other wodden lumber	1	3	0
Item Two feather bedds two boulsters five wooll quilts seaven pillowes & a little feather quilt wth three blanketts & a olde counterpointe	10	0	0
Item foure longe Cushions one high chaire two lowe chaires five high stooles & two lowe stooles all suteable covered wth blacke velvett	3	0	8
Item one high chaire & two lowe stooles of Crimson velvett embroidered	0	13	4

Plate 6. Thomas Viscount Savage's inventory, 1635/6: the beginning of the section on Melford Hall. The inventories of the three houses were copied on one roll, still in very good condition. *(By courtesy of Cheshire and Chester Archives and Local Studies)*

thowsand sixe hundreth and thirtieth five,[172] veiwed and apprised by Robert Wareyn Docter of Divinitie, Roger Aggas, Edward Paynell, Francis Johnson and Andrew Byatt as followeth:

	£	s.	d.
[In the hall] [*G21*][173]			
Inprimis in the hall three long tables, foure formes, one square table, one chest with some olde decayed vyalls, one paire of andirons & a fireforke	3	0	0
In the armorye [*G9*][174]			
Item old armes for three horsemen, some other old armes, 29 browne billes, sixe pistolls & some other lumber	1	10	0
In the armorie chamber [*G8*]			
Item one long table, one forme & one liverye bedstead	0	10	0
In the wardrope [*?F8 and 9*][175]			
Item three old bedsteades, one old standard & and [*sic*] some other woodden lumber	1	3	0
Item two feather bedds, two boulsters, five woollquiltes, seaven pillowes & a little leather quilt with three blankettes & a cloth counterpointe	10	0	0
Item foure longe cushions, one high chaire, two lowe chaires sixe high stooles & two lowe stooles all sutable, covered with blacke velvett	3	6	8
Item one high chaire & two lowe stooles of crimson velvett embroidered	0	13	4
Item five needleworke stooles & one little stoole of yellow velvett, three nedleworke long cushions & eight other old long cushions	3	0	0
Item one testar, single valence & five curtaines of old greene taffate with one other very old topp & valence & two clouded taffate curtaines	0	10	0
Item two covers of purple velvett for two formes, one Turkie carpett & nineteene backes & seates for chaires & stooles of turkye worke	2	0	0
Item three canopies & two counterpointes of severall coloured taffaters	3	10	0
Item one old iron backe & three paire of cobirons and feathers to stuffe a pillowe	0	13	4
In my Ladie Savages chamber [*?F18*]			
Item five peeces of tapistrye hangeinges with two window curtaines of striped stuffe	6	13	4

172 Using modern dating, January 1636.

173 With dais G22.

174 G2 and G3 were garderobe towers.

175 The wardrobe was usually situated near the private quarters of the lady of the house. Lack of necessary fireplaces in this area is apparently due to the later demolition of two stacks: they were between G5 and G7 (seen on eighteenth-century illustrations) and between G9 and G18, where a bricked-up fireplace originally serving F18 still exists.

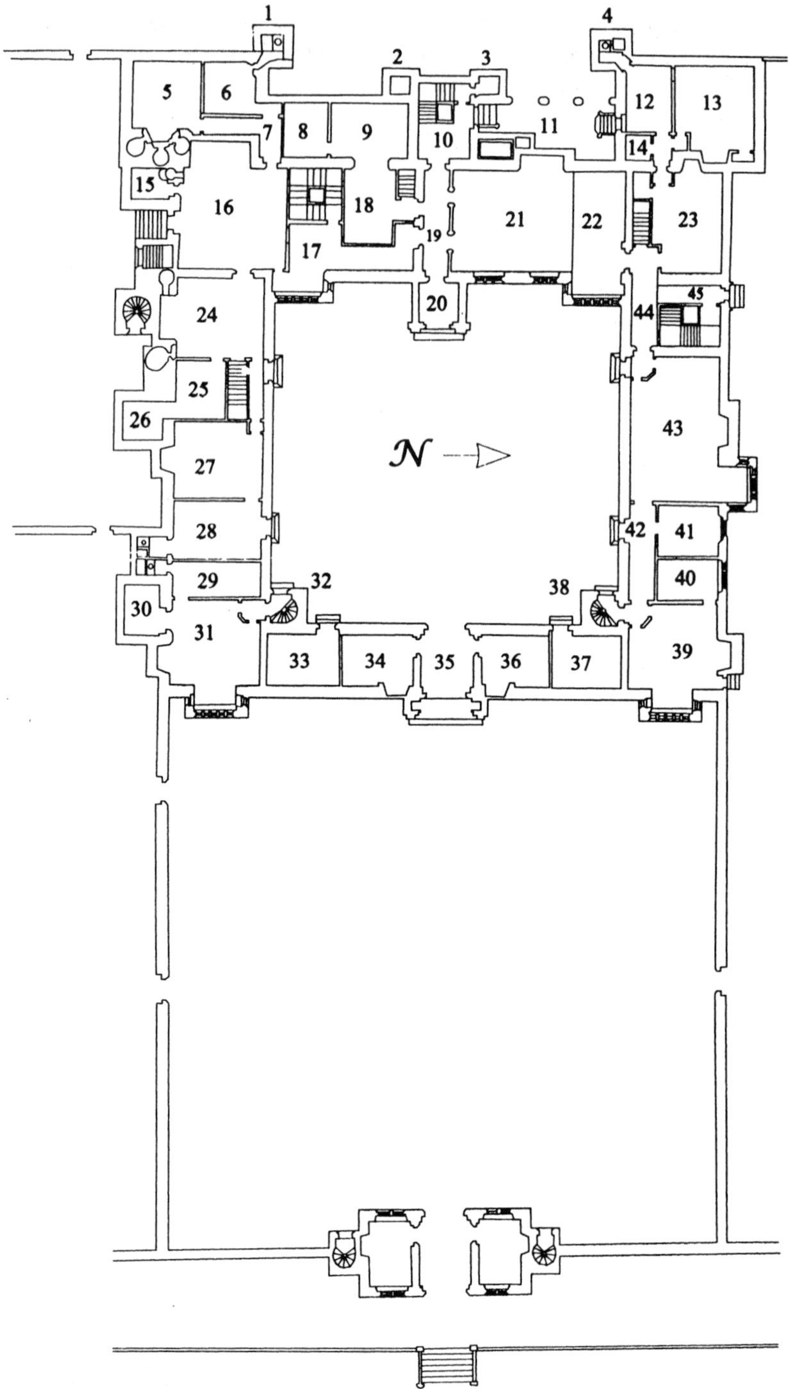

Plate 7. An adaptation of John Thorpe's plan of Melford Hall, c. 1606, with the ground-floor rooms numbered. These numbers are used in Doc. 60 and in Appendix 1 (pp. 155–8).

	£	s.	d.
Item one standing bedstead with topp backe, double valence, bases & counterpointe of crimson satten embroidered with armes, five taffate curtaines & one picture	13	6	8
Item two feather beddes, two bolsters, foure pillowes, two quiltes, foure blankettes, one rugg & one old white taffate counterpointe	13	6	8
Item three Turkye carpettes, two chaires, foure high stooles & three lowe stooles of sundry sortes, a cupbord, two little tables, an emptie chest, a skreene & a frame for a boxe	2	10	0
Item a capp panne, a paire of bellowes, andirons, tonges & fire shovell with brasse topps	0	16	0
Item three close stooles,[176] two presses & a groome porters table	1	0	0
In my Ladie's withdraweing chamber [*?F16*][177]			
Item five peeces of tapistry hanginges, one couch bedd with valence, sixe high stooles, two lowe chaires, two cushions, three carpettes & a windowe curtaine all of greene cloth	15	0	0
Item one table, one cupbord, a skreene, one picture, bellowes, tonges & andirons with brasse topps	0	16	0
In my Ladie's gallery [*F19*][178]			
Item a presse with glasses & earthen stuffe in it, three cupbordes, foure frames, one table, foure chaires, 11 stooles & nine boxes, chestes & trunkes emptie or with unvaluable trifles	4	0	0
In my Ladies closett [*F20*][179]			
Item two little tables, two cushions, a skreene, some glasses, two or three dozen of china dishes, bellowes, fire shovell, tonges & andirons with brasse topps, one iron panne to ayre roomes & 9 pictures	3	0	0
In the chamber in the southend of the gallery [*S16*][180]			
Item one bedstead with testar, valence and curtaines of old tawney cloth, hangeinges of striped stuffe, a traverse curtaine of the same, two window curtaines, foure tables, two chaires, two stooles, foure little carpettes, one close stoole & one paire of andirons with brasse toppes, fire shovell, bellows, tonges & a picture	4	0	0

176 Docs. 38 and 39 reveal that Lady Savage suffered greatly from a urinary complaint, which possibly explains the need for three close stools. A similar arrangement existed in her rooms at court.

177 F15 was a ground-floor extension.

178 With no window or fireplace and used as a store-room. Originally the minstrel's gallery and presumably walled-up to the roof by Thorpe. 'My Ladies Gallery' perhaps alluded to a partitioned-off section of the gallery adjoining F20, reserved for the ladies to watch male activities in the hall.

179 An attractive room with a fireplace and view of the main entrance, apparently used as a store-room.

180 A chamber screened-off by a curtain at the south end of the gallery.

	£	s.	d.
In the great chamber [*F43*][181]			
Item five peeces of tapistry hangeinges, parte of the storye of Absolon[182]	30	0	0
Item foure Turkye carpettes & 4 windowe curtaines of yellowe saye	20	0	0
Item two high chaires, 14 high stooles & two little foot stooles of blacke velvett & yellowe fringe	4	0	0
Item one long table, two side tables, two paire of andirons, fire shovell, tonges all of brasse, with a paire of bellowes & snuffers	4	0	0
In the chappell chamber [*F40–41*][183]			
Item one wind instrument, one high chaire, one high stoole, two lowe chaires, two lowe stooles & three landskipp pictures	2	10	0
In the withdrawing chamber to the great chamber [*F23*]			
Item foure peeces of tapestrye hangeinges, the other parte of the storye of Absolon	15	0	0
Item two Turkye carpetts, two window curtaines of yellowe taffate	4	10	0
Item one couch, one high chaire, foure backe stooles, sixe high stooles all of purple velvet embroidered	20	0	0
Item two paire of brasse andirons, fire shovell, tonges, bellowes, a skreene & one cupbord	1	0	0
In the gallerie [*S16–23*][184]			
Item one groome porters table with a carpett of crimson velvett embroidered, one Turkie worke carpett	2	10	0
Item foure long cushions of cloth of gould, sixe other long cushions, three of velvett & three of satten embroidered	3	0	0
Item foure high chaires, two high stooles & seaven low stooles, some of cloth of gould, some of silver velvett & some of crimson satten embroidered	4	0	0
Item 23 pictures of sundry sizes & a lookeing glasse	10	0	0

181 The most important room in the house, with an oriel window, and perhaps including F41. Sir William Parker named a later room in this area 'Queen Elizabeth's Bedroom', suggesting that Elizabeth I occupied this area during her visit in 1578.

182 Absolon is the French for Absalom. He was the son of King David. He had his half brother killed for having violated his sister. Later he turned the sympathies of the Israelites and rebelled against his father. His father's forces defeated him at the battle of Ephraim; while fleeing after this he caught his hair in a tree branch. His horse continued on without him. Jacob found Absalom hanging from the tree and killed him.

183 The name suggests that this room served as the gallery to a two-storeyed pre-Reformation chapel occupying G39–42, an area which apparently pre-dates the turret 38 and associated east wing. No mention of a room in F39 suggests this area formed the upper part of the chancel (*cf.* Mr Noye's Chamber, G39). See Appendix I, p. 155.

184 The gallery was connected by staircase 10 to areas occupied by the family in the north wing and a garderobe in turret S2. It also had access via a newel stair in turret 3 to a fine vantage point from the flat roof above, referred to by Howell in his letter: 'It [the park] is opposite the front of the great house, whence from the gallery one may see much of the game when they are a hunting.' Sir William Parker states: 'A tradition has long attached to Melford Hall that at one time during the rebellion, a company of Parliamentarian soldiers were quartered in what is called the "Long Gallery" of this house. This gallery is 135 feet long.' Areas S39–45 are unmentioned in the inventory, which suggests they had no contents or nothing of value.

	£	s.	d.
In the purple chamber at the gallerie end [*S13*][185]			
Item five peeces of tapistrye hangeinges, five Turkye carpettes & a window curtaine of purple taffate	22	0	0
Item one bedstead, foure quiltes, one boulster, two pillowes, a testar backe, double valence, three large curtaines & foure small curtaines all of purple cloth embroidered, two chaires, foure stooles & one carpett all sutable to the bedd & all covered with bayes	30	0	0
Item one groome porters table, one cupbord, one close stoole, one paire of brasse creepers, fire shovell & tonges with brasse toppes & a paire of bellowes	1	6	8
In the inner chamber to it before [*S12*][186]			
Item five peeces of old tapistry hangeinges, two peeces of darnickes, a feather bedd, boulster, two blankettes, one rugg; testar, valence & curtaines of striped canvas, one chaire, three stooles of silver tobyne & one other high stoole, with a little table	10	0	0
In the closett belongeing to this chamber [*S14*]			
Item one little table, one needle worke carpett & two stooles of silke Irish stiche	1	10	0
In the gould bed chamber [*F13*]			
Item five peeces of tapestrye hanginges, three Turkye carpettes, two crimson velvett carpettes and two window curtaines of cloudie taffatye	30	0	0
Item one bedstead, one feather bedd, one bolster, one pillowe, one quilt, three blankettes, one rugge, one testar backe, valence & five curtaines of gould chamlett crimson, a chaire & foure stooles sutable	22	0	0
Item a table, a cupbord, andirons, fire shovell & tonges	0	13	4
In the inner chamber belongeing to the former [*F12*]			
Item one bedstead with testar, backe, valence & five curtaines of russett cloth & two stooles sutable, one bedd of feathers, one bolster, one pillow, two blankettes & one rugge	6	13	4
Item foure peeces of tapistrye hangeinges, a dornix carpett, a taffeta window curtaine, one cupbord & one close stoole	3	0	0
In the weomens chamber [*F24–25*][187]			
Item two bedsteades, one testar, valence & five curtaines of redd cloth with two back stooles sutable, two feather beddes, two boulsters, one pillowe, five blankettes & a rugge	12	0	0

185 A very important guest-room possibly furnished and named in the hope of a royal visit. Access existed from this room to the adjoining gallery as would be expected, and the newel stair in turret 4 gave access to the Gold Chamber on the floor below, and to a vantage point on the flat lead roof above.

186 With access to a newel stair rising from this level in turret 4.

187 'The Women's Chamber' perhaps alluded to a room originally occupied by women servants involved in the nurseries, since converted for family use. The newel stair adjoining 24 gave access from first-floor family areas to the service yard, bypassing the ground-floor kitchen and its adjuncts. This stair presumably continued to second-floor level offering the same facility to the quarters of women servants.

	£	s.	d.
Item one cupbord, one little table, two high stooles, a little lowe stoole, one cushion, a dornicks curtaine & one close stoole, andirons, bellowes, fire shovell & tonges	0	15	0
In the great nurserie [*F25–27*]			
Item one bedstead with a testar, valence & five curtaines of yellowe say, one feather bedd, one boulster, two blankettes with a tapestry coverlett & 5 pillowes	6	0	0
Item one cubbord with an old cloth carpett, one little table, a window curtaine of old tapistrye, two high stooles & a backstoole, one chest & a paire of cobirons	0	12	0
In the little nurserie [*F27–28*]			
Item one bedstead with testar, valence & curtaines of cloth, one feather bedd, one bolster, one pillowe, two blankettes, a coverlett of durance, a cupbord, two dornicks carpettes, a paire of creepers, bellowes, fire shovell & tonges	5	10	0
In the gentlewomens chamber [*F31*][188]			
Item two bedsteades, one testar & valence of old silver chamlett with curtaines of bustian, one testar, valence & curtaines of yellowe say, two feather beddes, two boulsters, three pillowes, foure blankettes, one rugg & one tapistrye coverlett	14	0	0
Item two old window curtaines & a carpett of dornickes, one cupbord, two tables, one lowe stoole, andirons, fire shovell & tonges with brasse toppes, & a picture of Lucretia[189]	0	15	0
In the utter chamber to it before [*F30*][190]			
Item one feather bedd, one boulster, two blankettes, one rugge, a livery bedstead, canopie & curtaines of greene say, one old chaire & a little cupbord	5	10	0
In the two brushing chambers [*?F8*][191]			
Item two tables, two formes, one stoole, two skreenes & one great presse	1	6	8
In my Lord's chamber [*F5*]			
Item five peeces of tapestrye hangeinges, three Turkie carpettes & three greene carpettes & two window curtaines of greene saye	16	0	0

188 Nurseries were associated with quarters occupied by women servants and gentlewomen. No access existed from this room to the adjoining newel stair.

189 Lucretia in Roman legend was the beautiful wife of the nobleman Lucius Tarquinius Collatinus. She was raped by Sextus Tarquinius, son of Lucius Tarquinius Superbus, tyrant of Rome, and stabbed herself after extracting an oath of vengeance against the Tarquins from her father and husband. This was a popular cautionary theme felt suitable for young women.

190 Accommodation for a maid.

191 Presumably near the wardrobe.

	£	s.	d.
Item one bedstead, the testar & valence of greene velvet, five curtaines of taffeta & a counterpointe of the same, one feather bedd, one quilt, one boulster, two blankettes, two fustians	14	0	0
Item one chaire, two high stooles, two lowe stooles of nedle worke, one close stoole, two cupbordes, a paire of brasse creepers, bellowes, fire shovell & tonges	1	10	0
In his chamberer's chamber [*F6*]			
Item one trundle bedstead, one feather bedd, one bolster, one pillow, two blankettes, one tapistry coverlett & a joined stoole	3	0	0
In my Lord's closett [*S6*][192]			
Item one table with a blewe cloth carpett, one chaire, one picture, one trunke, five emptie boxes & cabinettes for papers & a few small bookes	1	0	0
In my Lord's withdraweing chamber [*S5*][193]			
Item foure peeces of tapestrye hangeinges, five Turkie carpettes & two window curtaines of taffeta	22	0	0
Item one couch of silver velvett with three cushions to it sutable, one chaire, sixe high stooles & three lowe stooles all of nedleworke	4	0	0
Item one paire of playeing tables, one table, one cupbord, one paire of andirons, one paire of brasse creepers, fire shovell, tonges & bellowes	2	10	0
In the chamber within the little parlour [*G13*][194]			
Item one purple & gold bedstead, the testar and valence of purple velvett embroidered, with five curtaines & a counterpointe of purple taffate	19	0	0
Item one feather bedd, two quiltes, one bolster, one pillowe, two blankettes, two fustians & one white rugg	10	0	0
Item foure peeces of tapestrye hangeinges, five turkye carpettes, two window curtaines, one chaire, two stooles & one carpett all of purple velvett, one close stoole, one table, one cubbord, andirons, fire shovell & tonges with brasse toppes	30	0	0
In the inner chamber to that before [*G12*][195]			
Item one liverye bedstead, one feather bedd, one bolster, one pillowe, two blankettes, one rugg & a stoole	5	0	0

192 With access to a garderobe under the newel stair, rising from this level in turret 1.

193 Approached via the newel stair in turret 1 and with access to the Gallery S16–23. Bricked-up fire-place in east wall. Areas S24–31 were unmentioned in the inventory, which suggests that they had no contents or contents of no value, but their intended use is evident by provision of a garderobe to serve this part of the house.

194 This secluded withdrawing room had the most costly furnishings in the house.

195 With access to a garderobe in turret G4, the Loggia G11 and then, presumably, to the private garden.

	£	s.	d.
In the little parlour [*G23*]			
Item foure peeces of tapestrye hangeinges, one Turkie carpett & two greene carpettes	7	0	0
Item one couch of wrought velvett with a cushion sutable, one chaire & three stooles of nedle worke, sixe backe stooles of tawney leather, one table, one cupbord, a paire of andirons & tonges with brasse toppes & two mapps[196]	4	0	0
In the great parlour [*G43*][197]			
Item one table, one side bord, one cupbord, a Turkey carpet, 4 greene cloth carpettes, 5 window curtaines of greene cloth, two high chaires, 18 high stooles, two lowe back stooles & two footstooles all of cruell Irish stitch, 4 pictures, one mapp of the world,[198] a paire of great brasse andirons, a lesser paire with brasse topps & a paire of tonges	10	0	0
In the corner chamber within the great parlour [*within G43*]			
Item three peeces of tapestrye hangeinges, two Turkye carpettes & one windowe curtaine of yellow saye	10	0	0
Item one bedstead, the testar, valence & five curtaines of redd cloth laced, one featherbedd, one quilt, one boulster, two pillowes, two blankettes & a redd rugge, two chaires & two backestooles sutable to the bedd	10	0	0
Item one table, one cupbord, a paire of andirons, tonges, fire shovell & bellowes	0	10	0
In the inner chamber to that before [*within G43*]			
Item one livery bedstead, one feather bedd, one boulster, two blankettes & a greene rugge, one table, one chaire, one high stoole & a close stoole	4	0	0
In the two chambers by the inner gate[199]			
Item two liverye bedsteades, two feather bedds, two boulsters, foure blankettes & two tapestrye coverlettes, one cupbord, two tables, two stooles & two paire of creepers	7	10	0
In the Stone Court chamber [*?F35*][200]			
Item one bedstead, the testar, valence and curtaines of yellowe say, one feather bedd, one boulster, one pillow, two blankettes, one yellowe rugge, one little table with a dornicks carpett, one window curtaine of dornicks & one joined stoole	6	0	0

---

196 Perhaps the still existing maps of the estate, commissioned by Sir William Cordell in 1580 and Sir Thomas Savage in 1613. However there is another surviving map, incomplete, dated 1615.

197 Shown as a single room by Thorpe but apparently later divided into three rooms, as suggested by lines faintly drawn in pencil on his plan.

198 There was another map of the world at Rocksavage; these possessions suggest that horizons were widening as the new world opened up.

199 Accommodation for two servants by, meaning near, the inner gate. Pierse shows the outer drive passing through a succession of gateways to ultimately arrive at a gate leading to the service yard. If this gate was called 'The inner gate' this accommodation existed nearby.

200 The position of this room is questionable. If the entrance court inside the gate-house was stone-paved, 'Stone Court' might allude to it. As no fire irons are mentioned, and no stack is shown by Thorpe or Pierse, the proposed identification of this room as F35 is strengthened.

	£	s.	d.
In Mr Noyes chamber [*G39*][201]			
Item one bedstead, the testar, valence & curtaines of greene cloth, one chaire & two lowe stooles sutable, one feather bedd, two boulsters, one blankett, a greene rugge, a windowe curtaine of greene say, one table, a cupbord, two greene carpettes, andirons, fire shovell, tonges & bellowes	8	0	0
In the two inner chambers to that before [*G 40 and 41*][202]			
Item two liverie bedsteades, two feather beddes, two boulsters, foure blankettes, a tapistrye coverlett, a yarne coverlet, a blew rugg, one table, six Turkie worke stooles & one old dornicke curtaine	7	0	0
In the stewards chamber [*G31*][203]			
Item one bedstead, the testar, valence & curtaines of yellowe say, one feather bedd, one boulster, two pillows, two blankettes, two window curtaines & two carpettes of dornickes, one table, one cupbord, one presse, one chaire, two blacke stooles & six high stooles all of redd leather, foure little stooles, a wicker chaire, andirons, a paire of creepers, fire shovell, tonges & bellowes & a chamber clocke[204]	12	0	0
In the inner chamber to that before [*G30*][205]			
Item two livery bedsteades, two feather beddes, two boulsters, foure blankettes, two rugges, foure peeces of dornickes, one chest & one joined stoole	7	0	0
In the scullerie chamber [*G28*][206]			
Item one liverye bedstead, one feather bedd & boulster, one flocke bedd, two boulsters, two blankettes and two coverlettes, one old cupbord & a stoole	2	0	0
In the cookes chamber [*G27*][207]			
Item two bedsteades, two feather beddes, two boulsters, sixe blankettes, one flocke boulster, two coverlettes & one canopie of dornickes & one presse	6	0	0

201 Evidence suggests that this room formed the east end of a two-storeyed pre-reformation chapel (cf. Chappell Chamber F40–41). The Savage family may have seen the pending arrival of valuers as a good reason to conceal the existence of a chapel in this area, or the use of the room may have changed. Noye was a Protestant who had earlier been steward of Thomas's estates; see Docs. 11 and 50, and Notes on People below.

202 Apparently quarters for two members of the steward's staff.

203 Quarters for the steward of the estate in the customary position near the service areas.

204 The only clock recorded in the inventory; those used by the family would presumably have formed part of their baggage.

205 Quarters for two members of the steward's staff. G29 is unmentioned in the inventory, which suggests that it had no contents or contents of no value.

206 Quarters for perhaps two members of the cook's staff but originally the scullery, where kitchen utensils were kept; when the inventory was taken, these utensils were stored in the kitchens and pastry.

207 Well-appointed quarters for a cook and his servant, with a canopy over one bed, suggesting use by Lord Savage's personal chef who may have formed part of his retinue. No mention of fire-irons might suggest that this room was not in use when the inventory was taken.

	£	s.	d.
In the butler's chamber [*G25 and 26*][208]			
Item one livery bedstead, one feather bedd, one boulster, one blankett & one rugge	2	0	0
In the still house [*?C12–14*][209]			
Item one table, two cupbordes, five stooles, eighteene fruite dishes, twentie foure water glasses, some two dozen of fruite glasse plates, foure stilles & a limbecke & other lumber there & boxes	4	0	0
In the first chamber of the gatehouse and the inner chamber to it [*G36 & 37*][210]			
Item two bedsteades, one testar, double valence, five curtaines of yellowe saye, two feather beddes, three bolsters, one pillowe, three blankettes, one white rugge & one tapistrye coverlet, one chaire & two stooles sutable to the bedd, a carpett, a table, two window dornicke curtaines, a close stoole, a paire of creepers, tonges, fire shovell & bellowes	8	0	0
In the toppe chamber over it [*F36 and 37*][211]			
Item one feather bedd & bedstead, one bolster, two blankettes & a rugge	1	10	0
In the second chamber in the gatehouse and in the inner chamber to it [*G33 & 34*][212]			
Item two bedsteades, one testar, valence & curtaines of buffin, two feather beddes, three boulsters, one pillowe, three blankettes, two rugges, one table, one cupbord, two old carpettes, one chaire, two stooles, a paire of andirons, tonges, bellowes & a close stoole	7	0	0
In the toppe chamber over it [*F33 and 34*][213]			
Item one bedstead, one feather bedd, two bolsters, one blankett, one rugg & one stoole	2	5	0
In the porters lodge and chamber over against it[214]			
Item two bedsteades, one old valence, two fether beddes, two bolsters, one pillowe, two blankettes, one rugge, one coverlett & two formes	4	0	0

208 Proximity of an oven perhaps explains the lack of a fireplace and the need for only limited bedding.

209 Distilling was a skill thought proper for the lady of the house and her gentlewomen, so her still-house tended to be close to her lodgings. 'House', although suggesting an out-building, might refer in this case to a basement room with a fireplace, connected by a stair to areas occupied by the family. Preparation of dessert dishes in the still-house would explain fruit glass plates required by the new fashion for Italian desserts.

210 Originally quarters for a porter, but now converted to family use. Proposals added in pencil on Thorpe's plan were carried out: a new door was inserted in the partition between G36 and G37, and the door between G35 and G36 was bricked up. The need had passed for elaborate protection, when the main inner and outer doors were secured from G35. The deeply rebated jambs to the main door perhaps suggest an original portcullis.

211 A dormitory-like room served by the newel-stair in G38 which continued to a probably flat roof above. Queen Mary granted Cordell a licence to keep twelve retainers.

212 Originally quarters for a porter, but now converted to family use. Proposals added in pencil on Thorpe's plan were carried out, corresponding with works to G36 and G37.

213 Corresponding with F36 and 37.

214 Reference to the two-roomed porter's lodge to the east of the hall, apparently by Thorpe, who included a sketched proposal for the façade of this building on his plan. This apparently replaced a considerably larger lodge depicted by Pierse in 1613. 'Over against it' means 'opposite'.

	£	s.	d.
In the pond chamber[215]			
Item one bedstead, testar, valence, curtaines, hangeinges to the chamber, three windowe curtaines & a carpett all dornickes, one feather bedd, one boulster, one pillowe, two blankettes, one yarne coverlett, two tables, three stooles & a paire of creepers	6	0	0
In the two chambers next to it[216]			
Item three bedsteades, two feather beddes & one flocke bedd, three feather bolsters, five blankettes, two tapistry & one yarne coverlett, a table & a forme	4	10	0
In the two chambers underneath these[217]			
Item one bedstead, two tables, a cupbord, two curtaines & two carpettes of dornickes, one chaire, two stooles, one close stoole, fire shovell, tonges, bellowes & a paire of creepers	1	0	0
In the maides chamber in the granaries[218]			
Item three bedsteades, one testar, valence and curtaines of dornickes, three feather beddes, three boulsters, sixe blankettes, two coverlettes & a rugge, one table, one great standard, a stoole & a paire of creepers	10	0	0
In the granaries[219]			
Item two skreenes, two fannes, two shovells, two formes with feather seates, two bushells, some lead, old iron & other lumber	9	0	0
In the bakehouse[220]			
Item one flocke bedd, two boulsters, one bedstead, one coverlett, foure boulting hutches, tubbes, troughes & searses with other implementes of a bakehouse	1	13	4
In the brewhouse			
Item an old haire to drye maulte, brewing vessells and other implementes for a brewhouse	10	0	0

215 This room was apparently above the gateway of a detached seven-roomed building depicted by Pierse, standing near the ponds to the east of the service range. This is apparently the building referred to as 'the Abbot's grange' in the survey for Abbot Curteys in 1441/2, and 'The Old House' by Sir William Cordell in his will of 1580. An adjoining walled-garden to the north was apparently directly associated with this building. It had a doorway to the service yard and two to the front of the hall, secured from the Pond Chamber side.

216 First-floor rooms flanking the Pond Chamber.

217 Ground-floor rooms flanking the gateway.

218 Perhaps a first-floor room in the south wing of the building containing the Pond Chamber. Quarters for three probably 'outside' maids employed in the dairy or laundry. 'In the granaries' could imply accommodation in a building also containing separate storage areas or bins, for grain, etc.

219 Perhaps on the ground-floor of the south wing of the building containing the Pond Chamber. If threshing in this area is suggested, the east-west orientated floor of the gateway was ideally suited for this purpose, with the stack-yard perhaps situated nearby to the east, flanked by the drive and ponds.

220 In the range of service buildings, as was the brewhouse.

	£	s.	d.
In the gardners chamber and husbandmans[221]			
Item three flocke beddes, three boulsters, three blankettes & two old coverlettes	1	10	0
In the laundry[222]			
Item tubbes, a table & other implementes for that office	5	0	0
In the dairie[223]			
Item one churne, a cheesepresse, keelers, trayes, tubbs, cheesemotes & other implementes for that office	3	0	0
In the two kitchins[224] and pastrye[225] [*G16, 24 and 5*]			
Item rackes, spittes, tramells, fryeing pannes and all implementes belongeing to that office, with one old dornickes skreene, a little table & three formes	4	0	0
In the wett larders [*C27–31*][226]			
Item a barrell of vargis, waightes and scales, powdering tubbs & other implementes for that place	1	15	0
In the pantry [*G18*][227]			
Item a presse for lynnen, a table, a chest, a cupbord, a bread bynne and other implementes for that office	2	10	0
In the beere and wine sellars [*C ?*][228]			
Item beere in 27 hoggesheades, fourteene pipes,[229] & a few rundlettes for cider, emptie, almost two hoggesheades of wine, a cupbord with glasses, keelars & other necessaries for sellars	13	0	0

221 Two rooms in the service range, one for the head gardener and the other for two members of the farm staff; further staff presumably came daily from the town.

222 The building nearest the hall in the south-west service range; shown by Pierse with a drying-yard adjoining to the west.

223 In the service range.

224 On Thorpe's plan, 16 is annotated 'Kyt' and 24 'bakehouse'. The bake-house had been moved to an out-house by the date of the inventory to make room for a further kitchen. G15 is unmentioned in the inventory, which suggests that it had no contents or contents of no value, but with its door secured from within probably served as sleeping quarters for a servant to oversee the kitchen at night.

225 Thorpe inserted three ovens to form a pastry, and annotated the room 'pastry' on his plan. Until the fashion for baking arrived from the continent, the pot and spit had sufficed. No. 6 is unrecorded in the inventory, which suggests that it had no contents or contents of no value, but this room probably served as sleeping quarters for a servant to oversee the pastry at night.

226 Connected to kitchen G24 by a stair. The greater part of this large five-roomed cellar was apparently unused at this date. Previous part-use as a dairy is suggested by a window and external doorway, obscured by later extension G30.

227 Original buttery and pantry areas were disturbed by insertion of a staircase G17; no mention is made of a buttery in the inventory.

228 In part of the cellars underlying the greater part of the west wing. This area was vastly more than sufficient to meet requirements of the house, which suggests they originally formed the ground-floor of an earlier house. The butler gained access by the stair descending from G18.

229 Some 2887 gallons of beer and 105 gallons of wine. Probably a mainly low-alcohol type of beer drunk in place of water and later known as 'small beer'.

	£	s.	d.
In a great standard at the lower end of the hall [*? in G18*][230]			
Item one rugg, foure blankettes, three pillowes, one cushion, one skreene cloth greene, five curtaines & three little carpettes of striped stuffe, thirteene little cushions of say and dornickes, a testar, valence, curtaines for a slope bedd of a partie coloured lynnen stuffe, an old greene carpett & one Irish mantle	5	0	0
In the groomes chamber and stables[231]			
Item one feather bedd, two feather bolsters, two flocke beddes and one bolster, two blankettes & two old tapistry coverlettes	2	5	0
Item two saddles for my lordes horse, seaven old liverye saddles, one side saddle & two pillions, one presse, one chest & other stable implementes	1	15	0
In the banquetting house[232]			
Item one marble table & five guilt woodden chaires	2	0	0
Item in plate 439 oz[233] at 4s 10d [*per ounce*]	106	2	0
Item in brasse	17	10	0
Item in peauter	21	0	0
Item lynnen in & with sundry trunkes & chestes	61	19	0
Item in corne[234]	140	16	0
Item waxe candles and torches	0	14	0
Item in tallowe candles	3	0	0
Item nettes and a pond boate	2	10	0
Item wood	16	0	0
Item timber	6	0	0
Item hay and strawe	9	0	0
Item cartes, tumbrells, plowes, harrowes & other necessaries therunto belongeing	8	0	0
Item carte horses, sixe	15	0	0
Item saddle horses, eleaven	40	0	0
Item sixe coltes	9	0	0
Item a bull & tenn cowes	30	0	0
Item two heifers, two bullockes & three yeerlinges	10	0	0
Item tenn sheepe, three hogges and some pullen	6	0	0
Item debtes and credittes	109	19	10
Item a lease of Glemsford Parke[235] & certaine woodes for thirtie yeares after the expiracion of a lease, now in being for some 13 or fourteene yeares	200	0	0
Item some few old cast suites of my lordes apparrell & a peece of yellow damaske	10	0	0

230 A large cupboard perhaps built into the recess in this room.

231 Detached building shown by Pierse to the east of the hall. According to Howell, 'the stables butt upon the park'.

232 Octagonal two-storeyed building shown by Pierse and still standing to the north-west of the hall.

233 This is less than one tenth of the weight of plate inventoried at Tower Hill. None is recorded at Rocksavage.

234 Corn valued at £140 in 1635 amounts to about 11 ton, occupying a floor area of some 15 square metres.

235 Glemsford is a parish adjoining Long Melford to the west.

	£	s.	d.
Item in salte fishe	0	7	0
Item in corne upon the ground groweing	7	0	0
Item in all other old implements & lumber not particularly expressed before	7	0	0
The totall somme of the inventory of the goodes at Melford	1571	18	2

An inventorie of all the goodes, chattells & househould stuffe of the right honorable Thomas Lord Viscount Savage, lately deceased, within his house at Tower Hill, London, taken the fourteenth day[236] of November Anno Domini 1635 and apprized by Valentine Haward of London draper, Roger Drayton of London skynner, Francis Hall of London goldsmith & Edward Paynell as followeth:

	£	s.	d.
In the gallerie[237]			
Imprimis one couch chaire & two long cushions, three chaires & eight stooles of purple velvett	4	10	0
Item two chaires & tenn stooles of cheney worke	0	10	0
In the great chamber			
Item sixe peeces of tapestrye hangeinges, one long carpett & five little ones, three longe cushions & three short ones & twentie stooles of old cloth of bodkine	15	3	8
Item one paire of iron andirons with great lowe brasse toppes & one little fire cradle of iron	0	14	0
Item old taffate windowe curtaines & one iron rodd	0	3	4
In the withdrawing chamber			
Item five peeces of tapestrye hangeinges	12	0	0
Item foure small Turkie carpettes	2	0	0
Item two window curtaines	0	6	8
Item one featherbedd, two feather bolsters, one fustian thicke quilt[238]	5	0	0

236 The inventory of the Tower Hill house clearly says, using words not numerals, that it was taken on 14 November which may have been before Thomas Savage's death. His death is given in several records as occurring on 20 November, but this was the day his entrails were interred under the chancel of St Olave's, Hart Street, and it is possible he died a few days earlier. Either the inventory was taken before he died, which is unusual but not unknown, or the inventory is in error. This may have occurred when the three inventories, separately made, were written on one roll. We suggest that the date 24th, written in numerals in secretary hand, could be misread as the 14th, and that the 24th is a more likely date for the inventory to have been made.

237 The values given in this inventory are in general markedly lower than those given at Rocksavage and Melford, and the word 'old' is more often used when describing goods. It is possible that Thomas and Elizabeth had not refurnished the Tower Hill house, that most of its contents had been inherited from Lady Lumley and may have been at least two generations old. Alternatively, or additionally, the appraisers in London may have been more used to seeing the contents of an aristocratic house than their peers in Cheshire and Suffolk, and were comparing the Tower Hill house with others of similarly placed individuals.

238 This inventory lists no bedsteads, although beds (feather mattresses) are mentioned. Presumably the appraisers assumed that bedsteads were part and parcel of the house and were therefore not moveable goods. Although this is unusual, it is not an unknown practice.

	£	s.	d.
Item one double valence & testar of crimson satten imbroidered, five taffeta curtaines & one taffeta quilt all crimson coloured	8	0	0
Item one high chaire & two lowe stooles of crimsen velvett	1	0	0
Item one paire of brasse andirons, one paire of iron creepers & one paire of tonges	1	2	0
In the chamber within the withdraweing chamber			
Item sixe peeces of tapestrye hangeinges, three Turkye carpettes & three greene carpettes all very old	6	0	0
Item one little downe bedd & boulster, one blanket & one old tawney rugg	5	0	0
Item five curtaines, one valence & testar of old dornicks	0	8	0
Item one paire of andirons, tonges & bellowes	0	2	0
In Mr Hoppers chamber[239]			
Item the dornickes hangeinges for the whole chamber & one quilt	1	0	0
Item one paire of iron creepers, a fireshovell, tonges & bellowes	0	1	6
In my lord's lodgeing chamber			
Item three chaires & sixe stooles of greene cloth	1	5	0
Item one paire of iron andirons with brasse topps, one paire of creepers, fireshovell, tonges & bellowes	0	8	0
Item two travers iron rodds & one window curtaine rodd	0	10	0
In my lord's backe chamber			
Item sixe peeces of very old hangeinges of tapestry	3	0	0
Item one old feather bedd & bolster, one old blankett & two old rugges	1	16	0
Item one old brasse cappe pann & one iron fire shovell	0	10	0
In the great nursery			
Item certaine very old hangeinges	2	0	0
Item two old carpettes & one window curtaine with the rodd	0	2	6
Item two feather beddes, two boulsters, two pillowes, foure blankettes & two rugges	4	10	0
Item five curtains, valence & curtaines of dimittie & one old sea canopie	0	15	0
Item one paire of andirons with brasse topps, tonges & a paire of bellowes	0	6	0
In Mistress Dorothies chamber[240]			
Item certaine striped stuffe hangeinges for the chamber with one curtaine for a window & two little carpettes all of the same stuffe	2	0	0
Item one bedstead, testar, curtaines & valence of the same striped stuffe	1	10	0

239 Presumably Christopher Hopper; see Notes on People below.

240 Thomas and Elizabeth's eldest living daughter, Dorothy Savage. See Introduction, Docs 63 and 65, and Notes on People below.

	£	s.	d.
Item one featherbedd, one boulster & pillowe, two blankettes & one rugg	4	0	0
Item 4 little low leather chaires, two little tables	0	12	0
Item one paire of iron creepers, fire shovell & tonges all with brass topps	0	5	0
In the little nurserie			
Item certaine very old hangeinges & two window peeces	0	15	0
Item one old mattres, a featherbed, bolster & pillowe, two blankettes & one rugge	2	15	0
Item 5 curtaines, testar & valence of tawney cloth, one chaire & three little old stooles	1	0	0
Item one paire of iron andirons with brass topps, one fire shovell, tonges and bellowes	0	4	0
In Grace's chamber[241]			
Item one featherbed, two bolsters & one pillowe two blankettes & a covering	2	15	0
Item five curtaines, a testar of dornix & one old lowe chaire	0	5	0
In Mistress Grace Savage's chamber[242]			
Item certaine peeces of very old hangeinges & two old carpettes, one old window curtaine, one high chaire & two old lowe stooles	0	15	0
Item one mattres and featherbed, bolster & two pillowes, one rugge & two bankettes	3	0	0
Item a little old fire shovell & tonges	0	1	0
In my lord's closett			
Item two wainscott presses with drawers for writeinges	1	15	0
Item certaine bookes there	5	0	0
Item an old cabinet & great standish corded with leather	1	0	0
Item one crimson velvet night bagg with a combe case of the same, one nedle vorke purse & two perfumed skinnes	3	0	0
Item one old chaire & old stoole	0	3	4
Item one diamond hatt band	130	0	0
In the parlour			
Item two Turkie carpettes	1	6	8
Item three old chaires, one paire of andirons & tonges topte with brasse, one fire shovell & one little iron cradle	0	13	4
In the parlour chamber			
Item one suite of tapistrye hangeinges containing five peeces	18	0	0
Item one other suite of tapestry hangeinges containing sixe peeces	12	0	0
Item one other old peece of tapistry hangeing	1	0	0

241 It is difficult to identify this Grace; possibly a female attendant.

242 Grace is probably Thomas's sister, who married Richard Wilbraham. See Notes on People below.

	£	s.	d.
Item foure Turkie carpettes	5	0	0
Item two travers curtaines & one window curtaine of greene kersey	2	10	0
Item foure quiltes, two feather beddes, one bolster	10	0	0
Item foure chaires great & small, three stooles & one skreene all of redd cloth	3	5	0
Item one paire of iron andirons & one iron fire grate	0	5	0
In the closett within the parlour chamber			
Item one peece of old tapistry hangeing & one old chaire & one old greene carpett	0	8	0
Item one iron chest	3	0	0
Item two trunkes with some old apparrell of a deceased sarvant of my lordes	1	10	0
In the old wardrope			
Item two feather bolsters & one old bedd	1	10	0
Item one sedan of murrey cloth	1	5	0
Item five old curtaines with a canopie covering	0	10	0
Item one wood skreene with an old cover of greene cloth	0	10	0
In the new wardrope			
Item sixe peeces of tapistry hangeinges of the storye of Abraham & Isaac	20	0	0
Item five peeces of other tapistry hangeinges	12	0	0
Item five blankettes old & new & one old quilt	2	10	0
Item five curtaines & one testar for a bedd, of redd cloth with gould lace & lined with clouded taffate, with valence to the same	7	0	0
Item one compleate furniture for a bedd with counterpaine & double valence & with cases for the postes of ginger lind cloth	7	0	0
Item one crimsen satten counterpane for a bedd	2	0	0
Item one redd perpetuana window curtaine & one old peece of hangeing	0	15	0
Item five curtaines, testar & valence of redd cloth, a redd rugg & a skreene cloth redd	2	5	0
Item one old window curtaine of crimson taffate	0	7	0
Item three small Turkey carpettes	1	15	0
Item an embroidered sumpter cloth, with my ladies armes	0	6	8
Item three feather pillowes	0	8	0
Item sixe backe chaires of yellowe & tawney silke	1	16	0
Item two high chaires & two lowe chaires with two lowe stooles of Irish stitch silke	2	0	0
Item all my lordes weareing apparrell & weareing linnen	100	0	0
Item three iron andirons	0	6	0
In the armorye			
Item all the armour as it now standes, by the advice of two armorers, a gunne maker & a sadler	40	0	0

	£	s.	d.
In Mr James Savages chamber[243]			
Item two mattresses, two feather beddes, two bolsters, two blankettes & two rugges	5	0	0
Item five curtaines & valence, a chaire, a stoole, a paire of andirons, a fire shovell & tonges	0	12	0
In the laundry chamber			
Item two featherbedds, two boulsters, two pillowes, three blankettes, one rugge & a coverlett	4	10	0
Item one paire of iron creepers	0	1	0
In the chamber by the backe gate next Tower Hill			
Item five curtaines, valence & testar of yellowe say, 8 peeces of old verduris & two old Turkye carpettes	1	10	0
In the cookes chamber			
Item one featherbedd, two bolsters, one blanket & a rugge	2	0	0
In the footemens chamber[244]			
Item one featherbedd, two little bolsters, one blanket & one rugge	1	5	0
In the porters lodge			
Item two feather beddes, two bolsters, one blankett & one rugg	3	0	0
In Mr Hopton's chamber[245]			
Item one featherbedd, one bolster, three blankettes, one rugge, one canopie of dornix & one chaire	2	15	0
In the tailors chamber			
Item one featherbedd, two bolsters, two old blankettes & a rugge	1	15	0
In Mr Mannings chamber[246]			
Item one featherbedd, one bolster, one pillowe, one blankett, two rugges & certaine old hangeinges	2	1	0
In Mr Fletchers chamber[247]			
Item one featherbedd, one bolster, a blankett & rugge	2	0	0

243 For James Savage, son of Thomas and Elizabeth, see Notes on People below.

244 Doc. 83 mentions uniforms for six footmen.

245 Thomas Brook, gent, who died in 1633, was steward to Thomas Savage. In his will he left 'To my good frend Mr Arthur Hopton £6 13s 4d': TNA PROB 11/163/21. Hopton was presumably an upper servant of the family, like Thomas Brookes, but his name does not appear either in relation to the Thomas Savage's funeral procession or in any Rocksavage accounts.

246 Mr Manning is likely to have been Mr Mainwaring, or Manwaring. This family were important gentry in Cheshire. Thomas Savage's sister Elizabeth married as her first husband Thomas Manwaring of Martin Sands, near Over, in Cheshire; he is said then to have served Sir John Savage, her father. A Mr Manwaring, who could very likely have been one of their sons or another close relative, carried one of the main heraldic banners (of Savage and Manners) in the funeral procession and another walked bare-headed on the left just ahead of the cortege; either could have been the occupant of this chamber. The Manwarings of Over Peover were one of those rare lines, like the Savages, who could trace their lineage in the male line to the Norman Conquest.

247 In Thomas Savage's funeral procession Mr Fletcher walked bare-headed on the right, just ahead of

	£	s.	d.
In the kitchiners chamber			
Item a featherbedd, a bolster, two blankettes & a rugge	1	5	0
In the stable			
Item one bedd, one bolster, one blankett & a coverlett	1	10	0
Item three quarters of oates & a load of hay		[*blank*]	
In the pantrye			
Item a featherbedd & bolster, a blankett & a coverlett	1	15	0
In the woodhouse			
Item wood and seacole	20	0	0
In the sellar			
Item fourteene hoggesheades of beere	6	0	0
Item sixe dozen of candles	1	10	0
In the kitchin			
Item all the brasse & copper	10	0	0
Item all the iron there	2	0	0
Item all the peauter there	6	0	0
Item sixteene cheeses	2	0	0
In severall trunkes in the house			
Item all kind of househould linnen	50	0	0
Item 4878 ounces ¾ of silver plate at 4^s^ 11^d^ the ounce[248]	1205	18	7
Item all kind of lumber throughout the house not before expressed	2	0	0

The goods at the court[249]

	£	s.	d.
In my ladies chamber			
Item five peeces of tapistrye hangeinges	18	0	0
Item five small Turkye carpettes somewhat old	2	10	0
Item one bedstead with a testar, double valence, five curtaines, two high chaires, a backe stoole & two stooles, all of crimson damaske fringed	16	0	0
Item three featherbeddes, three bolsters, foure pillowes, two thicke quiltes, three paire of blankettes & 3 rugges	14	0	0
Item two traverse curtaines of redd kersey with a curtaine rodd, one old peece of dornix & a dornix canopie	2	0	0

the cortege and parallel with Mr Manwaring. One William Fletcher acted as appraiser of Sir John Savage's inventory in Chester in 1616, and others appear in the Rocksavage accounts as tenants, but as the name is so common it is impossible to identify the occupier of this chamber.

248 This is over ten times as much plate as at Melford, and there was none at Rocksavage. This suggests that the bulk of the family's plate moved with them around the country.

249 We cannot be certain which royal palace contained these rooms. Because the section starts with 'my ladies Chamber' it is possible to assume that all the rooms were used by Elizabeth Savage, but the suite of rooms may have accommodated both Thomas and Elizabeth. If they were shared, Whitehall Palace seems the most likely candidate, and the fact that Elizabeth had a key to that palace in 1637 might encourage this view. However Queen Henrietta Maria used Greenwich a good deal, and other London palaces, so the rooms could have been in one of those.

	£	s.	d.
Item a little table, a little cupbord, a little skreene, a paire of creepers, fire shovell, tonges & bellowes	0	11	0
In the inner chamber			
Item three peeces of very old hangeinges, two old livery bedsteades, a stoole with three pannes, two chamberpottes, a greene cotten curtaine & rodd with two little tables	2	10	0
In the outer chamber			
Item striped hangeinges in the entry, two Turkie carpettes, a dornixe windowe curtaine & rodd & a greene carpett	2	0	0
Item a bedstead with dornix valence, testar & two curtaines, a feather bedd, bolster & two blankettes & one rugge	3	0	0
Item two backe chaires, five folding stooles all redd leather, a skreene frame, a little table, fire shovell, tonges & andirons with brasse topps	1	0	0
In the kitchin			
Item two [*damaged*] folding bedsteads, two small feather beddes, two bolsters, foure pillowes & two rugges	0	18	0
Item brasse & iron stuffe there	1	0	0
Item all other woodden stuff & lumber	0	5	0
Item two coaches & harnes for ech & one padd saddle[250]	35	0	0
Item in redie money	52	0	0
Item in debtes & credittes	50	0	0
Item in a lease neere Brainford[251] of a mansion house & some two or three acres of lands for thirtie seaven yeares at Michaelmas last, and some nine acres more or tenn for twentie yeares at our Ladie [*day*] next	800	0	0
The totall somme of the goodes at the house by Tower Hill & at Court comes to	2865	8	7
The totall somme of the severall inventories come to	6600	7	5

An adaicon unto this inventorie

	£	s.	d.
Imprimis all the jewells of the right honorable Ladie Viscountess Savage dowager which were veiwed and apprised the [*illeg.*] 1636 by Francis Hall of London goldsmith & [*illeg.*] & [*illeg.*] to the value of	506	13	4
[*damaged*] in ready money	198	7	7
Total amount	[*illeg.*]		

[*The probate statement in Latin at the end of the inventory is damaged and largely illegible. It is dated 1636, and signed Edward Woodhay, registrar*]

250 The coaches are here but no horses. Presumably they were stabled outside London. Eleven saddle horses are included in the Melford Hall inventory.

251 This is the house at Brentford Bridge inherited from Jane Allington and leased originally to William Noye and now to his son.

Doc. 61. Grant to Elizabeth Savage by Charles I of the right to income from 'shore minerals' for thirty-one years, February 1636.

In 1636 at least one of Elizabeth's schemes to improve her finances succeeded, and she received this grant, which is recorded in a Signet Office Doquet Book, in February 1636. We do not know how much money Elizabeth eventually made from this, if anything, but during 1637 Elizabeth gained more rights to copperas; see Doc. 68. Another document of the same date, held at Birmingham, is shorter but specifically mentions the seashore; it describes the stones in more detail, while omitting the last section of the Signet Office document. This illustrates the value of comparing locally available copies of official documents with those held in central archives.

No.1: [TNA: SO 3/11]

A graunt unto the Ladie Viscountess Savage & her assignes for 31 yeares of all minerall stones lying upon the sea sandes or shoares or anie other place within England & Wales being his majesties soyle or where his majestie hath prerogative, with power to her to dispose of the same for the making of copperas or otherwise, with inhibicion to all others to gather the said minerall stones without her licence. There is reserved the rennt of £13 6s. 8d. paiable at Xmas yeerely. And that if the said ladie or her assignes shall hereafter make it appeare that shee or her assignes [*six words deleted*] is able fully to furnish the kingdome at moderate rates with the said minerall stones, that then his majestie will restrayne the importacion thereof from forraine partes, shee paying his majestie soe much yeerely rennt as by a medium to bee cast upp for the last yeares hath bin answered for customes & other dueties in any one yeare for the said minerall stones imported, saving all such lawfull right as anie person shall clayme to the said minerall stones by graunt from the crownne or by anie other lawfull meanes. By order of Mr Secretary Coke & by him procured [*?*]subsc by Mr Attorney Generall.[252]

No.2: [BCA: 602993 No. 131, DV 894]
A patent graunted to the Lady Elizabeth Dowager Viscountesse Savage one of the ladies of the queenes bedchamber & her assignes (for the terme of 31 yeares next ensueing) of all the minerall stones gouldstones, copperas, stones and sulphur stones lying or being within or uppon the soyle, ground, sand, or shoare adjoyning uppon the sea, or within or uppon any other place being his majesties soyle, or wherein his majestie hath prerogative, within England and Wales. Paying therefore yearelie unto the exchequer £13 6s. 8d.[253]

Witnessed by the king at Westminster, 18 February in the eleventh year of his reign by writ of the privy seal
Wolseley[254]

252 Sir John Bankes was attorney general at this time.

253 Caroline Hibbard says that the category 'lady of the bedchamber' does not 'officially' exist in the financial records; 'the queen's establishment books do not include or list these women and they receive no official recompense for the position. But the household ordinances of 1631, an official source if not a financial one, refer to the ladies of the bedchamber. In early 1637 this group included the duchess of Buckingham, the marquess of Hamilton, Lady Mary Herbert, the countess of Carlisle, the countess of Holland and Lady Savage.' Our thanks to Prof. Hibbard for this reference.

254 For Wolseley, see Notes on People below.

[*on the reverse*]
Lady Savage
lease registered

Doc. 62. Inquisition Post Mortem (IPM) of Thomas, Viscount Savage, 1636. [TNA: CHES 3/103/12; in R. Stewart-Browne (ed.), *The Cheshire Inquisitions Post-Mortem, 1603–1660*, vol. 3, Record Society of Lancashire and Cheshire (London, 1938), 44–51]

An IPM gives a summary of all the landholdings of any recently deceased major tenant of the crown, with details of their rights to the lands. Most of the text given here is not a complete transcription, but (with permission) an almost exact replica of the abbreviated text given in the Lancashire and Cheshire Record Society volume noted above, the only alterations have been minor changes in the format to bring it into line with the editorial conventions of this volume. To this has been added a complete translation of sections relating to the Suffolk properties which the Lancashire and Cheshire Society did not print.

Inquisition taken at Chester Castle, in the Common Hall of Pleas, 7 October, 12 Charles I [*1636*] before Thomas Savage, William Whitmore, Henry Lee, Henry Birkenhead, esqs., Thomas Aldersey esq., escheator, & George Parker esq., feodary, by virtue of the king's commission to enquire after the death of Thomas, Viscount Savage, by the oath of William Marbury of Marbury, John Hurleston of Picton, Somerford Oldfeild of Somerford, Henry Leigh of Highleigh, John Daniell of Darresbury, William Glegge of Geaton, Thomas Trafford of Bridgtrafford, Thomas Marbury of Over Walton, Thomas Meoles of Wallesey, esq., John Nuttall of Cattenhall, Robert Venables of Rudheath, William Harcott of Wyncham, Robert Davies of Ashton, John Travers of Horton, Peter Hatton of Quistbirch & John Kelsall of Bridgtrafford, gentlemen.[255]

They say the said Thomas, Viscount Savage, was seised in tail male, with reversion to his right heirs, of the manor of Rocksavage *alias* Clifton & of the capital messuage of Rocksavage in Clifton & of the old park of Clifton called Clifton Park *alias* Rocksavage Park & of 2 other messuages, a dovecote, 100 acres of land, 20 acres of meadow, 100 acres of pasture, 20 acres of wood, 20 acres of marsh, 40 acres of moor & 20 acres of heath & furze in Clifton; & of the 3rd part of the manor of Runckorne & of 10 messuages, 10 gardens, 10 orchards, 40 acres of land, 20 acres of meadow, 40 acres of pasture, 100 acres of moor, 20 acres of marsh & 10s. rent in Runckorne, Over Runckorne, Nether Runckorne & Halton; & of the manor of Great & Little Barrow & of 50 messuages, 12 cottages, one dovecote, 2 watermills, 60 gardens, 60 orchards, 500 acres of land, 160 acres of meadow, 500 acres of pasture, 100 acres of wood, 100 acres of furze & heath & 20s. rent & the rent of 2 roses in Great & Little Barrow & Bromhill & of free warren in Great & Little Barrow & of a certain liberty to chase, take, kill & carry away deer of either sex found there; of the manor of Tarvin, with members, & of the Court Baron & Leet held there & all other liberties, franchises & royalties to the same manor belonging; of 40 messuages, 20 cottages, 2 dovecotes, 2 watermills, 60 gardens, 60 orchards, 200 acres of land, 100

[255] Thomas Savage might be Thomas Viscount Savage's son, because William Whitmore was his father-in-law, but he was a knight rather than an esquire. This man could also be a number of other relatives of the same name. Whitmore's wife had been sole heiress to the Beeston family of Beeston castle.

acres of meadow, 200 acres of pasture, 50 acres of wood & 300 acres of furze & heath in Tarvin & of a certain park in Tarvin called Tarvin Park & a free warren called Tarvin Warren, & of the rent of 100s. in Tarvin, Stapleford & Stockenhull; of 2 parts of the manor of Kingesley, in four parts divided; of the manor of Bradley by Frodsham; of 10 messuages, 4 cottages, 100 acres of land, 60 acres of meadow, 200 acres of pasture, 100 acres of wood, 20 acres of marsh, 1000 acres of moor, 200 acres of moss, 1000 acres of furze & heath & 40s. rent in the manor of Kingesley aforesaid & in Bradley by Frodsham, Bradley Orchard, Cattenhall, Crowton & Overton; of the manor of Shipbrooke; of the manor of Bostocke; of the manor of Leftwich; of the manor of Huxley & the 6th part of the barony of Nantwich & of 60 messuages, 10 tofts, 30 cottages, a windmill, 3 dovecotes, 40 acres of land, 100 acres of meadow, 300 acres of pasture, 100 acres of wood, 500 acres of furze & heath, 30 acres of moor, 60 acres of moss, 20 acres of marsh, 20 acres of alders, £4 rent, 2lbs. of pepper & 1lb. of cummin in Shipbrooke, Bostocke, Leftwich, Huxley, Nantwich, Henhull, Poole, Aldlem, Wrenbury, Netherton, Woodhouses, Halton Park, Cattenhall, Woodes, Macclesfeild, Macclesfeild Park, Shurlach, Davenham, Warton, Moulton, Occleston, Norcroft, Newton, Norley, Croton, Cuddington, Hale, Mottram Andrew, Ollerbarrow, Lym, Wolstencroft, Stockport, Chorleton, Orton, Tilston, Thelwall, Gropenhall, Appleton, Knottesford, Ashley, Sutton by Macclesfield, Raynow, Hurdesfeild, Dishley, Wildbore-Clough, Angreave, Midgley & Wyncle. He was also seised of the manor of Hellesby & of 4 messuages, 3 cottages, 7 gardens, 7 orchards, 30 acres of land, 10 acres of meadow, 20 acres of pasture, 3 acres of wood, 10 acres of marsh, 10 acres of moor, 10 acres of moss, 100 acres of furze & heath & 6s. rent in Hellesby.[256]

So being seised, a fine was levied at Chester, 20 March, 1 Charles I [*1625–6*] before the King's justices there, between Francis earl of Rutland & William Noy esq., plaintiffs, & said Thomas, earl [*sic*] Savage, by the name of Sir Thomas Savage kt. & bart. & Elizabeth his wife & Sir John Savage kt., his son & heir apparent, deforciants, of the said premises, as by the said fine appears.

He was also seised, in fee, of the castle, manor & borough of Frodsham & of 30 messuages, 10 cottages, 20 burgages, a windmill, a dovecote, 60 acres of land, 20 acres of meadow, 60 acres of pasture, 3 acres of wood, 100 acres of furze & heath, 20 acres of moor, 20 acres of marsh & 40s. rent in Frodsham; & of 3 water grain-mills in Frodsham, all in the county of Chester.

He was also seised of the manor of Melford, county of Suffolk & lands, &c., in Melford, Alpheton, Shimplinge, Lavenham & Acton, in the county of Suffolk, & in Liston & Borley, in the county of Essex & conveyed the said manors of Frodsham & Melford, & the premises aforementioned to the said earl of Rutland & William Noy.

The said fines settled the manors of Rocksavage, Frodsham, Hellesby, Huxley, the 3rd part of Over Runckorne Manor, Frodsham Mills, with mulcture, sok & services thereunto belonging, 2 wooded closes in Cattenhall, called Cattenhall Woods, the demesne lands of Bradley Orchard in Bradley in Frodsham Lordship & all the premises, etc., in Rocksavage, Clifton, Frodsham, Netherton, Overton, Woodhouses, Bradley, Over & Nether Runckorne, Halton, Halton Park, Hellesby, Huxley & Cattenhall Woodes, on the said Viscount Savage, with contingent remain-

256 The figures in the IPM are obviously rounded, but suggest that in Cheshire, Thomas owned his capital messuage, Rocksavage, and 209 other messuages, 79 cottages, 138 gardens, 137 orchards, 8 dovecots, 4 watermills and 2 windmills, 1090 acres of land (arable), 1340 acres of pasture, 2132 acres of heath and furze, 1200 acres of moor, 475 acres of meadow, 358 of wood, 110 of marsh, 260 acres of moss, 10 tofts, 20 acres of alders, 20 burgages (in Frodsham) and had rents of £14 16s. 0d. per year.

ders, after his death, on the said Sir John Savage kt., in tail male, the heirs male of the said viscount, his right heirs; as concerning the manors of Barrow & Tarvin & the premises in Barrow, Tarvin, Maxfield & Macclesfield Park to the use of the said viscount, to the said trustees to provide a marriage portion of £1500 to each of the said viscount's unmarried daughters & after to the said Sir John Savage kt., in tail male, &c. [*as before*].

As concerning the manor of Melford & premises there, except Lynage Wood in Melford & Raymeadow in Aketon, to the use of the said viscount, with contingent remainders to his wife Elizabeth, to Katherine wife of the said Sir John, to the said Sir John, in tail male.

The said viscount was also seised, in tail male, of a messuage, garden & 47s. rent in Chester city & of the advowsons of Alpheton & Stansted, in the county of Suffolk.

He conveyed to John Minshull & others the manors of Kingesley, Shipbrooke, Bostocke, Leftwich & Occleston, the premises aforesaid in the county of Chester & in the city of Chester, the advowsons in Stansted & Alpheton, in the county of Suffolk, premises in Liston & Borley, in the county of Essex, in trust, to the uses of his will.

He was also seised in tail male of the office of bailiff of the Manor & Forest of Macclesfield & of the office of constable or keeper of the King's Gaol in the town of Macclesfield & of the fees, &c., to the said offices appertaining; & was also seised of the advowsons of Davenham Church & of the parish church of Barrow & of 2 messuages in Aunston & 20 acres of land, 5 acres of meadow, 20 acres of pasture, 2 acres of wood, 12 acres of furze & heath in Aunston & of the court leet & view of frankpledge & all thereunto appertaining within the said manors, vills & hamlets of Kingesley, Newton, Croton, Onson, Cuddington & Hellesby, held twice a year.

He was also seised of a windmill in Wydnes, in the county of Lancs.

The jurors say that Elizabeth, late the wife of the said viscount, survives & dwells at Rocksavage & Katherine, wife of Sir John, likewise; & Dorothy, Anne, Katherine & Henrietta Savage are daughters of the late viscount & survive & dwell at Rocksavage, & are still unmarried.

The said manor of Rocksavage & Clifton & the premises there are held of Henrietta Maria, queen of England, as of her manor of Halton, county of Chester, parcel of the Duchy of Lancaster, by half a knight's fee & worth yearly (clear) £11 5s. 4d.

The premises in Over Runckorne held in like manner by 40th part of a knight's fee & worth yearly (clear) 40s.

Those in Nether Runckorne & Halton held of the queen, as of her manor of Halton, in free socage, by fealty only & worth yearly (clear) 10s.

Those in Appleton held of the heirs of Peter Warburton esq., as of his manor of Appleton, in free socage, by fealty only & worth yearly (clear) 10s.

Those in Gropenhall held of the heirs of Sir Peter Leigh kt., as of his manor of Gropenhall, in free socage, by fealty only & worth yearly (clear) 20s.

Those in Lym & Thelwall held of the queen, as of her manor of Halton, in free socage, by fealty only & worth yearly (clear) 40s.

Those in Wolstencroft held of the king as of his earldom of Chester, in free socage, by fealty only & worth yearly (clear) 2s.

Those in Hale, Ollerbarrow & Ashley held of Sir Thomas Booth kt. & bart., as of his manor of Dunham Massie, in socage, by fealty & 2s. 6d. rent yearly & worth yearly (clear) £3 5s. 0d.

Those in Mottram Andrew held of Hugh Calverley esq., in free socage, by fealty only & worth yearly (clear) 13s. 4d.

Those in Macclesfield, except Macclesfield Park, held of the king, as of his manor of Macclesfield in free burgage & worth yearly (clear) £3; the bailiwick of the manor & forest of Macclesfield & all thereunto pertaining, held of the king, as of his earldom of Chester, by the service of being bailiff & collecting the rents & profits of the king there & worth nothing beyond reprises; the office of constable of the gaol there, held in like manner & also worth nothing; the tenements in Macclesfield Park held of the king in socage, by fealty & worth yearly (clear) £5.

The premises in Raynow, Hurdisfield, Sutton, Dishley, Wincle, Angreave, Midgeley & Wildbore Clough held of the king, as of his manor of Macclesfield in free & common socage, by fealty only & worth yearly (clear) £3.

Those in Stockport held of Edward Warren esq., as of his manor of Stockport, in free socage & worth yearly (clear) 15s.

Those in Knottesford held of William Leigh of Booths, esq., in free burgage, by fealty & 12d. rent yearly & worth yearly (clear) 2s.

The manors & premises in Shipbrooke, Shirlach, Davenham, Wareton, Aldlem, Moulton, Henhull, Poole, Leftwich, Nantwich, Wrenbury & Chorleton, the 6th part of the barony of Nantwich, the advowson of Davenham held of the king, as of his earldom of Chester, by half a knight's fee & worth yearly (clear) £13.

The manors & premises in Bostocke, Huxley, Occleston, Norcroft & Orton held likewise & worth yearly (clear) £20.

The manors of Great & Little Barrow & premises there & in Bromhill & the advowson of Barrow church held of the queen, as of her Honor of Halton, by half a knight's fee & worth yearly (clear) £24.

The manor of Tarvin & premises there & in Stapleford & Hockenhull held of the king, as of his earldom of Chester, by half a knight's fee & worth yearly (clear) £5.

Two parts of Kingesley manor & premises there & in Cuddington, Norley, Newton, Cattenhall, Aunston & Croton held in like manner by 20th part of a knight's fee & worth yearly (clear) £3.

The manors of Frodsham & Bradley by Frodsham & premises there (except Frodsham mills) & in Bradley Orchard, Netherton, Overton & Woodhouses held of the king in chief, by knight service & worth yearly (clear) 100s. & the said mills held of the king, as of his manor of East Greenwich, in the county of Kent, in free socage, by fealty & rent & worth yearly (clear) 40s.

The premises in Chester city held of the Master of St John's without the North Gate of that city in free socage, by fealty only & worth yearly (clear) £3 4s. 8d.

The manor of Hellesby & premises there held of John, earl of Shrewsbury, as of his manor of Dunham on the Hill, in free socage, by fealty & 2s. rent & worth yearly (clear) 40s.

The premises in Tilston, tenure unknown, worth yearly (clear) 2s.

[*From this point on, an exact translation*]

And that the aforesaid manor of Melford aforesaid, and the aforesaid advowsons of Melford, Stanstead and Alpheton, and other premises in Melford and Acton aforesaid, are held, and at the time of the death of the aforesaid Thomas Viscount Savage were held, of the said lord king as of his manor of East Greenwich in the county of Kent, in free socage for fealty only, and not in chief or for military service, for all services, rents and demands whatsoever, and are worth per year in all profits over and above deductions twenty pounds. And that the aforesaid premises in Shimpling, Lavenham, Acton and Alpheton aforesaid with appurtenances in the county of Suffolk aforesaid are held, and at the time of the death of the aforesaid

Thomas Viscount Savage were held, of whom and for what services the aforesaid jurors are wholly ignorant, and are worth per year in all profits over and above deductions forty shillings.

And that the aforesaid premises in Liston and Borley with their appurtenances in the county of Essex aforesaid are held, and at the time of the death of the aforesaid Thomas Viscount Savage were held, of whom or for what services the jurors are wholly ignorant, and are worth per year in all profits over and above deductions four shillings. And that the aforesaid windmill in Widnes in the county of Lancashire aforesaid is held, and at the time of the death of the aforesaid Thomas Visount Savage was held, of the said lord king as of his manor of East Greenwich in the county of Kent in free socage for fealty and rent of twenty-three shillings and four pence, as is worth per year in all profits over and above deductions twenty shillings.

And the aforesaid jurors on their aforesaid oath further say that the aforesaid Thomas Viscount Savage named thus in the aforesaid commission, as said before, seised of all and singular premises respectively from such his estate, died so seised at Rocksavage aforesaid on the twentieth day of November in the now eleventh year of the said lord king, and that the aforesaid John Savage knight, now Viscount Savage, is his son and next heir of the said Thomas Viscount Savage named in the aforesaid commission, and is, and at the time of the holding of this inquiry was, of full age, that is to say of the age of twenty-four years and more.[257] And the jurors aforesaid on their aforesaid oath further say that the aforesaid Thomas Viscount Savage named in the said commission, on the day when he died, had or held no other or more lands or tenements from the said lord king, nor of any other persons in demesne, reversion or service in the said county of Chester or elsewhere, as was established in evidence by the aforesaid jurors on the holding of this inquiry.

In testimony of which, to one part of this inquiry the aforesaid commissioners as well as jurors placed their seals, and to the other part of this inquiry in the possession of the first juror the commissioners placed their seals, given in the day, year and place aforesaid.

Henry Leghe	Thomas Marbury	
John Hurleston	Thomas Meoles	John Travers
Somarford Oldfeild	John Nuthall	Peter Hatton
John Hamell	Robert Venables	John Kelsall
William Glegg	William Harcott	
Thos Trafford	sign of Robert Davies	

Doc. 63. Extract from a letter from Charles I to the earl of Pembroke, May 1636.[258] [Ogle and Bliss (eds), *Clarendon State Papers*, I, no. 729; Bodl., *CLSP* I, 547]

This says nothing about the recent death of Thomas Viscount Savage, but could be a result of Elizabeth Savage's pleadings of poverty or Queen Henrietta Maria's pressure on her husband to do something for the Dowager Viscountess. However, linking

[257] The place of death is an error: Thomas died at his house on Tower Hill.

[258] This is the draft of a letter, written partly by King Charles and partly by secretary Windebank; we do not know if a finished version was ever sent. If it was, a major error would have needed correction for it is addressed to the wrong earl. The 4th earl of Pembroke (who did not die until 1649) had four sons, all of whom became Lord Herbert of Shurland. Two died very young, and the third, Charles, died in January

this with Doc. 65 suggests that Dorothy's eventual husband was enamoured of her by this time; perhaps Charles was trying to divert Dorothy's attention from him by producing a new candidate for her attention.

1636 May
To the earl of Pembroke[259]

My Lord,
I cannot use a better arguement of my care of you and your family, than by taking into consideration that which mostly concerns you, and that is the marriage of your son, the Lord Herbert, which, though perhaps it may seem at this time unseasonable, considering he is not yet out of his mourning and true sorrow for the loss of his late dear and virtuous lady . . . The person I would recommend unto you is Mrs Dorothy Savage, daughter of the Lady Savage, whose birth and virtues are so well known, that there can be no doubt but when such a couple as your son and she shall come together, the conjunction will be very happy.[260] [*letter continues on other topics*] . . . You may be confident I will be ever cherishing my own work, for both your owne and my lady Sauvage's sake, who shall knowe nothing of this untill you shall thinke fitt . . . .

64. Letter from Thomas Earl Rivers to Charles I, 9 April 1637. [TNA: SP 16/352/50]

Earl Rivers, father of Elizabeth Savage, was obviously concerned about his daughter's well-being; he gave her a number of gifts of land before his death, and left her the bulk of his fortune, which Doc.55 suggests was large. He presumably felt that she also needed support at court. The letter was penned by someone else; the earl's signature at the end is noticeably weak.[261]

9th Aprill 1637
May it please your majestie,
Going now on my last dayes, with so much weakenes and decay that I can never hope to come into your majesties presence, I presume on your princely goodnes in these few lines, to present my humble service and thanks unto your majestie for the favour you have done my daughter, the Ladie Savage, who hath the honour to serve your majestie and, I trust, shall do when I am gon, with the same fidelity and devotion I ever caried toward your crowne and person.

For the better effecting of the which, I have disposed my estate upon her, for want of heire male of my owne bodie (of the which I have no hope) otherwise not, and have made it as sure as \I/ can in law, but the best assurance I can have is your majesties princely favour and protection, which I most humbly implore, if any question or

1635, with his wife surviving him (she was Mary daughter of the duke of Buckingham). The fourth son, Philip was born in 1620 and married in 1639. But Garrard (Doc. 65) says that Dorothy Savage nearly married the earl of Worcester's son, Lord Herbert; the eldest sons of the earls of Worcester were always Lord Herbert. It would seem probable that the letter should have been addressed to Henry Somerset, later 1st marquis of Worcester. His son Edward had been widowed in 1635, and married again in 1639. The Savages were related to the Somersets through Thomas's great grandmother.

259 For earl of Pembroke, 2nd marquis of Worcester, see Notes on People below.

260 For Lord Herbert and Dorothy Savage, see Notes on People below.

261 Thomas Darcy was probably approaching eighty by the time this was written, but he lived until February 1640.

troble should arise to hinder or abate any part of my intentions in the setling of my estate, as aforesaid, wherin if your majestie please, that I may rely upon your gratious word and promise in this my just \and/ reasonable desire, I shall with more comfort passe the rest of my few and evill dayes, and shall pray for all heavenly blessings, to be powred upon your majestie, your gratious queene and all your royall issue.

St Oses, Aprill 9, 1637
Your majesties most humble and devote subject, Rivers

Doc. 65. Extract from a letter from Revd G. Garrard to Thomas Wentworth, Lord Deputy (later earl of Strafford), April 1637. [W. Knowler (ed.), *The Earle of Strafforde's Letters and Dispatches, with an Essay towards his Life* (London, 1739), II, p.73]

Garrard was a frequent correspondent of Thomas Wentworth. This letter and others about this marriage reveal the importance both of religion and family approval for marriage. Dorothy Savage had been left a portion of £1500 by her father (Doc. 62); where the remaining £3500 came from we do not know.

Revd Mr Garrard to the Lord Deputy,
. . . Monday in Easter week, my Lord Andover, Berkshire's eldest son, was married by a popish priest to Mrs Doll Savage, eldest daughter to the Lord Savage lately dead, against consent of parents on both sides.[262] Never such an outcry was made about a marriage. My Lord of Berkshire, his lady, my Lady of Exeter, my Lady Salisbury, my Lady Carlisle, all highly incensed against this young lord, who had been passionately in love with her two or three year;[263] disinherited he must be, never looked on again by any of his friends, no maintenance, no house for them to live in; her mother also had commanded her from her house at Tower-hill, where they lay the first night of their marriage; nay, they were angry with my Lord Chamberlain, that he would lend them part of his house at Barnard Castle to lodge for a while in.[264] Setting aside her religion, the match was equal and honourable enough on both sides, her portion five thousand pounds. She had been nigh marriage twice, once to Dunlace when he was so, last year to my Lord of Worcester's son, the Lord Herbert, her younger sister married, so it behoved her to provide for herself.[265] His friends drive much at the marrying of a papist, but that which galls most is, whereby to provide fortunes for their younger children. All which is lost by this his disobedience to his parents. The king said he could not forgive him his disobedience to his parents, nor his fault in being married by a priest. The queen was heartily sorry for the affliction it brought upon my Lady Berkshire. My Lord's Grace of Canterbury also shewed himself a little in this business, for he writ to him, chiding him for the great disobedience he had shewed to his parents, and commanding him to come unto

262 For Lord Andover, later earl of Berkshire, see Notes on People below.

263 For Lord and Lady Berkshire, Lady Carlisle and Lady Salisbury, see Notes on People below.

264 The Lord Chamberlain was Philip Herbert, earl of Pembroke. Baynard's Castle was on the Thames towards the western end of the city wall; for several hundred years the building had been a palace and a home. Pembroke had previously had an adulterous alliance with the earl of Berkshire's daughter, which may have led him to befriend the earl's son.

265 For the possible marriage to Lord Herbert, see Doc. 63; for Lord Herbert and Dunlace, see Notes on People below.

him to give an account, when, where and by whom he was married.[266] But the queen, it is said, interceded that this might be pressed no farther. So my Lord's Grace was taken off. The Lady Savage is reconciled unto them, and hath admitted them into her house at Tower-hill, but no atonement yet betwixt them and his friends. . . .
London, April 28, 1637.

Doc. 66. Elizabeth Savage's account concerning her administration of her husband's effects, June 1637. [CCALS: DCH/O/27]

This survives in Cheshire but not in the records of the Prerogative Court of Canterbury. The original is very decayed: only parts of the document survive and they cannot be fully recovered, even with the use of modern digital techniques. Nevertheless the exemplification has been included here because it provides additional proof of Thomas Savage's debts when he died. The debts alone total nearly as much as the total valuation of the inventory.[267]

Exemplification of account of right honorable Viscountess Savage by William Laud, archbishop of Canterbury, June 1637.
[*damaged*; *the entire first part of the document is missing*.]

The Discharge	£	s.	d.
Imprimis paid for all Charges		[*illeg.*][268]	
Item paid for her charges right amountes after the death of the said deceased to recept the servantes togeather	32	2	2
Item paid for servantes wages due at his death	72	6	2
Item paid for takinge of lettres of administracion for two conturreries, for prizinge the goods in Chester, Suffolk and London and for engrossing the inventorie	21	1	[*illeg.*]
Item for fees solicitting charges and other travaileinge about the administracion	20	0	0
Item paid in parte of sundry debts due by bondes namely, [*vizt.*]			
to Sir John North, twentie poundes[269]			
to Sir Robert Pye, forty poundes			
to Sir Henry Knowle, one hundred and sixtene pounds			
to the Ladie Dorchester, three hundred and twentie pounds			
Mr Lasonbies agent, four pounde			
to William Payne of London esqr, two and thirty poundes[270]			
to Thomas Burton for G. Carter late of Melford, twelve poundes			

266 The archbishop of Canterbury was William Laud; see Notes on People below.

267 However this is unlikely to be a complete list of Thomas's debts. From 1639 onwards his eldest son John was involved in a long-running legal case with the administrators of Edward Wymarke; Thomas apparently died owing Wymarke £2000. There are numerous references to this case in the *Journal of the House of Lords* during the 1640s. See above, Introduction, note 316, p. lxi.

268 Taking the total of the legible sums from the 'sume of the discharge' leaves £1683, most of which was very likely the charges for the funeral. When the earl of Rutland was buried in 1632 his funeral cost £3544 (R. Houlbrooke, *Death, Religion and the Family, 1480–1750* (Oxford, 1998), p. 274).

269 See Notes on People, below, for information about people mentioned in this document, where identifiable.

270 This is very likely the William Payne of Middlesex who with Thomas and his cousin Edward Savage leased lands in Runcorn to Thomas Cheshire and others in 1630: CCALS, DCH/E/12.

	£	s.	d.
to Sir William Curteene, twentie poundes to Mr Doctor Eden, twenty poundes Sir William Slingesby, fourty poundes and to Mr James Halles of London gentleman, eight pounds, in all	632	0	0
Item to the Lord Coleraine	537	0	0
Item paid to Mr Richard Hayes of London gentleman	322	0	0
Item paid to Mr William Smythes of Kensington gentleman	256	0	0
Item to Mr Chrestopher Hopper of London gentleman	150	0	0
Item To Mr Edward Py of London Esqr	1040	0	0
Item paid to Sir John Thimbelby	500	0	0
Item paid to Mr Jefferie Werburton	410	0	0
Item paid to Sir Morrice Dromond	400 [*illeg.*]		
Item paid to Sir William [*illeg.*]	514	0	0
Item paid to Mr Auditor [*?*]Lacy	520	0	0
Item paid to Mr Frances Hall of Melford in Suffolk	627	0	0
Item William Cock and Antonie Sparrowe have a judgement in the Common Pleas of twelve hundred poundes uppon a bond a thousand, to paie[271]	600	0	0
Item William Cocke hath another judgement of one thousand poundes uppon a bond, to paie	600	0	0
Item for drawinge and engrossing this accompte quietus est, seale and other charges therabout	5	0	0
Sume of the discharge	£8742	2s.	10d.[272]
Soe this Accompt is in surplusage	£1467	8s.	6d.

[*damaged*]

Doc. 67. Letter from Sir Ranulph Crewe to Sir John Coke concerning Delamere Forest, 1637.[273] [BL: Add. MS 64915, 97]

John Crewe, forester of Delamere, was Sir Ranulph Crewe's son. This letter, probably written in August 1637, relates to a petition and patent which the authors have not found, but is presumably associated with Doc. 49. The overall sense of the petition is clear, if the detail and the grammar are not.

My humble duty doone to your honor, unto whom I am uppon all occasions exceedingly bownd & I hope God wyll reward you. By the letters your honor vouchsaffed to wryte unto me, I see the kynges pleasure & may discerne the strength of my Lady Savage who I dowbt not solecited the kyng, & hath her end.

The petition [*deleted*] exhibited by my soone for redresse of that exorbitant pattent procured by the late Lord Savage, & soome other thynges, was truth in every

271 The authors have not been able to find information about this case, despite searching the indexes to cases in the Common Pleas.
272 In the original document this sum is written under headings which are the initials of Latin numerals: M = thousands, C = hundreds.
273 For Sir Ranulph Crewe and Sir John Coke, see Notes on People below.

part, for I humbly thank God he loveth truth. The answere, mencioned in your letter, hath no truth in itt which is, that more were not demaunded then have continually bene allowed for soome hundreths of yeares, whereas the late Lord Savage was the fyrst man that procured a graunt of 20 buckes & does, 10 of the one & 10 of the other, whereas all former rangers had never more than 4, & those he kylles without calling the forrester thereunto & by that meanes may kyll att his pleasure & payes no fees to the poore keepers. Your honor may see by this petition which the bearer wyll shewe you, howe my Lord Savage upholdes the profession he made before you of respectes to me & my soone; wher as by his meanes \nowe lately/ the right of my soone in the bestowing of a principall keepers place in the forrest is sought to be invaded.

I knowe not howe farre you wylbe pleased to trouble your sellfe with the prefering thereof to the kyng, which my humble suit is you would vouchsaffe to do, if itt may stand with your honors liking, for that keepers dependent uppon my Lord Savage may hould places there, he may have venison enough, & the forrest suffer, & my soone may retayne the title, but not the right of a forrester, I most humbly beseech your honor helpe my soone of this rock which I presume wylbe doone, the kyng being well informed, ells he shall serve his majesty in his place off forrester with disgrace & no comfort, & thus remayning your honors dettor, which I would be glad in soome measure to pay, I humbly take my leave & rest
Your honors most humbly att command, Ranulphe Crewe

The place being graunted to an able man before the receipt of the kynges \letter/ me thinkes should be a satisfactory answere, with this that itt behoves the forester to make choyce of able & trusty keepers.
[*on the reverse*]
To the right honorable Syr John Coke knight, principall secretary to his majesty att courtt, humbly present.

Doc. 68A. Indenture between Charles I and copperas makers, 1637.[274] [BCA: 602993 No. 165, DV 894]

This and the next document record another of Elizabeth's successful schemes to acquire rights to money-making activities, although later documents suggest that the farm did not bring in as much income as had been expected, at least in the first year.[275]

An indenture betweene his majesty on the one parte and Tymothie Middleton esq., Augustine Garland, gent, James Monger, Richard Beresford, Robert Johnson, Thomas Golde, Edmond Rous and Richard Hankin on the other parte. Whereas the said parties are seized of and in severall copperas houses and copperas workes in Middlesex, Kent and other places, wherein they have made and doe nowe make copperas, doe hereby bargaine and sell to his majesty, his heires and assignes, yearely for the terme of 7 yeares to be accompted from the second of February last, such and soe many severall tonnes of good and merchantable copperas, *alias* greene copperas, *alias* iron rust copperas, as in a schedule annexed is mencioned to be agreed to be yearely made by each of the said severall copperas makers.

274 For copperas and the location of the works, see above, note 278 in the Introduction, p. lvi.
275 TNA, SO 3/12, f. 34 records a rebate of £262 10s. out of £1050 'due from the Lady Savage for the first yeares rent for the copperas farm and is in regards of her losses susteyned thereby'.

Which copperas, they for themselves severallie and not jointly doe covenant with his majesty, shalbe made in the severall copperas houses nowe belonging unto them scituate in the severall places aforesaid, and none other place, and accompting 2000 pound weight neate to everie tonne thereof, and after the rate of £5 10s. for every tonne of the said copperas before herein mencioned to be sould or contracted for as aforesaid.

All which said copperas in the said schedule mencioned to be contracted for, the parties above named doe covenaunt with his majesty and his agentes to deliver to his majesty or his agentes at such wharfes or keys betweene London Bridge and the east end of Wapping as by his majesty, his successors, agentes or assignes shalbe appointed. And they doe covenaunt not to make above a 1000 <li> tonnes yearely except the quantity of 3 tonnes neate above their severall proporcions expressed in the said schedule, unles a greater proporcion shalbe required by his majesty or his assignes. And they doe covenaunt not to sell any copperas to any person, but to his majesty, his successors or assignes upon paine of forfeiture of 12s. to his majesty for every 100 weight.

And his majesty upon the delivery of such copperas doth hereby covenaunt by his agent John Eldred of London, merchant, to pay for the same after the aforesaid rate of £5 10s. the tonne in ready money, or in default thereof by bills to be made, sealed and delivered by the said John Eldred as in such case is accustomed. And in default of payment of the said bills, it shalbe in \the/ power of the said parties to dispose of their copperas to any others, with divers other covenaunts for the better performaunce of this service, given on 27 day of July in the thirteenth year of King Charles, by writ of the privy seale.
Wolseley

[*on the reverse*]
May it please your Lordshipp,
The copperas men have sealed delivered & acknowledged their contract with his majesty, and the same shall bee forthwith delivered to be enrolled 28 November 1637.
John Bankes

Doc. 68B. Grant to Elizabeth Savage and others of the copperas farm, 1637.
[BCA: DV 894 (602993), No. 169]

May it please your Lordshipp,
The Lady Viscountess Dowager Savage, & Mr Edward Savage & Edmund Windhame her ladyships trustees, have sealed the counterpart of his majesties grant and assignment to them of the copperas farme.[276] And the same is acknowledged and \is/ [*deleted*] delivered to be enrolled 27 November 1637.
Jo Bankes

An indenture betweene his majesty of the one parte and the Lady Elizabeth Viscountesse Dowager Savage, Edward Savage and Edmund Windham esquier on thother parte, whereby his majesty (at the instance of the said viscountesse) doth

[276] For Edward Savage and Edmund Windham, see Notes on People below. These two men appear to have worked together in a number of business deals, not just as trustees for Elizabeth Savage: TNA, SO 3/12, f. 33 and TNA, SP 17/D/17.

grant and assigne unto the said Edward Savage and Edmund Windham and their assignes, all the tonnes of good and merchantable copperas, *alias* greene copperas, *alias* iron rust copperas, mencioned in a schedule to an indenture annexed dated 27 July last and in a schedule hereto annexed amounting in the whole to 1000 tonnes a yeare.

And his majesty doth hereby appoint the said Edward Savage and Edmond Windham and their assignes to take and receive whatsoever on his majesties behalfe is to be received by vertue of a contract made betweene his majesty and the copperas makers, to have and to hold the full benefitt of the said contract and the said severall tonnes of copperas to the said Edward Savage and Edmond Windham and their assignes from the second day of February last for the terme of 7 yeares, paying therefore yearely into his majesties exchequer a rent of £1050 upon the seacond of August and the seacond of February. The first payment to incurre from the seacond of February last, with divers other covenauntes herein expressed, given the 9 November in the thirteenth year of his reign, by writ of the privy seal.

Wolseley

[*on the reverse*]
Indenture, coperas makers
Registered
9 Nov, 13 Charles I (1637) [*in later hand*]

Doc. 69. Letter from Elizabeth Savage to Robert earl of Lindsey, 1639.[277] [TNA: SP 16/414/72]

Yet another investment is made in the hope of making money. This implies that Elizabeth was investing in fen drainage. The earl of Lindsey was involved in draining an area 'stretching between Kyme Eau and the River Glen' in south Lincolnshire and was given payment in the form of a grant of land in 1636.[278]

My Lord,
I have sent downe my servant this bearer to attend your lord and those who <r> are adventurrers with you, to demaunde the hundred acres which by consent was to be allotted unto mee, and I shall now expect to have it sett out accordingly, and if there bee any thing wherein I have fayled to performe what I ought to doe, and have not merrited my proportion as well as Mr German, I shall desire to bee informed therein; in the meane time let mee receave equall respect from you and them in the fairenes of the proceedinge, with mee, which I shall not doubt to have from your Lord becaus I am and ever shall be most ready to requite your courtesyes, being to the utmost of my power,
your Lords fathfull freind to serve you
Elizabeth Savage
Tower Hill, 10th of March, 1638

277 For Robert Bertie earl of Lindsey, see Notes on People below.

278 H. Darby, *The Draining of the Fens* (London, 1956), p. 48. The area was later called Lindsey level. The earl cut a 24–mile channel from the river Glen near Bourne to Boston, then enclosed the resulting land and built farms on it. The surviving map of the level names those with land, but does not include Elizabeth Savage: W. Dugdale, *The History of Imbanking and Drayning of Divers Fenns and Marshes* (London, 1662), pp. 417–19.

Doc. 70. Letter from Elizabeth Savage to Sir Francis Windebank, date uncertain. [TNA: SP 16/439/22]

In State Papers this letter is listed under 1639. The content would make sense if it was written in 1636, at the time of Elizabeth's petition about the freedoms of the city of London (Doc. 53). But the people to whom it has been referred are different and the language strongly suggests that she is a widow, so this must relate to a petition now lost. Sir Francis Windebank was secretary of state through this period.

Noble Sir,

I here the quene my mistris has done me soe great a favor as to get the kinge to <refer> send my petition to you, to whome I must ever acknowledge that I have bene infinitly bound, and now that as this is the greatest busines that ever I had, and the only thinge wherin I may hope to redeme my selfe of some of the great charge I have lived at in ther majesties service having spent very largely, and consederinge I have notheing from them but must run the hasard of ruening my selfe if I continue. Therfore I besich you be pleased to obtaine from his majestie that the examining of this petition may be referred to my Lord Cottington, Mr Attorney Generall, and if ther must be a third I desire it may be my Lord Prevy Seale for these I know as they will be noe waies partiall to me soe they will conseder I have great reason to be remembered with some thinge for my long exspence; this is a busines in the opinion of very good councell likely to pas if I have not bitter enimies, for I am assured most of the citty will stand for it and be glad soe great an abuse may be redused; I never had <any> \<deleted>/ openion of any good fortune to my selfe in any busines till now that I am soe happie as to be in your hands, assuring you I will not faile to be \a/ gratefull and most thankfull friend but will on all occations profes my selfe most fathffully.[279]

Your most affectionate friend,
Elizabeth Savage

[*on the reverse*]
Lady Savage
Memoriall, for Sir Francis Windebank Knt, principal Secretary of State

Doc. 71. Letter from Charles Savage to his grandmother Countess Rivers, 1641. [CUL: Hengrave 88, III, f. 88]

Charles and Richard Savage, youngest sons of Thomas and Elizabeth, were sent to Lisbon College during the winter of 1640–1, and arrived in December.[280]

Madam,

Pardon me, I pray you, that I did \not/ take my leave of your ladyship, upon my departure from England which indeede was no falt of mine, I being comaineded the contrarye by my superiors, even then when your Ladyship sent for me and my brother. But although it was the hindrance of others that I could not present myself in person to your Ladyship, yett it shall be my care that my letters shall not fayle to

279 The attorney general was Sir John Bankes; see Notes on People below.

280 In 1624 a college for English students desiring to study for the priesthood and for mission work in England was founded in Lisbon by Pietro Catinho, a member of an illustrious family. It was known as SS Peter's and Paul's.

be presented to your Ladyship, \though/ I be in a strainge countrey, and further seperated then before I was. I hope also, and doe no less desire that your Ladyship would vouchsafe to honour me sometimes with a letter from \you/ that I may be certified of your Ladyships good health and happinesse, which I pray God long to continue with you. Farewell, from Lisbon April 7 1641.
Your Ladyship's most dutifull and obedient grandchild,
Charles Savage
[*on the reverse*]
To the right honorable my most deare granmother the Countesse of Rivers these present
[*in another hand*]
Charles Savage his letter from Lisbon

Doc. 72. Licence to Elizabeth Savage and her son to build at Tower Hill, 1641. [UHA: DDSQ(3)/18/3]

Stuart planning permission! The summary of this licence is contained in a Signet Office book, held at TNA. It says that the licence was procured by Mr Secretary Vane and 'subscribed by Mr Attorney General upon significacon of his Majesties pleasure under his signe manuall'. However, a full copy of the licence has by some means found its way into the records of the Quintin family, now held at the Brynmore Jones library at the University of Hull. A map of 1666 shows six gables of a row of houses facing Tower Hill and others behind.[281]

Charles by the grace of God king of England, Scotland, Fraunce and Ireland, defender of the faith etc. To all to whome theis present shall come, greeting: whereas we are informed by the humble peticion of our right trusty and wellbeloved cozens John Earle Rivers and the Lady Elizabeth Viscountesse Savage his mother, to us latelie presented, that they are seized of the inheritance of land lying in the parishes of Saint Olave *alias* Saint Olaffe in Hartstreete and the Crossed *alias* the Crouched Fryers London and neare Towerhill London, upon the greater part whereof there are divers messuages and building which are very ancient and much decayed and ready to fall downe, and that the residue therof is wast ground, whereas if newe building were erected upon all the said land in an uniforme and convenient manner the same would be a great ornament to that place and much conduce to the common good of the cittie, but most especiallie for the conveniencie of the officers of our customehouse, their humble suite unto us is that we would be graciouslie pleased to graunt them licence, and others under their tytle, to erect and gett up such building in and upon the said land, conforming themselves to the forme prescribed by our proclamations.[282] And to have libertie to make use of such common sewers adjacent as shalbe most usefull and expedient for that purpose.

The consideracion thereof we having referred to our commissioners for building or any three or more of them, our Lord Treasurer of England, the earle of Arundell and Surrey, the earle of Dorsett and Sir Henry Vane knight being foure of the commissioners aforesaid, whoe to the end they might \give/ us the better

281 Map of London by Wenceslaus Hollar.
282 For the Crossed/Crutched Friars, see Introduction, p. lxxxiii. James I and Charles I had issued rules for building in London: J.F. Larkin and P. Hughes (eds), *Stuart Royal Proclamations* (2 vols, Oxford, 1973). For example, I, 485–8.

satisfaccion, did commend the further consideracion of the peticion aforesaid unto sondry others of our commissioners, and were thereupon certified by Sir William Acton, Sir Henry Garwaye knight, and Inigo Jones esquire, that they have taken a particuler viewe of the ground mencioned in the peticion aforesaid, conteyning on the south side toward Towerhill two hundred and thirty foote, and on the east side toward Crotched Fryers two hundred and nynetie foote, and on the north side one hundred eighty two foote, and on the west side three hundred and thirty foote or neere thereabout.[283]

And doe finde that upon the said ground there hath been anciently and is nowe standing a great mansion house with gardens and outhouses thereunto belonging toward Towerhill, and the other parte toward Croched Fryers is whollie built upon with divers tenements, warehouses and stables nowe in possession of the said Lord Rivers. All which building, being nowe of tymber, the said Lord Rivers intends to demolish and upon that ground desires to build about fifty houses of bricke, or bricke and stone, according to our proclamations for building, whereof eight of them to be in front toward Towerhill.

And the said Earle Rivers is contented to leave an angle of ground being about one hundred and thirty foote square into the publique way leading to Towerhill, whereby the street wilbe much enlarged. And the said Sir William Acton, Sir Henry Garwaie and Inigo Jones beleive that those building may be convenient for the officers of our customehouse. And if we should be graciouslie pleased to graunt leave unto the said Earle Rivers to build, then they the said Sir William Acton, Sir Henry Garway and Inigo Jones conceive it fitt that upon the front toward Towerhill there be built but only five faire houses which may serve for men of quality. And upon the rest of the said ground fortie-two houses or thereabout. And alsoe the said Sir William Acton, Sir Henry Garway and Inigo Jones thinke fitt that the streete intended to be made from Crotched Fryers into the Chayne Way leading to Towerhill be at least twenty foote wide. And for the sewers, they being by them the said Sir William Acton, Sir Henry Garwaie and Inigo Jones conceived to belong to the cittie of London, they can determyne nothing, but leave the same to them therein concerned, as by the same certificate transmitted unto us by the said Lord Treasurer, the Earle of Arundell and Surrey, the Earle of Dorsett and Sir Henry Vane knight, our principall secretary of state more at large appeareth.

Knowe ye that we graciouslie inclyninge to the humble suite of the said John Earle Rivers and the said Lady Elizabeth Viscountesse, his mother, for good consideracions us thereunto moving of our especiall grace, certaine and [*?*]meere mocion, have given and graunted and by theis presents for us our heires and successors do give and graunt to the said John Earle Rivers and the lady Viscountesse his mother, their heires or assignes, full licence, liberty, power and authority, that they, either every or any of them and their either every or any of their workmen from tyme to tyme, and att all tymes hereafter, shall and may, lawfully, quietly and peaceably, frame, erect, newe build and gett up seaven and forty houses upon the said parcell of land mencioned in the said certificate lying in the parishes of Saint Olave *alias* Saint Olaff in Hartstreete and the Crossed *alias* the Crowched Fryers London aforesaid neare the Towerhill aforesaid, conteyning on the south side toward Towerhill two hundred and thirty foote, and on the east side toward Croched Fryers two hundred and nyntie foote, and on the north side one hundred eighty and two foote, and on the

283 For Arundel and Surrey, Juxon (Lord Treasurer), Dorset, Vane, Acton, Garway and Jones, see Notes on People below.

west side three hundred and thirty foote or neare thereabout, viewed and certified as aforesaid. And upon the front whereof toward the Towerhill aforesaid our will and pleasure is there shalbe erected and built five houses and noe more and those to be faire houses fitt for men of good ranke and quality \to live/.

The front of the same five houses and buildings and likewise of the two and fortie houses aforesaid by theis present licenced and authorized to be erected and built, to be beautifully erected with bricke or stone, or bricke and stone, according to the forme and manner and the true intent and meaning of our proclamations for building in and about our cittie of London in that behalfe published and as thereby we directed and appointed.

And we doe further for us, our heires and successors graunt unto the said John Earle Rivers, the Lady Viscountesse his mother and to either of them and either of their heires and assignes respectively by theis present, that theis our present letters patent of graunt and licence and every clause, article, matter and thing therein conteyned shalbe taken, construed, allowed and adjudged in all our court or elsewhere most stronglie against us, our heires and successors and most favourably, [*?*]benignesie and beneficially to and for the said John \Earle/ Rivers, the Lady Viscountesse his mother and either of them, their and either of their heires and assignes and their either and every of their tenant and farmors and every of them respectively. Any lawe, statute, graunt, provision, proclamacion, act, ordinance, restriccion or other thing to the contrary in any wise notwithstanding.

Provided alwaies and our will and pleasure is that the streete intended to be made by the said John Earle Rivers, the Lady Viscountesse his mother, their heires or assignes, from Crochied Fryers unto the Chayne Way leading to Towerhill aforesaid, be above twenty foote wide. Any thing in theis present conteyned to the contrary in any wise notwithstanding. Although expresse mencion of the true yearely value or certainty of the premisses or any of them, or of any other guift or graunt by us or by any of our progenitors or predecessors to the said John Earle Rivers and the Lady Viscountesse his mother or either of them heretofore made in theis present is not made, or any statute, act, ordinance, provision, proclomation or restraint to the contrary thereof heretofore had, made, ordained or provided or any other thing, cause or matter whatsoever in any wise notwithstanding. In witnes whereof we have caused theis our letters to be made patent. Witnes our selfs at Westminster the one and twentith day of Aprill in the seaventeenth yeare of our raigne.

By writ of the privy seal
Wolseley.

Doc. 73. Elizabeth Savage becomes Countess Rivers, 1641. [TNA: SO 3/12, f. 144v]

Elizabeth's years of service to the queen, and her father's pleas to the king for her welfare, were rewarded in 1641 when she became Countess Rivers in her own right. Most of the appointments in the Signet Office books were procured by office holders, and it seems rare for the queen to be named in this role.

April 1641
Viscountess Savage
A graunt to the Lady Elizabeth Viscountesse Savage of the dignitie of Countesse Rivers, and her yonger sonnes & daughters and her sonnes wives are to take place & precedencie as the sonnes and daughters & the sonnes wives of an earle of this

kingdome of England, in as ample manner as the like dignity was granted by his Majesty to the Lady Viscountesse Maidstone of the dignity of Countesse of Winchelsey.[284] And for the better supportacion of that dignitie his majesty is pleased to graunt unto her the yearely somme of £20 out of the exchequer. Subscribed as above upon significacon of his majesties pleasure under his signe manuall. Procured by the queenes majesty.

Doc. 74. Indentures between Earl Rivers and others and John and Robert Cordell about the rental and then sale of Melford Hall, 1641–9. [Guildhall Library: MS 9848]

Details of four indentures of 1641–9, relating to the rental and sale of Melford Hall and its lands, are together here both because they show the process by which Melford and its lands left the Savage/Rivers family, and because they are part of one surviving document into which they were copied. The records come from an early eighteenth-century document, which gives the abstract of title of the later Sir John Cordell, who died in 1704, to the ownership of Melford Hall. The marginal notes are by an eighteenth-century lawyer who completed the whole document, and explain why the seventeent-century originals do not survive. These details form the first part of the document which goes on to record agreements and indentures made after 1660.

Abstract of Sir John Cordell's title
[*marginal note*: 27 Nov 1641 this deed]
By indenture between John Earle Rivers & Catherine Countess Rivers his wife, Richard Lord Viscount Lumley, Thomas Lord Brudnell, Gilbert Gerrard & John Pickering gent of the one part & John Cordell alderman of London & Robert Cordell his only son & heire apparent of the other part, for £15,000 paid to Earle Rivers and 5s. to Lord Lumley and Brudnell & Pickering and Gerrard.[285]

The said Earle Rivers, Countess Catherine his wife, Lord Lumley, Lord Brudnell, Gerrard and Pickering have granted, bargained, sold, enfeoffed and confirmed unto the said John Cordell and Robert Cordell, their heires & assignes, the mannor or lordshipp of Long Melford with the rights, members and appurtenances of the same in county Suffolk, the advowson of the church of Melford and all the messuages, mills, lands, tenements & hereditaments of the said earle & countess, Lord Lumley, Lord Brudnell, Gerrard and Pickering in Long Melford, Shimplin, [*sic*] Lavenham, Aketon *alias* Acton, Alpheton and Glemsford or elsewhere in the county of Suffolk, to hold to the said John & Robert Cordell & their heires forever.

And the said earle covenants that the estate is free from all incumbrances except the estate for life of Elizabeth Countess Rivers in the mannor house & parke of Melford, the game of deer therein & the presentacions to the next avoidance of the church of Melford, and covenants that he & his wife will levy a fine before the 2nd February following.

284 The document mentions the precedence of Elizabeth's younger children; her elder son was already an earl.

285 Sir Richard Lumley became Viscount Lumley of Waterford in the summer of 1628. See Notes on People, below, for details of these individuals. It is interesting that Lord Lumley was still very much involved in Savage family affairs.

[*marginal note*: 27 Nov 1641. A copy examined with the record and attested. This deed was likewise lost in the fire but the enrolment may be seen.]

By indenture inrolled in Chancery 1st December following, the said earle, Lord Brudnell, Lord Lumley, Pickering and Gerrard doe for £15,000 bargaine & sell the premises to John & Robert Cordell and to them and their heires.

[*marginal note*: 12 May 1644. This deed this deed [*sic*] is also lost but the inrollment may bee seen]

By indenture inrolled in Chancery the 15 May following made between the said Earle Rivers & Elizabeth Countess Dowager Rivers his mother of the one part, and the said Robert Cordell son & heire of the said John Cordell deceased of the other part. Reciting the two precedent indentures and also an indenture of defeazance dated with the said two other indentures & delivered at the same time with them, containing a proviso that on payment of £15,000 & interest the estate should be reconveyed. And alsoe reciting the said Countess Dower's [*sic*] estate for life, and further reciting that upon an account slated there was due from the Earle Rivers unto the said Robert Cordell £20,488 12s. And having so recited the said earle doth release and discharge the said Robert Cordell (in his peaceable possession), all condicions and provisoes for redeeming the premises. And the said earle & countess dowager for £8511 8s. in full for the purchase did grant, bargaine, sell, release & confirme unto the said Robert Cordell the aforesaid mannor & premises and the placeing the warden and brethren of the hospital there and to him & his heires forever.[286]

[*marginal note*: 12 May 1649. A copy examined with the record & attested.]

By indenture then dated, inrolled in chancery the 15th May aforesaid & made between the said Earle Rivers & Elizabeth Countess Dowager his mother of the one part, & said Robert Cordell of the other part, reciting the said 3 indentures dated 27 November 1641, and also reciting that by one other indenture dated the said 27th November 1641 made between the said Sir John Cordell (then John Cordell, alderman) & said Robert Cordell of the one part & said Earle Rivers, Lord Lumley, Lord Brudnell, Gilbert Gerrard and John Pickering of the other parte, sealed & delivered with the said first & second recited indentures.

It was provided & agreed that if the said earle, his heires or assignes should pay unto the said Sir John Cordell, his heires or assignes at his then dwelling house the summe of £15,000 & other the summes of money therein mencioned on the dayes therein expressed, that then after such payment the estate, terme, interest & demand of the said Sir John Cordell & Robert Cordell & their heires in said mannor, lands and premises should be released & conveyed to said Earle Rivers, his heires & assignes.

Notwithstanding which conveyance, the said Elizabeth Countess Rivers did remaine lawfully seized for her life in said capitall messuage & mannor house of Melford aforesaid with pertinances & in the parke called Melford Parke & the deer & game there & in certain other comodityes, easements & other things thereto belonging. And further reciting that [*if the*] said £15,000 & said other summes or any part were not paid at the days & place therefore limitted by the said last recited

286 The Hospital of the Holy Trinity on Melford Green was established by Sir William Cordell before his death, although trustees were only appointed in his will of 1581.

indenture or at any time after, soe that upon a just account before the executing thereof made between said Earle Rivers & Sir John Cordell & Robert Cordell thereof & of other summes thereby acknowledged to have been received & disbursed by said Sir John Cordell in his lifetime & to and for the said Earle Rivers & Countess Rivers, it appeared that there was due and owing to said Sir John Cordell at his decease £20,488 12s.

It is witnessed that said Earle Rivers for consideracions therein mencioned did remise, release, exonerate & discharge unto the said <Sir> Robert Cordell in his full & peaceable possession & seizin then being, & to his heires all & every the condicions, covenants & provisoes in the said therein recited indentures made by or between the said partyes contained, and all benefitt, possibility, advantage & power of reentry into or redempcion of the premises or any part thereof in law or equity, by reason of any provisoes or condicions in any the before \therein/ recited indentures or any other specifyed, or any speech or agreement concerning the same or by any reason or any equitable construction or intent or any of them.

And also the said Earle Rivers & Elizabeth Countess Rivers in consideracion of £8511 8s. to them then paid by Robert Cordell for the absolute purchase as well of the said mannor as of the said capitall messuage, advowson, parke, messuages, lands & premises & all other the messuages, lands, tenements & hereditaments of what nature or kind soever of them, the said earle & countess or either of them, in Melford, Shimpling, Lavenham, Asceton *alias* Acton, Alpheton & Glemsford aforesaid or any of them, did fully, clearly & absolutely grant, bargaine, sell, release & confirme unto the said Robert Cordell & his heires, the said mannor of Melford & capital messuage & advowson aforesaid, and all the parke called Melford Parke & deer & game there, and all woods & underwoods & the ground & soyle of the same, and the full & free donacion, placeing & disposicion of the wardens & poor people in the almshouse & almesguifts of the Hospitall of Melford, all other the lands, tenements & hereditaments of the said earle & countess or either of them, and all royaltyes, privileges & immunityes scituate & being or arising in the townes, parishes, feilds or hamletts of Melford, Shimpling, Lavenham, Acton, Alpheton & Glemsford or elsewhere in county Suffolk, and all their estate, right, title, interest, inheritance, clayme & demand whatsoever of, in or to the same, to hold unto & to the only use & behoofe of the said <Sir> Robert Cordell, his heires and assignes for ever.

Doc. 75. Elizabeth Savage's petition to the House of Lords about the sacking of her houses at St Osyths and Melford, 1642. [HLRO: HL/PO/JO/10/1/132, 29 August 1642]

A graphic account is presented of the collapse of law and order in and around the Stour valley, and of the resulting losses allegedly suffered by Countess Rivers.

To the right honorable the lords in Parliament assembled, the humble peticion of Elizabeth Countesse Rivers dowager.

Representing to your lordshipps justice, that the petitioner haveing for some time past retired herselfe into the country, with purpose and hope there to enjoy the remainder of her widdowed life in such a way of quiet privacy as might best become her condicion, and yet be agreeable to her quality and estate, was on Monday 22th of August instant driven (for safety of her life) to fly from her house at St Osithes in the county of Essex where she presumed (with your Lordshipps' honorable favour) to say she lived without any publique scandall or wronge to that honour she hath the fortune to weare.[287] Few howres past, before a rude multitude (raysed for the most part in and about Colchester) who threatned her death, had broken in and ransacked her house, torne from thence, and dispoyled her of all her furniture, hangeings, plate, mony, apparrell, linnen and other household stuffe, even to the least parcell, driven away her cattell, carted & shipt away her goods and provision of corne, digged upp and destroyed her gardens, and other plantacions, and laid that place (the seate of her family) wholly waste.

The relacion of that outrage was scarce arrived at the petitioner, before the like seized upon her at her other house at Melford, neere Sudbury in Suffolk, whether, on Wednesdaie morning after, repaired a multitude of like disposed persons, threatning her death, who (before she had fully escaped their sight) were entred her house, and have from thence alsoe robbed & carried away all the remainder of what was hers; insomuch as she doth in all faithfulnes protest before your lordshipps, shee hath not left unto her so much as change of apparell, or ought else, wherewith to sustaine herselfe, haveing thus beene rifled, and lost to the value of £50,000, besides the miserable destruccion in her houses, which were beautifull, and the undoeing of all her servantes, whose verie pocketes were searched, & they also rifled of all they had.

And to make her miserie full, even the petitioner's owne tenantes refuse to paie theire rentes to her, as being some of them threatned, and feareing destruction likewise, if she received releife from them (though by her owne rentes), and others happily well contented to take that occasion to withhould from your petitioner what they ought to pay her.

The application of a remedie, in soe outragious and unparalleled a fact, the petitioner's distracted thoughtes doe (in all humilitie) awaite from your lordshipps'greate wisedome, justice and honour; yet presume for the present humbly to praie, that by order from your lordshipps an enquiry may be made after the offenders, for satisfaccion of the publique justice in such a manner as to your lordshipps shall seeme meete; a power of strict search for, and restitucion of, the petitioner's goodes & estate, by all justices of peace, mayors, customers, searchers, cheife & pettie constables & other officers, with speciall recommendacion therein to Harbottle Grimston esquire, recorder of the towne of Colchester, and other the justices of both the said counties of Essex & Suffolk.[288]

That the petitioner's servantes and agentes (who now goe under perill of their lives) may by your lordships' command and protection repaire to the petitioner's houses, ymploy themselves in those searches, give informacion to the justices, and cause waite to be laid with tradesmen in London & elsewhere, as there shalbe cause. And that notwithstanding the discouragement by the outrages aforesaid, the petitioner's tenants maie be required to make paiement of their rentes to the petitioner according to lawe and theire respective leases.

[*on the reverse*]
29 August 1642
Countesse Rivers
Expedite

[287] The best summary of the attacks on Elizabeth's houses at St Osyth and Melford, along with the related disturbances in Colchester and elsewhere, is in J. Walter, *Understanding Popular Violence in the English Revolution, The Colchester Plunderers* (Cambridge, 1999), pp. 11–60.

[288] For Sir Harbottle Grimston, see Notes on People below.

Doc. 76. The House of Lords order to assist Elizabeth Savage, 1642. [HLRO: HL/PO/JO/10/1/132, 9 September 1642]

An order of the Lords and Commons in Parliament, for the finding out and regaining the goods of the Countesse Rivers taken from her houses in Essex and Suffolke, and for incouraging her tenants to pay her rents.

Friday, 9 September, 1642

Upon the humble petition of Elizabeth countesse Rivers dowager, who hath been in an unlawfull and disorderly manner dispoyled of all her goods, to a very great valew, from her houses at St Osiths in Essex, and Melford in the county of Suffolke, herselfe put in feare of her life, and her servants damnified.

It is ordered by the Lords and Commons in Parliament, that strict and narrow search shall be made by all sheriffes, deputy-lieutenants, majors, justices of peace, customers, searchers, high constables, petty-constables, and other his majesties officers, for the goods of the said countesse Rivers so taken away, in all and every such place and places, and in such creekes, vessels, waggons and carts, as the servants or agents of the said countesse, or any other person or persons shall give notice of, as justly to be suspected to harbour the same. And the said goods, or any part thereof being found, and appearing to be the goods of the said countesse, shall be forthwith redelivered unto her, her said servants or agents, who by vertue and authority of this order are to be permitted without interruption to repaire to any of the houses of the said countesse, or any other place or places, and with the assistance of some of the officers aforesaid, to imploy themselves in the searching for the said goods, and discovery of all places, and persons suspected, and to give information thereof, to all majors, justices of peace, and other his majesties officers aforesaid, and to cause waite to be laid with the trades-men in London, and elsewhere, as they shall thinke fit, for the finding out and making stay of the said goods so taken away as aforesaid.

And it is ordered, that this businesse be by the Lords and Commons in an especiall manner recommended to the care of Harbottle Grimpston, esquire, recorder of the towne of Colchester, and other the justices of the peace of the counties of Essex and Suffolke, for the finding out of the said goods, and for the deterring of all persons from committing the like offences hereafter. And lastly, the Lords and Commons doe likewise recommend to the said Mr Grimpston, and other the justices of peace neere adjoyning, to give such encouragement to the tenants of the said Lady Rivers, for payment of their rents to her, notwithstanding the discouragement (mentioned in her petition) by reason of the disorder and spoile aforesaid, that there may be no cause of her ladiship's further complaint in that behalfe.[289]

John Brown, Clerk of the Parliaments

Doc. 77. Letter from Francis Savage to Sir Harbottle Grimston, claiming extreme necessity, 1643. [CUL: Hengrave 88, II, f. 152]

Francis Savage was Thomas's and Elizabeth's third son. Doc. 24 records the arrangements Thomas Savage made to support Francis, which include income from

289 Elizabeth petitioned the House of Lords on several later occasions up until 1646, saying that her goods had not been returned and her tenants were still not paying their rent. For example: HLRO, HL/PO/JO/10/1/203, 3 April 1643.

the Melford estate after the death of his mother. His grandmother, Countess Rivers, was probably in her eighties by this date; she died in 1644. This Francis was probably the Francis Savage gent. who was living in Acton, near Long Melford, in 1663.[290]

Whorthy Sir,
Your former favors wich, when I was in England and had the honnor to wait on you in person, is caus of this my presumtion to begge your assistance, and to request you, of all loves to bee a meanes unto my grand mother to see this honnest bearer, Mr Cowper, is payed a hundred and 25 powndes, wich I have receaved hear in thes parts of him in my extreame great necessity. I shall never bee troublesome in the like nature with her ladyship, but acknowlegge my selfe everlastingly bond for this favor and to you sweet Sir soe highely ingaged that I am obliged all dayes of my liffe to subscribe my selfe.
Your most humble and most affectionat servant,
Francis Savage
Paris, this 12 of February, 1642

Dear Sir, as you tender my good, I beeseache you to bee pressing with my grandmother to satisfie this bearer for the bill hee has of me, and I shall not faile after my comming over to wait on you and tender my humble thankes.
[*on the reverse*]
To my much respected and whorthy frind Sir Harbottel Grimstone thes present.

Doc. 78. Letter from the Lord Holland to Sir Thomas Barrington urging support for Elizabeth, 1643. [BL, Egerton 2646, Barrington Papers f. 197]

This is another document which appears to have been written at speed by the author; Elizabeth had some protestant sympathisers, if not allies. Holland may have been both, as he was her cousin.

Cosen,
The sufferinges of my Lady of Rivers are suche, as itt must to a hart so just and worthy as I conceive yours to bee, have a great operacion upon it. Therefor I doe recomend \her/ unto you, as to a person that I knowe maye oblige her by <the writinge her>, \your care/ in the [?]rates that will bee set upon her land. Shee hathe by the violence of the peaple lost the value of fiftye thousand pounds and thoughe her religion doe differ from ours, yet is it governed withe more modestye and temper then I ever sawe it in any person, then reasons besydes a relation of bloud and longe frendship unto her makes mee thus earnestly desyre you to asist and favour her all you maye, in the whiche you will extreamly oblyge your most affectionat cosen and servant Holland, this 19 of April.
[*on the reverse*]
To my worthye frend and cosen Sir Thomas Barrington[291]
[*another hand*] from the Lord Holland, 19 of Aprill 1643

290 In 1668 a Richard Savage sued Sir Robert Cordell for an income of £100 a year from his Melford estates. It is possible that he was son of Francis Savage, who definitely had had a charge on the estate (see Doc. 24), but Charles Savage also had children and may have had a claim.
291 For Lord Holland and Sir Thomas Barrington, see Notes on People below.

Doc. 79. Petition by Elizabeth to the House of Lords, 1645. [HLRO: HO/PO/JO/10/1/186, 7 May 1645]

After her original petition to the Lords in 1642 (Doc. 75), Elizabeth petitioned several more times. This one gives details of how her income was being used to repay her debts. This was a successful petition; in May 1645 the House of Lords told the committee for Essex not to press Elizabeth for payment as they were 'resolved to assess her as a peer'.[292]

To the right honorable the Lords assembled in Parliament
The humble peticion of Elizabeth Countesse Rivers

Sheweth that your peticioner, besides her very great losse in her personall estate, haveinge but bare 800 li per annum out of her lands, for the maintenaunce of herselfe and family, the rest goeth to pay her debt, accordinge to a deed by her formerly made, and allowed as well order [*sic*] of the comittee of Lords and Commons for Sequestracions of 26 Junij 1643,[293] as alsoe by ordinance of both houses of parliament of 13 January last,[294] whereby alsoe your peticioners trustees are to account, half yearely, to the standinge committee of Essex for the proffittes of her lands, as well past as to come, to the end that the debtes and 800 li per annum beinge paid, the state may have such benefitt thereby, as by the ordinance of sequestracion is ordayned; yett your peticioners trustees are assessed and have lately received a tickett for the loane of 200 li out of your peticioners estate, towardes the assistance of the Scott, according to the ordinance of the 2nd of December last.[295]

Now the premisses considered, and for that your peticioner is a peeresse of this realme, and that there is an expresse provisoe in the same ordinance, in these wordes, namely, provided that noe peers of this kingdome, members of either house of Parliament, or assistant or attendant of either of the houses, bee assessed by this ordinance, but by the respective houses whereof they be members or assistant, or attendantes, and the other peeres by the house of peeres.

Wherefore your peticioners humble suite is that your lordships would take the premisses into consideracion and to order and direct that the comittee in Essex for that service may forbeare any proceedings upon the said assessment, and that your lordships wilbe pleased to give such direccion herein as is agreeable to justice and the priviledge of peerage. And your peticioner shall dayly pray, etc.

292 Result of the petition: *Journal of the House of Lords*, 7 (London, 1802), 7 May 1645.

293 The Committee for Sequestrations was formed in March 1643 and later renamed the Committee for Compounding with Delinquents. The lands of Parliament's opponents were confiscated and run for the profit of Parliament unless the owner could pay considerable fines.

294 *Journal of the House of Lords* records Elizabeth's sequestration order on 13 January 1645. Her debts amounted to £16,000 'principal', and the order confirms that she had been allowed an income of £800 a year. Her trustees were ordered to present their accounts to the standing committee for Essex every six months. After the debts were cleared the sequestration could take place. The standing committee was given the power to investigate the truth of the debts and Elizabeth's income from lands inherited from her mother. Sequestration order: *Journal of the House of Lords*, 7 (London, 1802).

295 3 December 1644, 'The Lords have sent down an ordinance concerning the raising of monies for our brethren the Scotts; to which they agree, with some amendments; in which they desire the concurrence of this house': *Journal of the House of Commons*, 3 (London, 1802), pp. 712–13.

Doc. 80. Elizabeth petitions the House of Lords to be allowed to stay in London, 1646. [HLRO: HL/PO/JO/10/1/203, 3 April 1646]

On 31 March 1646 the Commons passed an order excluding a variety of people, including papists, from the cities of London and Westminster for a month from 3 April.[296] *This petition must have been written in response, as was another from Elizabeth's daughter Dorothy, Viscountess Andover, who also petitioned the Lords to be able to stay in London.*

3 Aprill 1646
Countesse Rivers
Expedite
To the right honorable the peeres now assembled in Parliament
The humble peticion of Elizabeth Countesse of Rivers
Sheweth that the houses of your peticioner in the countyes of Suffolke \and Essex/ together with her whole personal estate are utterly wasted and distroyed to a very great value (as is not unknowne to your lordships), so that if your peticioner and her family should bee enforced to departure from her place of present residence, shee beeing destitute of any other place of habitacion must bee exposed to a misery not to bee expressed.

Now for as much as your peticioner hath taken the negative oath of the 5th of Aprill last[297] beefore the commissioners for the great seale, and for her servants to have taken likewise the same beefore the committee of examinacions and your peticioner hath undertaken for them,[298] your peticioner humbly prayes a license from this honorable house whereby her selfe and family may bee permitted to remayne in her house att Queen Street, shee haveing neither a bed to ly in nor an house to preserve her from the injuryes of the wether in any other place.[299]
And your peticioner shall ever pray, etc.
Elizabeth Rivers

Doc. 81. Petition of Mary Countess Rivers to the House of Lords, 1647. [HLRO: HL/PO/JO/10/1/227, 6 March 1647]

This Countess Rivers was the second wife of Earl Rivers, and Elizabeth's daughter-in-law. Halton Castle had fallen to Parliament after sieges in 1643 and 1644. Earl Rivers was obviously hoping eventually to regain the possessions he lost at that time. This is the first of three documents about these goods; it is not clear whether they had come from Halton Castle or from nearby Rocksavage, which is possibly the more likely.

296 Order of the Commons: *Journal of the House of Commons*, 4 (London, 1802), pp. 495–7.

297 The negative oath obliged 'all or every person of what degree or quality soever, that hath lived or shall live within the king's quarters, or been aiding, assisting or adhering unto the forces raised against the Parliament, and hath or shall come to inhabit or reside under the power and protection of Parliament' to swear that they would not directly or indirectly assist the king. For the terms of the oath, see S.R. Gardiner (ed.), *The Constitutional Documents of the Puritan Revolution, 1625–1660* (Oxford, 1906), p. 289.

298 The committee of examinations was set up 'to take the examinations of all prisoners, and suspected persons, that constables and other officers may receive despatch': *Journal of the House of Commons*, 2 (London 1802), pp. 825–6.

299 This is very likely to be Queen Street in Covent Garden; see Introduction, p. lxii.

6 March 1646
Mary Countess Rivers
To the right honorable the lords nowe assembled in Parliament, the humble petition of Mary Countess Rivers

Sheweth that upon the humble peticion of John Earle Rivers your peticioner's husband, certifieinge your lordshipps that his goods were imbesiled and sould by Henry Brooks of Norton in the countie of Chester esquire and his agents, contrary to the articles of rendicion of Halton Castle for the use of the Parliament, where your peticioner's said husband's said goods were to be preserved without loss till he had made composicion for them, which said articles remaine before your lordshipps.[300] And for that one William Rudges a broker in Long Lane had bought parte of th~~em~~ said goods, your lordshipps by your order of the 8th of February last were pleased to order that the said goods and everie parte of them should be kept and preserved for the use of the said Earle Rivers without alteracion of propertie' untill he had perfected his composicion or the pleasure of the howse further knowne.[301]

Nowe for that your peticioner's said husband is not yett ready for composicion, for reason some parte of his evidence which he is to make use of therein for the setting forth of his estate are not yett sent us from the comittee of Chester who have the same in custodie, and that nowe the said Mr Brookes together with Richard Brooks his brother and the said Rudges and theire agents doe practize to defraude your peticioner of the said goods, notwithstandinge your lordshippes order, and that your peticioner hath by her selfe and others offered to give him the said Rudges fiftye pounds more then he paid to the said Mr Brooks or his agents for the said goods.

Your peticioner therefore most humbly imploreth your honors that for the preservacion of the said goods (being all the howshold goods of your peticioner's said husband without which he is never able to be houskeep[*sic*] in respect of his great sufferinge since theis distractions and his other great engagements of debts), your honors wilbe pleased to order that the said Mr Brookes, William Rudges and all other persons who have anie parte of the said goods, maie restore the same to your peticioner, shee payeing the moneys to the said Rudges which he hath paid to the said Mr Brookes for the same or to any of his agents *bonafide* [*two lines deleted*], and to appointe the restitucion of them unto her, which favor your peticioner humbly craves of your honors.

Doc. 82. Petition by Mary Countess Rivers to the House of Lords, 1647. [HLRO: HL/PO/JO/10/1/230, 15 April 1647]

Just five weeks after the last petition, Mary or her husband had come to an agreement with William Rudges about the sale of the goods.

15 April 1647
Mary Countess Rivers
Expedite

To the right honourable the Lords now assembled in Parlament

300 Sir Henry Brooks of Norton bought Halton Castle after the civil war, but it was returned to the crown at the restoration.
301 For William Rudges, see Notes on People below.

The humble peticion of Mary Countess Rivers
Sheweth that wheras your lordshipps were pleased by order of this house to prohibite the sale of the goods of your peticioner's lord taken at Halton Castle and sould by Mr Brooks unto one William Rudges, soe it is that since the said order your peticioner hath agreed with the said William Rudges that the said goods shall bee sould unto Sir John Cordell knight, whoe will not proceed to buy the same of the said Rudges without the order and licence of this honorable house. Shee therefore prayeth that by your lordshipps order the sayd Sir John Cordell may bee permitted to buy the same.
And shee will etc.
Mary Rivers [*signed*]

Doc. 83. List of goods sold by John Earl Rivers to Sir John Cordell, 1647. [CCALS: DCH/O/13]

The parlous state of Earl Rivers' finances must account for this sale, which is of goods taken from him when Halton Castle was won by parliamentary troops in 1643.[302] *It is therefore most likely that the tapestries and linen came from Rocksavage, near Halton. It is not possible to identify any of the tapestries with those listed in the inventory of 1635–6, because the latter contains so many sets of tapestries. This list includes clothing for six footmen; the inventory includes mention of a footmens' chamber at Tower Hill, with just one feather bed, but nothing specific at Rocksavage.*

This indenture made the eight and twentieth day of Aprill in the three and twentieth yeare of the raigne of our soveraigne lord Charles by the grace of God of England, Scotland, France and Ireland kinge, defendor of the faith etc. betweene the right honorable John Earle Rivers of the one part and Sir John Cordell of the cittie of London knight and one of the aldermen of the same cittie of thother part, witnesseth that the said earle, for and in consideracion of the somme of six hundred and fiftie poundes of lawfull monie of England paid by the said Sir John Cordell before the ensealing of theis presents to William Rudges cittizen and [*blank*] of London by the appointment and direcion of the said earle, hath bargained and sold and by theis presentes doth fullie and absolutelie bargaine and sell unto the said Sir John Cordell all and singuler the goods and household \stuffe/ perticuler mencioned and expressed in a schedule hereunto annexed.[303]

To have and to hold the same unto the said Sir John Cordell, his executors and assignes as his owne proper goodes, provided neverthles and upon condicion that if the said earle, his executors, his administrators or his assignes shall well and trulie paie or cause to be paid unto the said Sir John Cordell, his executors, administrators or assignes, att or in his nowe dwellinge house in Milkestreet London the somme of seaven hundred and twoe pounds of lawfull monie of England on the fourth daie of Maie which shalbe in the yeare of our Lord God one thowsand six hundred fortie and eight, that then this present indenture, bargaine and sale shalbe utterlie void,

302 Mary Countess Rivers, John's wife, petitioned the House of Lords in March 1647 asking for the goods taken from Halton Castle to be preserved; in April she petitioned that they should be sold to Sir John Cordell. See Docs 81 and 82. Whether this is the whole or part of those goods we do not know.
303 For William Rudges, see Notes on People below.

frustrate and of none effect, anie thinge here in conteyned to the contrary thereof in anie wise notwithstandinge.[304]

And the said earle for himselfe and his heires, executors and administrators doth covenant, promise and graunt to and with the said Sir John Cordell, his executors, administrators and assignes by theis presentes, that he the said earle, his executors or assignes shall and will well and truelie paie or cause to be paid unto the said Sir John Cordell, his executors, administrators or assignes the said somme of seaven hundred and twoe pounds of lawfull monie of England att the time and place before lymitted and appointed for the payment therof. In witness whereof the said parties to theis present indentures interchangably have sett their handes and seales the daie and yeare first above written in the year of our lord 1647.

A schedule indented, mencioning and expressinge perticulerlie the goodes and household stuffe bargained and sold by the indenture hereunto annexed.

Imprimis seaven peeces of rich arras hangings with gold in them
Item six peeces tenn foot deep
Item six peeces with greate beastes in them tenn foote deepe
Item seaven peeces eleaven foote deep imagry
Item five peeces tenn foot deep imagry
Item five peeces tenn foot deep imagry
Item five peeces tenn foot deep imagerye
Item five peeces of huntinge
Item a furniture for a great bedd: five curtens and double valence, testor, head cloth, counterpaine, cover for post all of silke and gold stuffe trymed with a silke and gold cauld fringe
Item twoe blew velvett carpettes sutable with a gold silke fringe about them, a great chaire, twoe backe chairs, twoe high stooles, twoe lowe stooles of blew velvett trymed upp with silke and gold fringe sutable to the bedd
Item one great travis curten of watchett and yellow damaske
Item one orange colored suit imbrodered with peeces of black velvett and silver twist and silke onely, onely [*sic*] there is head peece, vallence and tester
Item one orange colored sarsnett counterpaine
Item a testor, a large curten and a fine quilt, a counterpaine of crimson wrought velvett lined with fustion
Item a crimson sasnett quilt
Item a greene taffity counterpaine
Item a liver coloured velvett carpett
Item five black coates for footmen richlie wrought with gold and silver
Item six footmens suits of redd cloth with gold lace
Item one codling colored counterpaine of sasnett
Item one counterpaine of the same being willow cullored
Item one very fine large carpett
Item foure great Turkey carpettes
Item twoe and twentie smale carpettes fine and course
Item three long cushions of crimson velvett stuffed with feathers
Item six crimson velvett wrought with gold stufft with feathers

304 Milk Street runs north from Cheapside. John Stow, in his ‘Survey of London’ says, ‘Now to return to Milk Street, so called of milk sold there, there be many fair houses of wealthy merchants.’

Item five long cushions of cloth of tissue and stuft with feathers
Item one long green velvett stuft with fethers
Item one crimson sattin cushion stufft with feathers
Item four long needleworke cushions stufft with feathers
Item four smale needleworke cushions stufft with feathers
Item a long crimson shagg rugg
Item a green sett rugg
Item a crimson sett rugg
Item three great covers of cloth of tissue with silke and silver fringes

Linnon
Item two diaper table clothes five yardes long and twoe and a halfe broad
Item two diaper table clothes three yardes and halfe long and twoe yardes and three quarters broade
Item one table cloth of the same three yardes and halfe long and twoe yardes and one quarter broade
Item foure table clothes of the same seaven yardes long and twoe yardes broade
Item seaven square board clothes of the same and 2 yards broad
Item seaven more table clothes twoe yardes and halfe longe and twoe yardes broade
Item one side board clothe two yardes long one yard broade

Fine diaper
Item three table clothes seaven yardes long twoe yardes and halfe broade
Item one table cloth six yardes long and twoe yardes broade
Item one table cloth five yardes long and two yardes one quarter broade
Item one table cloth twoe yardes and halfe long and two yardes broade
Item one table cloth twoe yardes three quarters long and two yardes broade
Item one square table cloth two yardes long one yard broade
Item one side board cloth one yard and halfe long and two yardes broad
Item one towell foure yardes long
Item foure towells three yardes long
Item three towells five yardes long
Item one towell eight yardes long
Item one towell twoe yardes and halfe long
Item one towell three yardes three quarteres long
Item one towell seaven yardes long
Item one side board cloth one yard three quarters long and twoe yardes broade
Item one side board cloth two yardes long one yardes one quarter broad
Item six dozen of diaper napkins
Item one towell of fine diaper five yardes halfe long
Item one more of three yardes long
Item one of seaven yardes long
Item one of tenn yardes long
Item eight dozen and halfe of diaper napkins
Item foure dozen of finer napkins
Item eight dozen of course napkins
Item three dozen of old course flaxen napkins
Item foure old flaxen towelles
Item three paire of old pillowbeers and two paire of flaxen
Item one paire of fine flaxen ones
Item one damaske table cloth seaven yardes long and two yardes broade

Item one side board cloth twoe yardes long and twoe yardes broade
Item foure dozen of damaske napkins
Item one fine damaske table cloth tenn yardes long 2 yards broade
Item one side board cloth two yardes long and two yardes broade
Item one side board cloth two yardes long and halfe yard broade
Item three of the same 2 yardes and one quarter long
Item five dozen of fine damaske napkins
Item one fine damaske towell five yardes and halfe long
Item one fine damaske towell six yardes long
Item one damaske towell eleaven yardes long
Item one damaske towell seaven yardes and one other six yardes
Item twoe of three yardes long
Item five fine holland pillowbeeres wrought with silke and gold
Item one fine holland pillowebeer wrought with crimson worsted in graine
Item a counterpaine and cupbord cloth and three pillowbeeres of fine holland wrought with black worsted
Item a counterpaine of fine holland wrought with crimson worsted in graine
Item fortie five great slipps wrought with needleworke and a parcell of smale ones all wrought with silke
The guilded bedstedd in the countrie[305]
The chaire frames guilt.

305 Had this bedstead been rescued from St Osyth or Melford, or had it been in London or Cheshire in 1642?

GLOSSARY

In the original documents individual words often had more than one spelling. In this Glossary, the more common forms have been chosen. Cross-references are given to related words elsewhere in the list. In cases of special interest or uncertain meaning, the number of the relevant document is also included.

Sources

Middle English Dictionary (University of Michigan Press, 1999)
Oxford English Dictionary, on CD-ROM (Version 2.0) (Oxford 1999)
D. Yaxley, *A Researcher's Glossary of Words Found in Historical Documents of East Anglia* (Dereham, 2003)

accompt: account, money reckoning.
acre: a measure of land area, 4,840 square yards, approx. 0.4 hectare.
act: any legal device or, specifically, a statute passed by Parliament.
advysed: advised, prepared, informed.
advowsons: rights of presenting a priest or minister to an ecclesiastical living. *See also* **benefice** *and* **patronage**.
aggott: agate; a precious stone; **aggaton:** ?a variety of agate.
alder: (*alnus glutinosa*) a tree suited to wet places.
alderman: in London, the chief officer of a ward, or division of the city.
alienacion: the transfer of ownership into other hands.
alias: otherwise, also known as.
anagram: transposition of the letters of a name to create a disparaging phrase (Doc. 50).
andirons: fire-dogs, in pairs, standing either side of a fireplace to support logs; often decorated with finials or **topps** (q.v.).
Annunciacon of Our Lady: a church festival commemorating the announcement of the Incarnation of Christ, celebrated on 25 March; also known as Lady Day, one of the four **quarter-days** (q.v.).
anuyte, anuyty: annuity; a yearly grant, allowance or income.
appendante: pendant (piece of jewelry, Doc. 4).
apprised, apprized: appraised; assigned a money value, especially by an official valuer or appraiser.
appurtenances: minor properties or rights, belonging to others more important, and passing with them; appendages.
Arches, court of: court of appeal of the archbishop of Canterbury, which met in Bow church (St Mary Arches).
arrearage: arrears.
armes: (a) weapons and armour; (b) coats-of-arms bearing heraldic symbolism.
armorie, armorye: a secure room where arms and armour were kept in a great house.
ague: an acute or violent fever.

arras: rich tapestry fabric; with figures and scenes woven in colours.
articles: separate sections in a legal document giving particular terms or conditions.
assize: a session held periodically in each county, for administering civil and criminal justice, by justices of assize.
assurance: a legal guarantee or conveyance for securing title to property.
attorney general: legal officer of the state, empowered to act in all cases in which the state is party.
attorneyment of tenants: attornment; the transference of tenants to a new lord (Doc. 5).
averages: services done by tenants with their beasts of burden, from Latin *averium* (Doc. 1).
avoidance: vacancy of an ecclesiastical benefice.
backe: (a) hangings at the back or head of a bed; (b) an iron sheet behind a fire.
backes and seates for chaires and stooles: fabric covers, often of **Turkie work** (q.v.).
backe chaires: chairs with a back and no arms, having an upholstered or covered back.
backe stooles: stools with a back and no arms, having an upholstered or covered back.
backsides: the back-yards and out-buildings attached to dwellings; can also include privies.
bailiff: the principal executive officer of a manor (under the lord).
bailiwick: the area under the control of a **bailiff** (q.v.).
bakehouse: bakery; a building or room with an oven, where bread was baked.
Baptist, Feast of the Nativity of St John: a church festival commemorating the birth of that saint on 24 June; Midsummer day, a **quarter-day** (q.v.).
bargain: to reach agreement to sell.
bare: bare-headed in an heraldic procession.
baron: a title of the lowest of the five degrees of nobility; **barony:** the estate of a baron.
baronet: a titled order; the lowest that is hereditary.
bases: hangings around the bases of beds.
Bath, Order of the: a high order of British knighthood; so-called from the bath which preceded installation.
battery: ordnance, artillery (Doc. 51).
bayes: baize; a thickish woollen cloth with a short nap on one side.
bedchamber (royal)**:** to which gentlemen and ladies were appointed as servants.
bedd: the mattress of a bed, usually filled with down; a feather-bed.
bedstead: the wooden framework of a bed.
behoof: use, benefit, advantage.
benefice: an ecclesiastical living, generally known as a rectory or vicarage.
bench: (a) a long seat for several persons, with or without a back; (b) the seat where judges sit in court, e.g. The King's Bench.
bergamot: *citrus bergamia*; a citrus tree which yields a fragrant oil.
billes: weapons consisting of a long wooden shaft topped with a curving blade; the shaft was often painted, hence '29 browne billes'.
blacke gowne: an over-dress, to be worn by women at a funeral.
blacke jacke jugges: large leather jugs for beer etc., coated externally with tar.
blankettes: woollen cloths often white or undyed, used as the principal coverings of beds.
blew: blue.

Blewmantle: the dress and title of one of the four pursuivants of the **College of Arms** (q.v.).

boale: bowl.

bodkine: baudkin; a rich embroidered cloth made with a warp of gold thread, and weft of silk.

***bon christien* pear:** *bon chrétien*, a variety of pear introduced to France from Italy.

bonde: bond, covenant, agreement; the document recording such an agreement.

book: can also refer to a legal document by which land or titles were conveyed.

boones: boons; services due from tenants to their lords.

borded bedstead: a bed with a solid panel either at the head, or at both ends; or a bedstead with boarded or panelled sides.

border: a braid of hair worn around the female forehead, sometimes ornamented with jewels (Doc. 4).

boulster: a long stuffed under-pillow.

boulting hutch: a chest for storing sifted or 'bolted' flour.

brasill: a type of hard wood from Brazil; 'eleaven brasill stooles'.

brasse toppes: brass finials on hearth equipment such as andirons and fire-shovels.

brethren: brothers; fellow members of a charitable institution, such as the Holy Trinity Hospital at Long Melford.

brewhouse: a building or room in which ale or beer was brewed.

bruerye: heath, heathland (Latin *brueria*).

brushing chambers: rooms where clothes were brushed, cleaned and stored.

buffin: a coarse worsted cloth, used for curtains.

bullockes: bullocks, usually bull calves but can be of either sex.

burgage: tenure whereby tenements in towns were held for a yearly rent; hence 'in free burgage'; a property so held.

bushel: a vessel which measured capacity, especially for grain; contained four pecks or eight gallons.

bustian: an imported cotton fabric, used for curtains.

butler: a servant who had charge of the wine-cellar and dispensed liquor.

buttery: a room for storing drink (Old French, *boterie*, from Latin *butta*, *bota*, cask).

bynne, broad: bin for storage.

cabinett: a cupboard or box for the safe custody of private papers, books and valuables; e.g. 'cabinett of China worke' (Doc. 60).

caddoue: caddow; a rough woollen covering or coverlet.

cage: dog-cage with bars; presumably refers to the practice of keeping dogs caged in the house.

calamy: *lapis calamarinus*, or calamine; this is combined with copper to make brass.

callico: calico; a light cotton cloth imported from Calicut in India.

canopie, canopye: canopy; a suspended covering over a bed, or part of curtaining.

canvas: strong unbleached fabric made from hemp or flax, used for mattresses and curtains.

capitall: capital, chief; applied to a principal dwelling, etc.

capricio: capriccio; a sudden prank.

capp panne: cap pan; a dairy or cooking vessel possibly with a domed lid; listed among hearth equipment (Doc. 60).

carnation: carnation coloured.

carpett: carpet; a thick fabric commonly of wool, which covered tables, beds or floors.

cartes: carts; strong, usually two-wheeled vehicles used in farming operations; **carte horses:** horses used to pull carts.

cases: fabric coverings or loose-covers on posts of beds, close stools, etc.

cast suites: cast-off suits of clothing.

cattells: cattle, animals; e.g. 'cattells and chattells'.

cauld: cord; as in 'cauld fringe' to a bed (Doc. 83).

chamber: a room for private use or 'withdrawing', often the innermost of two rooms with connected use; frequently associated with a person ('Mr Barneys chamber') and containing a bed or beds. *See also* **great chamber**.

chamberer: a household servant, akin to a valet.

chamberlain: a high-ranking servant-officer who managed the private quarters of his lord or lady and was closely associated with him or her; (a) **Lord Chamberlain of England**: an hereditary office attendant on the king or queen; (b) **Lord Chamberlaine of our [queen's] howshould**; (c) **vice-chamberlen** or deputy chamberlain of the queen's household. Also (d) **chamberlenn of London** or city treasurer.

chamlett: camlet; a fine and costly eastern fabric made of a mixture of silk, camel's or goat's hair, and gold and silver.

chancellor: a high royally-appointed official; (a) **Lord Chancellor of England and Keeper of the Great Seal:** the highest officer and judicial functionary in the kingdom; (b) **Chancellor of the Exchequer** in charge of the king's finances; also (c) **chancellor** of the queen's court and keeper of her great seal.

Chancery: the court of the Lord Chancellor, the highest court of judicature next to the House of Lords; also a court of record; twelve **Masters of Chancery** assisted the lord chancellor in hearing cases.

chappell: chapel, a room in a private house devoted to religious worship (for a Catholic family in Melford Hall).

chase: hunting-ground, a tract of unenclosed land for hunting wild animals and game.

chattells: chattels; property of any kind, goods, money, land, etc.

cheesemotes: cheese-moulds; also **cheese presse**.

cheine: chain of gold to wear around the neck or waist.

cheney worke: chain-work, formed by looping with a single thread; or in the Chinese style.

childers children: grandchildren.

china worke: (a) china-ware in reference to dishes and **voiders** (q.v.); (b) in the Chinese style, as in 'one cabinett of China worke'.

churne: butter churn.

Cipresse: cypress-wood (chest).

cisterne: cistern; tank or large vessel for the storage of water.

closes: enclosures; pieces of land, usually in single ownership, enclosed by hedges and ditches.

close stoole: close-stool; a portable lavatory in the form of a padded seat or box containing a removable pan; **with three pannes**, presumably refers to spare pans.

closet: a room for privacy or retirement; a small room for storage.

cloth of gould: a fabric interwoven with threads, wires, or strips of gold, used for stools, cushions and curtains.

clouded: having cloud-like decoration (on taffeta, Doc. 60).

cobirons: pairs of irons, either free-standing or leaning against the back of the hearth, with hooks to support spits in front of a fire.

codling coloured: having a brownish-colour similar to that of the apple variety (applied to a counterpane, Doc. 83).
cofferer: keeper of the coffer or chest, a treasurer.
coles: coal; **cole mynes**, coal mines. *See also* **seacole**.
College of Arms: a collegiate institution founded in 1483–4 which regulates the use of armorial bearings, arranges state ceremonials and organises major funerals; its officers under the Earl Marshall comprise Kings of Arms, Heralds of Arms, and Pursuivants of Arms.
coltes: young horses up to about the age of four.
commission, commissioner: group appointed by authority to carry out a specific work or investigation; an individual member of such a body.
commodities, comodityes: articles or raw materials capable of bringing profit.
Common Pleas, court of: a court seated at Westminster for the trial of civil causes; one of the three superior courts of common law in England.
composition: agreed costs.
comptrouler: controller of an heraldic funeral.
constable: an officer appointed to keep the king's peace, and to perform various administrative duties in his district; **chief constable** or **high constable:** operated within a hundred; **pettie constable:** operated within a parish or township; also **constable** of a gaol.
consul: an agent appointed by a sovereign state to a foreign town to protect the interests of its subjects there.
contingent remainder: *see* **remainder**.
controuler: *see* **comptrouler**.
conturreries: countries or counties (Doc. 66).
copperas: the green proto-sulphate of iron or ferrous sulphate, also called green vitriol, used in dyeing, tanning, and making ink.
coppie of court rowle: copy of court roll; refers to copyhold tenure, a form of customary land-tenure recorded in a manorial court-roll; the tenant received a copy of the relevant entry.
corps: corpse, in a funeral procession.
councilman: a member of the council of a corporate town.
council of state: a body of men chosen to advise and assist a sovereign.
counterpointe: counterpane; a quilted cover for a bed.
countess: the title of the wife or widow of an earl, or of a woman holding the position in her own right.
court baron: a manorial court held before the lord or his steward, and attended by the freehold tenants of the manor.
court cupboard: an open cabinet with tiered shelves for the display of plate, etc.
court house: building specifically for the holding of local manorial courts.
court leet: a court with jurisdiction over petty offences and the civil affairs of a manor or wider district, held before the lord or his steward.
court roll: the record of decisions taken at a manorial court, written on a parchment or paper roll, and later in a book.
covenant: an agreement between two or more persons, a contract.
cover, covering: a fabric cover for forms, stools and bed posts, etc.
covering baskettes: to cover **voiders** (q.v.) which were containers for clearing dining tables; could also be to cover food before eating.
coverlett: coverlet; the uppermost covering for a bed, often highly decorative and described as 'tapestry'.
cozen: cousin.

cradle: a small iron grate, usually for a coal-fire.
crassinges: probably applies to iron ties or rods in stonework (p. 78, footnote 157).
creacion money: an annual payment made by the Crown to a newly created peer (Doc. 25).
creepers: pairs of small fire-dogs placed on the hearth between the **andirons** (q.v.).
cruell: crewel; thin worsted yarn of two threads used in tapestry and embroidery.
crymosin: crimson.
cupbord: originally a flat board or table, but later tiered and enclosed by doors, for storage and display of pottery, pewter, etc.; **cupboard cloth:** cloth to cover the open shelves of a cupboard. *See also* **court cupbord**.
curtaines: curtains or hangings around a bed or window, usually decorative. *See also* **windowe clothes**.
cushions: stuffed fabric cases to give support when sitting, reclining or kneeling; **square cushions** and **long cushions**, the latter probably for window-seats.
customer: a customs-house officer; an official who collects customs or dues.
cyttie, cyttye: a city.
damask: originally a rich silk fabric woven with elaborate designs, produced in Damascus; later a fabric of linen and worsted made in England.
Dame: the legal title prefixed to the name of the wife of a knight or baronet, for which 'Lady' is also in common use.
daub: a mixture of clay and chaff used to plaster walls. *See also* **wattle**.
dean: the head of the chapter or body of canons in a cathedral church.
decayed: decreased in number.
defeazance: defeasance; rendering null and void (legal).
deforciants, deforcyantes: persons who deprived others of estates; usually defendants in a process by which a fine of land was levied to assume the title.
demesne: land in a manor occupied or held 'in hand' by the lord himself.
deodandes: personal chattels, which having caused the death of a human being, were forfeited to a manorial lord (e.g. if a man fell from his cart and died, both his cart and horse were forfeited); from the Latin 'to be given to God'.
Deputy, Lord: one deputed to exercise authority on behalf of the sovereign (for example in Ireland, Doc. 55).
devyse: device or strategy; **devysed:** devised, arranged.
diaper: linen fabric with a pattern (usually diamond-wise) formed by different directions in the threads.
dignity: aristocratic status to be appropriately maintained.
diminittie: dimity; a stout cotton fabric, woven with raised stripes or fancy figures; usually used undyed, for beds and bedroom hangings.
diocese: the district under the pastoral care of a bishop, subdivided into archdeaconries, deaneries and parishes.
disarmed: to be deprived of arms and armour.
distemperature: infection, illness (Doc. 36).
distreine: distrain; to seize goods or lands; *see* **distress**.
distress: the act of seizing goods or entering property in order to force the owner or tenant to honour some obligation.
dornick, dornix, darnick: a silk worsted or partly woollen fabric, originally manufactured in the Flemish town of Doornijk.
dovecote: a building in which pigeons were bred, so that their young could be taken for food.
dower: the portion of a deceased's property in which his widow could claim a life-interest, normally a third of the total; *see* **dowre**.

dowre: dowry; the money or property the wife brings to her husband on marriage.
downe: down; soft under-plumage of fowls, used for stuffing mattresses and pillows.
duke: the title of the highest of the five degrees of nobility.
durance: a stout durable cloth.
dyett: diet; provisions or victuals in daily use, as a collective whole.
earl: the title of one of the five degrees of nobility; ranks higher than viscount but lower than marquis.
earthen stuffe: earthenware.
easement: right or privilege; especially right-of-way over property owned by another.
East Indian canopie: canopy originating in the Far East, or in a Far Eastern style (accompanied curtains, Doc. 60).
emolumentes: profits, gains.
enfeoff, enfeoffed: *see* **feoffee**.
engross: to write a fair copy of an official or legal document.
entry: taking formal possession of lands or tenements.
equity: general principles of justice to supplement the law.
escuchion of presedence: escutcheon of precedence; a shield displayed in an heraldic funeral procession, ?bearing coats of arms in order of precedence (Doc. 56).
esquire: a man belonging to the order of gentry, ranking immediately below a knight; also applied to various officers in the service of a sovereign.
estate: (a) status or rank; (b) landed property; (c) possessions or wealth.
Ester tearme: Easter Term; a movable term in law-courts falling between Easter and Whitsuntide.
eviccon: eviction; recovering or re-possessing lands or property.
exemplification: an attested transcript of an account, resulting from a widow's administration of her husband's estate.
Exchequer: financial department or treasury of the king (Doc. 44) and of the prince of Wales (Doc. 16); **Chancellor of:** keeper of the king's exchequer; **Remembrancer of:** officer of the exchequer who collected debts due to the sovereign.
executor: one who is given the task of executing, or carrying into effect, the provisions of a will; **executrix:** a woman charged with the same responsibility.
fag end: the extreme and lower end of a major house, containing kitchens and other offices (Doc. 15).
fannes: fan-shaped baskets used in winnowing corn.
fealty: the obligation of fidelity on the part of a tenant to his lord; suit and homage made to a lord.
feast: a saint's day such as the Nativity of St John the Baptist, or a day celebrating events in the life of Christ such as Pentecost.
feather bedd: a mattress stuffed with feathers.
fee: land or estate held of a superior lord. *See also* **fee deer** and **knight's fee**.
fee deer: deer taken as a perquisite by the ranger of a royal forest (Doc. 49).
feedinges: grazing-grounds or pasture lands.
feefarme rentes: fee-farm rents; perpetual or fixed rents.
fee simple: freehold estate; the nearest possible to actual ownership under the crown.
feild bedstead: a portable or folding bedstead chiefly for use in the field; a camp bed.
fellow: (a) employee, man; (b) an equal (person).

feofees: feoffees, trustees; persons entrusted or enfeoffed with freehold estates and who then held the estate on behalf of the original grantors; such arrangements constituted **feofmentes**.

figg satten: ?figured or patterned satin.

fine, fyne: (a) an amicable composition or agreement of a suit; (b) sum of money paid on entering into a lease or other agreement; (c) **fyne with proclamacions:** a fine publicly proclaimed before the county justices. *See also* **deforciants**.

fire cradle of iron: an iron fire-grate. *See also* **cradle**.

fireforke: a pronged instrument used for poking a fire.

fire shovell: a shovel for placing coals on a fire, removing ashes and perhaps carrying fire.

flaxen: used of cloth made of flax; linen of napkins, towels, etc.

Fleete: a debtors' prison on the east bank of the River Fleet in London.

flocke: flock; refuse of wool used for stuffing mattresses and bolsters.

formes, fourmes: benchs; long seats for several people without a back.

forepryzed: foreprised; taken for granted, anticipated.

frankpledge, view of: a court where every member of a manor or larger district was answerable for the good conduct of, or damage done by, any other member; held with a **court leet** (q.v.).

freedome (of the Citty): grant of freedom to practice a trade in the city of London; hence **freemen** of the city.

free socage: *see* **socage**.

free warren: *see* warren.

French bedstead: a bedstead with a simple wooden box-like frame; in the French style (Doc. 60).

franchesies, franchises: privileges, exemptions.

fruite glasse plates: flat pieces of glass on which concentrated fruit syrup was dropped and left to crystallise (Doc. 60) (*ex inf.* Peter Prears).

frustrate: invalid, null and void (of an agreement).

fryzt: friezed or rubbed, to raise the nap of cloth (Doc. 4).

furniture for a bedd: bedding and hangings of a bed; **furniture for a horse:** harness.

furze: gorse, *ulex europæus*; used to describe manorial waste and thus coupled with heath(land).

fustian: (a) a kind of coarse cloth made of cotton and flax; (b) a blanket made of fustian.

fyne: *see* **fine**.

gallerie, gallery: (a) a narrow balcony-like room above the screens' passage and overlooking a hall; (b) a long, upper-storeyed room to give indoor exercise and to display portraits; (c) a balconied walk at roof level affording good views of parkland.

Garter … King of Armes: the title and rank of the principal king of arms; referred to as 'Mr Garter' (Doc. 56); *see* **College of Arms**.

Gatehowse: a prison at Westminster.

geldinge, gueldinges: castrated male horse(s).

gent., gentleman: (a) man of gentle birth, entitled to bear arms, but not ranking among the nobility; (b) man of gentle birth attached to a royal household, e.g. **gentleman of the bedchamber**, **gentleman usher** and **gentleman of the privie chamber**.

gentlewomen: women gentle by birth, who attended a lady of rank.

geoven: given.

goodes: moveable property. *See also* **chattels**.
good store: abundance, large quantity.
goulde: gold.
graine: grain, a scarlet dye also called Kermis ('crimson worsted in graine', Doc. 83).
granaries: granaries; buildings where grain was stored.
grange: (a) barn, granary; (b) farmhouse with outbuildings belonging to a religious house or feudal lord.
great chamber: principal reception room of a major house; at Rocksavage described as 'the great dineing chamber'.
great parlour: principal sitting or dining room of a major house.
great seal: seal used to authenticate documents of the highest importance in the name of the king or queen; kept by a chancellor or keeper of the great seal. *See also* **pryvy seale**.
groome: groom; a servant who attends to riding and carriage horses; **groom of the bedchamber:** a servant of the royal bedchamber.
groome porters table: a type of gaming table connected with the groom-porter, originally an officer appointed by the monarch who regulated gaming and decided any disputes which arose.
groundes, growndes: parcels of land, sites.
guilte: gilt, gilded.
halberde: a weapon with a combined axe and spearhead, mounted on a shaft 6–8 feet long.
hall: (a) main room or entry, where servants dined; (b) the residence of a manorial lord, such as Melford Hall.
haire: a sieve of fine-woven haircloth for straining liquids; for example malt was laid to dry on such a sieve in a malt-kiln.
hanginges: draperies with which bedsteads, walls and windows were hung.
harmlesse: free from liabilities and losses.
hatchments: the armorial bearings of a deceased person, carried at the funeral.
headcloth: a cloth hanging at the head of a bed, usually mentioned with a tester.
heath: open uncultivated waste land. *See also* **bruerye** and **furze**.
heifers: young cows, that have not calved.
healme and creast: a helmet surmounted by a crest, carried at an heraldic funeral.
herald: *see* **College of Arms**.
herbage: grass or pasture, and the right of using it.
hereditamentes: any kind of property that can be inherited.
heriot: at the death of a customary tenant, the obligation to pay his best beast to the lord of the manor.
high chaire: chair with a high back. *See also* **lowe chaires**.
hogges: hogs; castrated male pigs reared for slaughter.
hoggesheades: hogsheads; large casks usually for beer, each containing 52½ imperial gallons.
holland: linen fabric originally from the province of Holland in the Netherlands.
holland wooll bedd: linen-covered mattress stuffed with wool.
homage: the body of tenants attending a manorial court.
honour: (a) lordship of several manors held under one paramount lord; (b) dignity of a title, e.g. an earldom.
hoppes: hops; the ripened cones of the female hop-plant, *humulus lupulus*, which give a bitter flavour to beer.

horse of estate: horse in rich harness led in funeral to display the deceased's position or **estate**.

hospital: a charitable institution for the housing and maintenance of the needy.

hundred: a subdivision of a county, used for administrative and legal purposes, which held its own courts and appointed its own constables and bailiffs; and ownership of a hundred.

hundred waight: hundredweight; a unit of weight equal to 112 pounds or 8 stones.

huntinge: cloth embroidered with scenes of the hunt.

humour: temperament, personality.

husbandmans [chamber]: farmworkers' chamber on the home farm (Doc. 60).

imagry: large-scale figured work on tapestries.

immunity: exemption from a service, obligation, jurisdiction, etc.

impaling: combining two or more coats-of-arms on one shield to show marital connections.

impost inwards: import duty (Doc. 51).

impostome: impostume; a purulent swelling or cyst.

impound: to seize and retain stock until payments are paid.

***imprimis*:** in the first place, firstly (Latin); used to introduce the first of a number of items, as in an inventory.

in chief: tenure by which land was held directly of the king by military service.

incumbrances: any burdens on property, in the shape of claims, liabilities, mortgages, etc.

indenture: a deed between two parties written twice on the same piece of parchment and then cut apart in a sinuous line; when brought together the edges tallied exactly and showed that they were part of the same document. Can also be **tripartite indenture**.

indorsement: a signature at the end (literally, back) of a document.

indy pott: a pot to hold 'inde' or indigo, a blue dye obtained from India.

infanta: a daughter of the king of Spain; specifically, the eldest daughter who is not heir to the throne.

***inquisitio post mortem* (IPM):** inquisition after death; an official inquiry held after the death of a **tenant-in-chief** to ascertain what property the deceased held, and the lawful heir.

inure: to come into operation, to take effect, or become accustomed or habituated.

inventorie: inventory; a written list of goods, chattels and possessions, especially those of a deceased person as required by ecclesiastical courts.

Irish mantle: a kind of blanket or plaid worn by the rustic Irish.

Irish stiche: a canvas stitch used for working the particular zigzag patterns also known as Florentine work; white embroidery on a white ground.

iron backe: a fire-back; a thick cast-iron plate placed against the back of a chimney, usually decorated.

iron panne to ayre roomes: iron pan containing hot embers to warm or air rooms.

issue, yssue: (a) children or lineal descendants; (b) proceeds; profits arising from land, rents, services, fines, etc.

Jesuit: member of the Catholic religious order of the Society of Jesus.

jewell: a decorative object set with precious stones, chiefly for personal adornment; **jewell of the storie of Suzanna:** a miniature painting of the subject (from the Apocrypha) in a frame set with jewels.

jugges, blacke jacke: large leather jugs coated externally with tar.

joinctures, joynctors: jointures; the holding of estates by two or more persons in joint-tenancy.

joined stoole: joint-stool, made of parts joined or fitted together by a joiner, as distinguished from one of more primitive carpentry.

justice of peace: magistrate, appointed to serve in a particular district, county or town; **justices, lord chief:** judges who presided over the common-law courts of King's Bench and Common Pleas.

kersey: coarse narrow worsted cloth, woven from long wool and usually ribbed.

keelers: shallow bowls in which liquids, particularly milk, were set to cool.

Kinges Benche: the supreme court of common law in the kingdom; the King's Bench prison was in London.

knight: rank conferred by the sovereign, in recognition of personal merit or services.

knight service, the military service which a knight was bound to render as a condition of his fee.

knight's fee: under the feudal system, the amount of land for which the services of an armed knight were due to the sovereign; not necessarily implying a particular acreage.

knowledged: acknowledged.

laced: hangings or clothes ornamented or trimmed with lace.

landskipp pictures: landscape pictures; a painting with scenes in a landscape.

leades: large open leaden vessels used in brewing.

lett: (as noun): hindrance, obstacle.

lettres of administracion: authority to administer the estate of a deceased person.

letters patent: open or public letters.

liberties: districts within a county exempt from the jurisdiction of the sheriff, and having a separate commission of the peace (e.g. Liberty of Bury St Edmunds).

limbecke: alembic (from French *alembic*) or still, a glass apparatus for distilling liquors such as toilet waters and medicines; it consisted of a gourd-like flask surmounted by a cap (the alembic proper) which had a pipe leading to a condensing vessel. *See also* **stille** and **water glasses**.

link: a torch made of tow and pitch, much in use for lighting people along the streets.

linnon, lynnen: linen; cloth woven from flax.

liverye: (a) items such as beds and saddles intended for the use of servants; (b) the legal delivery of property into a person's possession. *See also* **Wardes and Liveries, court of.**

load of hay: equal in weight to 36 trusses or 18 hundredweight.

longe cushions: probably intended for window-seats.

lookeing glasse: mirror.

lord lieutenant: the chief executive authority in a county, and head of the magistracy, appointed by patent from the sovereign.

lordship: (a) the dignity and functions of a manorial lord; (b) used also as a title, 'your lordship'.

lowe chaires: chair with low backs. *See also* **high chaire**.

lowe stooles: foot-stools, or stools with low backs as in 'two lowe back stooles'.

Ludgate: a debtors' prison in the city of London.

lumber: odds and ends, usually lumped together in an inventory because of their small value.

lymytte: to assign within limits.

lynnen: *see* **linnon**.

maior, major, mayor: the head of the municipal corporation of a city; **Lord Mayor** is a title limited to the cities of London, York and Dublin.

manor: a landed estate held by a lord, who himself held it of a superior lord, often the sovereign; sometimes the term refers to the actual manor house.

mappe: map 'of the world' (Doc. 60).

marchantts, marchants: merchants.

Marshalsey: a prison in London.

marckes: marks; a mark is a unit of account (not a coin) equal to two thirds of a pound, 13s. 4d.

marquis: the title of one of the five degrees of nobility, ranking higher than earl but lower than duke. The wife or widow of a marquis is a 'marchioness'.

master: a man having control or authority; also applied to officers of a sovereign: **master of horse:** the title of the third official of the royal household who managed the king's horses. *See also* **Rolles, Master of; Chancery, Masters of**.

match: rope so prepared that when ignited at one end, was not easily extinguished, and burnt at a uniform rate; used to fire guns.

matriculated: admitted by enrolment as a student of a university.

mattres, mattresse: an under-mattress; a case of coarse material, stuffed with hair or the like and quilted, used as the underlay of a featherbed.

maulte: malt; barley prepared for brewing into ale or beer.

meadowe: grassland for mowing.

medowing, herbage of the: grass of meadow-land, and the right to mow and graze it.

member: an outlying part of a manor or estate.

messuadge, mesuages: messuage; (a) site on which a dwelling-house and ancillary buildings were erected; (b) such a house and its adjuncts; **capitall messuadge:** the head-house of one who owned several properties.

metes: bounds, boundaries.

Micheal, Feast of St: Michaelmas; a church festival celebrated on 29 September; a **quarter-day** (q.v.).

Middle Temple: one of the four legal societies with exclusive right to admit persons to practice at the bar.

millnes: mills, driven either by wind or water.

moile: 'toil and moil'; labour, drudgery.

moores: uncultivated high or wet land.

moss: bog, marsh and the herbage afforded in such places.

moveables: applies to personal possessions as opposed to real property.

moyetie, moyety: moiety; a half, one of two equal parts.

mulcture: multure; the right to extract a toll on flour ground at a mill.

murrey: the deep red or purple colour of mulberry; cloth dyed that colour.

muscadell grapes: muscat grapes which were used to make a sweet white wine.

***mutatis mutandis*:** with the necessary changes made (Latin); due alteration of details.

nag: a small riding horse or pony.

neate: clean; free from dirt or impurities (copperas, Doc. 68A).

nedle worke: needlework.

Newgate: a prison in London.

night bagg: a travelling-bag containing necessaries for the night, such as a 'combe case'.

noble: a gold coin, equivalent to 6s.8d.

nonage: under the age of twenty-one; or period of legal infancy.

Norroy: the title and rank of a king of arms; *see* **College of Arms**.

orator: one who pleads a cause, and presents a petition.

ordinary, in: in regular attendance or service.
ould: old (e.g. 'ould rent of assize').
ounce: a unit of Troy weight; one twelfth of a pound.
***ouster-le-maynes*:** (French, *outre les mains*, 'out of the hands'), a judgement or writ which delivered land out of a guardian's hands to a rightful claimant (Doc. 1).
overseer: supervisor of the proving of a will.
overworne: much worn, worn out.
oxen: a castrated bull used for draught purposes or reared for food.
padd: *see* **pillions**.
pallatine: (county) palatine; a county such as Cheshire over which a lord had privileges which were originally royal.
pannage: the right of pasturing swine in woodland or forest.
panne: pan; a metal or earthenware vessel, for domestic uses, usually broad and shallow and often open; e.g. **capp pann**; 'iron panne to ayre roomes'; **perfumeing pannes** (q.v.).
pantry: a room in which bread and other provisions were kept; contained 'bread bynne'.
particular: a statement, setting forth points or details of a matter.
partie coloured: partly of one colour and partly of another; variegated.
pastrye: pastry; (a) a room where bread, cakes, biscuits, etc. were made, before baking in a **bakehouse** (q.v.); (b) a room which was also a general food-store.
patente, pattente: open, public; as in **letters patent:** an open letter or document.
patronage: the right of presenting a qualified cleric to an ecclesiastical benefice. *See also* **advowsons**.
patten: pattern, design (in embroidery).
pear, *bon christien*: *see* ***bon christien***.
peauter: *see* pewter.
Pentecost: Whitsunday, a Christian festival commemorating the descent of the Holy Spirit, observed on the seventh Sunday after Easter.
perceive, perceived: synonymous with 'receive' and 'received'.
perfumed skinne: perfumed leather.
perfumeing pannes: pans in which some substance was burnt to emit an agreeable odour, or to disinfect, fumigate; *see* **panne**.
perpetuana: a durable woollen fabric manufactured in England.
Persian carpets: coverings for tables, beds or floors made in Persia, or in a Persian style; *see* **carpett**.
pertinences: appurtenances.
pewter: silver-grey alloy of tin with other ingredients, chiefly copper and lead.
piller: pillar, support; 'my onely piller'.
pillions: small saddles or pads attached to rear of a saddle for a second rider.
pillowbeeres: pillowcases.
pipe: a large barrel or cask, usually for wine, containing 126 old wine-gallons or 105 imperial gallons.
placeing: placing or appointing a person.
plate: silver utensils for table and domestic use including ornaments etc.
playeing tables: playing or gaming tables designed for the use of chequers (e.g. backgammon or chess), and at which players frequently laid bets. *See also* **groome porters table**.
plea: a case presented in court.
plea roll: roll on which actions in the court of Common Pleas were entered. *See also* **Common Pleas, court of**.

plowes: ploughs.
popish: having allegiance to the pope and the Church of Rome.
pourleiw: *see* **purleiu**.
powdering tubbs: a tub in which meat was powdered, i.e. salted or pickled.
premisses: houses, tenements or buildings with surrounding land and other appurtenances.
prerogative court: the court of an archbishop for the probate of wills, etc.
presentacions: presentations; as when a patron offers a clergyman to a bishop, to be instituted in a vacant benefice of his gift.
presentes: used in the sense of 'this actual document' or 'these writings'.
president: the appointed governor of a province or division of a country; **President, Lord, of the North.**
presse: a large usually shelved cupboard; especially one placed in a recess in the wall, for holding clothes, books etc.
pretend: profess right or claim to a title or the like.
principall: a capital sum of money, as opposed to interest or income.
privateering: actions of privately owned ships which a government commissioned, by 'letters of marque', to operate against a hostile nation, especially in the capture of merchant shipping.
privie, privy: private; **the privie chamber** of the king and queen; **privie councell:** a body of men who advised the crown; **pryvy seale, privie signett:** the private seal of the sovereign; also **Lord Prevy Seale**.
prizinge: appraising; estimating the monetary value of.
prothonotary, protonotary: chief clerk or registrar of the courts of Chancery, Common Pleas and King's Bench.
provisoes: conditions upon which the validity of a document depends.
pullen: poultry.
purleiu, purliewe: a tract of land on the fringe of a forest.
pursuivant: a junior officer of the **College of Arms** (q.v.), such as **Blewmantle** and **Rouge Dragon**.
quadripertyte: quadripartite; refers to a document drawn up in four corresponding parts, one for each party.
quarter: (a) a fourth part, e.g. of units of length or time; (b) a unit of dry measure containing 8 bushels; (c) a distinct district.
quarter day: one of the four days dividing the year into quarters, on which the payment of rent and other quarterly charges fell due: Lady Day, Midsummer, Michaelmas and Christmas.
quarter sessions: a court held quarterly before two or more justices of the peace.
quartering: the dividing of an heraldic shield into quarters, to denote the marriage alliances of a family; also **quartered**.
***quietus*:** quit, settled (Latin); ***quietus est*:** 'it has been settled'; a discharge or a quittance given on payment of sums due, or clearing of accounts.
quilt: an outer bed-covering or counterpane, of various materials such as fustian, linen, taffeta and even leather.
quyte clayme: 'quit claim'; to give up a possession, title, etc.
rackes: irons, usually placed above fireplaces, to support cooking-spits when not in use.
rainger: ranger; a forest officer or keeper of a park (Doc. 43).
recognyzances: bonds or obligations entered into and recorded before a court.
recorder: a magistrate or judge having jurisdiction in a city or borough such as Colchester (Doc. 75).

recoverie: gaining possession of property or a right by a court judgement, with a single or double **voucher** (q.v.).
rectories: ecclesiastical livings whose **tithes** (q.v.) remained intact and unappropriated.
recusant: a person, usually but not necessarily a Roman Catholic, who refused to attend services of the Church of England; from Latin *recusare*, to refuse.
redie monie: ready-money or cash.
Red Lyon: a prison in London.
reentry: the act of re-entering upon possession of land etc., previously granted or let to another.
releasse: to convey or make over an estate or right to another.
releefe, relief: assistance in various forms given to persons in a state of poverty or want.
remainders: routes specified by testators for the eventual descent of estates or interests; **contingent remainders:** such routes dependant on conditions, not absolute.
remembrancer: *see* **Exchequer**.
remise: transfer of property.
rent of assyze: a fixed rent.
Requests, Master of: a leading officer of the court of Requests, held for the relief of persons petitioning the king.
revercion: the right of succeeding to an estate or title.
rod: as in 'by the rod'; refers to the ceremony of transferring copyhold land, by handing over a 'rod' or baton to signify the land itself.
role: roll; a support for a gown or petticoat, used instead of a farthingale (Doc. 39).
Rolles, Master of the: the head of the twelve chancery masters who assisted the Lord Chancellor in hearing cases.
Rouge Dragon: the title and badge of one of the pursuivants of arms of the **College of Arms** (q.v.) (Docs 56–7).
royalties: profitable rights owned by a landowner, e.g. to take minerals.
rugge: a rough woollen material, coarse frieze, used as a coverlet for a bed.
rundlette: runlet; a small cask containing 18½ gallons.
russett: coarse homespun woollen cloth dyed a reddish-brown, grey or neutral colour.
sacke: a white wine similar to sherry; imported from Spain, Portugal or the Canaries.
saddle horses: a riding or coach-horse.
St Hillary: Hilary (term); the first of the four terms or sessions of the law-courts, named after the feast of St Hilary, 13 January.
salte fishe: fish salted and thus preserved.
sarsnett: sarsenet; a very fine and soft silk material made both plain and twilled, in various colours.
sarves: service.
satten: satin; a silk fabric with a glossy surface on one side; woven so that the warp almost completely covers the weft.
say, saye: a cloth of fine texture made of wool, woollen mixture or linen, resembling serge.
score: twenty; **threescore** therefore amounting to sixty.
scrowlebacke chaire: chair with a scroll-shaped back.
seabaulks: seabanks; sea defences.
sea canopie: canopy made of ?**say**.

seacole: coal brought in by sea-going ships.
seale: wax imprint by which a document was sealed.
searses: searces; sieves or strainers for sifting flour and removing the bran; kept in a bakehouse.
searchers: officers appointed to search for goods pilfered from Countess Rivers (Doc. 75).
seates: loose fabric covers to cover chairs or stools. *See also* **backes and seates**.
sedan: sedan chair; a portable closed vehicle to seat one person, borne on two poles by two bearers.
seised of, seized of: in possession of.
seizin: seisin, possession of land, as opposed to ownership.
seizures: confiscation or forcibly taking lands or goods.
sellars: cellars; basement or underground rooms for the storage of beer, wine, etc.
services: duties required of a tenant by his feudal lord, consisting of either money or labour. *See also* **knight service**.
sett out: set out (land); to measure or delimit.
sett: coarse woollen fabric dyed or 'set' in woad; used for rugs; *see* **rugge**.
severalty: individual and independent tenure of land, sharing no rights of grazing, etc. (Doc. 13).
shagg: worsted cloth with long and coarse nap.
sheriffes: representatives of royal authority in counties and major towns.
shipt: shipped, transported by sea.
shovell: (a) a fire-shovel, often mentioned with tongs and bellows; (b) a wooden shovel for corn.
side bord, side table: a board or table placed against the wall of a room, used for serving food, storage or display; also **side bord cloth**.
signe manuall: the royal signature (Doc. 73).
signett, privie: a small seal used by the sovereign for private purposes and for certain official documents; hence **clerk of the signet**, whose duty was to write grants or letters patent sealed in this way; *see* **privie.**
sithence: since.
skreene: (a) a fire-screen, a wooden frame covered with cloth, to protect faces from the heat of a fire; (b) a partition separating the entry-passage of a house from the hall; (c) a sieve in a granary.
skynner: skinner; one who prepares and deals in animal skins.
slated: recorded (account); alludes to writing on a slate.
slipps: slips; long pieces of embroidered cloth.
slope bedd: a bedstead with a canopy sloping down from the head.
snuffers: instruments for snuffing-out candles.
socage: a kind of land-tenure which imposed certain defined services, other than **knight-service**; also **free and common socage**.
sok: soc; certain rights of jurisdiction which by custom belonged to the lord of a manor, and which were specified in the grant of a manor by the crown.
sparver: a bed-canopy suspended by cords from the ceiling.
spittes: spits; sharp-pointed steel rods, for thrusting through meat to be roasted at a fire; usually supported by **cobirons** (q.v.).
stallages: stands which supported barrels of beer and wine.
stands: wooden frames or supports for chests and other furniture (Doc. 60).
standard: a large chest or trunk.
standing bedstead: standing high from the floor, to contain a truckle- or trundle-bed beneath. *See also* **trundle bedstead**.

standing cupp with a cover: tall drinking cup with a stem, base and cover.
standish: a stand containing ink, pens and other writing materials; inkstand.
staple, statutes of the: a bond of record, acknowledged before the mayor of the staple, giving the obligee power to seize the land of the obligor if his debt was not paid at an appointed time (Doc. 1). *See also* **statutes merchant**.
state, secretary of: originally the office of king's secretary, made effectively supreme under Elizabeth I and held jointly by two officials; 'principall secretary of state'.
statutes marchant: statutes merchant; a bond of record, acknowledged before the chief magistrate of a trading town, giving the obligee power to seize the land of the obligor if his debt was not paid at an appointed time (Doc. 1). *See also* **statutes of the staple**.
steward: (a) one who administers a manor or estate on behalf of his lord; (b) one charged with overseeing an heraldic funeral; (c) **high steward** of the queen's household; (d) steward of a borough (Congleton).
stille: still; an apparatus for distilling medicines, toilet waters, etc.; also **still house**. *See also* **limbecke** and **water glasses.**
stitche: stitch used in sewing or embroidery (Doc. 60). *See also* **cruell**, **Irish stiche** and **tentestitch**.
strayes: animals found wandering away from the custody of their owners, liable to be impounded and, if not redeemed, forfeited to the lord of the manor. *See also* **waifes**.
straynable: liable to be distrained; *see* **distreine**.
stuffe: (a) textiles of long wool or worsted; (b) a collective noun for materials of many different kinds, e.g. of metal, earthenware, wood, etc.
suer: sure, certain.
sugar loves: sugar-loaves; sugar boiled and then moulded into a conical mass.
sumpter cloth: a saddle-cloth; embroidered with the arms of its owner (Doc. 60).
supted: supped; had supper.
surrender: formally giving up an estate or lease to another person.
surrogate: a person given authority to act in place of another.
surveyor generall: the principal or head surveyor in the queen's household.
sute, suyte: suit; (a) a set of matching items; (b) a legal prosecution or 'sutes in lawe'.
sweete bagge: a small bag filled with scented herbs such as lavender or other aromatic substances; made of crimson satin with gold and silver (Doc. 4).
table: the top or board to a table, the legs and rails being called the frame.
taffatte, taffater: taffeta; a thin, plainly woven material, stiffened by extra weft threads; of varying grades and finishes.
tail male: entail male; an estate settled on a number of male persons in succession, so it cannot be bequeathed at pleasure by any one possessor.
talbott: talbot; a hound or hunting-dog; **blacke talbott of goulde**, a jewelled ornament in the form of a black hound. *See also* **jewell**.
tallowe: tallow; a hard fat derived from animals, mainly used for making candles and soap and for dressing leather.
tanner: one who tans hides to convert them into leather.
tapestrye: a fabric with designs or pictures in the weave; used for wall hangings, curtains and seat covers.
targett: a kind of shield, used in heraldic displays.
tawney: tawny; a shade of brown.
tenant-in-chief: in the feudal system, one who held lands directly of the crown.

tenement: a holding or property held in tenure, but not always including a dwelling.
tentestitch: tent-stitch, petit-point; needlework in which a pattern was worked by stitches across the intersections of threads of worstead cloth.
terme: terms of agreement, agreed conditions.
tertion: tertian ague or fever.
testar: tester; a fabric or panelled canopy over a bed, supported on the four posts of the bedstead.
thannunciacion: *see* **Annunciacion of Our Lady**.
thappurtenances: *see* **appurtenances**.
threescore: sixty.
timber: larger pieces of wood for structural purposes.
tinsell: a rich material of silk or wool interwoven with gold or silver thread, often used for bed hangings.
tissue: a rich kind of cloth often interwoven with gold or silver; made on a draw loom with a weft figure; used for furnishings.
tithes: the tenth part of all produce or wages for the year, due to the rector or vicar of a parish and payable in kind or in cash.
title: legal right to the possession of property; the evidence of such right, i.e. title-deeds.
tobyne: tabby; a general term for striped silk taffeta; three stools of 'siver tobyne' (Doc. 60).
toftes: sites of houses and their out-buildings.
tonges: fire-tongs; used to grasp coal or wood for a fire.
topps: (a) brass finials on tongs and andirons; (b) cloth coverings to the canopies of beds; hence, 'topp and valence'.
topte: topped.
torches: hand-held lights each consisting of a stick bound with inflammable substances.
tramells: adjustable iron hooks to hang pots and kettles over fires.
trapt: (horses) adorned with trappings.
travis curtaine: traverse curtain drawn across a room on a metal rod.
travers iron rodds: iron rods from which to hang curtains traversely across rooms.
trayes: (a) trays for carrying plates, cutlery, etc.; (b) shallow vessels for liquids standing in dairies and butteries.
treasurer: an official entrusted with finances; **Lord High Treasurer of England:** the third great officer of the crown, controlling the revenues of the sovereign; **treasurer and receavour generall** of the queen (Doc. 35).
trenchers: plates or platters of wood, metal or earthenware.
Trynety terme: Trinity term; the fourth of the terms or sessions of the law-courts.
trundle bedstead: a low bed running on truckles or castors, usually pushed beneath a high or standing bed when not in use; often for the use of servants and children; also known as 'truckle beds'.
trunkes: leather-covered chests with rounded tops, for storing cloths, linen, etc. and for carrying necessities when travelling.
tumbrells: two-wheeled farm-carts drawn by horses; designed to tip backwards to empty their loads.
tunnes: tons; a measure of weight equal to 20 hundredweight.
turbarie: turbary; the right to dig peat or turf for fuel, leased for a term of years.
Turkie work carpettes: carpets or coverings made of richly coloured wool, and having a deep pile to resemble velvet; either imported from Turkey or made in a Turkish style.

underwoodes: coppices or spring-wood; small trees and shrubs growing beneath higher timber-trees and cut to the ground in rotation to encourage regeneration.

valence: valance; the border or fringe of drapery hung round the canopy or top of a curtained bed.

vargis: verjuice; a juice of crab-apples and unripe fruit, fermented into a sharp vinegar and much used in cooking; kept in a barrel.

velvett: a textile fabric having a dense and smooth piled surface, much used for clothes and furnishings.

verder, verduris: verdure; decoration depicting green vegetation in tapestry, embroidery, etc.

view of frankpledge: *see* **frankpledge**.

vill: village, township; as in the phrase 'manors, vills & hamlets'.

vintners: dealers in wine.

virginalls: a keyboard musical instrument in a case or box, which was normally placed on a table as it had no legs; the strings were plucked rather than struck; a single instrument is often referred to as 'a pair of virginals'.

viscount: the title of one of the five degrees of nobility; ranking higher than baron but lower than earl.

viscountess: the title of the wife or widow of a viscount, or held in her own right.

voiders: china vessels in which fragments of food and used cutlery and plates were placed when a table was cleared; had two 'covering baskettes' (Doc. 60).

voucher: a person or document vouching for the correctness of a fact concerning the possession of land or rights (Doc. 8); this can be done by a single or double voucher. *See also* **recoverie**.

vyall: viol; a musical instrument having five to seven strings, held between the knees and played with a bow.

waifes: pieces of property found ownerless, and which, if unclaimed within a fixed period, fell due to lord of the manor. *See* **strayes**.

waite: watch for stolen goods.

walk: (a) formal alley in a garden (Doc. 15); (b) physical compartment of a forest (Doc. 43).

wardrope: wardrobe; a room where textiles and other goods were stored and repaired, often containing a privy; usually situated near the private quarters of the lady of the house.

Wards and Liveries, court of: a court established by Henry VIII for the trial of causes relating to wardships; abolished in 1660.

warmeing panne: a shallow container of brass filled with hot embers and attached to a long handle to warm beds.

warren, free: the right granted by the crown to a manorial lord of keeping and hunting small game (rabbits, hares, pheasants, etc.) in a defined area; also **free park**.

wast groundes: open, uncultivated land such as heaths, moors and commons; an important economic resource for the owners of manors and estates.

watchett: a light blue or greenish colour, and cloth of the same used in furnishings; **watched:** dyed accordingly.

water glasses: glass bottles to hold distilled medicinal and toilet waters (*ex inf.* Peter Priers).

wattle: rods or stakes, usually split lengthwise, which were sprung and tied into the timber-frame of a building and then daubed with clay. *See also* **daub**.

waul: wail, howl or cry.

waynscott, weinscott: wainscot; a superior quality of foreign oak imported from Russia, Germany and Holland, used to make furniture and panelling.

weareing linnen: wearing linen or underclothes, as opposed to outer garments or 'weareing apparell'.

wett larders: rooms where drink and liquid food were stored.

wich, wich wood: wych-elm (*ulmus montana*).

willow cullored: willow-green; a colour resembling that of willow-leaves.

windowe clothes: alternative name for the more common 'window curtaines'.

withdraweing chamber: a room to which individuals and groups could withdraw from the hall or great chamber, to obtain greater privacy; sometimes described specifically as for the 'king', 'my lord' or the 'ladies'.

wood: (a) firewood, in the form of logs, faggots, etc., kept with 'seacole' in a 'woodhouse'; (b) woodland, and important economic resource for the owners of manors and estates.

worsted: a closely twisted yarn spun of long-staple wool; cloth made from that yarn.

wrought: embroidered; applied to furniture and clothing.

yarne: spun threads, probably of wool, used in the making of coverlets ('yarne coverlets', Doc. 60).

yeerlings: calves one or two years old.

yeoman: a man holding a small landed estate; walked with grooms at an heraldic funeral.

York: the title and rank of one of the heralds of arms; *see* **College of Arms**.

yssue: *see* **issue**.

APPENDIX I

Melford Hall in 1636

Although originally constructed with four wings around a central courtyard, the core of Melford Hall in many ways closely reflects that of smaller houses of its period, with a main hall to the right of the entrance and service quarters to the left. Precisely which parts of the present building are the work of the abbots of Bury St Edmunds before the Reformation, which were built for Sir William Cordell in the mid-sixteenth century, and which were added for Sir Thomas Savage, is still a matter of vigorous debate – even after a recent survey commissioned by the National Trust, using accurate hi-tech measuring equipment.[1]

However it is now possible to suggest how individual rooms were used in the early-seventeenth-century Hall by using some of the results of the recent survey alongside three documentary sources: John Thorpe's plan of about 1606,[2] a birds-eye drawing of the building on a map of 1613, and the probate inventory of Sir Thomas Viscount Savage taken in 1636. Our identifications are given with the transcription of the inventory (Doc. 60) both in footnotes and in numbering attached to sub-headings, and on Pl. 7 (overleaf) with the rooms correspondingly numbered.[3]

Once visitors to the Hall had passed through two gatehouses and crossed the inner courtyard, they entered at the principal door (G20), and found the hall to their right (G21–22); beyond the hall were the more private family rooms on the ground floor, the great and little parlours and related rooms (G12, 13, 23, 43). These were well furnished and were probably used to receive visitors when the grandeur of the first-floor great chamber (F43) was not needed. G13, the chamber within the little parlour, is the most expensively furnished room in the house, and it overlooked the private gardens.

To the left of the entrance were the service-quarters (G5–6, 15–18, 24–29) and, we suggest, the armoury (G8–9). The ground-floor rooms overlooking the main entrance were the steward's chamber in the south wing (G30–31) and the room called Mr Noye's chamber in the north wing (G39–41).[4] The steward would be ideally placed for a direct view of the main gate. Mr Noye's chamber may not have usually been furnished as it was when the inventory was taken. We have suggested (see Introduction, p. lxix, above) that this area may originally have been a chapel. If so, and if it was still in use in the 1630s, it would have presumably been furnished for the Roman Catholic faith. To disguise its real role, it could have had its furniture replaced before the appraisers came to the house. Alternatively, the space could still have existed but its role could have been changed; a room at the front of the house

1 See Introduction, pp. lxviii–ix above.

2 Plan of Melford Hall by John Thorpe: SJSM, T249, T250 (Pl. 2, p. lxxii).

3 In this appendix ground-floor rooms have a G before the number, those on the first floor an F before the number; second-floor rooms have an S before the number and C indicates a cellar.

4 For William Noye, see above, Introduction, p. xxiv, Docs 11 and 50 and, below, Notes on People. He had died in 1634.

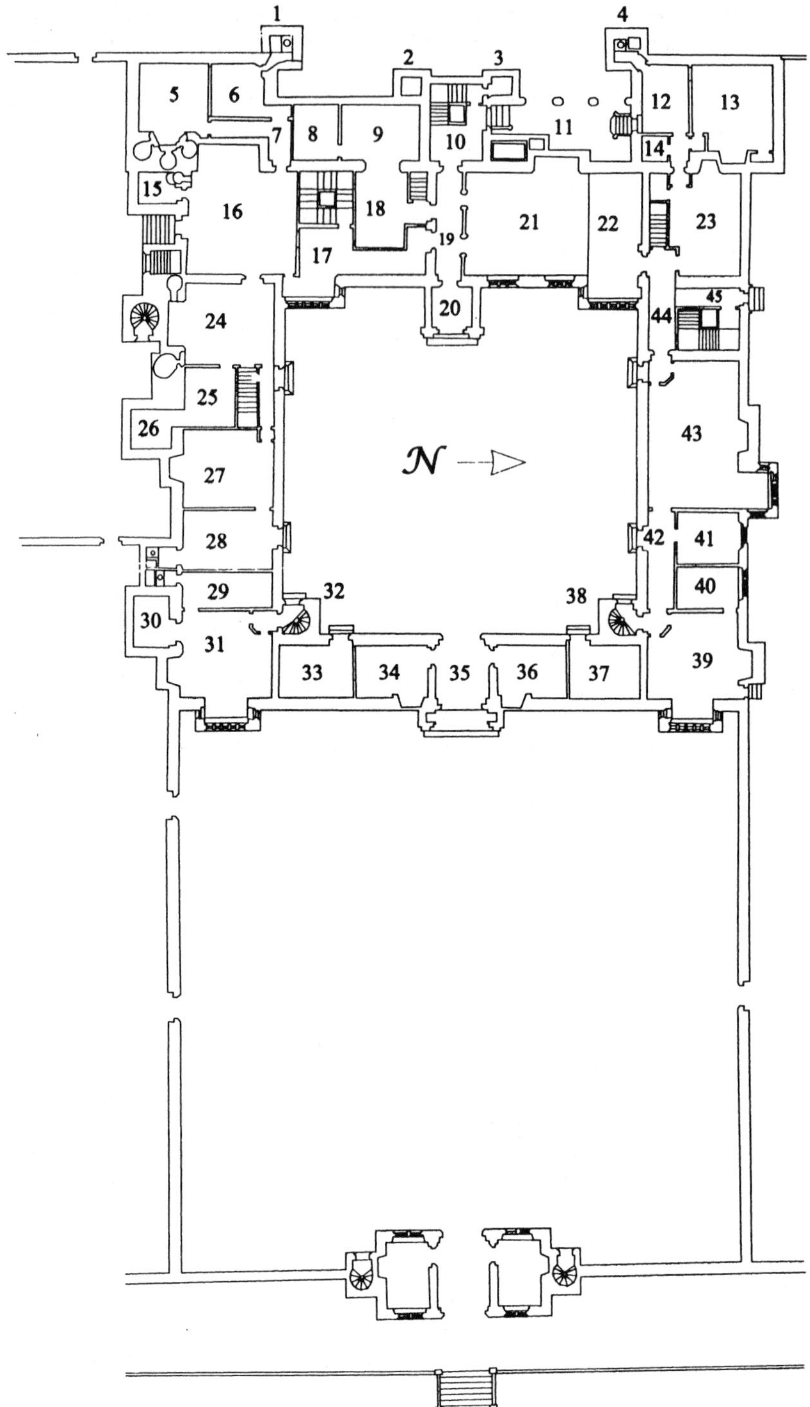

Plate 7. An adaptation of John Thorpe's plan of Melford Hall, c. 1606, with the ground-floor rooms numbered. These numbers are used in Doc. 60 and in Appendix 1.

with large windows may not have been the most tactful place for catholic worship in protestant England. In this case it may have been furnished as the inventory suggests.

The east wing, called the gatehouse (G33–34, 36–37 and rooms above) had probably originally been designed for the porters in control of the main entrance. Later, presumably after the construction of the porter's lodge to the east, the ground-floor rooms appear to have been converted to family or visitor use. Thorpe's plan did not extend to the outlying buildings, so we have no evidence for the layout of the outer gatehouse or stables, pond chambers or granaries.

Thorpe's drawing illustrates only the ground floor, so our knowledge of upper rooms is more speculative. The hall (G21–22) was two stories high, so divided the wings at first-floor level. The most expensively decorated rooms in the house were on the first and second floors to the north and west of the hall, laid out and furnished in anticipation of important visitors. From the dais in the hall (G22), visitors could go up the most important staircase (G45) and turn east into the great chamber (F43), the most public of the grand rooms. At its far end was the chapel chamber (F41–2); this may have been a gallery of the chapel below (G39) either at this time or at an earlier period.

Those allowed into the more private rooms could turn west at the top of the grand staircase to the withdrawing room of the great chamber, and, more private still, the gold bedchamber. Assuming that Melford followed the usual rule that the more important you were, the more private and expensively furnished your quarters, this room would have been for the most important people attending on a visitor of high status. From its inner chamber there is a stair to the purple bedchamber above and its associated rooms (S12–13), which would have been used by royal or aristocratic visitors. These grand bedchambers had good access to the principal room for the reception of important visitors, the great chamber already mentioned (F43).

We suggest that Thomas and Elizabeth Savage had their quarters on the first and second floors in the south-west corner of the house (F5–6, F16–20, S5–6). From F16 Elizabeth would have had good access to the south wing, which housed the nurseries and womens' chambers (F24–28, 30–31). Her attendant gentlewomen may have assisted in the supervision of the children's chambers. Thomas's and Elizabeth's youngest surviving children were in their early teens when Thomas died. The older children presumably visited with their progeny, but even so the nurseries were probably less important in 1635 than they had been twenty years earlier, and seem to have been converted to more general family use. To the north of Thomas's and Elizabeth's apartments was the wardrobe (F8–9).

On the first floor the hall separated the private family rooms from the guest and public spaces, but on the second floor these areas were connected by a gallery (S16–23). This provided space for exercise in poor weather, and the flat lead roof above meant that the family or important visitors could also take outdoor exercise with some privacy. It has previously been suggested that the main gallery of Melford Hall was in the east wing (demolished between 1635 and 1735),[5] and that it was from here that James Howell had earlier watched people hunting in the park (Doc. 15). The inventory indicates three rooms on the first floor of this wing, but a close examination of the 1613 map strongly suggests that the east wing also had a flat roof, an ideal vantage point from which to watch hunts. There will also have been a

5 Parker, *Melford Hall*, p. 332.

view from the lead-flat roof of the west tower (10), possibly for those of higher status.

The inventory does not mention attics, although traditionally many house-servants had their quarters in such roof-spaces. It is possible that the attics were empty, and that all the servants came in from the village or lived in the outer buildings, or in first-floor rooms in the east wing (F33–34, 36–37) which could well have been dormitories. Maids, presumably employed outside, were certainly housed in the granaries, and grooms near the stables. In contrast, the cellars of the house are mentioned in the inventory but their functions can only be inferred. We suggest that the wet larders were under the south wing accessed from the kitchens (C16, C24), that the beer and wine cellars were accessed from the pantry (C18) and ran under the southern end of the west wing, and that the still-house (C12–14) was in the cellars underlying the north-west tower.

Outside the main house were further service areas. Seven chambers in the 'Pond Building' were reasonably furnished and may have been used for visiting family or the upper servants of important visitors.

APPENDIX II

Notes on People

We have included here details about each individual for whom we have gathered information additional to that given in the Introduction or the documents, plus brief details of some of the major family members whose stories emerge in the documents and the Introduction. As elsewhere, Thomas and Elizabeth Savage are mentioned without their surname unless it is needed to avoid confusion. After each set of details is a note of where in the book the individual is mentioned.

Peers are listed by their family name, but cross-referenced from their title. Wives of peers are listed by either their original family name or the name of the family they married into, depending on their name when the documents in this volume were written. For Index of Persons, see p. 207

Abbott, Sir Morris, 1565–1642: an eminent and very wealthy merchant, one of the original directors and later governor of the East India Company and lord mayor of London. One of three high-achieving sons of a clothmaker from Guildford; one brother became bishop of Salisbury and another archbishop of Canterbury. In 1621 Abbott became MP for Hull. He was the first man to be knighted by Charles I when he became king. (Doc. 59)

Acton, Sir William, alderman of London; possibly he was the same man as the Sir William Acton who defended Macclesfield for the king in the civil war. (Doc. 72)

Aggas, Roger, 1568–1637: yeoman farmer of Long Melford who left some £500 in cash plus his lands when he died in 1637. Several times overseer of the poor and also churchwarden. Lived on the west side of Melford Green, very near Melford Hall, and held copyhold lands from the manor of Melford Hall. (Doc. 60)

Aiton/Ayton, Sir Robert, 1570–1638: poet and courtier. While a student at St Andrews university, Aiton wrote a poem praising James at his coronation, which brought him favour. Knighted in 1612, and became private secretary to both Queen Anne (wife of James I) and Queen Henrietta Maria. He is best known as a poet, 'one of the earliest Scots to use standard English as a literary medium'. (Docs 35, 42, 44)

Alcock, William gent, possibly the same William Alcock who witnessed the marriage settlement of Thomas and Elizabeth in 1602, or a relation. He was working for Thomas in Frodsham from at least 1616, and was described as 'of Frodsham' when leased part of Frodsham castle in 1626. Mentioned by Thomas as his servant in 1626 when a new window for Chester cathedral was paid for and he was deputy steward of Halton the following year. Although not an executor of the duke of Buckingham, he appears on lists of administrators of the duke's goods and chattels in the late 1620s. (Docs 1, 24, 30)

Aldesley, Thomas, 1600–75: prominent Cheshire gentleman, possibly related to Laurence Aldersley who features in Hakluyt's voyages. Their pedigree says that the family had lived at Aldersey in Cheshire since the time of Henry III. This Thomas served as sheriff of Chester in 1627/8, as an escheator of Cheshire under Charles I, and as mayor of Chester in 1640/1. On the county committee in 1642–3, and acted as a supernumerary to the deputy lieutenants. Reported to be a man of modest estate but distinctly of gentry stock. (Doc. 62)

Allington, Lady Jane, d. 1602: Thomas's maternal grandmother. Sister of Sir William Cordell and mother of Mary, wife to Sir John Savage. Inherited land and property in Melford and London from her brother and left it to her grandsons, Thomas Savage and Philip Stanhope. Widow of Richard Allington who had died in 1561. (Introduction and Docs 2, 4, 5, 7, 8)

Allington, William, relative of Jane Allington. In her will Jane Allington mentions her 'brother' William Allington. He is her brother-in-law. (Doc. 4)

Anderson, Sir Edmund, 1530–1605: judge; at Lincoln College Oxford, then the Inner Temple in 1550. Had a great knowledge of the law. Became serjeant-at-law to Queen Elizabeth I in 1579, before becoming a judge in the early 1580s. Knighted in 1582 when he became Lord Chief Justice of the Common Pleas. He was involved in many high-profile trials, including those of Mary queen of Scots, Essex and Raleigh. (Doc. 5)

Arderne, John, prominent Cheshire gentleman. One of the Ardernes of Alvanley, where the family had been established since the time of Edward III. May have been the John Arderne who was among the moderates in Cheshire in the civil war, but this could have been his son. The Ardernes were among the leading puritan families of Cheshire. (Doc. 7)

Andover, Lord: *see* Charles Howard.

Antrim, earl of: *see* Randal McDonnell.

Arundel, earl of: *see* Henry Fitzalan.

Arundel and Surrey, earl of: *see* Thomas Howard.

Aston, Herbert, 1614–89: second son of Sir Walter Aston (q.v.). Went with his father on his second embassy to Madrid in 1635. Married Catherine Thimbleby/Thimelby, sister of Sir John Thimbelby, son-in-law to Thomas and Elizabeth (q.v.). Author of the verse *On the Death of the Countess of Rivers*. (Introduction)

Aston, Sir Thomas, d. 1613: prominent Cheshire gentleman. Of Aston Hall, near Frodsham. Possibly uncle of the Sir Thomas below. (Doc. 1)

Aston/Ashton, Sir Thomas, d. 1645: sheriff of Cheshire and MP. Of Aston Hall near Frodsham. This younger Sir Thomas was son and heir of John Aston of Aston esq. (possibly brother to the older Sir Thomas) who was server to Queen Anne of Denmark, wife of James I. Born in 1600, Thomas succeeded his father in 1615. At Oxford in 1617, Lincoln's Inn in 1620. Served as sheriff of Cheshire in 1635–6 and MP for Cheshire in 1640 in the Short Parliament; he died at Stafford. A religious conservative, he defended episcopacy in 1641. (Doc. 56)

Aston, Sir Walter, later Baron of Forfar, d. 1639: ambassador to Spain in 1620–5 and again in 1635–8. 'A true and fast friend to the duke of Buckingham'. He is said to have earned £6 a day when ambassador, but at other times had to accept lower-paying jobs including keeper of the mulberry gardens and silk worms at St James, which paid £60 a year. His son and daughter both married siblings of Sir John Thimbleby, son-in-law to Thomas and Elizabeth. The Astons were a catholic family from Tixall in Staffordshire. (Introduction)

Ayres, Sir John, probably the Sir John Ayres who attacked Sir Edward Herbert, Lord Herbert of Cherbury, in 1611. Ayres thought that his wife was looking too favourably on Herbert; he and four armed men attacked Herbert but were beaten off. The privy council investigated and found Ayres guilty, and his father disinherited him. (Doc. 47)

Bacon, Anthony, 1558–1601: MP and one of the earl of Essex's party. Eldest son of Sir Nicholas Bacon and his second wife; brother of Francis Bacon (q.v.) and step-brother of Sir Nathaniel Bacon. Anthony was always in delicate health. He was at Trinity College, Cambridge in 1573 and at Gray's Inn with his brother in 1576. In 1579 he left England to travel on the continent, partly gathering intelligence for Francis Walsingham. He returned in 1591, very ill of gout. In 1593 he became MP for Wallingford, and entered the service of the earl of Essex, whom he served for the rest of his life. His considerable correspondence is held in Lambeth Palace archives. (Introduction)

Bacon, Sir Francis, later Viscount St Albans, 1561–1626: lawyer, statesman and philosopher. Younger son of Sir Nicholas Bacon and his second wife; Sir Nathaniel Bacon was his step-brother. Student at Trinity College, Cambridge, later at Gray's Inn. His writings are much better remembered than his political activities. He served as solicitor general, attorney general and lord chancellor of England. (Introduction)

Bankes, Sir John, 1589–1644: lawyer; made attorney general to the infant Prince Charles in 1630, and succeeded William Noye as attorney general to the king in 1634. He bought Corfe Castle and became chief justice of the common pleas. (Docs 61, 68)

Barrington, Sir Thomas, bart, d. about 1644: of Barrington Hall at Hatfield in Essex. Knighted before 1621, MP during the 1620s, and again from 1640, and became a Parliament man. Succeeded to his baronetcy in 1628. His mother was Oliver Cromwell's aunt. (Doc. 78)

Barney, John, servant to Thomas and Elizabeth. Housekeeper at Rocksavage from the early 1630s and also clerk of the kitchen there. At St Osyth's Priory when it was sacked in 1642; mentioned as one of Elizabeth's servants. (Introduction, Doc. 60)

Bath, earls of: *see* William and Henry Bourchier.

Bedford, countess of: *see* Lucy Russell.

Beeston, Sir Hugh, d. 1626: brother and heir of the man of the same name who died in 1608. The Beestons were another of the élite catholic families of Cheshire. Hugh was receiver general for the crown for Cheshire and North Wales. His daughter Margaret married William Whitmore; their daughter Bridget was his heir. She married as her second husband Sir Thomas Savage, son of Thomas and Elizabeth; they founded the line of the Savages of Beeston Castle. (Introduction, Docs 19, 21, 29, 57)

Bell, Arthur, 1590–1643: catholic martyr. Son of William Bell and Margaret née Daniell; his mother was sister to Francis Daniell of Acton near Long Melford (q.v.). Her family were descended from the Daniells who held Clifton, later the Savage family home, until a Daniell heiress married Sir John Savage in the 1380s. Arthur was sent in 1614 to St Omer, and afterwards went to Spain to complete his studies and be ordained; he was received into the Franciscan order in 1618. Spent some years at Douai, where he became professor of Hebrew. In 1632 he went to Scotland, but returned to England in 1637; he was arrested in 1643 and executed. (Introduction)

Berkshire, earl of: *see* Charles Howard, Thomas Howard.

Bertie, Robert, 1st earl of Lindsey, d. 1642: son of Lord Willoughby of Eresby and his wife Mary, daughter of the earl of Oxford. Although he went to Cambridge and Gray's Inn, he was primarily a military man. In 1612–26 he served in Denmark, Norway and the United Provinces; he later commanded the fleet, was vice-admiral for the Rhé expedition and in command of the navy at La Rochelle. In 1625 he tried but failed to acquire the earldom of Oxford, but did inherit the office of Lord Great Chamberlain from that family. To go with the position he needed an earldom and he received his title in 1626. He was lord lieutenant of Lincolnshire for many years. He fought for the king in the civil war and died of wounds received at Edgehill. (Doc. 69)

Bingley, Sir John, knighted in January 1618 at Theobalds; 'of the Exchequer'. (Introduction)

Birkenhead, Henry, esq, 1599–1660: prominent Cheshire gentleman of Backford in Cheshire, where the family had been established since the time of Richard II, according to their pedigrees. A JP before the civil war and a supporter of William Brereton in Cheshire during it, sub-commissioner of accounts in 1643–8 and much involved in disbursing funds in the 1640s. An active supporter of the protectorate. His wife Margaret was a daughter of Randle Mainwaring of Over Peover. (Doc. 62)

Blount, Charles, 8th Lord Mountjoy and 1st earl of Devonshire, 1563–1606: a favourite of Elizabeth I, he fought in the Low Countries before going with Essex to the Azores. In 1598 he took over from Essex in Ireland fighting against Hugh O'Neill, rebel earl of Tyrone. Defeated Tyrone in the north, as did Sir George Carew in the south. As earl of Devonshire he was one of the English negotiators at the Somerset House peace conference with Spain in 1604. His long-term mistress was Penelope Rich, sister of the earl of Essex and wife of the 1st earl of Warwick, cousin to Thomas Lord Darcy. (Introduction)

Booth, Sir George, bart, 1566–1652: member of one of the élite Cheshire families. Knighted at the end of Elizabeth's reign and created a baronet in 1611; his family were based at Dunham Massey. Served as sheriff of Chester in 1597 and 1622, and custos rotulorum of the Cheshire bench in the 1620s and 30s. He sat on the commission to investigate Thomas's dealings with the inhabitants of Frodsham in 1616. When Thomas went to Cheshire to help bring in the Forced Loan, Sir George was nominated collector. He was succeeded, during the Commonwealth period, by his grandson, also Sir George; it is easy to confuse the two in the civil war period. (Doc. 17)

Booth, Sir Thomas, bart, probably related to Sir George Booth, and as such a member of an important Cheshire family. (Doc. 62)

Bourchier, Henry, 5th earl of Bath, ?1587–1654: A cousin of the 3rd earl (q.v.), he inherited his title in 1637 when the 4th earl, William's son, died without a male heir. At Trinity College, Dublin in 1597, was knighted in 1621 and became a privy councillor in 1641; by 1644 he was one of the commissioners for the defence of Oxford (for Charles I). He married in 1638 Rachel Fane, daughter of Francis Fane, earl of Westmorland (q.v.). She wrote masques to be performed by children. (Introduction)

Bourchier, William, 3rd earl of Bath, 1557–1623: inherited his title from his grandfather John Bourchier, who died in 1560, having outlived his eldest son. His grandfather's third wife, Margaret, was widow of the Thomas Kitson who died in 1540 and the couple lived at Hengrave, so William presumably knew Sir Thomas Kitson well. William was educated at Bury St Edmunds and Ely before going to Cambridge. In 1585 he fought in the Netherlands and a year later was vice admiral and lord lieutenant of Devon. Around 1580 he secretly married Mary Cornwallis, Kitson's sister-in-law. This marriage was quickly annulled and in 1582 he married Elizabeth Russell, daughter of the earl of Bedford. (Introduction)

Bridgeman, John, bishop of Chester, 1577–1652: originally from Exeter, he studied at Cambridge before returning to Exeter as a canon; then moved to Peterborough. In 1615 he was one of James I's chaplains, and became rector of Wigan. Had a reputation for being 'negligent in his duties as a repressor of non-conformity'. Became bishop of Chester in 1619. His bishopric was poor, which may have exacerbated conflicts with the town governors. Although the bishop is not normally involved with the fabric of a cathedral, Bridgeman did a great deal of building and repair at Chester. (Introduction, Docs 30, 33, 37)

Brooke, Thomas, gent, d. 1632: steward or man of business to Thomas. Probably related to the Brooke family of Norton Priory, not far from Rocksavage. His will shows that he had loaned at least £1200 to Thomas 'my honorable good lord and master'. A single man when he died (in Melford) he may have been son of the Thomas Brook of Norton who died in 1622. (Introduction, Docs 7, 14, 36)

Brownloe/Brownlow, Richard, 1553–1638: a lawyer who studied at the Inner Temple. Became chief prothonotary of the Court of Common Pleas in 1591 and was reputed to make an annual profit of £6000 from the office, which he held until his death in 1638. At death his entrails were buried in Enfield and his body taken to Belton House, Lincolnshire, which he had bought. (Doc. 52)

Brudenell, Lord Thomas, most likely Thomas, Baron Brudenell of Stonton, later 1st earl of Cardigan. He succeeded to his father's Huntingdonshire lands and his uncle's estate at Deene in Northants. Became a baronet in 1611 and was knighted the following year. His wife was daughter of Sir Thomas Tresham, another catholic. He was over 80 when he died in 1663. Anne Savage (q.v.), daughter of Thomas and Elizabeth, later married his son Sir Robert Brudenell, who had become a catholic (she was his second wife). This was a long-lived family: Robert Brudenell died in 1703 aged nintety-six. (Doc. 74)

Buckingham, countess of: *see* Mary Villiers.

Buckingham, duchess of: *see* Katherine Manners.

Buckingham, marquis of, duke of: *see* George Villiers.

Byatt, Andrew, d. 1670: merchant and trader who held land in Long Melford; called Mr Byatt on the 1640 list of ship money paid. He and his wife baptised 12 children in Melford in 1617–37 but he also had lands in neighbouring Lavenham, and by the time of his death he lived in Hartest, a smaller community nearby. He issued trading tokens, and examples survive from 1652 and 1667. In his will he called himself a grocer; the will mentions property in Melford, Bury St Edmunds, Thetford, Sudbury and Great Yarmouth. (Doc. 60)

Calverley, Hugh, esq: the Calveleys were another of the élite families of Cheshire, but Calverley itself had passed to the Davenport family by this time. This is probably Sir Hugh Calverley, 1613–48, before he received his knighthood. Sheriff of Cheshire in 1642. His wife Elizabeth was a daughter of Henry earl of Huntingdon. (Doc. 62)

Caldwell/Cauldwell, Dan, friend of James Howell**.** Documents in Essex Record Office record a Daniel Caldwell, esq. of Horndon on the Hill, who was on an assize jury in 1629. Possibly the same Daniel Caldwell who died in 1634. (Doc. 15)

Cardigan, earl of: *see* Thomas Brudenell.

Carew, Sir Matthew, d. 1618: lawyer, son of a Cornish family. At Westminster school, then at Trinity College, Cambridge where he was a fellow for ten years. He then studied at Louvain and other European universities for twelve years. He accompanied the earl of Arundel (q.v.) to Europe. He entered practical law in the Court of Arches but soon became a chancery master. Knighted in 1603. (Doc. 8)

Carew/Carey, Sir George, later Baron Clopton and earl of Totnes, 1555–1629: soldier son of a churchman. Fought in Ireland from 1574, and was knighted in 1586. In 1590 he was an Irish privy councillor, but in 1592 he moved back to England as lieutenant general of ordnance. Treasurer at war in Ireland in 1599, then lord deputy until Mountjoy's appointment, and president of Munster in 1600. He retired in 1603 and took to court life as vice-chamberlain of Queen Anne's household. In 1604 he became Baron Clopton of Stratford and eventually in 1626 became earl of Totnes. It was this George Carew who took over as keeper of Nonsuch after the death of John Lord Lumley in 1609. (Introduction, Doc. 8, 35)

Carey, Sir Robert, ?1560–1639: a military man, and cousin of the earl of Suffolk, who was MP for Morpeth in several Elizabethan parliaments. It was Carey who rode to Scotland to tell James I of Elizabeth's death. He was involved with Prince Charles's household in 1605–22, when he was made baron of Leppington. His post of chamberlain to Charles, prince of Wales, went to Thomas Savage. A year later Leppington went to Spain with Charles and Buckingham. In 1626 he became 1st earl of Monmouth. He wrote his memoirs, which survive. (Introduction)

Cary/Carey, Sir George, d. 1617: of Cockington, Devon; prominent in Devonshire and Ireland. Three men of this name were active in the west country at this period. This Sir George came from a family which had been at Cockington since the early 15th century. When Sir William Cordell made his will in 1580 Cary was one of his executors, with Jane Allington. Cordell had sold land in Devon to Cary, whom he may have known as a fellow lawyer. Cary was treasurer at war in Ireland in 1588, was knighted the same year, was lord justice in Ireland in 1603 after Mountjoy's departure, then lord deputy of Ireland. His second wife was Lettice Rich, daughter of the 1st earl of Warwick and his wife Penelope. Penelope Rich was sister to the earl of Essex who was executed in 1601, and long-term mistress of Charles Mountjoy; she and her husband were divorced in 1605. This Sir George was second cousin to Henry Cary, 1st viscount Falkland, q.v. (Introduction, Docs 4, 5, 8)

Cary/Carey, Henry, 1st Viscount Falkland, ?1575–1633: son of Sir Edward Carey of Hertfordshire who had been master of the Jewel House to James I; Henry's sister was married to George Manners, earl of Rutland (q.v.). Henry was at Exeter College, Oxford and then Gray's Inn. He went to Ireland and was knighted in Dublin in 1599. He was a privy councillor in 1617/18 and later comptroller of the household; made viscount Falkland in 1620 and lord deputy in Ireland from 1622–9. In 1625 his wife left him, and openly professed her catholic faith. He died after falling out of a tree while hunting with the king at Theobalds. (Introduction)

Cary/Carey, Jane: presumably a daughter or other relative of Sir George Carie of Cockington. (Doc. 4)

Cary/Carey, Richard: presumably a son or other relative of Sir George Carie of Cockington. (Doc. 4)

Cary/Carey, **Thomas:** of Gray's Inn, presumably a son or other relative of Sir George Carie of Cockington. (Doc. 4)

Carleton, Dudley, later viscount Dorchester, 1573–1632: 'the most sagacious and successful diplomatist in Europe'. Carleton was made ambassador to Venice in 1610. Much of his correspondence survives, particularly that with John Chamberlain (q.v.). He was created Lord Carleton in 1626 and Viscount Dorchester in 1628. Shortly afterwards he was made chief secretary of state, responsible for foreign affairs. His second wife was the widow of Lord Bayning. (Introduction, Doc. 41)

Carleton, Anne, née Glemham, d. 1639: 2nd wife of Dudley Carleton, viscount Dorchester. Her first husband was Paul, later viscount, Bayning. She married Dorchester in 1630; when she died Elizabeth attended her funeral. By her first husband she had three daughters; one married Henry Murray and was later created countess of Dorchester for life by Charles II, another was mother to Barbara Villiers, the duchess of Cleveland, one of Charles II's mistresses. (Doc 66)

Carlisle, countess of: *see* Lucy Hay.

Carlisle, earl of: *see* James Hay.

Cavendish, Sir Charles, 1553–1617: son of William Cavendish and Bess of Hardwick, he married Margaret Kitson, Elizabeth's mother's sister, so uncle to Elizabeth. Margaret died soon after the marriage. By his second marriage to Catherine Baroness Ogle he had a son William, later the 1st earl of Newcastle, a royalist general in the civil war. Cavendish was step-brother and brother-in-law to Gilbert

Talbot 7th earl of Shrewsbury. The earl's father George, the 6th earl, married Bess of Hardwick as his second wife, and Gilbert's wife was Mary Cavendish, Charles's sister. (Introduction)

Cavendish, Christian, countess of Devonshire, 1595–1675: born Christian Bruce, her father was the 1st Lord Kinloss, master of the rolls, and her brother Thomas became the 1st earl of Elgin. She married William Cavendish (q.v.) in 1608; he died in 1628, two years after inheriting his title as earl of Devonshire. Their son, another William, did not marry until 1639, so in 1635 Christian would have been the only countess of Devonshire. (Introduction)

Cavendish, William, earl of Devonshire, 1590–1628: grandson of William Cavendish and Bess of Hardwick, and nephew of Charles Cavendish (q.v.), he became Baron Cavendish of Hardwick in 1605. In 1608 he married Christian Bruce (q.v.). His father had become earl of Devonshire in 1618, and this William inherited in 1626. (Introduction)

Cecil, Sir Robert, later Viscount Cranborne and 1st earl of Salisbury, 1563–1612: second son of William Cecil, Lord Burghley; his mother was Cecil's second wife. He was at St John's College, Cambridge and Gray's Inn in the early 1580s, then travelled to France. In 1586–7 he was an MP. In 1591 he was knighted and joined the Privy Council, and by 1596 was the queen's principal secretary of state, a role he held until his death in the next reign. In 1603 he received a barony, became Viscount Cranborne the next year and earl of Salisbury in 1605. He originally owned the house called Theobalds, but exchanged it with the king for Hatfield. (Introduction, Docs 5, 6, 12)

Cecil, William, Viscount Cranborne then 2nd earl of Salisbury, 1591–1668: only son and heir of Robert Cecil. Educated at Sherborne, St John's College, Cambridge and in Paris. Was KB and a student at Gray's Inn in 1605, known as Viscount Cranborne from that year when his father became earl. He travelled extensively in Europe but returned in 1610 to become an MP. Lord lieutenant of Hertfordshire from 1612, KG 1625 and joined the Privy Council the following year. In the civil war he sided with Parliament and received many honours and commissions. His first wife was Catherine Howard, daughter of the earl of Suffolk; his second wife Catherine née Knyvett. (Introduction)

Chamberlain, John, 1553–1627: described by the *DNB* as a 'letter writer'. He matriculated at Trinity College, Cambridge in 1570 but did not graduate. The *DNB* author calls him 'the Horace Walpole of his day' and says 'it is obvious from his father's will that he inherited means which were sufficient for his support, and he appears to have led a quiet, private life in the society of his friends'. However he is also known to have been active in acquiring news; he was one of the 'Paul's walkers' who frequented St Paul's each day to gain and exchange news of people and events. (Introduction)

Cheshire, Thomas, d. 1664: prominent Cheshire gentleman, bailiff of Halton Castle from 1615 to 1630 or later, also the king's bailiff and collector of his rents within the honour of Halton and Whitley. One of the appraisers of Sir John Savage's goods at Rocksavage in 1615. In 1622 and probably at other times he was 'deputed officer for Sir Thomas Savage'. In 1631 he paid Thomas to put his cows on the Rocksavage lands. (Doc. 60)

Cholmondeley, Sir Robert, 1584–1659: member of an élite Cheshire family. Son of Sir Hugh Cholmondeley, he was at Oxford in 1600; he succeeded his father in 1601 and became baronet in 1611. Served as sheriff of Chester in 1621 and MP for the county of Cheshire in 1625–6. He became Viscount Cholmondeley of Kells (in co. Meath) in 1628. Raised troops for the royalists in Cheshire, and became Baron

Cholmondeley in 1645 and earl of Leinster the next year. His wife Catherine was daughter of John Lord Stanhope of Harrington, possibly related to Thomas Savage's cousin Philip Stanhope. (Doc. 56)

Clare, earl of: *see* John Holles.

Coke, Sir John, 1563–1644: at Trinity College, Cambridge, then entered the service of Lord Burghley. He became commissioner of the navy under James I, was many times MP and became master of requests. In 1625 he was chosen, reportedly by Buckingham, as a principal secretary of state, and was regarded in parliament as the mouthpiece of the government. He was unpopular, and is remembered as one of the men who helped drive apart Charles I and Parliament. (Introduction, Docs 61, 67)

Colchester, Viscount: *see* Thomas Darcy.

Coleraine, earl of: *see* Hugh Hare.

Colman, William, poet whose collection 'La Danse Macabre, or Death's Duel' included an epitaph to Jane Lady Winchester. Very little seems to be known about him. (Introduction)

Conway, Sir Edward, later Baron Conway and Viscount Conway, d. 1631: originally from Warwickshire, he made his living as a soldier, and was colonel of a regiment of foot at Cadiz, where he was knighted in 1596. He succeeded his father in 1603 and later spent some time in command of British forces in the Netherlands. He was an MP three times and then acted as ambassador to Brussels and Prague in 1622, the year he became a privy councillor. He was secretary of state from 1623–8 and gained numerous other honours, including being lord lieutenant of Hampshire from 1625, when he was made Baron Conway; two years later he became Viscount Conway. From 1628 until his death he was lord president of the council. (Introduction, Doc. 23)

Cordell, John, d. 1551–3: father of Sir William Cordell and Jane Allington. Possibly from Enfield, where Cordells appear in the records from at least 1411, but the Savage genealogy suggests that his father was from Melford. The first mention of John in Melford is in 1519, as witness to a will. In the 1525 subsidy he appears as a senior servant of the Clopton family at Kentwell Hall. Throughout the 1530s and 1540s he appears as witness or executor to many wills. He received a grant of arms in 1548. (Introduction)

Cordell, Sir John, d. 1644: city merchant; son of Sir Thomas Cordell, who had been a very prominent city merchant, an investor in privateering and 'a pioneer of sugar refining in England'. The family was descended from one of Sir William Cordell's uncles. Sir John was, like his father, an alderman of the city of London. He lived in Milk Street, and St Lawrence in Old Jewry was his parish church. Portraits survive at Melford Hall of both John and his wife Sarah, daughter of Robert Bankworth of London; she died in 1646. (Introduction, Docs 59, 74, 82, 83)

Cordell, Sir Robert, bart, d. 1680: son of Sir John Cordell. Robert bought Melford Hall from Earl Rivers in 1649 and was active in Melford until his death. He was high sheriff of Suffolk in 1653 and MP for Sudbury in 1661 and 1678. Buried in St Lawrence in Old Jewry, like his father. His descendents held Melford Hall until the mid-eighteenth century. (Introduction, Doc. 74)

Cordell, Sir William, d. 1581: studied at Cambridge then Lincoln's Inn; called to the bar in 1544. The next year he leased the manor of Melford Hall and was MP for the first time. Received a grant of arms in 1549. MP for Steyning in the early 1550s. In 1553 he became solicitor general to Queen Mary, and a governor of Lincoln's Inn. About this time he was knighted, and in 1557 became master of the rolls and a privy councillor. In the next parliament he was speaker of the Commons and MP for

Suffolk. He continued as master of the rolls under Elizabeth. A land speculator. Thomas was his sister's grandson. (Introduction, Docs 4, 5, 7, 9)

Cornwallis, Lady Jane, 1581–1659: second wife and widow of Sir William Cornwallis who died in 1611; she later married Nathaniel Bacon. Her correspondence survives. A much younger sister-in-law to Elizabeth Kitson. (Introduction, Doc. 54)

Cornwallis, Sir Frederick, 1611–62: son of Sir William Cornwallis and his wife Lady Jane, later Bacon (q.v.). His father's sister Elizabeth married Sir Thomas Kitson and was grandmother to Elizabeth Savage. Frederick inherited the family estates in 1626, was created a baronet the next year, and was knighted in 1630. In 1627 he inherited the Cornwallis house at Thorpe in Norfolk after the death of his aunt Mary countess of Bathon. He was MP in 1640, then followed Charles II into exile and served as his treasurer of household. After the Restoration he served again as an MP, became a privy councillor and Baron Cornwallis of Eye, Suffolk. His sister Elizabeth married as her second husband Richard Viscount Lumley (q.v.). (Introduction, Doc. 54)

Cornwallis, Mary, d. 1627: sister to Elizabeth Kitson, known as the countess of Bathon. Daughter of Sir Thomas Cornwallis. Sir Thomas Kitson had persuaded William Bourchier, 3rd earl of Bath (q.v.) to marry Mary 'secretly at night' at Hengrave, but this marriage had been rapidly annulled and the earl remarried in 1582. Mary disputed the annulment for the rest of her life. Sir Thomas Cornwallis wrote about a case in the Court of Arches concerning the marriage, at which the earl's mother attempted to bribe the judges. The earl's mother was Frances Kitson, sister of Sir Thomas Kitson and sister-in-law to Elizabeth Lady Kitson; thus Frances Kitson's son had married her sister-in-law's sister. In his will Sir Thomas Kitson accepted that the Bath marriage had been partly his idea, and that it had caused Mary many problems; he left her £300 which may have been in partial recompense. In 1601 Sir Thomas Cornwallis and his daughter were still being reprimanded by the Privy Council for their behaviour to the earl of Bath and for Mary's insistence on calling herself countess of Bath. (Introduction)

Cornwallis, Sir Thomas, 1519–1604: a staunch catholic who started his official life as comptroller of the household to Princess (later Queen) Mary. In 1549 he was taken prisoner at Norwich while trying to put down Kett's rebellion. Made sheriff of Norfolk and Suffolk in 1553, he was later MP, privy councillor, diplomat and negotiator. In 1554 he was one of two privy councillors sent to negotiate with Sir Thomas Wyatt the younger during his rebellion. In Elizabeth's reign he retired to Suffolk. His daughter Elizabeth married Thomas Kitson of Hengrave, and was Elizabeth Savage's grandmother. (Introduction)

Cosin, John, 1594–1672: born in Norwich, and went to Caius College, Cambridge as a Norwich scholar. He became a fellow of Caius, then moved to become first secretary and librarian to the bishop of Lichfield and later domestic chaplain to the bishop of Durham. Cosin was a personal friend of William Laud and Richard Montagu (q.v.). In the 1630s he became master of Peterhouse College, Cambridge and later vice-chancellor of Cambridge university and chaplain to Charles I. In 1640 he became dean of Peterborough. He left England in 1644 and lived in Paris ministering to members of the Church of England exiled there. He became bishop of Durham in 1660. (Introduction)

Cottington, Sir Francis, ?1578–1652: started his career as an English agent in Spain, and became consul in Seville in 1612; returned to England to be one of the clerks of the Privy Council. In 1622 he became secretary to the prince of Wales and became both knight and baronet the next year. An enemy of Buckingham, but went with him and Charles to Spain in 1623 as part of the team negotiating for the

Spanish marriage. He gained more offices after Buckingham's death, becoming chancellor of the exchequer, ambassador to Spain and a baron in 1631. He several times converted to catholicism at times of serious illness, and died in Spain in the care of the Jesuits. (Introduction, Docs 44, 53, 70)

Coventry, Thomas Lord, 1578–1640: son of Sir Thomas Coventry, one of the justices of common pleas. At Balliol College, Oxford in 1592, and moved to the Inner Temple two years later. He became a barrister and received many official honours and appointments, being knighted in 1617. He was solicitor general in 1617–21 and then became attorney general until 1625, when he joined the privy council and became lord keeper of the great seal, a post he kept until his death. In 1628 he was created Baron Coventry of Aylesborough. (Doc. 47)

Cranborne, Viscount: *see* Robert Cecil, William Cecil.

Cranfield, Sir Lionel, 1575–1645: later earl of Middlesex. A London merchant and financier who became associated with George Villiers (later Buckingham, q.v.) and through him became a privy councillor and lord treasurer in 1621, and earl the following year. He became unpopular with James and Buckingham because he tried to preach economy, and was impeached by Parliament in 1624. (Introduction)

Crewe, John, esq: son of Sir Ranulph Crewe; he was ranger of the forest of Delamere, this role inherited from his wife Mary's Done family after 1630. Thomas Savage was ordered to take more responsibilities for Delamere in 1631 because the chief forestership was being contested at that time, so Crewe's assumption of the post cannot have been automatic. He was a moderate in 1641–2 and was only rarely active for Parliament from 1642–60. Sheriff of Cheshire in 1652. Described as a disillusioned Parliamentarian, he refused to serve as a JP in 1645 but accepted the role when reappointed after the Restoration. (Introduction, Docs 49, 67)

Crewe, Sir Ranulph, 1558–1646: Cheshire-born lawyer who became lord chief justice and several times speaker of the House of Commons. He was second son of a tanner of Nantwich, but his mother was a Manwaring. He studied at Lincoln's Inn and was called to the bar in 1584; he became MP and maintained his links with Lincoln's Inn (where he sponsored Thomas in 1597). He was knighted in 1614, when he served as speaker of the House of Commons during the 'Addled' parliament; he later became sergeant at law, and was on several commissions which tried important people. He was made lord chief justice of the Kings Bench in January 1625 but was dismissed the following year for opposing the Forced Loan and appears to have retired. In 1630, when he was at odds with the city of Chester, Thomas was called on to bring an end to the quarrel. (Introduction, Doc. 67)

Crisp, Sir Nicholas, ?1599–1637: a merchant whose family had lands in Gloucestershire and traded in London. He was active in the Africa trade from at least 1625. In 1632 he and five others gained exclusive rights to trade with Guinea. In 1640 he and colleagues paid Charles I for the right to have the income from customs; on this security they advanced the king £253,000 which was used to pay for the navy and other public uses. Knighted in 1641 and elected as MP in the Long Parliament, but expelled very quickly as a monopolist. During the civil war he raised large amounts for the king. He was made a baronet in 1664. (Introduction)

Croft/Croftes, Sir James, c.1560–1624: third son of the Sir James Croft who died in 1591 having been lord deputy of Ireland and controller of Queen Elizabeth's household; the family lived at Croft Castle in Herefordshire. James Croft was at Gray's Inn, married twice and died in 1624. Through the influence of his father he became MP for Brackley in the 1580s, and accompanied his father on a peace mission to the Netherlands in 1588. James was knighted by James I and given custody of Lady Arabella Stuart; her escape led to his imprisonment in the Fleet prison. However he kept his role as a gentleman-pensioner to James I, and served as pall-bearer at the funeral of Queen Anne of Denmark, wife of James I. James was a family friend of Thomas Lord Darcy, of James Howell, and of Thomas and Elizabeth Savage. One of his brothers was a catholic who moved to France. (Introduction, Docs 10, 60)

Curteene/Courten, Sir William, 1572–1636: a merchant and creditor of both James I and Charles I; he lent them some £200,000. Curteene's father was a Protestant tailor from Flanders who fled to England in 1568; the family made french hoods and then moved on to trade in silk and linen. William first worked in Haarlem for his father; here he married the deaf and dumb daughter of a Dutch merchant, who provided a dowry of £60,000. In 1606 he returned to England to expand his business. He was knighted in 1622. Two years later one of his trading ships discovered the isle of Barbados; Curteene got letters patent to settle it and invested large sums, but his right was challenged by the earl of Carlisle (q.v.) who eventually won. In 1631 his business was estimated to be worth £150,000. Seven years after his death his estate was bankrupt, following his court cases against Carlisle and his attempts to get repayments from the crown. (Doc. 66)

Danby, earl of: *see* Henry Danvers.

Daniell, Francis, this branch of the Daniells (linked to the Cheshire family) were long-term owners of Acton Hall, in the parish of Acton which borders Long Melford. They were catholic and appear as recusants from the late sixteenth century. This Francis was said to have spent much of his life living abroad. Margaret Daniell married William Bell in 1582 and their fifth child was Arthur Bell (q.v.), who, with the help of his uncle Francis Daniell of Acton, became a Franciscan. (Docs 15, 24)

Daniell, John of Daresbury: the Daniells were a prominent Cheshire family, and their pedigree says that they had been at Daresbury since the time of Edward III. The first Sir John Savage of Clifton (d. 1386) acquired his Cheshire lands by marriage with Margaret, daughter and heiress of Sir Thomas Danyers, otherwise Daniells/Daniers, of Bradley, near Frodsham. Daresbury is adjacent to Halton, to the east. This John inherited in 1613 as a child, married a daughter of the Hattons in 1635 and was living in 1649; he may have been the John Daniell who died in 1681. (Doc. 62)

Danyell, Mr: possibly John Daniell of Daresbury or Thomas Daniell of Over Tabley. (Doc. 56)

Danvers, Henry, earl of Danby, 1573–1644: started his career as page to Sir Philip Sidney, and had other military interests; he was outlawed for murder but this was reversed and he went on with military activities in Ireland. In 1603 he became Baron Danvers, and in 1626 earl of Danby. He was a privy councillor from 1628 and a knight of the garter from 1633. He gave Oxford University the lands to make their Botanic Gardens. (Doc. 44)

Darcy, Elizabeth: *see* Elizabeth Savage.

Darcy, Elizabeth: *see* Elizabeth Lady Lumley.

Darcy, Thomas, Baron Darcy of Chiche, later Viscount Colchester and then Earl Rivers: father of Elizabeth. Details of his life are given in the Introduction. (Docs 1, 2, 10, 12, 25, 31, 54, 55, 57, 64)

Darcy, Lady Mary, d.1644; daughter of Sir Thomas Kitson and his wife Elizabeth née Cornwallis (q.v.), wife of Thomas Lord Darcy but separated from him before 1600. However she maintained her right to share his titles, and so became Viscountess Colchester and then Countess Rivers. She lived in Colchester for many years. Probably in her 80s when she died. (Introduction, Docs 31, 32, 36, 38, 39)

Darcy, Mary, one of Elizabeth's sisters; her second marriage was to Sir Thomas Maples. (Introduction, Docs 31, 32)

Davenant, William, 1606–68: poet, playwright, theatre manager. Shakespeare is said to have been Davenant's godfather. Davenant became a page in London in 1622 and later served a famous literary courtier, Fulke Greville, Lord Brooke. Meanwhile he was writing his early revenge tragedies such as *Albovine* (produced *c.*1629), and tragicomedies such as *The Colonel.* He attracted the attention of Queen Henrietta Maria and was appointed poet laureate in 1638. (Introduction)

Davies, Robert, 1573–1658: of Ashton and Tarvin in Cheshire. In the first half of the seventeenth century he bought land in Ashton, Manley and Horton in Cheshire from the Legh family and others. (Doc. 62)

Dekham/Dackombe, Sir John, ?1570–1618: started his career at the Middle Temple and then joined Sir Robert Cecil's staff. He became Cecil's solicitor and later his secretary, and was executor of his will. He was a gentleman of the bedchamber to Princes Henry and Charles, and in 1613 became master of requests. In 1615 he was made chancellor of the Duchy of Lancaster and was knighted in 1616. (Introduction)

Delves, Sir Thomas, knighted at Whitehall in 1609, 'of Cheshire'. The Delves of Doddington were one of Cheshire's leading gentry families. This Sir Thomas sat on the commission to investigate Thomas Savage's dealings with the inhabitants of Frodsham in 1616. He became a baronet in 1621 and was sheriff of Chester in 1637. A royalist during the civil war. (Doc. 56)

Denbigh, countess of: *see* Susan Villiers.

Denbigh, earl of: *see* William Feilding.

Dethicke, Johane, mentioned by Jane Allington as her servant in her will of 1602. Dame Mary Cordell, widow of Jane Allington's brother, mentioned a cousin Dethick in her 1585 will; there may be a connection. Since the name is not common, a link may exist to the father and son who were Garter Kings of Arms until 1612. (Doc. 4)

Devonshire, countess of: see Christian Cavendish.

Devonshire, earl of: see Charles Blount, Lord Mountjoy.

Devonshire, earl of: see William Cavendish.

Done/Donne, Sir John, d. 1629: of Utkinton, Cheshire. Knighted in 1617, when James I hunted in Delamere forest, where the Dones were heritary rangers. He married a daughter of Thomas Wilbraham of Woodhey. The Dones were one of the élite families of Cheshire. This Sir John sat on the commission to investigate Thomas Savage's dealings with the inhabitants of Frodsham in 1616, although he had sold Thomas some of his Frodsham lands. His son John Done esq. succeeded him as forester of Delamere, but died himself in 1630. Sir John's daughter Mary had married John Crewe (q.v.), who took the role of forester of Delamere after his brother-in-law's death, after some contest for the post. (Docs 20, 43)

Done, Sir Ralph, d. 1660: second husband of Thomas Savage's sister Elizabeth. Their two eldest sons died young, but their third son Thomas became auditor to Charles II and James II. (Doc. 56)

Dorchester, Lady: see Anne Carleton.

Dorchester, Viscount: see Sir Dudley Carleton.

Dorset, earl of: see Edward Sackville.

Drommond, Sir Morrice, 'a Scotchman' knighted at Hampton Court in July 1625. (Doc. 66)

Drury, Elizabeth, later Lady Exeter, d. 1654: daughter of Sir William Drury of Hawstead in Suffolk, she married William Cecil, earl of Exeter, grandson of Sir

William Cecil, Lord Burghley. Her three daughters became the countesses of Berkshire, Oxford and Stamford. (Doc. 65)

Ducke, Nick, 1570–1628: a Devonshire lawyer who matriculated at Oxford but did not take his degree; he then moved to Lincoln's Inn and was called to the bar. He eventually became a governor of Lincoln's Inn and recorder of Exeter, where he died. (Doc. 2)

Dunluce/Dunlace, Viscount: *see* Randal McDonnel.

Dutton, Mr: the Duttons were one of the élite families of Cheshire. This could be one of any number of Duttons of Hatton alive at this period. However one of the more likely is Peter Dutton, 1601–39, married to a daughter of Hugh Calverley. (Doc. 56)

Eden, Dr, probably Dr Thomas Eden, 1580–1645: ecclesiastical administrator, a master in Chancery and bishop's chancellor. He joined the Parliamentary side in the Civil War. (Doc. 66)

Edmonds/Edmunds, Sir Thomas, ?1563–1639: a diplomat employed by Walsingham and the Cecils. He was English agent to Henry IV in Paris in the 1590s and later Queen Elizabeth's Secretary for the French Tongue. An MP in several parliaments, he became ambassador to Brussels in 1605 and corresponded with John Chamberlain. He later became controller of the royal household and a privy councillor, and was MP through the parliaments of the 1620s where he was 'pro government'; he retired from public life in 1629. (Introduction, Doc. 44)

Exeter, Elizabeth Lady: *see* Elizabeth Drury.

Falkland, Viscount: *see* Henry Cary.

Fane, Sir Francis, d.1628; later 1st earl of Westmorland. Son of Sir Thomas Fane of Badsell in Kent, he was KB at the coronation of James I and became earl in 1624. He was married to Elizabeth, second wife and widow of John Lord Darcy, Thomas Lord Darcy's father. His daughter Rachel married Henry Bourchier, earl of Bath (q.v.). (Doc. 7)

Fanshaw, Sir Thomas: the Fanshaws, a catholic family, had land in Derbyshire and Essex, and Thomas's father had bought Ware Park in Hertfordshire. In 1628 he bought Barking manor and abbey. Thomas was surveyor general for James I; he was knighted in 1624. (Doc. 37)

Feilding, William, earl of Denbigh, ?1582–1643: son of Basil Feilding of Warwickshire and his wife Elizabeth, daughter of Sir Walter Aston of Tixall (q.v.). He studied at Emmanuel College, Cambridge and was knighted in 1607; married Susan Villiers (q.v.), sister to George Villiers, later duke of Buckingham. Denbigh's honours followed Buckingham's rise to power, and he was created earl in 1622, when he was also Master of the Great Wardrobe. In 1623 he went to Spain with his brother-in-law and Prince Charles. He was an admiral on several of Buckingham's naval expeditions, and in 1642 a volunteer in Prince Rupert's horse. He died in a skirmish near Birmingham in 1643. (Introduction)

Finch, Dame Elizabeth, 1556–1634: born Elizabeth Heneage, daughter and heir of Sir Thomas Heneage of Copt Hall in Essex, who had been a vice-chamberlain to the household and chancellor of the Duchy of Lancaster. In 1572 she married Sir Moyle Finch, who later became a baronet. She succeeded her father in 1599. Her husband gained many honours and positions, and died in 1614. Elizabeth was left a very rich widow. In 1623 she was created viscountess of Maidstone in her own right, and in 1628 countess of Winchilsea. (Doc. 73)

Finch, Sir John, 1584–1660: a Gray's Inn man who was called to the bar in 1611. He was MP in most parliaments from 1614, and was knighted in 1626, when he also became king's counsel, and attorney general to Queen Henrietta Maria. In 1627/8 he was speaker of the House of Commons and mediator between king and commons. Amongst other tasks he investigated the assassination of Buckingham. He became lord chief justice in 1634, succeeded Thomas Savage as chancellor to Henrietta Maria in 1635, became privy councillor three years later and lord keeper in 1639/40, through the influence of the Queen. (Introduction, Docs 35, 42, 44)

Fitzalan, Henry, 12th earl of Arundel, ?1511–80: his mother was daughter of an Earl Percy and Henry VIII was his godfather. Arundel held high honours under Mary and Elizabeth, and has been seen as the leader of the old nobility and catholic party in government. His only son died early, but his two daughters married, Jane the eldest to John Lord Lumley. He and Lumley were very closely associated for thirty years. Arundel bought Nonsuch from Queen Mary and left it to John Lord Lumley. His younger daughter Mary married Thomas Howard duke of Norfolk and their son Philip Howard inherited the earldom of Arundel in 1580. (Introduction)

Fletcher, Mr: probably the Thomas Fletcher who was reeve of Halton Castle in 1627. There is also a John Fletcher of Weston who was a Rocksavage tenant, and they are perhaps related. This John Fletcher was possibly the John Fletcher gent. of Weston (Runcorn) who died in 1666. (Docs 56, 60)

Forfar, Baron of: *see* Sir Walter Aston.

Fotherley, Thomas: a senior and long-time servant of the duke of Buckingham; he was left £500 in the duke's will, and was one of his executors. (Introduction, Doc. 40)

Freeman, Sir Ralph, d. 1667: at the Middle Temple in 1606. His wife Catherine was a close relative of Buckingham's and Freeman was part of his circle. Appointed a master of requests in ordinary in 1618, served in this capacity until the civil war, and was re-sworn into the role in 1660. MP for Winchelsea in 1625 and 1628. One of the few MPs who was also a gentleman of the bedchamber, so took messages from the Commons to the king. Held a variety of commissions and auditorships, including one which led him to become master of the mint in the later 1630s and early 1640s. A royalist in the civil war. Also published translations from the Greek. Freeman introduced Nicholas Towse (see Windham, below) to the duke of Buckingham 'on a hunting morning at Lambeth Bridge'. Sir Ralph's report of this encounter informed the historian Clarendon's account of Sir George Villiers' ghost. (Docs 35, 44)

Gager, Thomasine, née Cordell, d. 1601: sister to Sir William Cordell. Married first an unknown husband surnamed Watson and then, by the mid 1550s, Gilbert Gager of Melford. William Gager, the Latin dramatist, was her eldest son (q.v.). Her brother in his will left her £26 13s. 4d. a year. Problems existed between Thomasine and her brother, and later between her daughter and son-in-law and Sir William's executors. (Introduction)

Gager, Dr William, 1560–1619: nephew of Sir William Cordell of Melford Hall, son of Thomasine Gager (q.v.). William was a Latin dramatist, a scholar at Westminster, then a student at Christ Church, Oxford. He got his MA in 1580, BCL and DCL in 1589. His Latin plays were successfully performed at Oxford, one in 1592 before the queen. In 1601 he became surrogate to Dr Swale, vicar-general of the diocese of Ely, and in 1606 chancellor of that diocese. Two of his siblings were recusants. (Doc. 4)

Gamull, William: mayor of Chester in 1608 and 1620, as his father had been in 1585. He married before 1606; his wife was one of the Grosvenors of Eaton. He died, still an alderman, in 1643. (Introduction)

Garland, Augustine, gent: possibly the Augustine Garland of Coleman Street, London, attorney, who died in 1637, or perhaps his son the regicide. The younger

Augustine was at Emmanuel College, Cambridge in 1618 and then Lincoln's Inn. When his father died he inherited lands in Essex. In 1648 he became an MP. He was one of the regicides who were not executed; he was imprisoned in the Tower of London. A warrant exists for his transportation to Tangiers in 1664, but it is not known whether he went. (Doc. 68)

Garway, Sir Henry: a draper of Broad Street in London, who became lord mayor in 1639–40, and governor of the East India Company in 1641–3. He was brother-in-law to his predecessor as governor, Sir Christopher Clitherow. Garway built a substantial house at Acton. (Doc. 72)

Gerrard, Gilbert: of Crewood Hall near Kingsley in Cheshire. He is often associated in documents with Sir John Savage, later Earl Rivers. His mother was from the Ireland family (see Thomas Ireland, below). He inherited from his grandfather, a lawyer who served as MP for Chester, as recorder of Chester and as lord chancellor of Ireland. Gilbert wrote in 1639 canvassing support for Earl Rivers' favoured candidates for the Cheshire elections. Made a colonel by Charles I in the civil war; his regiment served at Edgehill and the first battle of Newbury; later he was made governor of Worcester. Not to be confused with another Gilbert Gerrard who was a close associate of William Brereton in Cheshire during the civil war. (Doc. 74)

Glegge, John, of Gleaton: a John Glegge, tanner, who lived outside the city, became a councilman of Chester in 1624; he died not long after Thomas Savage. (Doc. 14)

Glegge, William, of Gleaton: sheriff of Chester in 1624/5. In the Civil war he was a JP, regarded as among the moderates in the 1640s. (Doc. 62)

Gondomar, Diego Sarmiento de, 1567–1626: Spanish ambassador to the court of King James I in 1613–18 and 1620–2. His power over the king and his pro-catholic opinions, made him unpopular. Thomas corresponded with him. He was recalled in 1622 and became a member of the Spanish council of state. (Introduction)

Goring, George, earl of Norwich, ?1583–1663: a student at Sidney Sussex College, Cambridge, went on to serve in Flanders and was knighted in 1608. By 1610 he was a gentleman of the privy chamber to Henry prince of Wales. Later he was involved in the marriage negotiations of Charles and Henrietta Maria, and was created Baron Goring in 1628. He became the queen's vice chamberlain, then her master of horse. He was in favour for the next ten years, and raised funds for the king. Became a privy councillor in 1639, and through the 1640s was estimated to have an income of £26,000 a year. (Docs 35, 44)

Grimston, Harbottle esq, 1603–85: son of an Essex baronet of the same name; at Emmanuel College Cambridge, then Lincolns Inn, where he was called to the bar. By 1628 he was MP for Harwich and he succeeded Coke as recorder for that town; by 1638 he was recorder of Colchester. He was MP for Colchester through the Long Parliament, and by 1642 was deputy lord lieutenant of Essex. He became a judge, was speaker of the House of Commons in 1660 and master of the rolls from that year. (Doc. 77)

Gurney, Sir Richard, 1577–1647: a zealous Royalist who was apprenticed to a silkman of Cheapside. He became a merchant and a liberal benefactor, and made his way in the City hierarchy, becoming an alderman, sheriff of London in 1633 and lord mayor in 1641, when he was knighted; he became a baron later the same year. He was later imprisoned by Parliament and died while incarcerated. (Doc. 59)

Gwynn, Robert: usher to the bishop of Chester, became Yeoman of the Pentice (the Clerk to the Pentice was town clerk of Chester). (Doc. 14)

Hall, Francis, gent, d. 1639: a gentleman who married into Melford in 1627. He was left a small legacy by Thomas Brooke (q.v.). He had landholdings in the town which were inherited by his wife, then his son. Although his occupation is not recorded, he could be the Francis Hall of London, goldsmith, who appraised Thomas Savage's goods. (Docs 60, 66)

Halles, James, gent. of London: unknown, possibly related to Francis Hall, above. (Doc. 66)

Hamilton, Dame Mary, 1613–38: daughter of Lord Fielding (later earl of Denbigh) and his wife Susan Villiers, sister to the duke of Buckingham (both q.v.). She was married aged seven to James Hamilton, 3rd marquess and 1st duke of Hamilton in the Scottish peerage, 2nd earl of Cambridge, who was next heir to the throne of Scotland after the heirs of James VI. Her husband was averse to the marriage contract and for several years the couple were on poor terms. Dame Mary became a lady of the bedchamber to Queen Henrietta Maria, and enjoyed the confidences of both king and queen. (Introduction, Doc. 51)

Hammersley, Sir Hugh, 1565–1636: from a Staffordshire family, he became lord mayor of London in 1627/8. (Doc. 59)

Harcott, William, of Wincham: born 1605, married 1629 and alive in 1669. (Doc. 62)

Hare, Hugh, 1st Lord Coleraine, 1606–67: he inherited a large fortune from a lawyer uncle; created Baron of Coleraine in the Irish peerage in 1625. (Doc. 66)

Hatton, Sir Thomas, 1583–1658: a cousin of Sir Christopher Hatton, lord chancellor to Queen Elizabeth. Thomas was surveyor general to Queen Henrietta Maria but though prominent before the civil war his support for the king was 'to say the least, tepid'. He was married to Mary daughter of a Sir Giles Allington (descended from Jane Allington's husband's brother). Her father was very heavily fined for marrying his own niece. (Docs 42, 44)

Hay, James, earl of Carlisle, ?1612–60: son of James Hay, earl of Carlisle and his first wife, Honora Denny of Waltham. In 1624 he was colonel of a regiment of foot in Germany; KB 1626. He was Viscount Doncaster when in 1632 he married Margaret daughter of the earl of Bedford, and inherited the title Lord Denny of Waltham from his maternal grandfather in 1637. In 1642–6 he was in the royal army as colonel of a regiment of horse. However he lived for much of the civil war in Barbados, which his family had won from William Curteene (q.v.) and returned to England in 1652. (Introduction)

Hay, Lucy, countess of Carlisle, 1599–1660: second daughter of Henry Percy, 9th earl of Northumberland, she married James Hay, earl of Carlisle (q.v.) in 1622 as his second wife. She was celebrated by numerous poets of the period. In the civil war she remained at court, but acted as a spy for Parliament, yet also betrayed Parliament to the royalists. She was arrested in 1649 and sent to the Tower of London, but released the following year. (Doc. 65)

Heath, Sir Robert, 1575–1649: a judge who became lord chief justice of the Common Pleas in 1631. He had been at St John's College, Cambridge, then the Inner Temple, and was called to the bar in 1603. By 1618 he was recorder of London, by 1620 MP for London and a year later he was knighted and made solicitor general. He was very opposed to recusants. (Doc. 25)

Herbert, Charles, Lord Herbert of Shurland, 1619–36: 3rd but only surviving son of the 4th earl of Pembroke (q.v.). KB in 1626 at coronation of Charles I, at Oxford in 1632. Married in 1635, in the Royal Closet at Whitehall, to Mary Villiers, daughter of the 1st duke of Buckingham by his wife Katherine née Manners (both q.v.), who was about 12. He died in Florence. (Docs 47, 63, 65)

Herbert, Philip, 4th earl of Pembroke, 1584–1650: named after his uncle Sir Philip Sidney, Herbert was a royal favourite who married Susan de Vere, daughter of the earl of Oxford, in 1604, when he also became MP. A year earlier he had become a gentleman of the privy chamber, and in 1605 gentleman of the bedchamber; that same year he became Baron Herbert and earl of Montgomery. In 1625 he was sent to France to ensure that Henrietta Maria got to England, and by 1626 was lord chamberlain of the royal household. Four years later he succeeded his brother as earl of Pembroke. At some stage before 1637 Philip Herbert had had an adulterous relationship with the earl of Berkshire's daughter. The Pembrokes' London home was Baynard Castle, on the Thames. Although Pembroke had regularly entertained Charles I at Wilton, he later became a Parliamentarian. (Introduction, Docs 63, 65)

Herbert, William, 3rd earl of Pembroke, 1580–1630: a godson of Queen Elizabeth I, he was at Oxford in 1593 and went on to the royal court, but was banished in 1597 for an affair with a maid of honour. However he recovered his position, and bore the great banner at Elizabeth's funeral. James I made him a gentleman of the privy chamber and KG, and gave him many offices and positions. Was lord chamberlain of the household 1615–26. He carried the crown at the coronation of Charles I. His wife Mary was daughter of Gilbert Talbot 7th earl of Shrewsbury (q.v.). (Introduction)

Holland, earl of: *see* Henry Rich.

Holles, John, 1st earl of Clare, 1564–1637: of Haughton in Nottinghamshire. At Christ's College, Cambridge and then Gray's Inn. He served in the Netherlands, fought against the Armada, in Ireland, in Hungary against the Turks and in Spain with Essex in 1597. He had been knighted in 1593. He served as MP for Nottinghamshire and later became comptroller of the household to Henry, prince of Wales. In 1616 he became Baron Houghton of Houghton (sometimes given as Haughton) and in 1624 earl of Clare. His wife was Anne, daughter of Sir Thomas Stanhope; another possible family connection to Thomas Savage's cousin. Father-in-law to Thomas Wentworth, earl of Strafford. His letters tell us that he was related to Thomas Lord Darcy. (Introduction)

Holt, William, possibly this is the William Holt (of a family from Gristlehurst, Lancashire) who appears in the Visitation of London in 1634. The Lancashire family included a Sir Thomas Holt who was of Gray's Inn, as this William was. Sir Thomas's son, John, became lord chief justice at the end of the seventeenth century. (Doc. 7)

Hopper, Christopher, servant to Lord Lumley, then to his wife, and mentioned in both their wills; a man of this name participated in Thomas Savage's funeral and was owed £150 by him at his death. A chamber in the Tower Hill inventory was called 'Mr Hopper's chamber'. Presumably the same man, but as Lumley died in 1609 could be a son or relative. (Docs 10, 56, 60, 66)

Hough, William: if he was of Thornton Hough in Cheshire, as well as of London, he was related both to the Wilbrahams and the Whitmores – William Whitmore's mother was a Hough. (Doc. 60)

Howard, Catherine, d.1673: daughter of Thomas Howard 1st earl of Suffolk by his second wife Catherine, widow of Richard Rich. In 1608 she married William Cecil, earl of Salisbury. (Doc. 65)

Howard, Charles, Lord Andover, later 2nd earl of Berkshire, ?1615–79: KB in 1626 at the coronation of Charles I. In 1637 Andover married Dorothy Savage, daughter of Thomas and Elizabeth, in a secret catholic ceremony. They had no heirs. MP for Oxford in the Short and Long Parliaments. Gentleman of the bedchamber in 1658, but not re-appointed after the Restoration. He died in Paris cared for by the monks of La Charité. (Introduction, Doc. 65)

Howard, Elizabeth, countess of Berkshire, d. 1672: wife of Thomas, 1st earl of

Berkshire, she was daughter and co-heir of William Cecil, 2nd earl of Exeter and his second wife Elizabeth née Drury (q.v.). (Doc. 65)

Howard, Frances, duchess of Richmond and Lennox: daughter of Thomas Howard, 1st Viscount Howard of Bindon. When she became third wife of Ludovic Stuart (q.v.) she was widow of Edward Seymour, earl of Hertford, whom she had married in 1601. (Doc. 58)

Howard, Thomas, earl of Arundel and Surrey, 1586–1646: great grandson of Henry Fitzalan (q.v.) and grandson of Jane Lumley's sister Mary. His fame was as an art collector rather than as a politician; he has been called 'one of the first and most famous of English connoisseurs'. Travelled widely in Europe, both for himself and in the 1630s in his role as ambassador for Charles I; in 1613–14 he had travelled in Italy with Inigo Jones. In 1638 he was a 'humiliating failure' as captain general of the English army against the Scots. He was married to Aletheia Talbot, one of the daughters of Gilbert Talbot (q.v.). In 1642 he accompanied Princess Mary to the Netherlands for her marriage to William of Orange; he did not return but went on to Padua where he lived until his death. (Doc. 72)

Howard, Thomas, 1st earl of Berkshire, 1587–1669: second son of the earl of Suffolk, and married Elizabeth daughter of William Cecil (q.v.). Made master of the horse to Prince Charles; KG in 1625 and earl of Berkshire in 1626. Related to Elizabeth Savage through the Rich family. (Doc. 65)

Howell, James, ?1594–1666: one of the first Englishmen to make a livelihood out of literature (*DNB*). Educated at Jesus College, Oxford, BA in 1613 and fellow in 1623. Was sent to mainland Europe to obtain materials and workmen for glassmaking and returned to London shortly before his contract with Thomas Savage. Howell travelled widely, but was in the Fleet as a debtor between 1643–51. Some suspect that many of his letters were composed then, rather than at the time they were purported to have been written. Howell became a clerk to the Privy Council and 'Historiographer Royal of England', a post created specially for him. (Introduction, Docs 15, 50)

Hurlestone, John, of Picton, d. 1669: inherited his estate from his father at the age of three. His mother was an heiress of the Massey family, who married as her second husband John Done of Utkinton (q.v.). His wife was daughter to Thomas Wilbraham of Woodhey. Possibly related to the Roger and William Hurleston who are mentioned in Chester City Council minutes. Roger Hurleston had been a good benefactor to the city and his brother William became a freeman. (Doc. 62)

Ireland, Sir Thomas, d. 1634: appointed bailiff-sergeant of Halton Castle in 1611; knighted in 1617 during James I's visit to Lancashire and Cheshire; became attorney general and vice-chamberlain of Chester. The Ireland family was of Bewsey near Warrington. King James stayed at Bewsey immediately before his visit to Rocksavage in 1617. His wife was Margaret Aston, a daughter of Sir Thomas Aston (q.v.). (Doc. 1)

Jeffreys, J.: possibly the John Jeffries esq. mentioned in the Chester city council minutes. (Doc. 1)

Jermyn, Sir Thomas, of Rushbrooke, Suffolk. His eldest son Thomas was second Baron Jermyn and his son Henry, 1604–84, became 1st earl of St Albans, having from 1639 been master of horse to Queen Henrietta Maria and later her lord chamberlain. He had many posts in Charles II's governments after the Restoration. (Doc. 44)

Jones, Inigo, 1573–1652: painter, architect and designer. Born in London, trained probably as a joiner; before 1603 had visited Italy to study painting and design. Was employed at the court of King Christian of Denmark and Norway, then moved back to England to work for that king's sister, Queen Anne, wife of James I of England. From 1615 until 1643 he was the king's surveyor of works. He designed many royal masques and worked on royal properties such as the Queen's House at Greenwich and the Banqueting House in Whitehall. He was involved in the regulation of new buildings in London and planned Covent Garden, the first London square. In 1641 when he was consulted about Tower Hill, he was still involved with the restoration of St Paul's, work which was lost in the great fire. (Introduction, Doc. 72)

Jonson, Ben, ?1573–1637: dramatist and poet. His stepfather was a bricklayer but he was educated at Westminster School (funded by William Camden). After this, to avoid having to train as a bricklayer, he went to the continent and joined an army in Flanders. Returned to London and began working for the stage no later than 1595. Wrote many plays, not all of which survive, but in James I's reign wrote masques for performance at court, often in cooperation with Inigo Jones (q.v.). (Introduction)

Josselin, Revd Ralph, rector of Earls Colne in Essex, diarist. (Introduction)

Juxon, William, bishop of London, 1582–1663: had a successful career at Oxford, including spells as vice-chancellor, before becoming dean of Worcester in 1627 and bishop of London in 1633. In 1636 he was made lord high treasurer of England, the last cleric to hold high secular office with a religious one. He attended Charles I on the scaffold. Was deprived of his bishopric in 1649 but at the Restoration in 1660 was made archbishop of Canterbury. (Doc. 72)

Kelsall, John, of Bridge Trafford gent, d. 1655: this John was grandson of the man who had bought his estate from Sir John Savage in 1550. (Doc. 62)

Killigrew, Sir Robert, 1579–1633: a courtier, as was his father. At Christ Church, Oxford, MP for Cornwall in 1601 and at various times afterwards, knighted in 1603. He became prothonotary of Chancery in 1618, a rewarding office which he held for life. Ambassador to the States General in 1625/6 and vice-chamberlain to Queen Henrietta Maria from 1630. (Doc. 44)

Knowle, Sir Henry: possibly Sir Henry Knolles of Berkshire, knighted in 1605. (Doc. 66)

Kilmorey, Viscount: *see* Needham.

Kitson/Kytson, Lady Elizabeth, d. 1628: née Cornwallis, widow of Sir Thomas Kitson (q.v.), Elizabeth Savage's maternal grandmother. Lived to see her great great grandchildren. (Introduction, Docs 32, 36)

Kitson/Kytson, Sir Thomas, d. 1601: Elizabeth's maternal grandfather. (Introduction)

Laud, William, archbishop of Canterbury, 1573–1645: after attending St John's College, Oxford, he moved academic posts and became a royal chaplain in 1611. During Buckingham's years of importance Laud was his chaplain. Made a privy councillor in 1627, bishop of London the next year and archbishop of Canterbury in 1633. Best remembered for his attempts to move the Church of England towards more ritualism. (Introduction, Docs 65, 66)

Leicester, countess of: *see* Dorothy Sydney.

Leigh/Legh, Henry, esq.: son of Richard Legh of Baggiley/Baguley. Probably Henry Leigh of Baguley who died in 1642, although he was of High Legh in 1636. (Doc. 62)

Leigh, Peter, esq.: could be Peter Leigh of High Legh who died in 1665, or his father who died in 1636. The younger of these two was married to Anne, daughter of Henry Birkenhead (q.v.). There are so many Leighs that it is difficult to distinguish them. (Doc. 62)

Leigh, William, esq. of Booths: presumably the William Leigh of Norbury Booths,

Cheshire who died in 1642, aged forty-two. He inherited from his father in 1621, and served as sheriff of Cheshire in 1636. His mother was née Brereton. (Doc. 62)

Leinster, earl of: *see* Sir Robert Cholmondeley.

Lewknor, Sir Richard: Lewknors from Sussex and Suffolk were knighted in James I's reign. This Sir Richard was probably serjeant-at-law in 1594/5, who was one of two men entrusted by John Lord Lumley with the upbringing and education of his cousin Richard Lumley. A Sir Richard Lewknor had organised the funeral of John Lord Lumley's first wife Jane, in 1577; this was presumably the same man but could have been his father. A Sir Richard Lewknor was chief justice of Chester in 1606. (Doc. 1)

Lindsey, earl of: *see* Robert Bertie.

Littler, Mr, probably Ralph, Richard or John Littler. Richard was a councilman of Chester, and later a 'leavelooker', responsible for collecting the sea customs of the city. Nobody could become sheriff of Chester without having served as leavelooker. He later became Clerk of the Pentice, or town clerk. Richard and John were brothers, sons of Ralph, and were both alive in 1636. The family was of Wallerscote, where they had been established since the time of Edward I; however Ralph sold the estate to Hugh Cholmondeley in 1637. (Doc. 56)

Lumley, Elizabeth Lady, d. 1617: sister to Thomas Lord Darcy, second wife to John Lord Lumley (q.v.); aunt to Elizabeth Savage. (Introduction, Docs 6, 10, 12)

Lumley, Jane Lady, d. 1577: daughter of Henry Fitzalan, earl of Arundel (q.v.). She and John Lord Lumley (q.v.) had children who all died young. She was a highly educated woman, and some of her translations of Greek tragedies survive in the British Library; she is included in the recent *Dictionary of British Classicists*. Her father gave the house on Tower Hill to Jane and her husband in 1575. An illustration of her funeral procession is in this volume, Pl. IV. (Introduction)

Lumley, John Lord, ?1534–1609: his father was executed for high treason in 1537, but a settlement was made so that John was able to inherit from his grandfather, who died in 1544. Three years later he was 'restored in blood' and created Baron Lumley, which honour was limited to his own heirs male. He first married Jane, daughter of Henry Fitzalan, earl of Arundel (q.v.), and was very closely associated with his father-in-law until his death in 1581. Lumley inherited both debts and grandeur from the earl, the latter including Nonsuch Palace. A major figure in Elizabethan England, he married as his second wife Elizabeth Darcy, sister to Thomas Lord Darcy. (Introduction, Docs 1, 2, 6, 10)

Lumley, Sir Richard, 1589–?1663: a relative of John Lord Lumley, from whom he inherited Lumley Castle and many other northern lands in 1609. Knighted in 1616, he was made Viscount Lumley of Waterford in 1628. His second wife Elizabeth was a daughter of Sir William Cornwallis of Brome, sister or half-sister to Sir Frederick Cornwallis (q.v.), and thus related to Elizabeth Savage. Lumley's descendants became earls of Scarborough. (Introduction, Doc. 74)

Mallet/Malet, Thomas esq, later Sir Thomas Malet: Queen Henrietta Maria's solicitor general, he later became a judge of the King's Bench. (Doc. 44)

Mallory, Thomas, dean of Chester cathedral from 1607–44: sixth son of a Yorkshire knight; after study at Cambridge he married a daughter of the bishop of Chester. By 1601 he was rector of Davenham and in 1603 became archdeacon of Richmond. From 1619 he was also rector of Mobberly in Cheshire where he lived until ejected by Parliament in 1642; the family were still connected with the parish in the 1950s. All his positions did not make him rich, presumably because he had at least twelve children. He worked closely with John Bridgeman, bishop of Chester (q.v.). (Doc. 14)

Manchester, earl of : *see* Edward Montagu.

Manners, Cecily, countess of Rutland, d. 1653: daughter of Sir John Tufton of Kent, and sister to the 1st earl of Thanet, she married Francis earl of Rutland as his second wife. (Doc. 47)

Manners, Francis, earl of Rutland, 1578–1632: father of Katherine Manners (q.v.), who married George Villiers, later duke of Buckingham. He and his brothers were implicated in Essex's plot in 1601 but managed to escape with a fine. At the Inner Temple in 1601, then became prominent at court. He was created KB in 1605 when Prince Charles received the same honour. James I visited him at Belvoir six times. He became KG in 1616, on the same day as George Villiers; in the next year he became a privy councillor and in 1623 was admiral of the fleet sent to bring Prince Charles home from Spain. A catholic. (Introduction, Docs 24, 40, 45, 47, 62)

Manners, Sir George, earl of Rutland, ?1580–1641: at Christ's College, Cambridge, then fought in Ireland under Essex, where he was knighted in 1599. Implicated in Essex's plot but managed to be bailed. Served several times as MP for Grantham. Succeeded his brother Francis (q.v.) as earl of Rutland in 1632. (Doc. 47)

Manners, Sir John, d. 1611: brother to Thomas Savage's grandmother. Thomas sold him many of his lands in Derbyshire and Nottinghamshire. (Introduction)

Manners, Katherine, d. 1649: daughter of Francis Manners earl of Rutland (q.v.) and his first wife, Frances daughter of Sir Henry Knyvet. A catholic like all her family, she married George Villiers, marquis and later duke of Buckingham, in 1620. Widowed in 1628. In 1635 she married Randal McDonnell (q.v.), 2nd earl of Antrim. Her daughter by Buckingham, Mall (Mary), married Charles Herbert (q.v.). (Introduction, Docs 38, 45, 47)

Manners, Sir Oliver: younger brother to Francis and George Manners (q.v.); he was knighted at Belvoir Castle, the Rutland home, on 23 April 1603. (Introduction, Doc. 2)

Mainwaring/Manwaring/Maynwaring, John: possibly brother or cousin of Philip, see below. The Mainwaring family of Cheshire was very large with numerous men of the same name. (Doc. 1)

Mainwaring/Manwaring/Maynwaring, Mary: daughter of Elizabeth and Thomas Maynwaring (q.v.), she was grand-daughter of Dame Mary Savage (née Allington) and Thomas's niece; she was thought to be the culprit in the theft of Dame Mary's jewels and plate in 1618. (Introduction)

Mainwaring/Manwaring/Maynwaring, Philip: probably fourth son of Sir Randle Manwaring, bart, of Over Peover. He married Ellen Minshull. He served as MP, was secretary to Thomas Wentworth (q.v.) and important in Irish affairs. Sheriff of Cheshire in 1639. In the civil war he was captain of the light horse in Cheshire; he served as a JP from 1645–7 and as a deputy lieutenant of the county. He was an opponent of William Brereton in Cheshire, being one of the more moderate party. One of Sir Randle's descendants, the baronet who died in 1726, was the 29th male heir of the Manwarings of Peover since the Norman Conquest. (Introduction)

Mainwaring/Manwaring/Maynwaring, Thomas: younger son of Mainwaring of Martin-Sands nigh Over, and related to the Mainwarings of Peover (above), he was first husband of Elizabeth Savage, sister to Thomas. He served Sir John Savage, their father. (Doc. 14)

Maples, Mary: *see* Darcy

Maples, Sir Thomas, d. 1635: second husband of Mary née Darcy, Elizabeth Savage's sister; from Stow Longa in Huntingdonshire. This marriage caused many problems and there are suggestions that Mary was much abused. Sir Thomas was made a baronet in May 1627. Correspondence in the Hengrave MSS suggests that he would have to be financially compensated for his wife leaving him. His will shows that he expected a house, gardens and orchard in Colchester after the death of Lady Rivers, which he tells his executors to sell. (Introduction, Docs 31, 32)

Marbury, Thomas, esq, of Marbury: either Thomas the elder, 1568–1636, or his son. The elder Thomas was also father of William Marbury (q.v.) by a different wife. Thomas the elder's first wife, Eleanor, was daughter of Peter Warburton (q.v.), his second was daughter of John Arderne (q.v.). The younger Thomas was William's heir, and died in 1667; his wife was a daughter of the Brookes of Norton. (Doc. 62)

Marbury, William of Marbury, d. 1645: there had been Marburys at Marbury since the time of Henry III. Like his brother Thomas, he married a daughter of the Brooke family. This William was a deputy lieutenant of Cheshire in the 1640s, and was part of the more moderate group among those who ran the county during the civil war. During 1644 he was one of the men responsible for paying the army while William Brereton, the Parliamentary leader, was away from Cheshire. (Doc. 62)

Martin, Henry, 1602–80: at University College, Oxford and then Gray's Inn before 1620, then travelled abroad. It was not until 1639 that he appears in national politics; the following year he was MP for Berkshire, and one of the most extreme members of the 'popular party'. He energetically opposed Strafford; his activities in parliament led to Charles I calling him a whore-master and wanting to try him for high treason in 1642. He was expelled from Parliament in 1643 but readmitted in 1646; resumed his leadership of the extreme party, and was prominent in the proceedings for the establishment of a republic. Martin was one of the regicides, and was convicted in 1660 but his sentence was suspended; spent the remainder of his life in prison. (Introduction)

May, Sir Humphrey, 1573–1630: politician and lawyer. At John's College, Oxford, then the Middle Temple. He was MP in every parliament from 1605 to his death. Knighted 1613. Chancellor of the Duchy of Lancaster from 1618; in 1625 he became a privy councillor. One of the government's main spokesmen in the Commons in the late 1620s. (Introduction)

McDonnell, Randal, 1609–82, Viscount Dunluce, later 2nd earl of Antrim and marquis of Antrim: mentioned as a possible husband for Dorothy Savage, in 1635 he married Katherine née Manners, duchess of Buckingham. He succeeded his father as earl of Antrim in 1636; fought for Charles I in the civil wars but later crossed to support Cromwell. Because of this he was imprisoned at the Restoration, but his lands were returned to him in 1665; it is suggested that Henrietta Maria, as Queen Mother, was influential in getting his lands restored to him. (Doc. 65)

McGeoghan, Arthur, OP: an Irish Dominican who came to England from Lisbon in 1633. Reported to have said that the king was a heretic and that it was lawful to kill him. Earlier, in Spain, he was heard to say that he would not return to England unless it was to assassinate the king. Executed in late 1633; he 'suffered the extreme penalty, . . . being torn in pieces by horses'. (Introduction)

Mead, Joseph, 1586–1638: a biblical scholar of Christ's College, Cambridge, 'a man of encyclopaedic information', he engaged in extensive correspondence and paid for weekly foreign intelligence. (Introduction)

Medici, Ferdinand, duke of Tuscany, d. 1609: a son of Cosimo Medici. He had been made a cardinal at the age of fifteen, but had never been ordained. When he succeeded his brother as Grand Duke of Tuscany in 1587 he resigned his cardinalate. He died in 1609 so the table may have been made to commemorate his reign. (Doc. 12)

Medici, Mary, queen of France, 1573–1642: daughter of Francis Grand Duke of Tuscany, she married Henry Bourbon in 1600. After her husband's assassination she became Queen Regent of France but she allowed too much influence to two Florentine 'adventurers', and her son Louis XIII caused one of them to be assassinated. Mary was exiled to Blois but escaped through Angoulême in 1617. Mother of Henrietta Maria (q.v.), she visited London on occasions, which caused problems in both France and England. (Doc. 45)

Meoles, Thomas, of Wallesey, esq. d. 1640: his family had been established at Meols in Cheshire since the time of Henry III, but Thomas had married a widow who came from Wallesey and appears to have lived there. (Doc. 62)

Middlesex, Earl of: *see* Lionel Cranfield.

Middleton, Timothy, esq.: appears in the king's indenture with the copperas makers. This may be a son of Sir Thomas Myddleton who was lord mayor of London and died in 1631. (Doc. 68)

Mills, William, d.1608: clerk to the Star Chamber; when he died the position went to Sir Francis Bacon. (Introduction)

Milton, John, 1606–74: poet. At Cambridge when he wrote his epitaph to Jane marchioness of Winchester. Earlier at St Paul's School, and is said to have been a poet from the age of ten. He was at Christ's College, Cambridge from 1625, BA in 1629 and MA in 1632. He went on to write poetry, pamphlets and political tracts, and to support Parliament and the Commonwealth. Blind from around 1651. Arrested after the Restoration but released, and went on to publish 'Paradise Lost' and other works. Thought of now as one of the greatest poets in the English language. (Introduction)

Minshall, John, members of this family were amongst the Cheshire élite, and were related to the Savages by an earlier marriage. This John is probably the one who lived 1582–1654 and married Francis daughter of Sir John Egerton. His children were all daughters; one married into the Cholmondeley family. (Docs 24, 56)

Mitchell, Robert, clerk to the town clerk of the city of London from at least 1615, deputy town clerk from 1630 and town clerk 1642–9. Made a freeman of the city through the Draper's Company on 21 November 1615. In 1627 he was granted the benefit of selling two freedoms of the city because of his 'ymploym[en]te and attendance' in the business of ship moneys: CLRO records. (Doc. 59)

Molyneux, Richard, of Sefton in Lancashire, later Viscount Molyneux of Maryborough, in the Queen's County, 1593–1636: listed as attending Thomas Savage's funeral. An Oxford man who was knighted in 1613, was MP for Wigan and other places. He served as recorder of the Duchy of Lancaster, became a baronet in 1622 and viscount at the end of 1628. (Doc. 56)

Montague, Edward, 1602–71, later 2nd earl of Manchester: at Sidney Sussex College, Cambridge in 1618, and MP for Huntingdon several times in the 1620s. Went to Spain with Prince Charles and Buckingham in 1623, made KB at Charles I's coronation. His first wife was a cousin of the duke of Buckingham; they married in the king's bedchamber in 1623. Through Buckingham's influence he became Baron Montague of Kimbolton in 1626. His second wife was daughter of the earl of Warwick, who leaned towards the puritans and from 1640 onwards Montague aligned himself with Parliament. (Doc. 45)

Montagu, Richard, 1577–1641: at Eton and then Cambridge, became dean of Hereford and then chaplain to James I. A defender of the Anglican faith, he argued that taxation is a matter of divine right. He was much attacked in the Commons, so presumably appreciated peers who defended him. He became bishop of Chichester in 1628, negotiated with the papacy for Charles I in 1635 and was made bishop of Norwich in 1638. (Introduction)

Morley and Monteagle, Lords: *see* Henry Parker and William Parker.

Mountjoy, Lord: *see* Charles Blount.

Needham, Sir Robert, later Viscount Kilmorley: one of a long established Cheshire family, his mother was one of the Astons of Tixall (q.v.). He married Eleanor daughter of Thomas Dutton of Dutton, another of the Cheshire élite families. Made Viscount Kilmorley in the peerage of Ireland in 1625. The Savages and Needhams had been closely related by marriage in the fifteenth century. (Doc. 56)

Nicholas, Sir Edward, 1593–1669: at Queen's College, Oxford and then the Middle Temple. He spent time in France and then in 1618 became secretary to Lord Zouche, warden of the Cinque ports. Zouche resigned in Buckingham's favour, and from 1624 Nicholas was Buckingham's secretary for the business of the Cinque ports and his office of high admiral of England. By 1625 he was secretary for the Admiralty and a year later a clerk of the Privy Council. Became MP for Dover in 1627/8. Buckingham left him a legacy of £500. He eventually became principal secretary of state to both Charles I and Charles II. (Introduction, Docs 28, 34, 46)

Norreys/Norris, Sir William, d. 1579: a descendant of the Sir Henry Norreys who was beheaded for his relationship with Anne Boleyn and son of the Sir Henry who had been Princess Elizabeth's guardian at Woodstock, and later her ambassador to France. He was with the earl of Essex in Ulster in 1574 and later became marshal of Berwick. He returned to Ireland and died of a fever in Newry on Christmas Day. His son became earl of Berkshire. (Introduction)

North, Sir John: probably son of another Sir John who died in 1597; this would make him brother of Roger North, the navigator. (Doc. 66)

Norwich, earl of: *see* George Lord Goring.

Noye, William, 1577–1634: a Cornishman who was at Exeter College, Oxford and then at Lincoln's Inn in 1594. Called to the bar in 1602 and kept up his role within Lincoln's Inn until his death. 'His rise in his profession was slow, and was not achieved without intense and unremitting application'. He was MP for Cornish seats from 1604 onwards, when he was also acting as steward for Thomas Savage. During the 1620s he led opposition to the court party on several occasions, so his becoming attorney general in late 1631 led to 'no little surprise'. He is reported to have asked what the wages were and to have hesitated before he accepted the post. Very unpopular with many, for he revived the forest laws, instigated a soap monopoly and was behind the introduction of ship money. He died in 1634 at 'his house in Brentford', which he was leasing from Thomas Savage. (Introduction, Docs 8, 10, 11, 24, 50, 60, 62)

Nuttall, John of Cattenall: there had been Nuttalls (or Nuthalls) at Cattenall in Cheshire since the early 16th century. This John was born around 1578 and was still alive in 1642. (Doc. 62)

Oldfield, Somerford, esq. 1604–74: the Oldfields were a prominent Cheshire family who held Somerford Hall. His mother Mary Somerford, heir of that family, had married Philip Oldfield of Bradwall in 1600. She was the Mrs Mary Oldfield for whom Francis Pilkington wrote a galliard. It was either this man or his son Somerford who was chief sergeant at law of Cheshire in the 1670s. (Doc. 62)

Olivares, Gaspar de Guzman Pimental, de Conde-Duque, 1587–1645: born in Rome, where his father was Spanish ambassador. As a second son he started preparing for the priesthood and studied at the University of Salamanca from 1601–4. However his older brother died and Olivares inherited the family lands and money. He married in 1607 a woman who was both his cousin and his neice. He became one of six personal attendants to Prince Philip in 1615; when in 1621 the prince became king Olivares became his chief minister, a position he maintained until 1643. (Introduction)

Oliver, Richard: a senior and trusted servant of the duke of Buckingham; was left £1000 in the duke's will and became one of his executors. (Introduction, Doc. 40)

O'Neill, Hugh, ?1540–1616: 3rd baron of Dungannon and (in 1585) 2nd earl of Tyrone. Reputed to be grandson of Con, 1st earl of Tyrone. This O'Neill spent many years working to become 'the' O'Neill of Ireland, and succeeded in 1593. Had spent time at Queen Elizabeth's court but later led armed opposition to the English in Ireland, which led to the war in Ireland fought by O'Neill and the Spanish against English troops led first by the earl of Essex and later by Lord Mountjoy. O'Neill surrendered to Mountjoy in 1603 at Mellifont, County Louth. (Introduction)

Owen, George, York Herald: often confused (says the *DNB*) with his father of the same name, who was county historian of Pembrokeshire. This George was appointed Rouge Croix in 1626 and York Herald in December 1633. He was later with Charles I at Oxford. (Doc. 56)

Parker, Catherine: *see* Catherine Savage.

Parker, Elizabeth, Lady Morley, d. 1648: widow of William Parker (q.v.). Daughter of Sir Thomas Tresham of Rushton, Northants and sister to Francis Tresham, one of the Gunpowder Plotters. Convicted as a recusant in 1625, the year in which her daughter Catherine (q.v.) married Thomas and Elizabeth's eldest son, John, later Earl Rivers. (Introduction, Doc. 24)

Parker, Henry, Lord Morley and Monteagle, d. 1655: eldest son of William Parker (q.v.); received the KB when Charles became prince of Wales in 1616. He was vice-admiral of the fleet which brought Charles and Buckingham home from Spain in 1623. (Doc. 24)

Parker, William, 4th Baron Monteagle and 11th Baron Morley, 1575–1622: widely known for his role in foiling the gunpowder plot in 1605. Married Elizabeth daughter of Sir Thomas Tresham (q.v.), and was very close to leading catholic families. (Introduction, Doc. 24)

Paule, Sir George, ?1563–1637: a servant of Archbishop Whitgift, the comptroller of his household and finally his biographer. Paule was MP in 1597, and knighted in 1607. He came to the attention of Buckingham, and through him obtained legal work for the crown; he was chief clerk for the inrolling of pleas. In 1623–4 and 1628 he was a member of the commission which examined Buckingham's estate and revenues. He was MP again in 1625 and 1627/8. (Doc. 22)

Paulet, John, 5th marquis of Winchester, earlier known as Lord Paulet, then Lord St John, 1598–1675: third but eldest surviving son of the 3rd marquis, Paulet was at Exeter College, Oxford, and then in 1620 became MP for St Ives. In 1622 he married Thomas's and Elizabeth's eldest daughter Jane (q.v.). He succeeded as marquis in 1629 but lived in comparative seclusion in an effort to pay off his father's debts. His wife died in 1631 and he married twice more. Best remembered for the defence of his home at Basing House in the Civil War. (Introduction, Docs 23, 57, 58)

Paulet, William, 4th marquis of Winchester, earlier known as Lord Paulet, then Lord St John, d. 1629: lord steward for the funeral of Mary queen of Scots. In 1601 he entertained Queen Elizabeth very lavishly at Basing House for three days, and caused long-term financial problems for the family. His wife Lucy was a daughter of Thomas Cecil, earl of Exeter. (Introduction, Doc. 23)

Pembroke, earl of: *see* Philip Herbert.

Pennington, Sir John, ?1568–1646: sailor, eventually admiral. First appears as captain of his own ship during Sir Walter Raleigh's voyage to Orinoco in 1617. He had recommendations from Buckingham, and in 1620 was a captain in service to the crown. Was captain of the Victory which took Count Gondomar, the Spanish ambassador, home to Spain. In 1626 as admiral of a squadron in the downs, captured some 20 ships which were sold, so managing to pay his sailors. (Doc. 40)

Percy, Algernon, later earl of Northumberland, 1602–68: his father's third son but surviving heir. Queen Elizabeth was his godmother (by proxy). At St John's College, Cambridge in 1615, made KB the following year. Served as MP on several occasions in the 1620s. Became master of the horse to Queen Henrietta Maria in 1626, when he took his seat in the Lords as Baron Percy; privy councillor in 1636. Succeeded his father as earl of Northumberland in 1632. Became involved with the navy, and lord high admiral of England, but gave this honour up when he supported Parliament in the Civil Wars. However he supported the Restoration. (Doc. 35)

Phesant, Peter, gent, ?1580–1649: son of a barrister of the same name, he followed his father to Gray's Inn, and was called to the bar in 1608. Rose in the legal hierarchy and became a recorder in 1624. In 1640 he became deputy of the sergeant-at-law, and the next year justice of assize in Nottinghamshire. He lived at Upwood near Ramsey in Huntingdonshire. (Doc. 59)

Philip IV, king of Spain, 1605–65: succeeded his father Philip III in 1621 at the age of sixteen; the first twenty-two years of his reign were dominated by his chief minister, the Conde-Duque Olivares (q.v.). Olivares was attempting to restore Spanish hegemony in Europe, and to defeat the Dutch. Philip's first wife was Elizabeth, daughter of Henry IV of France and sister to Henrietta Maria, queen of England; his second wife was Maria Anna daughter of the Holy Roman Emperor. He was a noted patron of the arts, particularly of Velazquez. (Introduction)

Pickering John, gent: a document of 1633 says he was 'servant to the right honorable the Lord Viscount Savage, and receyver of his lordshipps revenewes in the county of Chester'. He apparently continued working for the family after Thomas's death, as his name appears on the indenture whereby Earl Rivers leased Melford Hall to Sir John Cordell. (Docs 56, 74)

Portland, earl of: *see* Richard Weston.

Pory, John, ?1570–1635: a traveller and geographer. Was at Gonville and Caius College, Cambridge, and took his MA in 1595. To some extent a pupil of Richard Hakluyt, and translated a number of works on history and geography. In 1605 he was MP but he travelled widely, visiting Constantinople and America. Corresponded with Joseph Mead and others and made his living writing newsletters; prominent among the 'Paul's walkers' who picked up news and intelligence at St Pauls. (Introduction)

Pye, Sir Robert, 1585–1662: a close ally of Buckingham. Remembrancer of the exchequer in 1618, knighted in 1621. Acted with Thomas Savage in many matters related to Buckingham, including as executor. Owned Faringdon House in Berkshire. Pye represented Woodstock in the Long Parliament and he 'remained at Westminster after the breach with the king and passed for a thoroughgoing supporter of Parliament'. His son Robert married Ann daughter of John Hampden; they lived together sixty years and died within weeks of each other in 1701. (Introduction, Docs 22, 40, 66)

Pye, Sir Walter, 1571–1635: called to the bar in 1597. From a family long established in Mynd, Herefordshire. Buckingham helped him to the post of attorney of the Court of Wards, which he held from 1621–35. Said to be one of the richest men in England. Most of the Pye references in documents involving Thomas relate to Sir Robert, but some could refer to Sir Walter.

Ratcliffe, John, d. 1633: alderman of Chester, mayor in 1611–12 and 1628–9, and elected as MP for that city in 1620. (Introduction)

Remington, Sir Robert: knighted at Cadiz in 1596, he later married Elinor, widow of the Sir John Savage who died in 1597 (q.v.), Thomas's grandfather. (Doc. 1)

Remington, Lady Elinor, née Cotgrave: widow of the Sir John Savage who died in 1597. She brought into the Savage family extensive lands in Southampton and Hampshire which went to Edward Savage, her husband's younger son and uncle to Thomas. (Doc. 1)

Rich, Henry, 2nd earl of Holland, 1590–1649: second cousin to Elizabeth Savage, both were descended from the 1st Baron Rich. Henry was at Emmanuel College, Cambridge, made KB in 1610 when Prince Henry became prince of Wales. By 1610 he was also an MP. In 1624 he became Baron Kensington, and ambassador to Paris; later that year made Earl Holland and a year later a privy councillor. Was high steward to Queen Henrietta Maria from 1629–48, and chancellor of the university of Cambridge for the same period. Many other roles and honours. Beheaded in 1649. (Introduction, Docs 35, 42, 44, 78)

Rivers, earl: *see* Thomas Darcy and John Savage.

Rivers, countess: *see* Mary Darcy, Mary Savage, Elizabeth Savage and Catherine Savage.

Rous, Revd John: after studying at Emmanuel College, Cambridge, returned to Suffolk to become incumbent of Santon Downham, where he served from 1625–43; his father was rector of a neighbouring larger parish. Rous's diary includes military and foreign news as well as notes of more general national and local happenings, plus a collection of satirical verse. (Introduction)

Rudges, William, of London. When John Earl Rivers surrendered Halton Castle to Henry Brooks, many of the earl's belongings were taken from him to be held until he paid his fines. Instead Brooks sold much to Rudges. (Doc. 81)

Russell, Lucy, countess of Bedford, née Harrington, d. 1627: daughter of Sir John Harrington of Exton, she married Edward Russell earl of Bedford in 1594. Her husband was fined £10,000 after having taken part in Essex's rebellion. (Introduction)

Rutland, earls of: *see* Manners.

Ryley, William, d. 1667: son of a herald, and a herald and archivist himself. After being a student at the Middle Temple, he moved to the Tower of London to become clerk of the records under the Garter King of Arms, keeper of the archives. He worked at the Tower until his death. In 1633 was made Bluemantle pursuivant of arms and in 1641 Lancaster herald. Became a Parliamentarian and in 1646 Norroy King of Arms. (Doc. 57)

Sackville, Edward, 4th earl of Dorset, 1591–1652: apparently one of the handsomest men of his time; educated at Christ Church Oxford. In 1613 he killed Lord Kinloss in a duel, but became MP the next year. Had a relationship with Venetia Stanley, afterwards wife of Sir Kenelm Digby. Was a military man who became ambassador to France. In 1624 he succeeded his brother, and spent the rest of his life trying to pay off his brother's debts. KG in 1625 and a privy councillor the next year. In 1628 became lord chamberlain to Queen Henrietta Maria, and went on to gain many more roles and honours. His wife was governess of the young princes from 1630. (Introduction, Docs 42, 44, 72)

Salisbury, earl of: *see* Robert Cecil and William Cecil.

Salisbury, Lady: *see* Catherine Howard.

Savage, Anne, 1617–96: daughter of Thomas and Elizabeth; in 1661 married Sir Robert Brudenell (see Lord Thomas Brudenell) as his second wife. Her husband became earl of Cardigan in 1663. (Docs 57, 62)

Savage, Sir Arthur, knight: of Cardington, Beds, and of Rhebane, Co Kildare, vice treasurer of Ireland at several times; related to Thomas Savage through shared great great grandparents; knighted at Cadiz in 1596; died March 1634, in the Fleet prison (presumably for debt). Had a son Sir Thomas (who might have been the one knighted in 1617), and a daughter who was ancestress of the earls of Rosse. (Introduction)

Savage, Catherine, née Parker, later Viscountess Savage and Countess Rivers; 1st wife to Sir John Savage, eldest son of Thomas and Elizabeth. Daughter of William and Elizabeth Parker (both q.v.) and mother of the third Earl Rivers. Her date of death is unknown, but Earl Rivers had married again before 1647. (Introduction, Docs 24, 57, 62, 74)

Savage, Charles: seventh and youngest surviving son of Thomas and Elizabeth, born *c.* 1622. Sent to the catholic college at Lisbon in 1640 and left for France in 1643. Had a daughter, but no record of his marriage has been found. (Introduction, Docs 57, 71)

Savage, Dorothy, ?1611–91: second daughter of Thomas and Elizabeth. Charles I tried to arrange a marriage for her in 1636; a year later she married Charles Howard, Lord Andover (q.v.) in the face of much opposition from his family and hers. Died at Ewelme, Oxfordshire, in 1691 aged eighty. Her portrait by Van Dyck is in this volume, Pl. III. (Introduction, Docs 57, 60, 62, 63, 65)

Savage, Edward, grandson of the Sir John Savage who died in 1597, cousin to Thomas. His father, also Edward, was younger brother to Thomas's father. This older Edward inherited the Savage lands at Beaurepaire, Hampshire, which Sir John (d. 1597) had received from his second wife, but lost them to his step-mother's family before 1618. The older Edward was an MP several times, and died in 1622. Edward junior was present at Thomas's funeral and acted in partnership with Elizabeth in many of her businesses. Associated with Edmund Windham from the mid 1620s at the latest. Presumably younger brother of Sir John Savage of Bradley, Southamptonshire (q.v.). (Docs 7, 56, 68)

Savage, Elizabeth, née Darcy, Viscountess Savage, later Countess Rivers, ?1580–1651: wife of Thomas Viscount Savage and one of the principal subjects of this book. (Introduction and many documents)

Savage, Elizabeth: daughter of Sir John Savage and his wife Mary née Allington, sister to Thomas Savage. Left £700 by her grandmother Jane Allington. She married first Thomas Mainwaring and afterwards Ralph Done (both q.v.). She was the main beneficiary of her mother's will in 1635. (Doc. 4)

Savage, Elizabeth, third daughter of Thomas and Elizabeth, born 1612: she took part in court masques with her sister Dorothy before she married Sir John Thimbleby of Lincolnshire, which was before August 1635. In 1645 she was assessed, by the Committee for the Advance of Money, as worth £1500 a year. Her portrait by Van Dyck is in this volume, Pl. III. She was alive in 1655, with an adult son. (Introduction, Doc. 57)

Savage, Francis, third son of Thomas and Elizabeth, born before 1609: lived in Paris in the early 1640s. Probably the Mr Francis Savage living in Acton near Long Melford, Suffolk in 1663. Richard Savage who sued Sir Robert Cordell for his inheritance of £100 a year from the Melford estates in 1668 may be his son. (Docs 24, 57, 77)

Savage, Grace: *see* Grace Wilbraham.

Savage, Henrietta Maria, later Sheldon, d. 1663: youngest surviving daughter of Thomas and Elizabeth, probably born around 1621. In 1645 she married Ralph Sheldon of Beoley in Worcestershire and Weston in Warwickshire (q.v.). The family was recusant, but are famous for introducing tapestry weaving into England in the sixteenth century. The couple had no children. Her portrait is in this volume, Pl. 1. (Introduction, Docs 57, 62)

Savage, James, 1609–38: buried in the chancel of St Olave's Hart Street, fourth son of Thomas and Elizabeth; he died without any children. (Docs 56, 57, 60)

Savage, Jane, later Lady St John and marchioness of Winchester, ?1604–31: eldest daughter of Thomas and Elizabeth, married John Paulet (q.v.) in 1622 and died nine years later. Her son Charles became 1st earl of Bolton. Jonson and Milton are the best known of at least five poets who wrote epitaphs or elegies on her death. (Introduction, Docs 23, 45, 57)

Savage, John, d. 1609: younger brother of Thomas; murdered by Ralph Bathurst. (Introduction)

Savage, John, illegitimate son of Sir John Savage, Thomas's father; known as John Savage of Barrow. It is likely to be this John Savage who is MP in the 1620s, not Thomas's eldest son. (Doc. 56)

Savage, John, Mr: a number of 'Mr' John Savage's could have been at Thomas's funeral; he could have been, for example, Thomas's illegitimate half-brother John (q.v.), or the son of Sir Arthur Savage (q.v.). (Doc. 56).

Savage, Sir John, d. 1597: Thomas's grandfather and a major figure in the governance of Tudor Cheshire; served seven times as sheriff of Cheshire and three times as mayor of Chester. In the 1560s he built Rocksavage on the site of the older Clifton as his family home. His first wife was Elizabeth Manners, daughter to the earl of Rutland. (Introduction)

Savage, Sir John, d. 1615: Thomas's father, son of Sir John Savage and Elizabeth Manners, daughter of the earl of Rutland. Married Mary Allington in the late 1570s. Lived a quieter, less public life than his father or his eldest surviving son Thomas, but served as an MP on several occasions. Was not knighted until 1599; was mayor of Chester in 1607 and high sheriff of Cheshire. (Introduction, Docs 1, 3, 4, 5, 9, 14)

Savage, Sir John, later Earl Rivers, 1603–54: eldest son of Thomas and Elizabeth, knighted in 1624 at Belvoir; succeeded his father as Viscount Savage in late 1635, and became Earl Rivers on the death of his grandfather six years later. Fought as a royalist in the civil war. Married twice; his first wife was Catherine Parker, his second Mary Ogle (both q.v.). (Introduction, Docs 9, 24, 55, 56, 57, 62, 72, 74, 83)

Savage, Sir John: the person taking part in Thomas's funeral procession is not likely to have been his eldest son, who would have become Viscount Savage at his father's death and would have been principal mourner; most likely to be Sir John Savage from Hampshire, the brother of Edward Savage (q.v.), and Thomas's cousin. This John was a knight by 1627, when his quarrel over the manor of Bradley in Hampshire was mentioned in the privy council. A law suit followed and William Noye was counsel to his opponent. This Sir John's father, also Edward, was second son of the Sir John Savage who died in 1597, and inherited lands in Hampshire. (Doc. 56)

Savage, Katherine, born 1620: daughter of Thomas and Elizabeth; it is reported that she became a nun. (Docs 57, 62)

Savage, Mary, née Ogle, Countess Rivers. Daughter of Thomas Ogle and a member of one of the major families of Northumberland; the Ogles could trace their roots to before the Norman Conquest. Second wife of Thomas's and Elizabeth's eldest son John, Earl Rivers. It is not known when John's first wife died, but Mary was married to him by 1647. She had earlier been one of Elizabeth Savage's attendants. She had one son, Peter. (Docs 81, 82)

Savage, Dame Mary, d. 1635: daughter of Richard and Jane Allington, wife of Sir John Savage (q.v.); after his death in 1615 she lived at Bostock in Cheshire, apart from a visit to London in 1618. Buried at Macclesfield on the same day as her son Thomas Viscount Savage. (Introduction, Docs 4, 5, 8, 9, 14)

Savage, Richard, son of Thomas and Elizabeth, baptised in 1622 but records at the catholic college at Lisbon suggest that he was born in 1620: sent to Lisbon with his younger brother Charles (q.v.) but was sent away because he could not be controlled. (Introduction, Docs 57, 71)

Savage, Thomas, Viscount, ?1579–1635: one of the principal subjects of this book. (Introduction and many documents)

Savage, Sir Thomas, second son of Thomas and Elizabeth; in 1624 married Bridget Whitmore granddaughter of Sir Hugh Beeston of Beeston Castle; she was widow of a son of the earl of Worcester. A number of Thomas Savages were knighted, including one at Belvoir in 1621; although he would have been rather young, and knighted before his elder brother, he seems the most likely candidate. (Introduction, Docs 19, 20, 21, 57, 62)

Savage, William, one of the younger sons of Sir John Savage and his wife Mary née Allington: was left a bequest by his grandmother Jane Allington in her will of 1602. Many available genealogies of the Savage family suggest that the Thomas Savage who was an early settler in New England was son of this William; however this Thomas's father was a blacksmith, which seems unlikely for the son of a Cheshire baronet. (Docs 4, 57)

Savage, William, born 1619; fifth son of Thomas and Elizabeth. (Introduction, Doc. 57)

Sheldon, Ralph, 1623–84: son of William Sheldon of Beoley in Worcestershire; the family were described as 'ancient, gentile and wealthy'; they were also catholic. A predecessor of the mid-sixteenth century had brought the art of tapestry-weaving to England and Sheldon tapestries are famous. Educated at home by the family priest; then during the civil war travelled in France and Italy, staying principally in Rome. In 1645 he returned to England to marry Henrietta Maria Savage, youngest daughter of Thomas and Elizabeth. During the second civil war he was involved with Charles's escapade up an oak tree, and after 1660 was nominated by Charles II as a member of the 'Order of the Royal Oak' – which order never came into being. His wife died in 1663. Sheldon then spent his money on building up his library and his work as an antiquary, for which he is still remembered. He was 'an honest and good man, of remarkable integrity, charitable to the last degree and a munificent favourer of learning and learned men'; was so widely renowned in Warwickshire and Worcestershire that he was called 'the Great Sheldon'. He left a remarkable collection of genealogical material to the College of Arms. (Introduction)

Shrewsbury, earls of: *see* Gilbert Talbot and John Talbot.

Slingesby, Sir William, possibly from the Slingesby family of Yorkshire who feature in the Talbot papers. (Doc. 66)

Smith, Richard, bishop of Chalcedon, 1566–1655: became a catholic while at Oxford. In 1586 went to the English College at Rome where he was ordained. Took his doctorate in Spain and later taught philosophy there. Returned to England in 1603 and soon became involved in disputes between regular and secular clergy. Head of a small college of English priests in Paris from 1613–31. In 1625 he was chosen vicar-apostolic for England and Scotland, was consecrated bishop of Chalcedon and returned to England. Lived mainly at the Bedfordshire home of Viscount Montague. Became involved in controversy within the catholic community about his rights as a bishop; this brought him to the notice of the government and he only escaped arrest by living in the French embassy. By 1629 he had returned to

France, where, during his dispute with the pope, he was protected by Cardinal Richelieu. (Introduction)

Somerset, Edward, 4th earl of Worcester, 1550–1628: his wife was Elizabeth Hastings, daughter of the earl of Huntingdon. Worcester was Queen Elizabeth's ambassador to Scotland in 1590. Their fifth son married Bridget Whitmore, grand-daughter of Sir Hugh Beeston (q.v.), but he died young and without children. His widow then married Thomas's and Elizabeth's second son Sir Thomas Savage. Another son married a daughter of Sir Walter Aston (q.v.) and became a brother-in-law of Elizabeth Thimbleby née Savage (q.v. as Elizabeth Savage). (Introduction)

Somerset, Edward, Lord Herbert of Raglan: son of the 5th earl of Worcester, and later 2nd marquis of Worcester, very rich leader of the catholic interest in London, and close to the Jesuits in the capital. He was the Lord Herbert who King Charles suggested might marry Doll Savage. Worcester House in the Strand has been described as a centre for London catholics. Edward Somerset was cousin to Sir John Winter (q.v.), who became Henrietta Maria's secretary. Edward's first wife died in 1635 and he married again in 1639. In 1640 the king called upon him to supply 2000 men to fight the Scots. (Doc. 63)

Somerset, Henry, 5th earl of Worcester, 1577–1646: from a very rich catholic family, based at Raglan Castle and in London. Raglan served as the Jesuit base in Wales. Thomas Savage was related to the Somersets both through Thomas's great grandmother, and through his daughter-in-law Bridget née Whitmore, who had been first married to a son of the 4th earl. The Somerset family provided extensive funding to Charles I, allowing him to pay for an army in 1641–2; Henry is reported to have given the enormous sum of £1,000,000. (Introduction, Docs 63, 65)

Squire, Nicholas, d. 1630: a servant mentioned by Jane Allington in her will of 1602, who later became housekeeper of Rocksavage until his death; many of his accounts survive. He was married and his wife had care of much of the linen in the house. (Introduction, Doc. 4)

St Albans, viscount: *see* Francis Bacon.

St Albans, earl of: *see* Thomas Jermyn.

St John, Lady: *see* Jane Savage.

St John, Lord: *see* John Paulet, William Paulet.

Stanhope, Sir John, d. 1611: of Shelford in Nottinghamshire. Married as his first wife Cordell Allington, younger daughter of Richard and Jane Allington (q.v.); they were parents of Sir Philip Stanhope (q.v.). Probably knighted in 1596 but others of the same name were knighted in 1603 and 1607. His niece Ann married John Holles, later earl of Clare (q.v.). (Docs 4, 5, 8)

Stanhope, Sir Philip, later 1st earl of Chesterfield, 1584–1656: cousin of Thomas Savage; their mothers were sisters and Jane Allington (q.v.) their common grandmother, from whom both inherited. Fought on the king's side in the civil war and had his estates sequestered. Married twice; the earls of Chesterfield are descended from children of his first wife, and the earls of Stanhope from his son by his second wife. (Introduction, Docs 4, 5, 8)

Stanley, James, Lord Strange, 1607–51: eldest son of William Stanley earl of Derby. The Stanleys were hereditary lords lieutenants of Lancashire and Cheshire. Lord Strange's grandmother was a Kytson of Hengrave, his mother a de Vere; this meant that he was related to Elizabeth Savage on both her paternal and maternal sides. From 1626 Strange shared with his father the roles of lord lieutenant of Lancashire and Cheshire and chamberlain of the county Palatine of Cheshire. He later became earl of Derby. He was a royalist and executed at Bolton. (Introduction)

Stanley, William, 1561–1642: succeeded his brother as earl of Derby. At Oxford, then Lincoln's Inn; KG in 1601. Many honours relating to Lancashire and Cheshire including being the lord lieutenant 1607–26 and jointly with his son 1626–42. Bought from his nieces the hereditary family lordship of the Isle of Man, where he spent much of his time. His wife Elizabeth was a de Vere, daughter of an earl of Oxford and Anne Cecil, daughter of William Cecil, Lord Burghley. (Introduction, Doc. 33)

Stafford, Sir Thomas, knighted at Dublin in 1611 by the lord deputy of Ireland. (Doc. 35)

Strafford, earl of: *see* Thomas Wentworth.

Stuart, Charles, King Charles I, 1600–49: second son of James I and his wife Anne of Denmark, became heir to the throne on the death of his elder brother Henry in 1612. In 1623 he accompanied his father's favourite, the duke of Buckingham, to Spain to negotiate a marriage with the Infanta. This failed and both he and Buckingham later argued for war against Spain. Charles became king in 1625, and married Henrietta Maria Bourbon, sister of the king of France. His reign ended in civil war with Parliament. Executed in 1649. (Introduction, Docs 16, 23, 33, 43, 47, 48, 52, 53, 61, 62, 63, 65)

Stuart, Esmé, 3rd duke of Lennox, 1579–1624: succeeded his brother in 1623 but died the following year. He was second son of the 1st duke of Lennox, who was very influential in the upbringing of James IV of Scotland. When James came to England in 1603, Esmé's brother Ludovic (q.v.) was amongst his most powerful Scottish nobles. Esmé was married to Katherine Baroness Clifton, who survived him and died in 1637. Doc. 58 is a letter to the duchess of Richmond, who may be Esmé's widow but is more likely to be Francis Howard, widow of his brother Ludovic, the second duke.

Stuart, Henrietta Maria, née Bourbon, queen of England, 1609–69: daughter of King Henry IV of France and his wife Marie de Medici. Married Charles I in 1625 when she was 16. For her first two years as queen she had a mainly French entourage but was forced to accept an English household in 1628. Even so, her household was a centre of catholic influence at court. Spent time in England and abroad during the civil war raising funds; remained out of the country after Charles I's execution. Returned to England when her son became King Charles II but did not stay. (Introduction, Docs 23, 35, 39, 42, 44, 45, 48, 62, 65)

Stuart, Henry, prince of Wales, 1594–1612: eldest son of James I and his wife Queen Anne of Denmark. Had his own household from 1603, when he also was admitted to the Order of the Garter. Was highly educated and showed much promise. Spent a considerable amount of time at Nonsuch, where the Lumleys were still living. (Introduction)

Stuart, James, King James IV of Scotland and James I of England, 1566–1625: succeeded to the English throne when Elizabeth I died without issue. Married to Anne of Denmark and had three children, Henry who died in 1612, Elizabeth who became Princess of Bohemia and Charles who succeeded him. Buckingham was his favourite from 1614 until the end of the reign. (Introduction)

Stuart, James, 4th duke of Lennox and duke of Richmond, born 1612: succeeded his father Esmé in 1624. Travelled after his time at Cambridge, became a gentleman of the bedchamber in 1625. In 1633 joined the privy council and went to Scotland with Charles I. Married Mary, daughter of the duke of Buckingham (q.v.).

Stuart, Ludovic, 2nd duke of Lennox and duke of Richmond, 1574–1624: very important at the Scottish court, Lennox travelled south with James I in 1603; was prominent amongst the Scottish courtiers in England. Lived at Ely House in

Holborn. His third wife was Francis Howard (q.v.). Doc. 58 is a letter to the duchess of Richmond, who may be Ludovic's widow or the widow of his brother Esmé, the third duke.

Suckling, Sir John, 1569–1627: son of a mayor of Norwich, father of John Suckling the poet and playwright. This John was at Gray's Inn, then became MP in 1601 and secretary to Robert Cecil, earl of Salisbury, in 1602. Knighted in 1615/16 and became master of requests in 1620. Two years later he was secretary of state and comptroller of the royal household, and by 1625 was a privy councillor. He was MP in most parliaments of the 1620s. His wife was sister to Sir Lionel Cranfield, who became earl of Middlesex and was at the peak of his power in the early 1620s. His son John Suckling, the poet, is credited with the invention of cribbage. (Doc. 22)

Sydney, Dorothy, later countess of Leicester, 1598–1659: née Percy, wife of Robert Sydney earl of Leicester. Her father was Henry Percy, earl of Northumberland and her mother was a daughter of the earl of Essex. She married Robert Sydney in secret in 1615; the marriage was not generally known about until the next year. Her husband was ambassador to Denmark and then to Holstein in 1632, and to Paris from 1636–41. She was in England when she wrote to her husband in 1637 about Dorothy Savage's marriage. Leicester went on to become a privy councillor in 1639, but supported Parliament. The family home was at Penshurst, where Dorothy had charge of two of the royal children (for Parliament) in 1649–50. (Introduction)

Talbot, Gilbert, 7th earl of Shrewsbury, 1552–1616: son of the 6th earl and Gertrude Manners, daughter of the 1st earl of Rutland, so a cousin to Thomas. A step-son of Bess of Hardwick (his father's second wife), he married his step-sister Mary Cavendish (Bess's daughter by a previous marriage). At St John's, Oxford in 1566 and Lincoln's Inn in 1577/8, he was MP for Derbyshire from 1572–83, KG in 1592 and a privy councillor in 1601–3. The family were one of the wealthiest in England, owning large amounts of Yorkshire, Derbyshire and Nottinghamshire. They had ten houses of good size, including two in London. (Introduction, Docs 6, 20, 21)

Thimbleby/Thimelby, Sir John, from a long-established Lincolnshire family, and a catholic; knighted at Belvoir in 1624 on the same day as John Savage, eldest son of Thomas and Elizabeth. Thimbleby married Elizabeth Savage (q.v.), their daughter, before August 1635, when Thomas Savage wrote introducing him to Sir Thomas Wentworth (q.v.). Of his four siblings two married into the Aston family of Tixall; one was the Jesuit known as Richard Ashby and another, Winifred, was abbess of Louvain in France. (Introduction, Docs 57, 66)

Thomson/Thompson, Thomas: son of Samuel Thompson who had been Windsor Herald in the reign of James I. Became Rouge Dragon in 1624 and Lancaster Herald in 1637. While Rouge Dragon he conducted a visitation of Cheshire, with the Cheshire Herald, Henry Chitting. (Doc. 56)

Thornborow, William: worked for Thomas Savage as keeper of Rocksavage Park and had a similar role at Halton Park. Several of his accounts survive in the Cheshire Record Office. (Doc. 56)

Thorpe, John, ?1565–?1655: by 1582 he was a clerk in the Queen's Works, where his grandfather, father and brother were masons; he worked there until 1600/01. Thorpe married in 1592; he and his wife had 12 children. The first of his drawings to survive comes from 1596. In 1601 he left the Queen's Works and sought patronage as a surveyor of lands and buildings; was soon being paid considerable sums for surveying lands for the king, and of the estates of both Prince Henry and Prince Charles, and for providing plans for existing houses and alterations for 'men of substance'. His work for James I continued; his plans of Theobalds in 1607 are very similar in style to those for Melford, which helps date the latter. In 1611 he became assistant surveyor general to the king for the midlands. In his later career Thorpe became more of an architect. (Introduction)

Tonstall/Tunstall, Sir John, 'of Surrey': knighted in 1619 at Theobalds. (Doc. 35)

Trafford, Thomas, d. 1645: there had been Traffords at Bridge Trafford, Cheshire since the time of Edward I, according to their pedigrees. Married a daughter of the Aldersey family in 1636; he died at Naseby. His daughter Alice married (as her second husband) Richard Savage, second son of John Earl Rivers. In the early eighteenth century their son John, a catholic priest, inherited the title of Earl Rivers; as this great-grandson of Thomas and Elizabeth had no children, the title died with him. (Doc. 62)

Travers, John, of Horton: presumably the John Travers of Horton, Cheshire who died in 1681, or possibly his father. (Doc. 62)

Vane, Sir Henry, 1589–1655: at Oxford in 1604, Gray's Inn in 1606 and knighted in 1611. Married Frances Darcy daughter of Thomas Darcy of Tollehurst Darcy in Essex. Vane bought the position of cofferer to Charles prince of Wales in 1617; became comptroller of the King's household in 1629 and its treasurer in 1639. An MP several times, he also served on peace missions in Europe in 1629–31. Appointed to the privy council in 1630 and held a wide range of administrative positions in the next decade. In 1640 was appointed secretary of state to replace Sir John Coke (q.v.). Supported the king in the early stages of the dispute with parliament, but eventually joined the parliamentary cause. (Introduction, Docs 16, 72)

Venables, Robert, esq. of Wincham: probably the Robert Venables of Wincham who died in 1687 but this could be his son. (Doc. 62)

Villiers, George, earl, then marquis, then duke of Buckingham, 1592–1628: son of Sir George Villiers and his wife Mary (q.v.), George was introduced to James I in 1614 and soon became the royal favourite. Appointed master of horse in 1616 and lord high admiral in 1619. James made him earl of Buckingham in 1617. In 1620 he married Katherine Manners, daughter of the earl of Rutland and a relative of Thomas Savage. In the latter part of James's reign and the early part of Charles's, Buckingham was said to be the most powerful man in England. He and Charles prince of Wales went to Spain in 1623 to arrange a marriage between Charles and the Infanta. This failed. Buckingham organised a series of military expeditions which ended in disaster, and Parliament tried to impeach him in 1626, but Charles I dismissed Parliament to save him. Buckingham was assassinated in 1628, reputedly the most hated man in England. (Introduction, Docs 16, 18, 26, 27, 38, 40)

Villiers, Mary, countess of Buckingham, ?1570–1632: originally Mary Beaumont, of a family from Glenfields in Leicestershire. She married three times, firstly (as his second wife) to Sir George Villiers of Brooksby in Leicestershire; by him she was mother to George, later duke of Buckingham (q.v.) and Susan, later the countess of Denbigh (q.v.). In 1618 (when her son had become marquis of Buckingham) she was created countess of Buckingham for life. She became a catholic, which caused problems for her son. (Doc. 45)

Villiers, Mary, 1622–85: daughter of George Villiers, 1st duke of Buckingham, and Katherine née Manners, daughter of the earl of Rutland. Married in 1635 at around twelve years old to Charles Herbert, Lord Herbert of Shurland. This marriage had long been planned, and was mentioned by her grandfather Rutland on his death bed. Her husband died the following year and in 1637 she married James Stuart, duke of Richmond; she later married a brother of the then earl of Carlisle. (Doc. 47)

Villiers, Susan, countess of Denbigh, d. 1655: daughter of Sir George and Mary Villiers, and sister of George, duke of Buckingham. Married William Feilding, later earl of Denbigh. Appointed as one of Henrietta Maria's ladies in 1626. Left England with Henrietta Maria in 1642 but seems never to have returned; her husband died in the civil war during 1643. Became a catholic while in France and probably died in Cologne in the spring of 1655. (Introduction)

Warburton, Sir Peter, d. 1621: a justice of the Queen's Bench during Elizabeth's reign, and serjeant-at-law to Elizabeth. Bought the manor of Grafton and other lands in Cheshire. Worked with Thomas Savage in an attempt to settle disputes within Chester city council in 1619–20, and died during that dispute. (Introduction)

Warburton, Peter, esq.: presumably related to Sir Peter Warburton (q.v.). (Doc. 62)

Warren, Edward, esq. 1605–87: of Poynton in Cheshire. His first wife was an Arderne and his second a Hough. (Doc. 62)

Warren, Revd Dr Robert, ?1565–1661: rector of Long Melford from 1618, presented by Thomas Savage; he was also rector of Borley in Essex. Was ejected from his living in 1643, and restored in 1660. Held an MA, although it is not known from which university. Warren was a JP and thought by some to be a papist; his house was searched (some reports suggest it was pulled down) in 1642 in the Stour Valley riots. His papers including the records for the Rectory Manor in Melford were destroyed; his household goods and five horses were stolen. He reported being 'huffed and shuffed about'. Records say that he was 96 at his death. (Doc. 60)

Webb, William: in 1656 Daniel King published *The Vale Royal of England; or the County Palatine of Chester*, performed by William Smith and William Webb, gentlemen. Since Webb seems to have been present at Sir John Savage's funeral in 1597 and writes in detail about Rocksavage in 1617, it is possible that *Vale Royal* was written a considerable time before it was published. (Introduction)

Wentworth, Sir Thomas, lord deputy of Ireland, then earl Strafford, 1593–1641: at St John's College, Cambridge, then the Inner Temple. Knighted in 1611 and MP several times between 1614 and the late 1620s. After opposing the government in the 1620s, he became lord president of the north and Viscount Wentworth in 1628, and a privy councillor a year later. In 1633 became lord deputy of Ireland. Created earl of Strafford in 1640, he was recalled to England to contain the Scots; he failed and was eventually tried, condemned by Parliament, and executed. (Introduction, Docs 55, 65)

Werburton, Mr Jefferie, possibly a Warburton, see above. (Doc. 66)

Westmorland, earl of: *see* Francis Fane.

Weston, Richard, Lord, later earl of Portland, 1577–1635: studied at the Middle Temple, then travelled in Europe. MP in 1601, was knighted in 1603. By 1618 he was joint commissioner, comptroller and surveyor of the navy. Two years later he was chancellor and under treasurer, and a member of the privy council. Closely linked to Buckingham, had catholic sympathies and was a member of the pro-Spanish party at court. By 1628 he was Baron Weston of Neyland and lord high treasurer. Reported to be nearly as unpopular as Buckingham, and not liked by Queen Henrietta Maria. In 1632/3 became earl of Portland, and by the next year was attached to the party of Laud and Wentworth (later Lord Strafford). (Introduction, Docs 42, 44)

Whitby, Edmund, esq.: from a family much involved in Chester's government, he served as recorder of Chester and was elected MP in 1620. (Introduction)

Whitmore, Bridget: daughter of William Whitmore and Margaret née Beeston, sole heir of Sir Hugh Beeston of Beeston Castle. Bridget was widow of Sir Edward Somerset, KCB, fifth son of Edward Somerset, 4th earl of Worcester; she then married Thomas's and Elizabeth's second son Thomas, which marriage founded the line of Savages of Beeston. (Introduction, Docs 19, 20, 29, 56, 57)

Whitmore, William, gent: father of Bridget Whitmore (q.v.). He was from a well-established recusant family in Cheshire; much of their lands and wealth had been inherited from the Hough family, into which William's grandfather had married. (Introduction, Docs 19, 20, 21, 29, 56, 57, 62)

Wilbraham, Lady Grace, née Savage, sister of Thomas Savage: she married Sir Richard Wilbraham (q.v.); outlived him by 19 years and died in Chester in 1662, the longest-lived of Sir John and Mary Savage's children. (Docs 4, 60)

Wilbraham, Sir Richard, 1579–1643: of Woodhey, Cheshire. The Wilbrahams are another of the élite families of Cheshire. This Richard's mother was a Cholmondeley. He married Grace Savage, sister to Thomas Savage, before 1601. Was knighted at Dublin in 1603 and succeeded his father Thomas in 1610. Was sheriff of Cheshire in 1615–16 and became a baronet in 1621. Was also related by marriage to Sir Richard Grosvenor, one of the more strongly anti-papist leaders in Cheshire. (Docs 4, 19, 20, 56, 60)

Wilbraham, Mr Thomas, ?1601–60: probably the Thomas who was eldest son of Sir Richard and Grace (q.v.). Married the daughter of Sir Roger Wilbraham in 1613 (both were very young). This Thomas inherited from his father in 1643, and as a royalist had his estates sequestered. (Doc. 56)

Williams, John, 1582–1650: originally from Conway, was at St John's College, Cambridge and ordained in 1605. He gained rapid promotion from James I and by 1617 was chaplain to the king. Became successively dean of Salisbury, dean of Westminster and in 1621 lord keeper of the Great Seal and bishop of Lincoln. Faced trouble in the late 1630s and spent time in the Tower, but was appointed archbishop of York in 1641. (Introduction)

Winchester, marquis of: *see* John Paulet, William Paulet.

Winchilsea, countess of: *see* Elizabeth Finch.

Windebank, Sir Francis, 1582–1646: student at St John's College, Oxford, where he formed close links with William Laud (q.v.). He moved on to the Middle Temple. Travelled abroad in 1605 and then became clerk of the Signet, and remained in that office for 21 years. Was not politically important until 1632 when he became secretary of state with Coke, succeeding Viscount Dorchester; knighted that same year. With Richard Weston and Francis Cottingham he was part of the pro-Spanish party at court. Died in Paris in 1646, shortly after having become a catholic. (Docs 48, 53, 70)

Windham/Wyndham, Edmund: acted with Edward Savage as one of Viscountess Savage's trustees in relation to the copperas agreements, and with Edward Savage in other matters. His wife was nurse to Prince Charles (Charles II) in the early 1630s. Sir John Coke calls him brother to Sir Arthur Savage; he may have been brother-in-law and thus a relation of Edward Savage. A letter of 1637 says that Windham was prepared to give £40,000 for lands in Sedgemoor, so he was obviously of some wealth; by 1637 he was also a gentleman of the privy chamber. He was from Kelford in Somerset but in 1652 was living in Boulogne, when he wrote confirming the tale of Mr Towse, a kinsman. Apparently in 1627 Towse was visited by the ghost of Sir George Villiers, the duke of Buckingham's father, who foretold the horrible end of his son. Towse was called before Buckingham to give evidence, and Windham, by the agency of Edward Savage, was able to visit the court and see Buckingham and Towse in conversation. (Doc. 68)

Winne/Wynne, Sir Richard, ?1588–1649: groom of the chamber to Charles while he was prince of Wales, and MP in 1619 and later. Wynne went to Spain with Charles and Buckingham in 1623. Became treasurer to Queen Henrietta-Maria. (Docs 42, 44)

Winter, Sir John: secretary to Queen Henrietta Maria after Sir Robert Aiton's death in 1638. A catholic, and associate of both the Jesuits and the papal nuncio, George Con, he was related to one of the gunpowder plotters, and was a nephew of the earl of Worcester. (Introduction)

Wolseley, Sir Robert, ?1587–1646: of Morton in Staffordshire. Clerk of the king's letters patent. Made a baronet in 1628. Became a colonel in the king's army. (Docs 61, 68, 72)

Worcester, earl of: *see* Edward Somerset, Henry Somerset.

Worcester, marquis of: *see* Henry Somerset, Edward Somerset.

Wyatt, Sir Thomas, 1503–42: poet, military man and diplomat. A student at St John's College, Cambridge, he became a courtier and diplomat at Henry VIII's court. Knighted in 1537. Best remembered for his poetry. Wyatt bought (or was given) the Crutched Friars site on Tower Hill after the dissolution of the monasteries. (Introduction)

Wyatt, Sir Thomas the younger, 1521–54: a soldier who fought in France in the 1540s. Although he had at first welcomed Queen Mary to the throne, he was to lead a rebellion against her in 1554, for which he was executed. Sir Thomas Cornwallis, Elizabeth Savage's great grandfather, was one of the two privy councillors who rode out to negotiate with Wyatt. It was probably after his death that the Tower Hill house fell into the hands of Henry Fitzalan, earl of Arundel. (Introduction)

BIBLIOGRAPHY

Manuscript sources

Archivo General de Simancas:
Estado Libro 374, ff. 79–80

Birmingham City Archives:
602993 No 131, DV 894, Grant of mineral stones to Elizabeth Savage (Doc. 61)
602993 No 165/169, DV 894, Grant of copperas farm (Doc. 68)
MS 3061/Acc 1901–003/167431, Marriage settlement, Ralph Sheldon and Henrietta Maria Savage

Bodleian Library:
Rawlinson B 138, f. 20, Thomas Viscount Savage's funeral proceedings (Doc. 56)

British Library:
Additional MS 64915, 97, Coke papers, letter from Sir Ranulph Crewe to Coke (Doc. 67)
Cotton, Otho B, xiv, Lands belonging to the Monastery of Sheen
Egerton 2552, Sir Thomas Savage's creation as a viscount (Doc. 25)
Egerton 2646, Letter from Lord Holland to Sir Thomas Barrington (Doc. 78)
Harleian MS 99, f. 94, entry onto Melford Green in December 1609
Harleian MS 1581, f. 258, Sir Thomas Savage to Buckingham about Charles, Prince of Wales (Doc. 16)
Harleian MS 1581, f. 282, Sir Thomas Savage to Buckingham (Doc. 18)
Harleian MS 2129, Funeral of Sir John Savage, 1597; Instructions concerning the hearse and funeral of a viscount
Maps 189a.11, Map of the hundred of Isleworth, 1635, by Moses Glover; facsimile of original at Syon House
Stowe MSS 812/12, 50, 56, 58, 63, 65, 66, Correspondence between Thomas Savage, Ranulph Crewe and Chester City Corporation

Cambridge University Library
Hengrave 88, vol. II, f. 132, Elizabeth Viscountess Savage to Countess Rivers (Doc. 38)
Hengrave 88, vol. II, f. 133, Elizabeth Viscountess Savage to Countess Rivers (Doc. 39)
Hengrave 88, vol. II, f. 152, Francis Savage to Harbottle Grimston (Doc. 77)
Hengrave 88, vol. III, f. 46, Thomas Viscount Savage to Countess Rivers (Doc. 31)
Hengrave 88, vol. III, f. 51, Richard Lynall to Countess Rivers (Doc. 32)
Hengrave 88, vol. III, f. 52, Thomas Brooke to Countess Rivers (Doc. 36)
Hengrave 88, vol. III, f. 88, Charles Savage to Countess Rivers (Doc. 71)

Cheshire and Chester Archives and Local Studies:
D5913, Genealogy of Thomas and Elizabeth Savage
DAR/A/16, Instructions to ranger of Delamere Forest, 1631
DAR/A/3/16, Instructions to ranger of Delamere Forest, 1639
DCH/E/10, Agreement between Lord Savage and tenants concerning the purchase of Runcorn manor
DCH/E/144, Interrogatories relating to court case concerning Runcorn, 1640
DCH/E/302, Book of Savage deeds (Docs 1, 2)
DCH/E/304, 305, 309, Replies of Thomas, John and Edward Savage to bill of complaint from Sir Richard Trevor
DCH/E/311, Will of Sir John Savage, 1615

DCH/E/314, Rocksavage housekeeper's accounts
DCH/E/316, Housekeeper's account for Rocksavage, 1627
DCH/E/324, Administration bond for Savage's estates
DCH/E/325, Will of Earl Rivers
DCH/EE/15, Manorial records, Tarvin
DCH/F/148, Frodsham given to Sir John Savage's wife, 1587
DCH/F/150, Injunction concerning Frodsham tithes, 1602
DCH/F/151, Lease of Frodsham, 1605
DCH/F/153, Assignment of lease, 1610
DCH/F/155a, Lease concerning Frodsham
DCH/F/158, Frodsham Castle accounts
DCH/F/159, Frodsham petition, 1614
DCH/F/170, Frodsham petition, 1616
DCH/F/215c/viii, Purchase of coals, 1633
DCH/H/199, Housekeeper's accounts for Rocksavage, 1624
DCH/H/200, Sir Thomas Savage's income from Cheshire lands
DCH/H/205A, Jointure of Elizabeth Savage (Doc. 3)
DCH/H/506, Financial arrangements concerning Elizabeth Viscountess Savage's debts
DCH/K/1/1, Rocksavage kitchen accounts
DCH/M/1/4, Rocksavage housekeeper's accounts, 1633
DCH/M/34/81r, Agreement between Sir John and Sir Thomas Savage concerning furniture (Doc. 9)
DCH/M/34/81v, Agreement between Sir Thomas Savage and his mother (Doc. 14)
DCH/M/35/1, Debts of John Viscount Savage
DCH/M/35/40, Linen given to Sir John Savage at his marriage and Rocksavage housekeeper's accounts, 1629
DCH/M/35/146, Records of executors of Edward Somerset
DCH/O, Records relating to the Savage and Cholmondeley families from outside Cheshire
DCH/O/13, Goods sold by Earl Rivers, 1647 (Doc. 83)
DCH/O/13, Indenture between Sir Thomas Savage and Elizabeth Lumley (Doc. 10)
DCH/O/27, Exemplification of account, Elizabeth Viscountess Savage (Doc. 66)
DCH/O/29, Increase to Lady Elizabeth Savage's jointure
DCH/O/42, Agreement between Sir Thomas Savage and Sir Philip Stanhope (Doc. 8)
DCH/O/42, Appointments concerning Queen Henrietta Maria's lands (Doc. 44)
DCH/O/75, Grant of Tower Hill house to John Lord Lumley and his wife Jane
DCH/O/75, Details of recovery, Common Pleas (Doc. 7)
DCH/P, Records relating to the Savage and Cholmondeley families from outside Cheshire
DCH/U/13, Appointment of councillors to Queen Henrietta Maria (Doc. 42)
DCH/U/37, Indenture between Sir George Carey and Sir Thomas Savage
DCH/X/15/5, Minutes, commission for sale of crown lands
DCH/X/15/10, Inventory of Thomas Viscount Savage (Doc. 60)
DDX 111/2, Marriage settlement of Sir John Savage, eldest son; settlement of portions for Sir Thomas's and Lady Elizabeth Savage's unmarried daughters
F1 D198 S, Sir Thomas Savage's letter to Cheshire justices (Doc. 17)
Savage WS1616–18, Inventories of Sir John Savage
Savage, WC 1635, Legal papers concerning the will of Dame Mary Savage

College of Arms:
MS I.8, f. 50, Funeral certificate of Thomas Viscount Savage (Doc. 57)

Essex Record Office:
D/DAc/239, Grant of land from Earl Rivers to his daughter
D/DAc/241, Grant of land from Earl Rivers to his daughter
D/DGhM45/6, Sale by Countess Rivers of lands in Great Oakley, 1648
D/DH/VID12, Exemplification of an order in Chancery relating to Sir Thomas Maples and Countess Rivers
D/DHf/T192, Indenture concerning income for Francis Savage (Doc. 24)

D/DU 207/43, Sale by Countess Rivers of lands in Fingringhoe, 1648
D/DZf/9, Sale by Countess Rivers of manor of Peldon, 1650
Q/SR 320/15–16, Indictments of individuals for thefts from St Osyth
Q/SR 320/61, Recognizance relating to the thefts from St Osyth
T/A 418/126/5, Indictment of John Eglond for theft and assault at St Osyth

Guildhall Library, Corporation of London:
Guildhall Library MS 9848, Abstract of title, Sir John Cordell (Doc. 74)

Hatfield House:
Petitions 1607, Petition from Sir Philip Stanhope to Lord Cecil (Doc. 5)
CP109/32, Letter from earl of Shrewsbury to Lord Cecil (Doc. 6)

House of Lords Record Office:
HL/PO/JO/10/1/132, 29 August 1642, Elizabeth Savage's petition after sack of houses (Doc. 75)
HL/PO/JO/10/1/132, 29 August 1642, Lords' response
HL/PO/JO/10/1/132, 9 September 1642, Printed order concerning the search for goods (Doc. 76)
HL/PO/JO/10/1/134, 5 October 1642, Draft order concerning the arms and ammunition of Countess Rivers
HL/PO/JO/10/1/148, 27 April 1643, Petition from Elizabeth, goods not returned
HL/PO/JO/10/1/186, 7 May 1645, Petition from Elizabeth, assistance to the Scots (Doc. 79)
HL/PO/JO/10/1/203, 3 April 1646, Petition from Elizabeth, applying to stay in London (Doc. 80)
HL/PO/JO/10/1/203, 3 April 1646, Petition from Dorothy Lady Andover, applying to stay in London
HL/PO/JO/10/1/203, 8 April 1646, Petition from John Earl Rivers in answer to petition of John Greene
HL/PO/JO/10/1/213, 10 September 1646, Draft pass for Lady Rivers to come from France
HL/PO/JO/10/1/227, 6 March 1647, Petition from Mary Countess Rivers about her husband's goods (Doc. 81)
HL/PO/JO/10/1/230, 15 April 1647, Petition from Mary Countess Rivers about sale of goods (Doc. 82)
HL/PO/JO/10/1/263, 19 June 1648, Permission for Elizabeth Countess Rivers to stay in London

Lambeth Palace Library:
MSS 647–662, Index to papers of Anthony Bacon

London Metropolitan Archive:
Acc 903, Records of Enfield Parochial Charities

Melford Hall, Hyde Parker Papers:
Grant of Melford Manor to William Cordell, 1554
Licence to empark at Melford (Doc. 13)
Map of Melford Hall estate, 1580
Map of Melford Hall estate, 1613
Map (unfinished) of Melford Hall estate, 1615
Map of Melford Hall, 1735
Melford Cartulary, part of a collection of evidences relating to abbot's manor of Melford (12th–15th cent)
Parker Biography, 1867, by Sir William Parker
Rental, 1442
Rental, 1613
Supplement to the History of Long Melford (1880–89), by Sir William Parker

Ministerio de Asuntos Exteriores:
MS 243, ff. 137v–142r, Speech of Count Olivares

Real Biblioteca, Madrid:
MS II-2108, no. 119, at d, Gondomar to Isabella, 31/21 Jan. 1622
Staffordshire Record Office: Bradford Papers:
D1287/18/2, Letters from Thomas Viscount Savage to John Bridgeman, bishop of Chester (Docs 30, 33 and 37).

Suffolk Record Office, Bury St Edmunds:
Acc 466, Court rolls of manor of Melford Hall

The National Archives:
C 142 Chancery: Inquisitions Post Mortem, Series II, and other Inquisitions, Henry VII to Charles I
C 142/377/50, IPM of Lady Elizabeth Lumley
CHES 3 Palatinate of Chester: Exchequer of Chester: Various Inquisitions
CHES 3/91/7, IPM of Sir John Savage
CHES 3/103/12, IPM of Thomas Viscount Savage (Doc. 62)
E 101 King's Remembrancer: Accounts Various
E 101/438/7, Establishment book of Queen Henrietta Maria
E 179 Exchequer: King's Remembrancer: Particulars of Account and other records relating to lay and clerical taxation, *c.*1190 – *c.*1690
E 179/180/152, Lay subsidy roll, Babergh, Suffolk, 1525
LC 2 Lord Chamberlain's Department: Records of Special Events
LC 2/5, Funeral of Anne, queen of James I
LC 2/6, Funeral of James I
LR 5 Office of the Auditors of Land Revenue and predecessors and successors: Vouchers and Accounts, subseries, Queen Henrietta Maria's Jointure
LR 5/57, ff. 9–10, Commission concerning Queen Henrietta Maria's revenues (Doc. 35)
LS 13 Lord Steward's Department: Miscellaneous Books, subseries, Establishment
LS 13/30, Records for 1629, included bouge of court records
PROB 11 Prerogative Court of Canterbury and related Probate Jurisdictions: Will Registers
PROB 11/103, f. 9, Will of Lady Jane Allington (Doc. 4)
PROB 11/63, f. 42, Will of Sir William Cordell
PROB 11/114, f. 72, Will of John Lord Lumley
PROB 11/129, f. 13, Will of Elizabeth Lady Lumley
PROB 11/154, f. 103, Will of Dame Elizabeth Kitson
SO 3 Signet Office and Home Office: Docquet Books and Letters Recommendatory
SO 3/11, Signet Office Doquet Book, Nov. 1634–Oct. 1638
SO 3/12, Signet Office Doquet Book, Nov. 1638–Dec. 1644
SO 3/12, f. 144r, Planning permission for Tower Hill
SO 3/12, f. 144v, Elizabeth Viscountess Savage created Countess Rivers (Doc. 73)
SP14 Secretaries of State: State Papers Domestic, James I
SP 14/57/59, Grant from Sir Thomas Savage to William Noye (Doc. 11)
SP 14/64/21, Letter from Elizabeth Lady Lumley to Salisbury (Doc. 12)
SP 14/141, Reversion of Lord Darcy's title to Savage, 1613
SP 14/215/23, Edward Nichols to John Drake (Doc. 34)
SP15 Secretaries of State: State Papers Domestic, Edward VI – James I: Addenda
SP 15/37/46, Letter of Elizabeth Viscountess Savage referring to Brentford
SP 15/75/212, Letter from John Chamberlain
SP16 Secretaries of State: State Papers Domestic, Charles I
SP 16/10/23, Jane Lady St John to Lord Conway (Doc. 23)
SP 16/53/17, Thomas Viscount Savage to the duke of Buckingham (Doc. 26)
SP 16/53/39, Thomas Viscount Savage to the duke of Buckingham (Doc. 27)
SP 16/53/41, Thomas Viscount Savage to Edward Nichols (Doc. 28)
SP 16/69, Minutes, commission for the sale of crown lands
SP 16/95/165, Letter from George Lord Carew to Sir Thomas Roe
SP 16/116/6, Executors of Buckingham to Captain Pennington (Doc. 40)
SP 16/140/10, Administration of Queen Henrietta Maria's estates

SP 16/143/44, Elizabeth Viscountess Savage, letter asking for mercy concerning a hanging (Doc. 41)
SP 16/148/56, Administration of Queen Henrietta Maria's estates
SP 16/169/68, Letter from Philip Manwaring
SP 16/181/444, Sir Thomas Savage as High Steward of Congleton
SP 16/185, Thomas Viscount Savage as executor of Buckingham
SP 16/197/287, Commissioners for lands held by Charles I as prince of Wales
SP 16/223/47, Thomas Viscount Savage to Edward Nicholas concerning Fisheries (Doc. 46)
SP 16/257/46, Petition of John Crewe to Charles I (Doc. 49)
SP 16/257/76, Elizabeth Lady Savage, petition concerning a pension (Doc. 48)
SP 16/271/45, Thomas Viscount Savage requesting deer from Eltham
SP 16/274/46, Petition from forester of Delamere against Thomas Viscount Savage
SP 16/282/80, Elizabeth Viscountess Savage's petition concerning brass manufacture (Doc. 51)
SP 16/303/65, Elizabeth Viscountess Savage's petition about freedom of the City (Doc. 53)
SP 16/306/1, Elizabeth Viscountess Savage's petition concerning position of prothonotary (Doc. 52)
SP 16/312/44, Lord Poulet to Duchess of Richmond (Doc. 58)
SP 16/312/58, City of London's reply to Elizabeth Viscountess Savage's petition (Doc. 59)
SP 16/352/50, Letter from Earl Rivers to Charles I (Doc. 64)
SP 16/414/72, Letter from Elizabeth Viscountess Savage to earl of Lindsey (Doc. 69)
SP 16/439/22, Letter from Elizabeth Viscountess Savage to Secretary Windebank (Doc. 70)
SP 16/521/134, Sir Thomas Savage and others to vice admirals (Doc. 22)
SP 16/531/83, Thomas Viscount Savage's petition to Charles I concerning Delamere (Doc. 43)

SP17 Secretaries of State: State Papers Domestic, Charles I: Large Documents
SP 17/D/17, Commission concerning brewers and sellers of beer

SP38 Signet Office: Docquets
SP 38/7, Reversion of clerkship of the star chamber
SP 38/15, Lord Cottingham's expenses

SP39 Signet Office: King's Bills
SP 39/2, Sir Thomas Savage created a viscount

University of Hull, Brynmore Jones Library: Quintin Papers (owner Sir Charles Legard):
DDSQ(3)/18/3, Licence to demolish Tower Hill house (Doc. 72)

University of Wales, Bangor:
Lloyd Mostyn MSS E688, Disarming of William Whitmore, 1612
Lloyd Mostyn MSS 9082, Whitmore–Savage correspondence (Docs 19, 20, 21, 29)

Archives of the Archdiocese of Westminster:
AAW A XXVI, nos 55, 64, Documents relating to the establishment of a catholic bishop in England

Printed primary sources

Acts of the Privy Council of England, 1603–4, 1613–40 (46 vols, London, 1890–1964)
Birrell, T.A. (ed.), *The Memoirs of Gregorio Panzani* (London, 1970)
Calendar of the Committee for Advance of Money (London, 1888)
Calendar of the Talbot Papers, HMC (London, 1971)
Cornwallis, J., *The private correspondence of Jane, Lady Cornwallis, 1613–1644* (London, 1842)
Dugdale, W., *The History of Imbanking and Drayning of Divers Fenns and Marshes* (London, 1662)

Ellis, H. (ed.), *Original Letters Illustrative of English History* (3 vols, London, 1824)
Gardiner, S.R. (ed.), *Constitutional Documents of the Puritan Revolution, 1625–1660* (3rd edn, Oxford, 1906)
Green, M.A.E. and Bruce, J. *et al.* (eds), *Calendar of State Papers, Domestic, 1547–1625* (27 vols, London, 1856–97)
Green, M.A.G. (ed.), *The Diary of John Rous*, Camden Society 66 (London, 1856)
Groombridge, M. (ed.), *Calendar of Chester City Council Minutes, 1603–1642*, Lancashire and Cheshire Record Society, CVI (Blackpool, 1956)
Historical Manuscript Commission Reports (HMC):
Fourth Report, Appendix, House of Lords MSS (London, 1874)
Fourth Report, Appendix, De La Warr MSS (London, 1874)
Eleventh Report, Appendix I, Skrine MSS (Salvetti Papers, 1625–1628) (London, 1887)
Twelfth Report, Appendix II, Cowper MSS II (London, 1888)
Twelfth Report, Appendix IV, Rutland MSS I (London, 1888)
Thirteenth Report, Appendix II, Portland MSS II (London, 1893)
Fourteenth Report, Appendix I, Rutland MSS IV (London, 1905)
Fourteenth Report, Appendix II, Portland MSS III (London, 1894)
Salisbury (Cecil) MSS, XVII 1604 (London, 1933)
Salisbury (Cecil) MSS, XXI 1609–1612 (London, 1970)
Lord De L'Isle and Dudley MSS, VI (London, 1966)
Marquis of Downshire MSS, VI (London, 1940)
Howell, J., *Familiar Letters on Important Subjects, wrote from the year 1618 to 1650* (2nd edn, London, 1650)
Journals of the House of Commons, 1547–1629 (London, 1802)
Journals of the House of Lords, 1578–1714 (London, 1742–)
Kingsford, C.L. (ed.), *A survey of London reprinted from the text of 1603, with introduction and notes by Charles Lethbridge Kingsford* (London, 1908)
Knowler, W. (ed), *The Earle of Strafford's letters and dispatches, with an essay towards his life* (2 vols, London, 1739)
Larkin, J.F. and Hughes, P. (eds), *Stuart Royal Proclamations* (2 vols, Oxford, 1973)
Matthew, H.C.G. and Harrison, B. (eds), *Oxford Dictionary of National Biography* (60 vols, Oxford, 2004)
McClure, N.E. (ed.), *The Letters of John Chamberlain* (2 vols, Philadelphia, 1939)
Milner, E., *Records of the Lumleys of Lumley Castle* (London, 1904)
Nichols, J.G. and Bruce, J. (eds), *Wills from Doctors' Commons – a Selection from the Wills of Eminent Persons Proved in the Prerogative Court of Canterbury 1495–1695*, Camden Society (London, 1863)
Nichols, J., *The Progresses, Progressions and Magnificent Festivities of King James the First, his Royal Consort, Family and Court* (London, 1828)
Notestein, W. (ed.), *Journal of Sir Simonds D'Ewes* (New Haven, 1923)
Ogle, O., Bliss, W.H. and Macray, W.D. (eds), *Calendar of Clarendon State Papers* (Oxford, 1869–76)
Ornsby, G. (ed.), *The Correspondence of John Cosin DD, Lord Bishop of Durham, Part I*, Surtees Society, LII, 1869 (Durham, 1869)
Petrie, Sir C. (ed.), *The Letters, Speeches and Proclamations of King Charles I* (London, 1935)
Piccope, G.J. (ed.), *Lancashire and Cheshire Wills & Inventories from the Ecclesiastical Court, the third portion*, The Chetham Society, LIV (London, 1861)
Rushworth, J. (ed.), *Historical Collections of Private Passages of State, etc* (8 vols, London, 1680–1701)
Ryland, J.P., *Lancashire and Cheshire Funeral Certificates, AD 1600–1678*, Lancashire and Cheshire Record Society (1882)
Rymer, T. and Sanderson, R. (eds), *Foedera* (20 vols, London, 1704–32, reprinted Newton Abbott, 1987)
Seddon, P.R. (ed.), *Letters of John Holles, 1587–1637*, Thoroton Society Record Series (3 vols, Nottingham, 1975–86)

Sharratt, M. (ed.), *Lisbon College Register, 1628–1813* (Southampton, 1991)
Stephen, L. and Lee, S. (eds), *Dictionary of National Biography* (63 vols, London 1883–1900)
Stewart-Browne, R. (ed.), *The Cheshire Inquisitions Post-Mortem 1603–1660, Vol 3*, Lancashire and Cheshire Record Society (1938)
Strype, J. (ed.), *A survey of the cities of London and Westminster: containing the original, antiquity, increase, modern estate and government of those cities. Written at first in the year MDXCVIII. By John Stow, citizen and native of London. Now lastly, corrected, improved, and very much enlarged* (London, 1720)
Summerson, J. (ed.), *The Book of Architecture of John Thorpe in Sir John Soane's Museum* (Glasgow, 1966)

Secondary sources

Airs, M., *The Tudor and Jacobean House, a Building History* (Stroud, 1995)
Akrigg, G.P.V., *Jacobean Pageant, or the Court of James I* (London, 1967)
Armstrong, G.F., *The Ancient and Noble Family of the Savages of the Ards* (London, 1888)
Ashton, R., *The City and the Court, 1603–1643* (Cambridge, 1979)
Aungier, G.J., *The History of Syon Monastery* (London, 1840)
Aylmer, G., *The King's Servants – the Civil Service of Charles I, 1625–1642* (London, 1961)
Aylmer, G., 'Buckingham as an administrative reformer', *English Historical Review*, April 1990, 355
Beamont, W., *A History of the Castle of Halton Castle and the Priory or Abbey of Norton* (Warrington, 1873)
Beamont, W., *An Account of the Ancient Town of Frodsham* (Warrington, 1881)
Birch, T., *The Life of Henry Prince of Wales* (London, 1760)
Birch, T. (Williams, R.F. (ed.)), *The court and times of Charles I* (London, 1848)
Chaney, E., *The Grand Tour and the Great Rebellion, Richard Lascalles and the 'Voyage of Italy' in the Seventeenth Century* (Geneva, 1985)
Cliffe, J.T., *The World of the Country House in the Seventeenth Century* (London, 1999)
Clifford, A., *Tixall Poetry* (Edinburgh, 1813)
Cogswell, T., *Blessed Revolution: English Politics and the Coming of War* (London, 1992)
Cogswell, T., *Home Divisions: Aristocracy, the State and Provincial Conflict* (Manchester, 1998)
Coope, R., 'The Long Gallery', *Architectural History Journal of the Society of Architectural Historians*, 1986
Cust, R., *The Forced Loan and English Politics, 1626–1628* (Oxford, 1987)
Cust, R. and Hughes, A. (eds), *Conflict in Early Stuart England, Studies in Religion and Politics 1603–1642* (London, 1989)
de Figueiredo, P. and Treuherz, J., *Cheshire Country Houses* (Chichester, 1988)
Dent, J., *Quest for Nonsuch* (London, 1970)
Dodd, J.P., 'Sir Giles Overreach in Cheshire', *Cheshire History*, Autumn 1993, 11–19
Dodd, J.P., *A History of Frodsham and Helsby* (Frodsham, 1987)
Dore, R.N., *Cheshire* (London, 1977)
Dore, R.N., '1642: the coming of the civil war to Cheshire: conflicting actions and impressions', *Transactions of the Lancashire and Cheshire Antiquarian Society*, 87, 1991, 39–63
Dovey, Z., *An Elizabethan Progress* (Stroud, 1996)
Dow, L., 'The Savage Hatchment at Long Melford', *Proceedings of the Suffolk Institute of Archaeology*, 1955, 214–19
Doyle, J.E., *The Official Baronage of England* (London, 1886)
Earwaker, J., *East Cheshire, Past and Present* (London, 1877)
Elrington, C.R. (ed.), *A History of the County of Cambridge and the Isle of Ely*, 6 (VCH, Oxford, 1978)
Fisher, N.R.R., 'The Queenes Court in her Councell Chamber at Westminster', *English Historical Review*, CVIII, no. 427, April 1993, 314
Gage, J., *The History and Antiquities of Hengrave in Suffolk* (London, 1882)

Gardiner, S.R., *The History of England from the Accession of James I to the Outbreak of the Civil War, 1603–42* (10 vols, London, 1883–4 and 1884–90)

Gibbs, V., Doubleday, H.A., White, G. *et al.* (eds), *Complete Peerage of England, Scotland, Ireland, Great Britain & the United Kingdom,* 2nd edn (13 vols, London, 1910 –59)

Girouard, M., *Life in the English Country House* (London, 1978)

Gittings, C., *Death, Burial and the Individual in Early Modern England* (London, 1984)

Gruenfelder, J., 'The Parliamentary Election at Chester, 1621', *Transactions of the Historic Society of Lancashire and Cheshire*, 120, Liverpool, 1969, 35–44

Hamilton, E., *Henrietta Maria* (London, 1976)

Harris, B.E. (ed.), *A History of the County of Chester* (VCH, Oxford, 1979)

Havran, M.J., *The Catholics in Caroline England* (Stanford, 1962)

Hibbard, C., 'The Role of a Queen Consort, the Household of Queen Henrietta Maria 1625–1642', in R.G. Asch and A.M. Birke (eds), *Princes, Patronage and the Nobility – the Court at the Beginning of the Modern Age* (Oxford, 1991)

HMC, *Principal Family and Estate Collections A–K* (London, 1996)

HMC, *Principal Family and Estate Collections L–Z* (London, 1999)

Houlbrooke, R., *Death, Religion and the Family in England 1480–1750* (Oxford, 1998)

Impey, E. and Parnell, G., *The Tower of London* (London, 2000)

Lockyer, R., *Buckingham, the Life and Political Career of George Villiers, First Duke of Buckingham 1592–1628* (London, 1981)

Lockyer, R., *The Early Stuarts* (London, 1998)

Loomie, J., 'The Spanish Faction at the Court of Charles I, 1630–6', *Bulletin of the Institute of Historical Research* 59, 1986, 37–49

Luxon, Thomas H. (ed.), The Milton Reading Room, http://www.dartmouth.edu/~milton, Nov. 2005

Lysons, D., *The Environs of London* (London, 1796)

Magee, B., *The English Recusants* (London, 1938)

McCulloch, D.N.R. (ed.), *The Chorography of Suffolk* (Ipswich, 1976)

Milton, A., *Catholic and Reformed: Roman and Protestant Churches in English Protestant Thought, 1600– 1640* (Cambridge, 1995)

Morrill, J.S., *Cheshire 1630–1660, County Government and Society during the English Revolution* (London, 1974)

O'Riordan, C., 'The Story of a Gentleman's House in the English Revolution', *Transactions of the London and Middlesex Archaeological Society*, 38, 1987, 165–7

Ormerod, G., *A History of the County Palatine and City of Chester* (2nd edn, London, 1882)

Parker, Sir W., *The History of Long Melford* (London, 1873)

Patterson, C., 'Conflict Resolution and Patronage in Provincial Towns, 1590–1640', *Journal of British Studies*, 37, 1998, 1–25

Peck, L.L., *Northampton: Patronage and Policy at the Court of King James I* (London, 1982)

Peck, L.L., *Court Patronage and Corruption in Early Stuart England* (London, 1990)

Pennant, T., *Some Account of London* (2nd edn, London, 1791)

Plowden, A., *Henrietta Maria, Charles I's Indomitable Queen* (Stroud, 2001)

Pounds, N.J.G. (ed.), Hyde Parker, R. and Adshead, D., 'Long Melford Hall', supplement to *Archaeological Journal*, 149, 1992

Quintrell, B., 'The Practice and Problems of Recusant Disarming', *Recusant History*, 17, 3, May 1985, 208–22

Redworth, G., *The Prince and the Infanta, the Cultural Politics of the Spanish Match* (New Haven, 2003)

Robinson, J.M., *A Guide to the Country Houses of the North West* (London, 1991)

Sharpe, K., 'The Image of Virtue, the Court and Household of Charles I, 1625–1642', in D. Starkey (ed.), *The English Court from the Wars of the Roses to the Civil War* (London, 1987), pp. 226–60

Sharpe, K., *Faction and Parliament: Essays on Early Stuart History* (Oxford, 1978)

Shaw, W.A., *The Knights of England* (London, 1905)

Smuts, R.M., *Court Culture and the Origins of a Royalist Tradition in Early Stuart England* (Philadelphia, 1987)

Southerden, J., *The Star Chamber* (London, 1870)
Starkey, H.F., *Old Runcorn* (Halton, 1991)
Strickland, A., *Lives of the Queens of England* (London, 1848)
Suckling, A., *The History and Antiquities of the County of Suffolk* (London, 1848)
Thornton, P., *Seventeenth Century Interior Decoration in England, France and Holland* (London, 1978)
Walter, J., *Understanding Popular Violence in the English Revolution, The Colchester Plunderers* (Cambridge, 1999)
Ward and Trent, *et al.*, *The Cambridge History of English and American Literature* (New York, 1907–21; New York: www.bartleby.com, 2000), chs 11 and 12
Watney, J., *A Sole Account of St Osyths Priory* (London, 1871)
Weikel, A., 'The Marriage of Mary Cornwallis', *Recusant History*, 23, 1996, 16–26
Wood, M., *The English Mediaeval House* (London, 1965)

Notes about the Indexes

In all three indexes, an asterisk denotes more than one reference to a page, while 'n' attached to a page-number refers to a footnote.

Index of Persons. A dominant spelling of each surname has been chosen from those used in the documents, or one closest to the modern equivalent. This is followed in brackets by the more important variants. Many of the individuals indexed were peers or from aristocratic families, so references are given under their family name, with cross-references from their titles. Where a married woman's original surname is known, it is used in the entry with a cross-reference. Women who appear in this volume as single, but were married later, are indexed under their first surnames. Where two people having identical names are listed, at least one is given special identification to help distinguish them. Where a person is mentioned several times in a single document, but not necessarily on each page, covering page-numbers are given. (For Notes on People, see pp. 159–95.)

Index of Places. Place-names are spelt in their modern forms. The great majority are in England, and are scattered over most parts of the country, but some relate to Europe and other parts of the world. Those in England have the county identified, except in the case of London; note that longer county names have been abbreviated as shown in the table below. A place-name is sometimes followed (in brackets) by earlier spellings taken from the documents, but these variants may not preserve a strict alphabetical order. Where a place is mentioned several times in a single document, but not necessarily on each page, covering page-numbers are given.

Abbreviations

Beds	Bedfordshire
Berks	Berkshire
Bucks	Buckinghamshire
Cambs	Cambridgeshire
Ches	Cheshire
Co Dur	County Durham
Corn	Cornwall
Derby	Derbyshire
Hants	Hampshire
Hereford	Herefordshire
Herts	Hertfordshire
Hunts	Huntingdonshire
Lancs	Lancashire
Leics	Leicestershire
Lincs	Lincolnshire
Midd	Middlesex
Norf	Norfolk
Northants	Northamptonshire
Northumb	Northumberland
Notts	Nottinghamshire
Oxon	Oxfordshire
Som	Somerset
Staffs	Staffordshire
Suff	Suffolk
Suss	Sussex (all)
War	Warwickshire
Worcs	Worcestershire
Yorks	Yorkshire (all)

INDEX OF PERSONS

INDEX OF PLACES

INDEX OF SUBJECTS